S0-CBX-423

Pseudonymity and Canon

An Investigation into the Relationship
of Authorship and Authority in Jewish
and Earliest Christian Tradition

by

David G. Meade

WILLIAM B. EERDMANS PUBLISHING COMPANY
GRAND RAPIDS, MICHIGAN

Copyright © 1986 by J. C. B. Mohr (Paul Siebeck),
P.O. Box 2040, D-7400 Tübingen, West Germany

This edition published 1987 by special arrangement with J. C. B. Mohr
by Wm. B. Eerdmans Publishing Co., 255 Jefferson Ave., SE, Grand Rapids, Mich. 49503

All rights reserved

Printed in the United States of America

Library of Congress Cataloging-in-Publication Data

Meade, David G.
Pseudonymity and canon.
Bibliography: p. 219
Includes index.
1. Bible — Authorship.   2. Bible — Canon.
3. Bible — Evidences, authority, etc.   4. Bible — Inspiration.
I. Title.
BS519.M43   1987   220.1   87-22355

ISBN 0-8028-3645-3

230.1
M461p

L.I.F.E. College Library
1100 Glendale Blvd.
Los Angeles, Calif, 90026

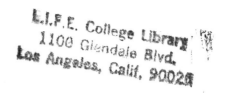

Preface

It would be amiss, particularly in a book dealing with attribution, not to mention in gratitude those who helped make this writing possible. Praise is first due, of course, to the Author of all things, since my story is really just a part of His story. Among mortals, pride of place goes to my supervisor, James D. G. Dunn, whose combination of intellectual rigor and pastoral concern provided the ideal climate for a "budding" young scholar. Thanks is also due to P. Maurice Casey, whose additional supervision was a welcome boon. Mention should be made of the selfless efforts of the staff at Nottingham University Library, particularly Glenis Pickering and Tony Barker, and of the helpful advice of my colleagues at St. John's Theological College, Bramcote. The patience of my typist, Rosemary Bagley, who time and again would cheerfully type another "final" copy, has been worthy of canonization. Such an opportunity to study abroad would not have been possible apart from a John Wesley Fellowship from the Foundation for Theological Education (Marshall, Texas), and I count it a privilege to be among their ranks. The support of family was also greatly appreciated. Finally, I gladly record my debt of love to my wife, Elizabeth, who for five years has denied herself and managed to make a home for me and the children in the midst of our postgraduate "exile." Her contribution is no less important for its anonymity, for in truth this book is *our* story. For this reason I gratefully dedicate this work to her (Proverbs 31:10b).

As canon criticism has clearly demonstrated, a work takes on a new life and meaning when included in a larger, authoritative corpus of literature. Therefore I am grateful to Georg Siebeck and to the co-editors of the WUNT series, Professors Hengel and Hofius, for including my 1984 doctoral thesis among such distinguished ranks. Except for condensation, revision of the manuscript has been minimal.

All biblical quotations are taken from the Revised Standard Version, except where noted. Abbreviations follow the guide published in S. Schwertner, *International Glossary of Abbreviations for Theology and Related Subjects* (Berlin: de Gruyter, 1974), or alternatively, the style sheet for contributors issued by Biblica, 1982.

August, 1985   David G. Meade
                                                      Houghton, New York

038041

080041

Contents

Chapter 1

The Problem of New Testament Pseudonymity

1.1 Defining the Problem

Ever since the advent of higher critical studies, there has been felt an ever present tension between the concept of canon and the discovery of pseudonymity in the NT[1]. A great deal of the confusion and controversy that has arisen is due to inadequate and contradictory definitions. Thus, for example, when Martin Rist makes the statement that a likely two-thirds of the NT is pseudonymous[2], one is quite taken aback until realizing that Rist has (quite wrongly) equated anonymity and pseudonymity, and lumped together false and/or mistaken ascription, interpolation, textual alteration, literary convention, and forgery all into the same category.

A more careful definition is that of K. Koch: "A text is pseudonymous when the author is deliberately identified by a name other than his own[3]." This would eliminate the designation "pseudonymous" from most of the NT and OT, and much of the OT Apocrypha and Pseudepigrapha as well. Though a great many of the books included in these are in fact incorrectly attributed, this is often due to the mistaken attribution of originally anonymous works and not from any calculated attempt to deceive.

Another distinction that needs to be made is between an invented pseudonym and a borrowed one. In modern literature pseudonyms are often *invented* to mask the author's real identity. The motives range from pure whimsy to a desire to avert certain prejudices, such as sexism[4]. In antiquity, however,

---

1 See D. Guthrie, "The Development of the Idea of Canonical Pseudepigraphy in New Testament Criticism", *The Authorship and Integrity of the New Testament.* Edit. K. Aland (London. SPCK, 1965) 14–39, reprinted from *Vox Evangelica I. Biblical and Historical Essays.* Edit. R.P. Martin (London. Tyndale Press, 1962) 43–59.
2 "Pseudepigraphy and the Early Christians", *Studies in New Testament and Early Christian Literature* Wikgren Fest. Edit. D. Aune (Leiden. E.J. Brill, 1972) 75–91.
3 "Pseudonymous Writing", *IDB Supp.*, 712.
4 Thus the pseudonyms Currier, Ellis and Acton were used by the Bronte sisters Charlotte, Emily, and Anne, because they confessed, "We had a vague impression that authoresses were liable to be looked on with prejudice." As cited by B. Metzger, "Literary Forgeries and Canonical Pseudepigrapha", *JBL* 91 (1972) 5.

pseudonyms were mostly *borrowed,* not invented. That is, works were deliberately and falsely attributed to other, recognized figures. Though the motives could be similar to those behind the modern *nom de plume,* the use of real, borrowed names places much of ancient pseudonymity in the realm of literary forgeries or pseudepigraphy[5].

Because of this distinction it might at first appear more helpful to restrict ourselves to one of these latter terms for our consideration of the NT phenomenon. However, each of the alternate terms also have their liabilities. Though the term "forgery" may accurately describe these writings from a literary-critical perspective, the moral overtones that it carries from modern experience and practice make it unsuitable for this discussion. Pseudepigraphy, on the other hand, is a more accurate and restricted term. Unfortunately, it is associated with the OT canonical terminology of Pseudepigrapha, which has other considerations besides authorship. Further, a great deal of the relevant secondary literature uses the terms "pseudonymity/pseudonymous", reflecting, no doubt, the preference of English usage. The truth is, it is almost impossible to restrict a discussion of ancient authorship to an exclusive use of either the "(pseudo)-nym" of the "(pseudo)-epigraph" word groups. For these reasons, the broader term "pseudonymity" and its cognates will be retained in this investigation, but with due regard to its distinctive configuration in antiquity. This means that *for our purposes,* pseudonymity and pseudepigraphy are equivalent, and both word-groups will be similarly used. The problem of pseudonymity is the problem of pseudepigraphy.

Even with a more circumspect definition of pseudonymity, the tension that its presence in the canon creates is not fully relieved. This is because of the inevitable clash of the fundamental principles of each concept. Inherent in the idea of pseudonymity is the use of deception, and in canon is the communication of truth. Put bluntly and emotively (though perhaps not accurately), the question is how forged documents can serve as vehicles of inspired religious truth? Or less emotively, what is the relationship between pseudonymity and canon? Two major positions or perspectives can be discerned in the relevant literature.

Theology, like politics, makes strange bedfellows. The first major perspective on pseudonymity and canon is that there is no correlation, or connection, between the two. Strangely enough, this position is held by both the far

---

5 For the motives and methods of forgeries in antiquity, see esp. W. Speyer, *Die literarische Fälschung im Altertum* (München: C.H. Beck, 1971); R. Syme, "Fraud and Imposture", *Pseudepigrapha I.* Edit. K. von Fritz (Vandoeuvres-Genève: Fondation Hardt, 1972) 1–17, with discussion 18–21; and Metzger above. For the phenomenon of pseudonymity in general, ancient and modern, see A. Taylor and F. Mosher, *The Bibliographical History of Anonyma and Pseudonyma* (Chicago: University of Chicago, 1951); and the bibliography in Metzger, "Literary Forgeries", 23–24; N. Brox (Edit.), *Pseudepigraphie in der heidnischen und jüdisch-christlichen Antike* (Darmstadt: Wissenschaftliche Buchgesellschaft, 1977) 335–342.

left and the far right of the theological spectrum. Each side differs only in which concept it is willing to retain at the expense of the other. The attitude of the right, as might be expected, is to reject the concept of pseudonymity outright, on dogmatic grounds. Representative is J. I. Packer: "We may lay down as a general principle that, when biblical books specify their own authorship, the affirmation of their canonicity involves a denial of their pseudonymity. Pseudonymity and canonicity are mutually exclusive[6]." This attitude settles the question from a certain theological perspective on canon, with no recourse to literary-critical studies. Though this rejection of modern tools is to be deplored, one ought not to be blinded to its genuine theological concern.

The position of the left differs only in what concept it is willing to preserve. In this case pseudonymity is paramount, and the perceived exclusivity of the concept of canon means that the latter is dropped from reckoning. Investigations never reach beyond the literary-critical stage. Representative is M. Rist, whose treatment of NT pseudonymity reveals his belief that though canonicity was an issue during an earlier church period, it is not of vital concern now. He makes no attempt to reconcile his literary views with a concept of canon[7]. This rejection of theological concern is to be similarly deplored, but one at least needs to recognize the value of an unswerving commitment to the use of literary criticism in the canon.

Fortunately the vast majority of scholars belong to the second major perspective, one that sees, or desires to see, some correlation between pseudonymity and canon. Though they represent quite widely differing perspectives, they all seem to agree that the issue is not adequately addressed until both literary and theological questions are answered. Representative is the statement of R.D. Shaw:

> It is freely granted that any form of literary composition which came most naturally to an inspired men, would be a proper vehicle for the conveyance of his message, whether poety or parable or the very plainest of plain speech. If there were no conscious transgression of any moral principle, it would be impossible to refuse inspiration to a pseudonymous writing on the mere ground of its pseudonymity[8].

The common task of this position, then, is to try to demonstrate how

---

6 *Fundamentalism and the Word of God* (1958) 184, as cited by D. Guthrie, "Development", 29. Though Guthrie would reject the dogmatic method of Packer, he in fact agrees with him. He states (30), "Consistency would seen to demand that any proved unauthentic works would be automatically excluded from the canon." Though he does not reject literary-critical methods, his demand for "assured results" (31) before he accepts the presence of pseudonymity in the canon shows where his real interest lies. Historical reconstruction deals in probabilities, never the absolutes that Guthrie demands.

7 "Pseudepigraphy". Thus he glibly relates (82–83) his idea that 2 Thessalonians is a pseudonymous work written to reject the true Pauline letter of 1 Thessalonians, without any sensitivity to what this would mean for the canon.

8 "Pseudeonymity and Interpolation", *The Pauline Epistles* (Edinburgh: T. & T. Clarke, 1903) 482. Though Shaw in fact doubts this can be shown.

pseudonymity could be a legitimate part of the early Christian's (and Hebrew's) moral conscience. It is here that the unanimity ends, and what follows is a survey of various attempts to "justify" the presence of pseudonymity within the canon.

1.2 Attempts at Resolving the Problem

A pre-critical attempt to resolve the tension, still found in isolation today, was to simply regard the writers of antiquity as unburdened with the "copyright" mentality of our modern era. The sheer bulk of pseudonymous writings was cited as proof that correct attribution was of little concern. This view has been decisively shattered by the work of W. Speyer[9]. He acknowledges that the vital element of our modern understanding of forgery is a sense of *geistiges Eigentum* or "intellectual/creative property". This, he demonstrates, developed in Greek culture as early as the sixth century B.C. The rise of a book trade and the formation of large libraries in the Hellenistic era contributed to this development. By the Christian era, ancient critics had developed literary tools for exposing forgeries not unsimilar to our techniques today.

A related attempt at appealing to a "pre-copyright" mentality is to restrict the phenomenon to oriental, and particularly, Jewish culture. M. Hengel in particular thinks that even in hellenistic Judaism "the consciousness of literary property and individuality of authorship was underdeveloped in comparison to the Greco-Roman world"[10]. Speyer would certainly agree that *geistiges Eigentum* was introduced to Judaism from Greek culture[11]. However, by the Hellenistic era the concept was well established in Judaism. Even though an "Israelite literary tradition", mostly characterized by anonymity, can be discerned[12], the pervasiveness of Greek culture and the evidence of a consciousness of *geistiges Eigentum* in Jewish and Christian literature of the Hellenistic era (cf. 2 Thess 2:2; Rev 22:18–19) make this appeal untenable[13]

Another uncritical approach to the problem was to assert that pseudonymity was just a transparent literary fiction, not intended to deceive anyone. This idea found wide currency in the English speaking world, particularly through the works of H.H. Rowley (for apocalyptic) and P.N. Harrison (for

---

9 *Fälschung.*
10 "Anonymität, Pseudepigraphie und 'Literarische Fälschung' in der jüdisch-hellenistischer Literatur", in K. von Fritz (Edit.), *Pseudepigrapha I,* 283.
11 *Fälschung,* 150.
12 M. Smith, "Pseudepigraphy in the Israelite Literary Tradition", in K. von Fritz (Edit.), *Pseudepigrapha I,* 189–215, with discussion 216–227.
13 See N. Brox, *Falsche Verfasserangaben. Zur Erklärung der früh-christlichen Pseudepigraphie* (Stuttgart: KBW, 1975) 69–70.

the NT)[14]. Yet J.S. Chandlish put the lie to this approach as early as 1891, when he wrote,

> ... when any work was given out as of ancient or venerable authorship, it was either received as genuine ... or rejected as an imposture ... and the notion of dramatic personation as a legitimate literacy device is never mentioned, and seems never to have been thought of as a defence of such compositions. If any author wrote a pseudonymous book in such a way, he must have been very unsuccessful in his purpose; for it was generally taken as a genuine work, or else rejected as feigned and worthless[15].

A more insightful attempt to explain Jewish pseudonymity (particularly apocalyptic) was that of R.H. Charles, who isolates three factors in its rise: (1) the belief that prophetic inspiration had ceased with Ezra, (2) the growing supremacy of the Law, and (3) the closure of the OT canon[16]. If books were to be accepted into the canon after the time of Ezra, they had to be written under a pseudonym that hearkened back before that time. Yet though the belief in the cessation of prophecy was widespread in the first two centuries B.C., that there was such a developed sense of law and canon is problematic[17]. If the purpose of pseudonymity was to get books accepted into the "canon", then they would have all been written in Hebrew, not Aramaic and Greek as well. Of course, this theory has no relevance at all to the problem of NT pseudonymity[18].

Without question the broadest and most popular theory of pseudonymity has been the religious/psychological approach. Both English and German writers have their own distinctive contributions. Among the English writers the most pervasive influence has been the work of D.S. Russell[19], whose theories on apocalyptic pseudonymity have been widely extrapolated to

---

14 E.g. H.H. Rowley, *The Relevance of Apocalyptic* (London: Lutterworth, 1955[2]) 14; P.N. Harrison, *The Problem of the Pastoral Epistles* (London: Oxford, 1921) 12. A German example is A. Meyer, "Religiöse Pseudepigraphie als ethisch-psychologisches Problem", *ZNW* 35 (1936) 262–279, reprinted in N. Brox (Edit.), *Pseudepigraphie*, 90–110, who regards pseudonymity as a dramatic-poetic creation.

15 "On the Moral Character of Pseudonymous Works", *Exp* (4th series) 4 (1891) 103. See also F. Torm, *Die Psychologie der Pseudonymität im Hinblick auf die Literatur des Urchristentums* (Gütersloh: C. Bertelsmann, 1932), reprinted in N. Brox (Edit.), *Pseudepigraphie*, 119 (19).

16 *A Critical History of the Doctrine of the Future Life in Israel, in Judaism, and in Christianity* (London: Black, 1913[2]) 202–204. See also *idem, OT Apocrypha and Pseudepigrapha*, Vol.II, vii–ix.

17 D.S. Russell remarks, "This picture which R.H. Charles draws of the 'autocracy' of the Law whose overwhelming authority was such as to make utterly impossible the utterances of God-inspired men cannot find any substantiation in fact." *The Method and Message of Jewish Apocalyptic* (London: SCM, 1964) 131. See also W.E. Oesterley, *The Jews and Judaism During the Greek Period* (London: SPCK, 1941) 74.

18 This applies as well to the "Camouflage" theory of apocalyptic, i.e. pseudonymity to avoid political reprisals. Besides, this theory is essentially superfluous (anonymity would work as well).

19 *Method*, esp. 132–139.

other Jewish and Christian writings. His psychological approach is defined in three concepts.

The first psychological concept is that of "corporate personality", an idea developed by H.W. Robinson and applied by Russell to pseudonymity. Robinson had argued from texts in Hebrew law, wisdom literature, and the Psalms that in the Hebrew psychology there was a blurring or mixing of the identity of the individual and the group[20]. Noting that apocalyptic literature exhibits a self-conscious witness that it is indeed a *bona fide* message from an ancient seer, Russell regards this as evidence of corporate personality.

> Just as all (in the apocalyptic tradition) could speak for the one (the ancient seer in whose name they wrote), so one (the individual apocalyptic writer) could speak for all. In this way the apocalyptists, in their writings, were trying to express what they believed the person in whose name they wrote would have spoken had he been living in their own day. As spokesman of the tradition, they were, in fact, spokesman of the seer himself, and could justifiably assume his name[21].

Whatever the truth in the claim of the apocalyptists to be representatives of tradition (see below), there is no way that this can be grounded in any concept of corporate personality, which has been decisively refuted on both exegetical and anthropological grounds. J. Porter has examined the legal texts upon which Robinson builds his case, and demonstrated that every one can be explained in ways other than corporate personality[22]. The anthropological refutation came in a brilliant article by J.W. Rogerson[23], who demonstrated that the concept is based on unsubstantiated foundations. "Corporate personality" is a legal term, based on Sir Henry Maine's theories of the development of law and corporate responsibility (*Ancient Law*). Robinson took this idea of *legal* identity and inappropriately applied it to *psychological* identity. His justification for doing so was the anthropological theories of L. Levy-Bruhl about "primitive mentality", who contended that primitive societies blurred the boundaries between individual personality and that of the group. Unfortunately for Robinson, Levy-Bruhl's theories have now been discredited. In any case, Levy-Bruhl never characterized the Hebrews as a "primitive" society.

A second and similar psychological concept offered by Russell is that of contemporaneity. Citing the work of T. Boman[24], he contends that the Hebrew mind did not maintain the strong division of time into the past, present and future familiar to most moderns. They were more concerned with the quality of time than the quantity, the "psychic content". If the

---

20 H.W. Robinson, *Corporate Personality in Ancient Israel* (Philadelphia: Fortress Press, 1964).
21 *Method*, 133–134.
22 "The Legal Aspects of the Concept of 'Corporate Personality'", *VT* 15 (1965) 361–380.
23 "The Hebrew Conception of Corporate Personality: A re-examination", *JThS* n.s. 21 (1970) 1–16.
24 *Hebrew Thought Compared With Greek* (London: SCM, 1960) 147–149.

"psychic contents" of the apocalyptist's time and that of his hero were similar, they could be equated[25].

However, Boman's arguments for contemporaneity were refuted by J. Barr[26], and Russell's further arguments are unconvincing[27]. "Contemporaneity" was in fact more of a feature of Israel's Near Eastern neighbours, whose religions were grounded in the cyclic timelessness of myth. Since Russell argues for the prophetic origin of apocalyptic, he himself should recognize that what distinguishes prophecy from myth is its tie to the peculiarity of history. That Hebrew writers could *identify with* historical events from the past is well recognized, but there is no way that they could *equate* them.

The third inter-locking psychological concept that Russell promotes is the "extension of personality", as evidenced by the use of the proper name in Hebrew. He notes that the Hebrew name was not a mere appellation but an "extension" of one's personality, indicating one's essential being. Since in the Greek period, Jewish children were increasingly named after ancient figures, Russell suggests that is may have been possible for the apocalyptists to appropriate the name of their hero to become an "extension" of his personality. He maintains that the ecstatic experiences of the apocalyptists may have supported this identification.

The "extension of personality" concept, however, falters simply for lack of substantial proof. There is no evidence that a Jew's "personality" could be extended in his name beyond his own blood ties, and Russell's demonstration of "extension" in Jubilees, 1 Enoch and 4 Ezra is extremely tenuous. Further, there is no evidence that the Hebrews could lose consciousness of their own individual identity and be taken over by another. Russell's appeal to ecstatic identification or *unio mystica* is in fact a key feature of the German psychological theories; thus it is appropriate to turn to these.

Of the four major German monographs written on the subject of pseudonymity, those of F. Torm[28], J. Sint[29], and W. Speyer[30] all feature ecstatic or oracular identification as a primary vehicle of pseudonymity in religious writings[31]. Since Speyer's views are the most recent and articulate, they will

---

25 *Method*, 136.

26 *Biblical Words for Time* (Naperville: Allenson, 1962) 96, 130–131.

27 *Method*, 134–137.

28 *Psychologie*.

29 *Pseudonymität im Altertum. Ihre Formen und ihre Grunde* (Innsbruck: Universitätsverlag Wagner, 1960).

30 *Fälschung*. See also "Religiöse Pseudepigraphie und literarische Fälschung im Altertum", in N. Brox (Edit.) *Pseudepigraphie*, 195–263, reprinted from *JAC* 8/9 (1965–66) 82–125; "Fälschung, pseudepigraphische freie Erfindung und 'echte religiöse Pseudepigraphie'", in K. von Fritz (Edit.), *Pseudepigrapha I*, 333–366, with discussion 367–372.

31 The fourth is that of N. Brox, *Falsche Verfasserangaben*. This is not to say that this is the *only* vehicle of pseudonymity promoted. Both Sint and Speyer also attribute certain pseudonymous Jewish writings to the category of innocent literary devices or pious fiction.

be treated as representative. According to Speyer, even after the rise of the consciousness of *geistiges Eigentum* there existed alongside of it (and indeed prior to it) the concept of religious inspiration. In Greek culture, a writer could regard himself merely as the instrument of a revealing God or Muse[32]. Yet this did not lead to pseudonymity. But in the Orient, the idea of a "writing God" was prevalent, which was not so much a literary form as an experiential reality[33]. This attribution of authorship to God is especially prevalent in OT legal material and prophetic "I-sayings". Religious pseudepigraphy found its highest expression in apocalyptic literature, with its visionary, ecstatic identification. This type of religious pseudonymity is called *echte religiöse Pseudepigraphie,* and is defined as follows:

> Führt die Vorstellung der Ergriffenheit weiter zu einer Identifikation von Schriftsteller und vorgestelltem inspirierenden Geist, der ein Gott, ein Engel, ein gottgeliebter Weiser der Vorzeit sein kann, so entsteht die "echte religiöse Pseudepigraphie". In diesem Fall versinkt der menschlichen Verfasser ganz in der ihn inspirierenden personalen Macht.[34]

Though it is not limited to any particular culture or time in history, there are admittedly some that are more favourable to the phenomenon[35]. *Echte religiöse Pseudepigraphie* really belongs to the area of mysticism[36].

The appeal of Speyer and the others to this type of religious pseudonymity is subject to a number of insurmountable objections. The foremost is against the facility with which all of the German authors move across various cultures. In particular, all three seek to enlighten *Jewish* pseudonymity by extrapolating from Greco-Roman literature, especially the orphic, hermetic, and sibylline material[37]. This phenomenological generalization leads to the mistaken use of a theory of *unio mystica* in Jewish writings, a concept which is not all evident. Though much Jewish literature is written under the conviction that God is the real speaker, there is no evidence that the author ever thought he was God. And even more damaging, there is no shred of evidence that a pseudepigrapher thought that he was possessed by the spirit of a pretended author[38].

Another problem is that even apocalyptic literature is not wholly visionary or oracular, and as Speyer admits, even these features can be forged. This leads him to try to define more carefully what *"echte religiöse"* signifies. For Speyer, "religious intent" is the key to discernment. To be *echt,* a writing must not display any *Tendenz.*

> Je deutlicher festzustellen ist, dass ein religiöses Pseudepigraphon nur Wünsche eine

---

32 "Religiöse Pseudepigraphie" (in N. Brox), 201.
33 *Ibid.,* 218–219, 225 ;*Fälschung,* 36.
34 "Fälschung" (in K. von Fritz), 359.
35 "Religiose Pseudepigraphie" (in N. Brox), 239.
36 "Fälschung" (in K. von Fritz), 345.
37 See J. Gribomont, "De le notion de 'Faux' en littérature populaire", *Bib* 54 (1973) 434–436 (response to Speyer, *Fälschung*).
38 M. Smith in response to W. Speyer, in *Pseudepigrapha I* (Edit. K. von Fritz), 371.

einzelnen oder einer Gruppe zu befriedigen sucht, das heisst z. B. merkantile, rechtliche, politische, kultische, apologetische, verherrlichende, verleumderische, kirchenpolitische, disziplinare Absicht durchsetzen sucht, um so eher wird von Fälschung zu sprechen sein[39].

Yet Speyer would be hard pressed to find many Jewish or Christian pseudepigraphs, especially in apocalyptic literature, that do not display at least one of these features, the fact of which he seems blissfully unaware.

Perhaps the most damning criticism of the idea of religious inspiration as the source of pseudonymity is that, in fact, it makes it *harder* to explain, as M. Smith remarks, "had these authors really experienced such visions it is hard to understand why they would not have said so in their own names, as Isaiah and Jeremiah and Ezekiel did[40]." Though a fruitful part of the religious/psychological theory does suggest that the sense of *geistiges Eigentum* may be altered by the author's perception of a divine source of his information or ideas, the dependence on para-normal, mysterical categories has not really explained how this can result in pseudonymity, even in the literary genres that most conform with the theory. Of course, it utterly fails when applied to the non-oracular genres of most Christian literature. This is why Torm regards NT pseudonymity as "psychologically impossible" (and thus rejects its presence)[41], Sint does not even deal with it, and Speyer regards almost all early Christian pseudepigrapha as forgeries[42].

Another approach to the problem of pseudonymity may be labelled the "school" theory. Taking notice of the emphasis on tradition in many NT pseudepigrapha, this theory attempts to explain their attribution on the basis of the practice in antiquity of a disciple publishing in his master's name[43]. True to the general trend of scholarship, substantiation of this theory is sought in Greco-Roman parallels, particularly the Greek philosophical schools. A number of similar NT schools are then suggested. There has long been proposed a Johannine school[44], and a school of Matthew[45]. H. Conzelmann proposes a Pauline school as the source of the deutero-Paulines[46], and E. Ellis

---

39 "Fälschung" (in K. von Fritz), 361–362.
40 In *Pseudepigrapha I* (Edit. K. von Fritz), 371.
41 *Psychologie,* esp. 146 (52).
42 "Der Mehrzahl der christlichen Pseudepigraphie der drei ersten Jahrhunderte fehlte die prophetische oder apokalyptische Rede gänzlich... Dennach sind wir zu dem Urteil berechtigt, in den meisten christlichen Pseudepigrapha Fälschungen zu sehen", "Fälschung" (in K. von Fritz), 365.
43 Especially the Pythagorean school.
44 O. Cullmann, *The Johannine Circle* (London: SCM, 1976); R.A. Culpepper, *The Johannine School* (Missoula: Scholars Press, 1975).
45 K. Stendahl, *The School of St. Matthew and Its Use of the Old Testament* (Uppsala: Gleerup, 1954).
46 "Paulus und die Weisheit", *NTS* 12 (1965–66) 233–234. See also G. Bornkann, *Paul* (New York: Harper and Row, 1971) 86. The Pauline school is often located at Ephesus. See A. Patzia, "The Deutero-Pauline Hypotheses: An Attempt at Clarification", *EvQ* 52 (1980) 33; E.J. Goodspeed, *New Chapters in New Testament Study* (New York: Macmillan, 1937) 38–39.

suggests that Paul's numerous co-workers formed its nucleus[47]. The evidence for a Pauline "school", however, is not so straightforward. Only five out of over one hundred Pauline associates stand in explicit subordination to him[48], and this is most likely a result of his instrumentality in their conversion, not a structured master-disciple relationship[49]. Indeed, we know from 1 Corinthians 1:12 ff. that Paul discouraged any organized form of personal loyalty. Certainly whole communities (e.g. the Pastorals) highly value Pauline teaching, but it is highly questionable whether these can be described under the rubric "school".

There are essentially three weaknesses to the school theory as an explanation of NT pseudonymity. First, there is no demonstrable link between the pseudonymous practice of *some* of the Greek philosophical schools (not all used it) and the proposed practice in the NT. Culpepper's extensive comparison really only demonstrates the parallel of the practices of reading, writing, teaching, and learning ; hardly a sufficient foundation. Indeed, he admits that it is difficult to trace any direct influence of these Greek schools on (Johannine) Christian practice[50]. The most frequently quoted source to assert this link is Tertullian, Adv. Marc. 6.5, "it is allowable that that which disciples publish should be regarded as their masters' work". Yet this statement is not directed to pseudonymous documents, but rather to justify the apostolicity of the *anonymous* gospels of Mark and Luke. Furthermore, these remarks are those of a *second century Latin father,* and may in fact have no real connection to the mind set of the (largely Jewish) writers of the NT[51].

This leads to the second, related weakness of the school theory, which is the virtual exclusion of the OT background in its reckoning. Culpepper does treat the "schools" of Philo, Hillel, and Qumran, but goes no further. Yet surely the New Testament writers would have been at least as affected by their Jewish background as by the surrounding culture. There has, in fact, long been evidence of several types of schools in Israel's history : legal[52], wisdom[53], and prophetic[54]. Though some would minimize or deny any presence

---

47 "Paul and His Co-workers", *Prophecy and Hermeneutic in Early Christianity: New Testament Essays* (Tübingen: J.C.B. Mohr, 1978) 3–22, esp. 13, 22. Reprinted from *NTS* 17 (1971) 437–452.

48 Erastus, Mark, Timothy, Titus, Tychichus(Acts 19:22; Tim 4:11, Phil 2:19; Col 4:8; Titus 3:12). For the fundamental independence of the co-workers from Paul, see W.H. Ollrog, *Paulus und seine Mitarbeiter. Untersuchungen zu Theorie und Praxis der paulinischen Mission.* (Neukirchen-Vluyn: Neukirchener Verlag, 1979).

49 Acts 9:25 does mention Pauline "disciples" (μαθηταί) but this seems more a Lukanism than evidence for a school.

50 *Johannine School,* 258.

51 See D. Guthrie, "Tertullian and Pseudonymity", *ET* 67 (1956) 341–342.

52 M. Weinfeld, *Deuteronomy and the Deuteronomic School* (Oxford: Clarendon, 1972).

53 G. von Rad, *Wisdom in Israel* (London: SCM, 1972) 17.

54 J.H. Eaton, "The Origin of the Book of Isaiah", *VT* 9 (1959) 138–157; J. Lindblom, *Prophecy in Ancient Israel* (Oxford: Blackwell, 1967).

of organized schools or master-disciple relationships in the OT[55], the early association of prophetic guilds (2 Kgs 6:1 ff., 1 Sam 10:10), the later collection and redaction of legal, sapiential, and prophetic material, and the ample evidence of scribal schools in surrounding cultures makes it likely that at least some of the literature (or some parts of that literature) in the OT is due to "schools".

Yet it is unlikely that even a revised school theory, taking into account the OT evidence, can serve as a helpful tool in explaining NT (or OT) pseudonymity. This is because of the third weakness: the term "school" itself. It is simply too technical to describe the complex phenomenon of the growth of tradition in Jewish and Christian writings. Even when we are able to isolate certain groups that might have been involved at various stages in the growth of collective works (in much of the OT, and in the gospels), there is little likelihood that even these works can be regarded as the sole product of these various "schools". To ascribe the bulk of pseudonymous writings to the work of various schools in either the OT or NT demands a type of organization and historical continuity that is simply not present in the evidence we possess. Though it is certainly compatible with it, the growth of tradition in Jewish and Christian writings cannot be explained simply in terms of the master-disciple relationship of an organized "school".

A final attempt at resolving the problem of pseudonymity is not really a single, uniform theory, but what might well be called the "eclectic" approach. Reacting negatively to the attempts of many to find a single, overarching explanation of pseudonymity, this approach emphasizes the complexity of the phenomenon, and suggests a number of different models. The recent work of N. Brox is representative of this approach[56]. While accepting some of the approaches listed above for some literature (including the idea of forgery), Brox relies heavily on three principal features to explain pseudonymity in early Christian writings. First is the almost universal "love of antiquity" present in every culture of the era. The general idea was that what was old was true, thus Christians, like their pagan counterparts, used pseudonymity to participate in the *überlegene Vergangenheit*[57]. Second is the similarity pervasive idea of the "noble falsehood". Expressed most clearly in the writings of the Pythagoreans and Platonists, they held that falsehood might be used in support of religion, i.e. the end might justify the means[58]. Brox sees this as the fundamental motivation of the "counter-forgeries" used by the early church against the heretics. In support of this he cites as the third principle the assertion that for the early fathers (2nd–4th century), the content of writings was more important than authorship. Programmatic

---

55 K.H. Rengstorf, "μαθητής", *TDNT IV*, 426–431.
56 *Falsche Verfesserangaben*. See also B. Metzger, "Literary Forgeries".
57 N. Brox, *Falsche Verfasserangaben*, 105–106.
58 *Ibid.*, 82 ff. See also J. Candlish, "Moral Character", 103–104; B. Metzger, "Literary Forgeries", 19.

is the counsel of the Apostolic Constitutions VI 16.1, "You ought not to pay attention to the name of the Apostle, but to the character of the contents and to unfalsified teaching[59]."

Though there is certainly an element of truth in Brox's assertions, particularly as they apply to post-NT Christian literature, one has a number of reservations about their applicability to the NT itself. It is hard to see how "love of antiquity" or early origins could have been such a strong motivating force to pseudepigraphers in the first century, writing only a few decades after the death of their pseudonyms. Similarly, the pervasiveness of the Greek idea of "noble falsehood" is hard to judge in first century Christian writings of a mainly Jewish origin. Though there was in fact a stronger emphasis on content than authorship in the era of the fathers, pseudonymity appears still to have been disreputable and therefore discouraged[60]. Even if Brox's principles were admitted to be applicable to NT pseudepigrapha, they would not in fact resolve the theological tension that these writings create. A final objection relates to Brox's methodology, an objection that is not limited to his approach. The recognition of this in fact leads to a suggestion for a more fruitful approach to the problem.

1.3 Toward a New Contribution

A feature of most of the critical theories under review is that they treat the problem of NT pseudonymity from the perspective of the history of literature of late antiquity[61]. While this can be regarded as a legitimate reaction to pre-critical attempts to insulate the scriptures from modern literary investigation, in practice it has led to a phenomenological approach that has resulted in a lack of appreciation for the subtle differences in Jewish and first century Christian writings from their surroundings. In particular, the method usually consists of a survey of Greco-Roman literature and/or the Christian literature of the era of the Greek and Latin fathers[62], whereupon parallels are then

---

59 N. Brox, *Falsche Verfasserangaben,* esp. 26–36. Other frequently cited texts in this regard are Salvian's ninth letter and Serapion's remarks in Eusebius, H.E. vi, 12.

60 Tertullian, De. Bapt. 17. The evidence here and above (n. 59) is ambiguous. See further the discussion in Chapter 6.

61 "... pseudepigraphische Schriftstellerei des christlichen Altertums nicht anders als die altchristliche Literatur insgesamt wissenschaftlich als ein Phänomen der Spatantiken Literaturgeschichte zu behandeln und zu interpretieren sei", N. Brox, "Methodenfragen der Pseudepigraphie Forschung", *ThRv* 75 (1979) 275.

62 E.g. Brox *Falsche Verfasserangaben,* spends only four pages on Jewish background, and *fifteen* pages treating Christian literature from the second to fourth century A.D.

"discovered" with the NT (and OT) documents and the explanation is given "this is that". Though no reputable scholar would deny the value of these surveys, the tendency has too often been a confusion of form with intent. There is no room for the recognition that a different, theological perspective can alter the way that similar, or even identical literary forms are used[63]. Further, a certain theological perspective may *cut across* literary genres, and thus render them ineffective as an indication of the author's intent[64]. As was said above, both literary *and* theological considerations must be brought to bear on the problem.

There have, in fact, been rumblings about this over-generalizing approach for some time. K. Aland in particular has proposed the novel counter-thesis that the Christian era from A.D. 50–150 should be regarded as a unique period for anonymity and pseudonymity[65]. Because of the conviction that a writer was really the *Werkzeug* of the Spirit, anonymity or pseudonymous attribution (not intended to deceive) to the ideal figures of the apostles was the rule.

> When the pseudonymous writings of the New Testament claimed the authorship of the most prominent apostles only, this was not a skillful trick of the so-called fakers, in order to guarantee the widest possible circulation for their work, but the logical conclusion that the Spirit himself was the author[66].

The rise of pseudonymity was simply the result of the shift from spoken to written word, when Christian prophets wrote down their charismatic utterances. Only with the writings of Tertullian do we find a shift of emphasis to orthonymous writings.

Unfortunately, Aland's theory commits the same error as many of his German predecessors. His dependence on an undifferentiated sense of inspiration for these authors is similar to earlier psycho-religious theories, and subject to the same criticisms. Furthermore, his theory does not really fit the historical facts. When faced with the self-attributed writings of Paul, he can only appeal to the now discredited distinction of Deissman between a real letter and an epistle. As H. Balz points out, the ironic result of Aland's theory

---

63 This focus on genre is apparent in Speyer and most others, who when faced with the writings of Paul and the deutero-Paulines, immediately assume that the use of the Greco-Roman epistolary *genre* implies a similar Greco-Roman *attitude* toward its use.

64 This is especially the failing of the religious/psychological approach. E.g. F. Torm, *Psychologie* (148), "Auch in die Fällen, die eine beabsichtigte Pseudonymität gemeinsam haben, muss man zwischen den verschieden Literaturgattungen scharf unterscheiden. Die psychologischen Voraussetzungen sind bei einem apokalyptischen Verfasser, einem Erzähler von legendarischen Geschichten, und einem Briefschreiber sehr verschieden." How does he know this?

65 "The Problem of Anonymity and Pseudonymity in Christian Literature of the First Two Centuries," *The Authorship and Integrity of the New Testament*. Edit. K. Aland (London: SPCK, 1965) 1–13, reprinted from *JThS* n.s. 12 (1961) 39–49.

66 *Ibid.*, 8.

is that Paul appears to be less filled with the Spirit than the pseudonymous and anonymous writers, since he is content to write under his own name[67]! Nor does the theory of charismatic anonymity/pseudonymity explain the Pastorals, with their elaborate framework of autobiographical and historical details. Indeed, Aland is forced to consider the Pastorals as sort of hybrids between his theory of origins and the motives that gave rise to the later NT Apocryphal writings[68].

The failure of Aland's theory should not blind one to some of his valuable suggestions, particularly in the idea of relating anonymity and pseudonymity, and both to early preaching. H. Balz has noted this connection, and stressed the growth of the Jesus tradition as an illustration[69]. He points out how the goal of the kerygma was to contemporize (*vergegenwärtigen*) the words of the Lord for it hearers, and that this led to the anonymity of much of the literature. Pseudonymity in this regard could be termed an extreme form of anonymity. Yet for Balz the majority of *apostolic* pseudepigrapha are not traditional in character, but *Tendenzfälschungen*. That is, they are not attempts to contemporize *apostolic* tradition, but apologetic foils for the pseudepigrapher's own ideas and interests. This judgement, however, is due more to Balz's dislike of "early Catholicism" than to an evaluation of the traditional nature of the material[70].

A more dispassionate treatment of the theme of tradition in NT writings is that of J. Zmijewski[71]. He agrees that the heart of the matter is the relation of NT pseudonymity to Christian preaching, or more precisely, to the preservation and propagation of apostolic tradition. Using the theme of "reminder" in 2 Peter (1:12–15, 3:1f.), he demonstrates the concern of the author for unfalsified tradition. Unfortunately, Zmijewski offers no mechanism for understanding how this extension of tradition could result in pseudonymity, other than a pneumatic *Werkzeug* concept similar to Aland.

The theories of Aland, Balz, Zmijewski and others[72] can be commended for their sensitivity to the peculiarity of Christian literature of the first century, and for focusing on tradition as the key to understanding NT pseud-

---

67 "Anonymität und Pseudepigraphie im Urchristentum. Überlengungen zum literarischen und theologischen Problem der urchristlichen und gemeinantiken Pseudepigraphie," *ZThK* 66 (1969), 419.

68 "Problem," 9–10.

69 "Anonymität," 433–434.

70 For example, see his remark that the deutero-Paulines are further removed from Paul's original theology than the heretics it opposes. *Ibid.*, 436.

71 "Apostolische Paradosis und Pseudepigraphie im Neuen Testament. 'Durch Erinnerung wachhalten' (2 Petr 1, 13; 3,1)," *BZ* 23 (1979) 161–171.

72 See also K. Koch, "Pseudonymous Writing"; K.M. Fischer, "Anmerkungen zur Pseudepigraphie im Neuen Testament," *NTS* 23 (1976) 76–81; F. Laub, "Falsche Verfasserangaben in neutestamentlichen Schriften. Aspekte der gegenwärtigen Diskussion um die neutestamentliche Pseudepigraphie," *TThZ* 89 (1980) 228–242; P. Grelot, "Tradition as Source and Environment of Scripture," *Concilium* 2/10 (1966) 5–15. The article of P. Pokorný, "Das Problem der neutestamentliche Pseudepigraphie," *EVTh* 44 (1984) 486–496, was unavailable for consultation.

onymity. Yet they fail to give a satisfactory answer for how and why tradition grew as it did, and why pseudonymity could be an expression of this. This is because the phenomenon is usually treated solely as a Christian one, with little investigation of its Jewish antecedents. This is by far the largest failing of most of the theories of pseudonymity that have been treated. Jewish background studies for the most part have been limited to (post-A.D. 70) rabbinic parallels and the apocalyptic literature. Even here the material (especially apocalyptic) has been treated more from the perspective of Greco-Roman parallels than for its own sake.

M. Smith has written an interesting analysis of Jewish literature that isolates a "Jewish literary tradition" characterized by anonymity[73], but he makes the same methodological mistake of trying to isolate this tradition by literary genre rather than content. Thus he makes no attempt at examining the role of tradition and revelation in Jewish writings, and is content to label as forgeries those pseudonymous writings which conform to Greco-Roman literary tradition (such as the letter form). Similarly, D. Guthrie recognizes the failure to investigate Jewish sources, and devotes a published essay to the topic[74]. Once again, however, the confusion over genre and theological intent is apparent, since the only Jewish literature that he compares with NT epistolary pseudepigrapha are the two sole examples of Jewish pseudonymous letters: The Letters of Aristeas and Epistle of Jeremiah. Yet even this reveals a parallel to the NT practice of supplementing or contemporizing a tradition through the use of pseudonymity. Unfortunately Guthrie discounts it.

This fundamental lack in the history of the investigations of NT pseudonymity is what this book proposes to redress. The central focus of this exercise will be to examine the relationship of revelation and tradition in OT and intertestamental literature, and to see how they relate to the concepts of authorship and authority. Hopefully, this will result in the isolation of a "pattern" of anonymity/pseudonymity, that is, of elements that can be regarded as distinctive of many, if not all, of Jewish religious pseudepigrapha. This "pattern" will then be compared with the NT documents to determine if a continuity of theological and literary perspective exists. Finally, the results will be evaluated in the light of the concept of canon, ancient and modern, in order to grapple with the tensions inherent in the issue of canonical pseudonymity.

---

73 "Pseudepigraphy," 189–215.
74 "Epistolary Pseudepigraphy," *New Testament Introduction* (London: Tyndale 1970[3]) 671–684. Guthrie also devotes a portion of his unpublished doctoral thesis to a survey of Jewish pseudepigrapha, but it mostly consists in a superficial assessment of their lower or epigonal spirituality, and does not really deal with the role of tradition and revelation. See *Early Christian Pseudepigraphy and Its Antecedents* (PhD., University of London, 1961). A recent repetition of Guthrie's ideas can be found in T.D. Lea, "The Early Christian View of Pseudepigraphic Writings," *JETS* 27 (1984) 65–75.

Three methodological principles need to be established at the outset. First, instead of repeating the error of fixation on literary genres, the Jewish literature will be approached from the traditio-historical perspective of three broad streams of tradition: prophecy, wisdom, and apocalyptic[75]. Second, even within these traditions not all the literature will be investigated, but "typical" documents associated with a well-known figure will be selected. Naturally this lays one open to the danger of distortion, but the alternate danger is to become superficial while trying to be comprehensive. Third, it is not the purpose of this study to prove or disprove pseudonymity in the case of individual documents, but to understand it. Obviously positions need to be taken for the sake of the larger investigation, but for the most part these positions will be assumed and not argued.

Chapter 2

Authorship, Revelation and Canon
in the Prophetic Tradition

Though a valid case could be made that the roots of canonical pseudepigraphy go back to the legal and historical documents of the Moses tradition[1], our investigations of Jewish background will begin with the prophetic tradition of Israel. This is because the Pentateuchal traditions are too complex in their relation to the historical figure of Moses to readily establish any principled relationship of authorship and tradition. In the prophetic tradition, however, we are dealing with much more concrete individuals, and the relation of the prophets to the books that bear their names is much more open to analysis.

The breadth of scholarly investigation of OT prophecy is overwhelming, and no attempt can be made to give a comprehensive overview[2]. Therefore after a general discussion regarding the nature of prophecy and the methodology for understanding the growth of the prophetic tradition and corpus, a detailed examination of only the Isaiah tradition will follow. Hopefully this two-fold approach will help us to suggest a "pattern" of anonymity/pseudonymity in the OT prophetic tradition, and then illustrate it more fully in the development of the book of Isaiah.

2.1 Prophetic Revelation and the Growth of the Prophetic Tradition

2.1.1. *The Nature of OT Prophecy*

What are some of the features of the relevation given to the prophets? Four have a direct bearing on the Israelite attitude toward authorship and

---

1 The book of Deuteronomy could be called the first canonical pseudepigraph.
2 The most comprehensive survey and bibiography is contained in the series of articles by G. Fohrer: "Neuere Literatur zur alttestamentlichen Prophetie", *ThR* 19

attribution. First, though it may sound like a truism, OT prophecy is described as from God. The most frequent designation of prophetic revelation is as "the word of the Lord"[3]. If we remember that a necessary element of forgery and the drive for proper attribution is a sense of *geistiges Eigentum* or creative proprietary claims, then we can better understand the prophet's attitude.

It is not the prophet's word, but Yahweh's (Jer. 1:9; 15:19; Isa. 59:21; Ezek. 3:17; Zech. 1:6)[4] and any attribution to the prophet is *already* at one remove from its perceived true author. Yet one might object that the Greco-Roman literature is full of references to the inspiration of the gods, and this does not materially affect the sense of human *geistiges Eigentum,* or the criteria for proper attribution and forgery. But note that the prophetic word is a word from *Yahweh,* and not from any other gods. The "monolatry" (if not monotheism) of the OT may well explain the difference between itself and other polytheistic literature, both Greco-Roman and Near Eastern. For the OT, the source of revelation was not only *divine* (as it could be in many cultures), it was also *unitary* (as it was in no other). The only true revelation was Yahweh's (Isa 41:21–29; Jer 23:23–27).

A second, related feature of prophetic revelation is that it expresses the *unified or coherent message* and/or will of Yahweh. R. Clements notes that it was a common attitude of the NT (Acts 3:24; Cf. 3:18; 1 Pet 1:10–12) and post-biblical Judaism (Sir 49:10; 48:17–25; 1 Q Hab) that OT prophecy had one unified and coherent message, and that this attitude can be traced back to the time of the prophets themselves, especially in the work of the Deuteronomic school (2 Kgs 17:13–15), and in the redaction of the prophetic corpus[5]. Now it is impossible to state uncategorically that this was the view of the original prophets themselves, but there is one particularly common prophetic concept that would give credence to the idea, if not in the

---

(1951) 277–346; 20 (1952) 192–271, 295–361; "Zehn Jahre Literatur zur alttestamentlichen Prophetie (1951–1960)", *ThR* 28 (1962) 1–75, 235–297, 301–374; Neue Literatur zur alttestamentlichen Prophetie (1961–1970)", *ThR* 40 (1975) 193–209, 337–377; 41 (1976) 1–12; 45 (1980) 1–39, 109–132, 193–225; 47 (1982) 105–135, 205–218. See also R. Clements, *A Century of Old Testament Study* (Philadelphia: Westminster, 1976) 51–57; R.R. Wilson, *Prophecy and Society in Ancient Israel* (Philadelphia: Fortress, 1980) 1–19.

3 Of the 241 times the term "the word of Yahweh" appears in the OT, 221 relate to a prophetic oracle. G. von Rad, *Old Testament Theology, II* (London: Oliver and Boyd, 1965) 87.

4 The frequent use of *Botenspruch* or messenger formula such as "thus says Yahweh" makes this clear. See J.F. Ross, "The prophet as Yahweh's Messenger", *Israel's Prophetic Heritage.* Fest. J. Muilenburg. Edit. B.W. Anderson and W. Harrelson (London: SCM, 1962) 98–107; A. Malamat, "Prophetic Revelations in New Documents from Mari and the Bible", *VTSupp* 15 (1966) 207ff; M. Weinfeld, "Ancient Near Eastern Patterns in Prophetic Literature", *VT* 27 (1977) 178–195.

5 "Patterns in the Prophetic Canon", *Canon and Authority. Essays in Old Testament Religion and Theology.* Edit. G.W. Coats and B.O. Long (Philadelphia: Fortress, 1977) 42–55.

prophets themselves, at least for their successors and/or redactors. This is the concept of the "council of Yahweh"[6]. Pictured as a heavenly replica of the proceedings of an oriental court, Yahweh is seen as the celestial King surrounded by his host of servants and advisors, a conference in which the prophet is invited to take part, and to convey the divine deliberations to men. This concept is not only found in pre-exilic, exilic, and post-exilic prophets (Amos 3 :7; Isa 6:1–13 ; 40:1–11; Ezek 1–3 ; Jer 23:18–20; Zech 3:7), it is also found in the creation myth (Gen 1 :26), the wisdom tradition (Job 1: 6–12; 2:1–7; 15:8; Sir 24:2), the Psalms (89:5–7) and significantly, the Deuteronomic picture of prophecy (1 Kgs 22:19–23). Now if the prophets and those that followed them felt that true prophecy was a participation in the council Yahweh, then a logical corollary of this, based also on the nature of God, was that there would be a certain unity or consistency to his revelation, i.e. it partook of a coherent message. Unity or continuity, however, does not mean uniformity. The prophet did not necessarily know the whole counsel of Yahweh, but rather that aspect that concerned his own generation (Amos 3:7). Nevertheless his prophecy would have been felt to fit into the larger whole, and in fact to be relevant to later generations[7]. This is why in Jeremiah 26:16–19 (whether authentic or not)[8] the oracle of Jeremiah regarding Jerusalem can be regarded by its hearers as substantiated by an appeal to a similar prophecy made by Micah (3:12) nearly a century earlier.

The fundamental coherence or continuity of prophetic revelation also fits into a third feature, its *autonomous* or *"living"* nature. There is no denying the importance placed on the historical connection of prophetic revelation to the person and life of the prophet, as both the call narratives and the later superscriptions make clear. Yet it must be emphasized here that there is never any biographical interest placed in the prophet for its own sake, but only as a means of authorizing the message as truly the word of Yahweh[9]. Though it undoubtedly needs its human beginning, the prophetic word soon takes on a reality apart from the personal scope of the prophet. "Once spoken and current, his word is, as we might almost say, depersonalized, and enters upon its own independent history"[10].

---

6 See H.W. Robinson, "The Council of Yahweh", *JThS* 45 (1944) 151–157.

7 Clements ("Patterns") feels this is the force behind much of the redaction of the prophetic corpus and oracles into a more unified woe/salvation sequence.

8 Clements, "Patterns", 421–422, thinks it is not.

9 See N. Habel, "The Form and Significance of the Call Narrative", *ZAW* 77 (1965) 317; G.M. Tucker, "Prophetic Superscriptions and the Growth of a Canon", *Canon and Authority. Essays in Old Testament Religion and Theology.* Edit. W. Coats, and B.O. Long (Philadelphia: Fortress, 1977) 65–68.

10 H.W. Robinson, *Inspiration and Revelation in the Old Testament* (Oxford: Clarendon, 1946) 170. But it is not "depersonalized" in the sense that its nature is devoid of the influence of the prophets' personality. This is why I am hesitant to accept R.E. Clements' emphasis on the inspiration of the *message* rather than the prophet ("Patterns", 45). An example of the independence of the prophets' message may be found in the instances where the prophet actually delegates the delivery of his ora-

Older scholarship traced this phenomenon to a supposed distinctive Oriental concept of the "word"[11]. Rather than simply serving as linguistic symbols, both human and divine words were considered as objective agents fulfilling their intent. Scholars were not even reluctant to refer to this independent quality of the word in the OT as a hypostasis[12].

Today a more circumspect scholarship would be reluctant to speak of the relative independence of the prophetic word as a hypostasis. Furthermore, it is clear that the function of the word is not due to any distinctive Oriental use of language, but to the *performative* function of *religious* language[13]. In other words, the divine/prophetic word has a relative independence and objectivity because it is regarded as an extension of the mind and attributes of the deity who is its source.

Given this qualification, the phenomenon of the autonomous (from the prophet) "word" of Yahweh is still an important one. As an extension of the divine attributes, the word of Yahweh is both creative (Ps 33:6) and effective (Ps 147:15f). Because of who Yahweh is, it can never be ineffective or fail in its objective (Isa 55:11). Even more significant, this word was an eternally valid one (Isa 40:8). As we shall see, it is this autonomous and eternal quality of the prophetic word that will give rise to its subsequent interpretation and reinterpretation (*Nachgeschichte*), beyond its original historical moorings. Even those prophecies that plainly found their original goal and fulfilment were retained and applied to new contexts, as though new meaning could always be derived from them[14].

An illustration of this "vitality" of the word of God is given in an article of similar title by P.R. Ackroyd[15]. He discusses the presence of three parallel prophecies recorded in the book of 1 Kings (14:11; 16:4; 21:24). The oracles are identical, and yet they occur on the lips of three different prophets, are uttered against three different kings, and take place in three different historical contexts. Rather than regard these as original, independent prophecies, or the unimaginative repetition of an editor short of materials, Ackroyd regards this as indicative of a conviction of the fundamental vitality of the word of God. The underlying premise of this thrice-repeated prophecy is that the northern kingdom is apostate or illegitimate, a fundamental theme of

---

cles to other individuals (Jer 21:1–14; 2 Kgs 9:1–10). See K.W. Schmidt, "Prophetic Delegation: A Form-Critical Inquiry", *Bib* 63 (1982) 206–218.

11 See esp. von Rad, *Theology II*, 80–98.

12 See H. Ringgren, *Word and Wisdom. Studies in the Hypostatization of Divine Qualities and Functions in the Ancient Near East* (Lund: Ohlssons, 1947) 157–164; L. Dürr, *Die Wertung des göttlichen Wortes im Alten Testament und im antiken Orient* (Leipzig: J.C. Hinrich, 1938) (N.V.)

13 See A.C. Thiselton, "The Supposed Power of Words in the Biblical Writings", *JThS* 25 (1974) 283–299.

14 von Rad, *Theology II*, 45. See further below.

15 "The Vitality of the Word of God in the Old Testament. A Contribution to the Study of the Transmission and Exposition of Old Testament Material", *ASTI* 1 (1962) 1–23.

the Deuteronomic history. Therefore either the prophets, or more likely, the editor, creatively refashions or reapplies this traditional oracle to new situations, and fits it into a larger salvation-historical perspective.

The fourth feature of prophetic revelation is also connected to the above, and may be described as its *interpretive* (and reinterpretive) nature. It ought to be noted that there is no technical language in the OT for the idea of revelation[16]. Nor is there any standard mode of revelation. J. Barr gives a helpful explanation of why this is so[17]. In our modern usage, revelation opposes the denial of God's existence and is used to distinguish divine knowledge from scientific knowledge. Yet in ancient Israel there was no disbelief in Yahweh's existence or doubt in his ability to reveal himself. Thus the emphasis is not on the actuality or even the mode of revelation, but on the interpretation of revelation that is everywhere present, with no sharp demarcation made between "special" and "general" revelation. This emphasis on discernment or interpretation gives OT revelation its multi-layered, traditional nature.

The interpretative process of prophetic revelation is not just a feature of later tradition, but is intrinsic to the whole development. C. Westermann stresses that, even in the basic prophetic oracle, the interpretive facilities of the prophet are required to make sense of the vision or audition. The message that is given is in some senses both the prophet's and Yahweh's[18]. Certainly we know that the oracles were shaped by the features of the culture in which the prophet lived, as recent sociological studies have reaffirmed[19].

In fact, not all of the prophetic revelation was derived from an oracular source. Not only did the prophets interpret their own encounter with the divine, they also demonstrate a mark of "inspired" reflection on the traditions they had received. C. Buchanan has demonstrated that even some oracles described as "visions" or the "coming of the word" are in fact the result of an "inspired" midrashic examination of earlier traditions[20]. In all of this it

---

16 See H. Haag, "Offenbarung in der herbräischen Bibel" *ThZ* 16 (1960) 251–258; W. Zimmerli, "Offenbarung im Alten Testament" *EvTh* 22 (1962) 15–31; R. Rendtorff, "The Concept of Revelation in Ancient Israel", *Revelation as History*. Edit. W. Pannenberg (New York: Macmillan, 1968) 23–53; R. Knierim, "Offenbarung im Alten Testament", *Probleme biblischer Theologie*. Fest. G. von Rad. Edit. H.W. Wolff (Munich. C. Kaiser, 1971) 206–235.

17 *Old and New in Interpretation* (London: SCM, 1966) 89–90.

18 *Basic Forms of Prophetic Speech* (London: Lutterworth, 1967). See also von Rad, *Theology II,* 75; and more speculatively, J. Lindblom, *Prophecy in Ancient Israel* (Oxford: Blackwell 1962) 137–148; reprinted separately as "Symbolic Perceptions and Literary Visions", *The Bible in its Literary Milieu.* Edit. J. Maier and V. Tollers (Grand Rapids: Eerdmans, 1979) 67–76.

19 See P.L. Berger, "Charisma and Religious Innovation: The Social Location of Israelite Prophecy," *American Sociological Review* 28 (1963) 940–948; R.R. Wilson, *Prophecy and Society;* D.L. Petersen, *The Roles of Israel's Prophets* (Sheffield: JSOT Press, 1981).

20 "The Word of God and the Apocalyptic Vision", *Society of Biblical Literature*

is important to note that tradition is often used but virtually never cited or attributed. This means that the prophets must have been aware that they were part of a *living* tradition process, a process to which they could add, and presumably a process that could add to their message once they were gone.

2.1.2 *The Growth of the Prophetic Tradition*

Whenever one reads a prophetic book, the first impression is one of over-whelming incoherence. Now there is no doubt that at least some of the or-acles that we have were written by the prophet himself (Isa 8:16–18; 30:8–17; Jer 36), or recorded for him. Indeed, it is likely that all of the prophets took care to have their prophecies preserved in some fashion, either orally or in written form. Yet the composition of the prophetic books shows that it is probable that they were not compiled by the original prophets. "They are not the kind of literary works which follow from the master plan of a single creative mind"[21]. There is no question, then, that the prophetic books are the literary expression of a long history of tradition. The real question is, did the later disciples, redactors, recipients, etc. of the prophetic tradition conceive of that tradition as a static *traditum*, or did they feel the same free-dom as the original prophet (at least in kind, it not degree) to enter into a dialogue with that tradition in order to interpret if for their own generation?

The traditio-historical method of OT studies has demonstrated that this is the case with unqualified success[22]. In short, the growth of the prophetic tradition is not due to a rigid transmission and accumulation of a *traditum,* but the living process of a *traditio.* The freedom of reinterpretation or actual-ization (*Vergegenwärtigung*) of the prophetic tradition is in evidence through-out the OT corpus. For example, the sayings of Amos and Hosea were given a new "Judaic" actualization after the northern kingdom had been destroyed. That is, their prophecies were expanded or reinterpreted to include Judah[23].

Examples of *Vergegenwärtigung* in varying degrees could be cited from most prophetic books. Many prophecies may well have remained virtually unaltered. How far the process of actualization could go will be demon-

---

    Seminar Papers (1978), Vol. II (Missoula: Scholars Press, 1978) 183–192. He cites 2 Isaiah's midrash on Exodus 15:1–16 (cf. Isa 42:10–13; 43:14–17; 51:9–10) and Jeremiah's midrash on Deut 28:26 (cf. Jer 7:32–33), Deut 28:64 (cf. Jer 9: 16), Deut 27:26; 4:20; 7:12 (cf. Jer 11.3–5), Deut 30:15 (cf. Jer 21:8), and Deut 4:9 (cf. Jer 29:13–14).

21 W. McKane, "Prophecy and the Prophetic Literature", *Tradition and Interpreta-tion.* Edit. G.W. Anderson (Oxford: University Press, 1979) 181.

22 The most famous of this method's proponents is, of course, Gerhard von Rad. See esp. *Theology II.* See also S. Mowinckel, *Prophecy and Tradition* (Oslo: Dybwad, 1946). An excellent introduction to the history and literature of this methodology may be found in D.A. Knight, *Rediscovering the Traditions of Israel* (Revised edition. Missoula: Scholars Press, 1975).

23 See S. Mowinckel, *Prophecy,* 72.

strated in the Isaiah tradition (below). At this point it is important to remark on the theological rationale for such a process. It is obvious that the various redactors or tradents of the prophetic tradition give no abstract or overt theological justification for their work. Indeed, any trace of their involvement at all is due to the labours of modern criticism, and not their own volition. Yet as we discussed, even the original prophets were less concerned with revelation in the abstract than they were with the possession of God's word *for them*. As we saw, four of the essential features of that revelation were its divine source, unified (not uniform) message, autonomous quality, and interpretive nature. If these qualities were felt to be part of the original prophetic oracles, then what evidence do we have that they were part of the thinking of the later tradents? The answer lies in the development of the prophetic texts themselves. We cannot look for theological proof-texts, but we can see how the prophetic oracles were actually handled. As will be demonstrated in Isaiah, these oracles were not rigidly regarded as a fixed *traditum*. Because of their nature as the word of Yahweh, they were considered to have an independent relevance and authority, apart from the original. The details are not always clear, but the growth of prophetic tradition has to be understood in the context of the interaction of original oracles, later tradents such as disciples or scribes, and the religious community that not only allows its identity to be shaped by this tradition, but by its outlook also indirectly shapes the tradition as well.

This is not to deny the uniqueness and necessity of creative, inspired individuals — as the original prophets undoubtedly were. But the emphasis in the process of tradition is decidedly not on the individual for his own sake, but on the community as it finds its identity in the unfolding word of God. All of the participants in the prophetic tradition are linked in this common identity[24].

However, one cannot deny that there were historical, biographical, or literary interests in the development of the prophetic tradition. In fact, a fundamental weakness of the traditio-historical approach is that it has lent itself to an entirely non-historical approach to OT interpretation. The stress on *traditio* has led some to depict the tradition process as entirely fluid, dictated only by the existential needs of the tradents[25]. This hermeneutic has fed directly into the development of process theology[26].

---

24 See S. Mowinckel, "Oppkomsten av profetlitteraturen," *Norsk Teologisk Tidsskrift* 43 (1941) 89, as cited and translated by D. Knight, *Rediscovering,* 256, n.1. See also H.J. Hermission, "Zeitbezug des prophetische Wortes," *KuD* 27 (1981/82) 96–110.

25 B.S. Childs maintains this was certainly not the intent of G. von Rad in his concept of *Vergegenwärtigung* (communicated in a lecture at the University of Cambridge, England).

26 For example, P. Hanson, *Dynamic Transcendence: The Correlation of Confessional Heritage and Contemporary Experience in a Biblical Model of Divine Activity* (Philadelphia: Fortress, 1978).

Therefore a much needed corrective can be welcomed in the recent rise of the discipline now called canon criticism[27]. A seminal work in this regard was B.S. Childs, *Memory and Tradition in Israel* (London: SCM, 1962). His examination of the root *zkr* in the OT demonstrated that what distinguished Israelite tradition from the mythic world view of its neighbours was its connection to real history. However, *Vergegenwärtigung* does not simply repeat the past, nor does it abandon it, but ... "each successive generation rewrites the past in terms of her own experience with the God who meets his people through the tradition" (89).

Canon criticism as it developed was not only a reaction to elements of the traditio-historical method, but also to the rigid literary approach to the problem of canon and authority. A great deal of confusion is engendered in any discussion of canon because of its two-fold meaning. From the perspective of the "history of the canon", canon is used in the sense of a *closed canon,* a group of static, authoritative documents to which nothing can be added and nothing subtracted, either as a group or as individual documents. But a second meaning of canon, preferred by canon criticism, is that it simply designates something as *authoritative.* The prophetic (and other) tradition became authoritative long before it had reached its final literary form, a fact that is ignored by traditio-historical criticism and the usual historical accounts of canonization.

Other writers have recognized this difficulty in the meaning of canon, and have suggested that the word "canon" be restricted to a closed collection, and the term "scripture" be used to designate writings that are in some sense authoritative[28]. The problem with this approach is that it is still tied to the perspective of *literature,* and many traditions were authoritative long before they took literary form. It is best to use the term "closed canon" to designate just that, and retain the wider use of "canon" or "canonical" to refer to authoritative tradition.

The value of canon criticism is that it fills the gap between the unrestricted growth of tradition envisioned by the traditio-historical method and the authoritative and ultimate restriction placed on that growth by the canonization of the final literary documents. In pictorial terms, for canon criticism the formation of the prophetic corpus is less like the filling of a mould with an

---

27 The two major figures in the movement are James Sanders and Brevard Childs, whose views are by no means entirely congruent. Childs' mature views may be seen in his *Introduction to the Old Testament as Scripture* (London: SCM, 1979). See also the series of review articles on this work in JSOT 16 (1980) and *Horizons in Biblical Theology* 2 (1980). See also his latest work, *The New Testament as Canon: As Introduction* (Philadelphia: Fortress, 1984). Sanders' major work is *Torah and Canon* (Philadelphia: Fortress, 1972). See also "Biblical Criticism and the Bible as Canon," *USQR* 32 (1977) 157–165; *Canon and Community* (Philadelphia: Fortress, 1984).

28 A. Sundberg, "The Bible Canon and the Christian Doctrine of Inspiration," *Interp* 29 (1975) 356.

amorphous tradition which is then hardened into an authoritative shape by the pronouncement of some ecclesiastical body, and more like the growth of a tree, expanding in layers to a level of maximal growth, but always taking its shape from the core. Traditions from their inception take on an increasingly authoritative and correspondingly less adaptable nature. The full grown tree may look a lot different from the sapling, but there is a fundamental continuity between the two.

As we shall discuss further in Chapter 6, the role of the religious community is crucial both to the growth of tradition and the development of canon. Those tradents who actualized the tradition in light of their own needs were also bound to it as the authoritative source of their identity. In other words, there was a developing sense of "canon-consciousness" among those responsible for the growth of the tradition.

The results of canon-criticism have important implications for an understanding of authorship and attribution in the growth of the prophetic tradition. We have already seen how the prophetic oracles were supplemented and reinterpreted to make them relevant to new generations, a major contribution of the traditio-historical method. Now the contribution of canon criticism reminds us that this process was not an indiscriminate one, but that the historical nature of Israelite religion and the developing "canon-consciousness" of those who handled the traditions served as stablizing elements in the tradition process in order to insure its continuity. If prophetic revelation was not restricted to the original oracles of the prophet, neither was it separate from them, and the retention of the literary, biographical, and historical elements in the prophetic works are an essential witness to this "canon-consciousness" of the tradents toward the core traditions[29].

The question as to why the autobiographical or orthonymous witness of some prophets are retained and others are not is a question that cannot be fully answered. It may be partly on the basis of their perceived special election (as witnessed by the call narratives) or by their ability to gather disciples around them. D. Petersen suggests that it is connected to the prophet's special relationship to the monarchy, and that when the monarchy was destroyed, orthonymous prophecy (and later all prophecy) died as well[30]. While it is true that anonymous supplementation of the prophetic corpus was more prevelant during and after the Exile[31], *Vergegenwärtigung* was a pre-exilic phenomenon as well[32]. It must simply be admitted that our understanding

---

29 This is not to say that all the core traditions are in fact historical, only that they are regarded as such.

30 *Late Israelite Prophecy: Studies in Deutero-Prophetic Literature and in Chronicles* (Missoula: Scholars Press, 1977).

31 J. Blenkinsopp, *Prophecy and Canon* (London: University of Notre Dame Press, 1977) talks of the increasing "scribalization" of prophecy.

32 R. Mason, "The Prophets of the Restoration," *Israel's Prophetic Traditon.* Fest. P.R. Ackroyd. Edit. R. Coggins, A. Philips, and M. Knibb (Cambridge: University Press, 1982) 139–140 denies any such vital link to the monarchy.

of the phenomenon of OT prophecy is too incomplete to gain a clear picture of the dynamic involved in the emergence of the classic prophetic personalities.

At least it is clear from our discussion of the formation of the prophetic corpus that within the individual tradition of an historically recognized prophet, it is certainly possible that the anonymity of those responsible for its actualization and redaction is directly due to a perceived continuity with the original prophetic figure. In other words, the prophet was still regarded as speaking to later generations. It is this perceived continuity of revelation and tradition that most likely stands at the heart of the formation and attribution of the prophetic corpus. Confirmation of this can be gained from an illustration of these features in the growth of the Isaiah tradition.

2.2 The Isaiah Tradition

The choice of the book of Isaiah to illustrate the growth and reinterpretation of the prophetic tradition is certainly not an original or innovative one. In 1936 H.W. Hertzberg published an essay precisely on the topic of *Nachgeschichte* in Isaiah 1–35[33]. Even before this, the book of Isaiah had been a cornerstone in the critical arguments over the authorship of the prophetic corpus. Ever since the work of Duhm, the multi-layered (and multi-authored) nature of Isaiah has been accepted. The editorial history of the book covers a span of five hundred years and a number of major redactions and additions.

However, until recently this emphasis on discovering the elements that can be *divided* in Isaiah has led to a corresponding de-emphasis on what unites the tradition[34]. It is usually not the constraints of format but critical presuppositions that lead to the publication of separate commentaries on Isaiah 1–39 and 40–66, as if they could be understood apart from each other. Besides the arguments of a few isolated conservatives who maintain the literary authenticity of the entire book[35], the main efforts to counter this trend have been by those who would attribute Isaiah to the work of a single prophetic "school"[36]. But their arguments are based on extremely

---

33 "Die Nachgeschichte alttestamentlichen Texte innerhalb des Alten Testaments," *Werden und Wesen des Alten Testaments*. Edit. P. Volz (BZAW 66. Berlin: A. Töpelmann, 1936) 110–121.

34 A notable exception is R.E. Clements, "The Unity of the Book of Isaiah," *Interp* 36 (1982) 117–129.

35 See O. Allis, *The Unity of Isaiah* (Philadelphia: Presbyterian and Reformed, 1950, reprinted Grand Rapids: Baker, 1972); E.J. Young, *Who Wrote Isaiah?* (Grand Rapids: Eerdmans, 1958).

36 See D.R. Jones, "The Traditio of the Oracles of Isaiah," *ZAW* 26 (1955) 226–246; S. Mowinckel, *Jesaja-Disiplene* (Oslo, 1926); J. Eaton, "The Origin of the Book of

fragile exegetical and historical grounds[37]. If there is a fundamental unity to the book of Isaiah, then it has to be sought along *theological* grounds, as R.E. Clements remarks[38]. This will be the approach taken below, as we seek to demonstrate the progressive reinterpretation of the Isaiah tradition and its implications for literary attribution.

2.2.1. *Isaiah of Jerusalem and First Isaiah (1—39)*

It must be stated at the outset that no attempt will be made to give a comprehensive account of the redaction of this or any other part of the book of Isaiah[39]. What is intended is merely an illustrative survey, using examples from redactions that are commonly, if not universally, posited. Furthermore, it is not the intent to give a comprehensive treatment of the life and thought of Isaiah of Jerusalem, or any of the other "Isaiahs", but merely to investigate their theological connections.

Though a pre-exilic "Josianic" or "Assyrian" redaction of Isaiah's oracles has been isolated[40], we will begin with what may be called the "Babylonian" redaction. It will be noted that the two main historical loci of Isaiah of Jerusalem's prophecies concern the Syro-Ephraimite crisis of 736 B.C. (the reign of Ahaz), and the invasion of Sennacherib in 701 B.C. (the reign of Hezekiah). Isaiah's message revolves around the fate of Jerusalem as she faces these crises. Repentance and trust in a holy God will result in deliverance (1 : 16—19) and stubborn reliance on self and human allies (first Assyria, then Egypt) will result in judgement and destruction (1 :20). There is a great deal of redactional evidence to show that Isaiah's prophecies were reinterpreted in the light of the Babylonian exile in the sixth century. This can be seen in a series of redactions ranging from a few words at the head of a collection of oracles (1:1 ; 2:1)[41] or as an interpretive appendage (23:13) to large additions of material (Chap. 35, 38—39).

Isaiah," *VT* 9 (1959) 138—157; *idem,* "The Isaiah Tradition," *Israel's Prophetic Tradition.* Fest. P.R. Ackroyd. Edit. R. Coggins, A. Phillips, and M. Knibb (Cambridge: University Press, 1982) 58—76.

37 See G. Fohrer, "The Origin, Composition, and Tradition of Isaiah I—XXXIX," *ALOUS* 3 (1961—62), 29—37; R.E. Clements, *Isaiah 1—39* (London: Marshall, Morgan and Scott, 1980). 4—5, 100—101.

38 "Unity."

39 Space alone, as well as lack of scholarly consensus, dictates against it. For example, the latest treatment of Isaiah 1—35 takes two volumes (nearly 900 pages) and claims to isolate no less than seven distinct redactional stages! See J. Vermeylen, *Du Prophète Isaie à l'Apocalyptique: Isaie I—XXXV, miroir d'un demi-millénaire d'expérience réligieuse en Israel* (Paris: Gabalda, 1977—78).

40 See H. Barth, *Die Jesaja-Worte in der Josiazeit* (Neukirchen-Vluyn: Neukirchener Verlag, 1977).

41 "Judah and Jerusalem" is an exilic term used to refer to the remnant whose center is Jerusalem. D.R. Jones, "Traditio of Isaiah," 238—239.

There are two main elements to this "Babylonian" redaction. First, Isaiah's prophecies of judgement are directly related to the destruction of Jerusalem in 587 B.C.[42] This is done in a number of ways. Isaiah's original oracles of judgement are coloured with features of the actual siege, such as famine ("stay of bread and water", MT 3:1). Oracles not directly connected with Jerusalem are now seen in the light of its destruction. Thus the "Women of Jerusalem" (3:16–17) now become Jerusalem herself (3:25–26), ravaged and destitute. A prophecy against a certain (royal?) servant (22:15–19) now becomes a prophecy of the downfall of the entire Davidic monarchy (22:25). Oracles whose original referent was Assyria are now overtly corrected to refer to Babylon (23:13). The connection with the events of 587 B.C. is made specific by the addition of the story of Hezekiah and the Babylon emmisaries (Isa 39 = 2 Kgs 20:12–19)[43]. Chapters 36–39 act as a hermeneutical link between the two main divisions of the book of Isaiah (the "Assyrian" book, 1–39, and the "Babylonian" book, 40–66). Borrowed from 2 Kings 18–20, they explain not only why the events of 587 B.C. are to be regarded as the fulfilment of Isaiah's prophecy, but also why the threatened destruction of Jerusalem *did not* take place in Isaiah's lifetime (because of Hezekiah's repentance).

We can certainly observe that the redactors of Isaiah's oracles saw a *formal* parallel between the Babylonian destruction of Jerusalem and Isaiah's threatened judgement by means of Assyria, as well as the attendent religious/ historical causes (corrupt leadership, defiled cult). Coupled with a conviction of the lasting vitality and applicability of the word of Yahweh, this might be enough to justify their work. Yet there is evidence to suggest that the link is even deeper. In Chapter 22:1–4, 12–14 we have what is most likely Isaiah's reaction to the deliverance of Jerusalem through Hezekiah's "cutting a deal" with the invading Sennacherib (2 Kgs 18:13–18)[44]. He warns the citizens that instead of rejoicing they should be mourning, because their attitude is still deeply offensive to Yahweh. Significantly he warns, "Surely this iniquity will not be forgiven you till you die". *In other words, in light of the circumvention of his original prophecies against Jerusalem, Isaiah threatens with a future judgement.* It is easy to see how the "Babylonian" redactors could see this fulfilled in their own recent events, and this is confirmed by the associations they make in this very chapter. In 22:5–8a, we have a redacted oracle with several allusions to the destruction of Jerusalem in 587 B.C.[45] Of paramount importance is the *theological* underpinning of this redaction. In the subsequent redactional addition (vv 8b–11) which

---

42 See esp. R.E. Clements, "The Prophecies of Isaiah and the Fall of Jerusalem in 587 B.C.," *VT* 30 (1980) 421–436.
43 See P.R. Ackroyd, "An Interpretation of the Babylonian Exile: A Study of 2 Kings 20, Isaiah, 38–39," *SJT* (1974) 329–352.
44 R.E. Clements, "Fall of Jerusalem," 429–432.
45 The battering of walls (v 5), the armies of Elam and Ker (v 6) and the removal of the covering (v 8a). See R.E. Clements, *Isaiah 1–39*, 182–185.

mocks the futile attempts to withstand the siege, reference is made to the "plan" (ר צ י) of Yahweh (22:11b, cf. 37:26).

Isaiah of Jerusalem is the first prophet to speak clearly of a "plan" or "counsel" of Yahweh (י ע ץ , ה צ ע y)[46]. Building on the concept of the heavenly council, Isaiah contrasts the plan of Yahweh to that of sinful Israel (7: 5) and Judah (30:1, cf. 29:15; 32:7), as well as to the plans of the nations (8:10; 19:3, 11). Though wicked men refuse to believe it, Yahweh has his sovereign plan (5:19), a plan that embraces world history (8:10; 19:12; 23: 8–9?).

This theme of a divine plan is an important one in the redactional material as well (14:24–27; 19:17; 23:8–9? ; cf. also 37:26), and the stress here is even more on the universal purpose of Yahweh. Thus it is easy to see how the "Babylonian" redactors of Isaiah's oracles could connect the destruction of 587 B.C. with his prophecies of judgement. It was all part of Yahweh's plan, which could not come to nought. Originally disclosed "long ago" (22: 11b) to Isaiah, it had now found its fulfilment a century and a half later in the Babylonian exile.

Few people would dispute that, even if Isaiah had not envisioned a future judgement, the reapplication of his oracles to the destruction of 587 B.C. does no violence to the essence of his message. A more controversial aspect of the "Babylonian" redaction, however, is the second major element: the systematic organization of the prophecies into a woe/salvation sequence, to reflect the hope of restoration after the Exile. Thus, for example, 2:1–4 promises an eschatological salvation after the judgement of Chapter One; 4:2–6 adds a word of grace to the oracles of judgement against the daughters of Jerusalem in 3:16–26; and Chapters 34 and 35 promise future redemption after a series of oracles against Israel and Judah (28–33).

It seems almost unquestionable that much of this optimism received its inspiration from the prophecies of 2 Isaiah. Though it was long thought that Isaiah 40–66 (or –55) was joined to the collected prophecies of Isaiah of Jerusalem through accidental linkage in a common scroll, the redaction of Isaiah 1–39 *in light of* 2 Isaiah makes it clear that the association is intentional. Chapter 35 is a clear example of themes of salvation introduced secondarily from 2 Isaiah[47]. As we remarked earlier, Chapters 38–39 serve as a redactional link to the Babylonian *Sitz*. P.R. Ackroyd has demonstrated that the intent is not only to refer to the judgement of exile (39:1–8), but the story of Hezekiah's illness and recovery (38:1–8) is meant as a paradigm of restoration as well[48].

The key motivation of this type of thinking is the idea of a returning rem-

---

46 See J. Fichtner, "Jahwes Plan in der Botschaft des Jesaja," *ZAW* 63 (1951) 16–33.

47 For example, the themes of the highway (v 8, cf. 40:3), streams in the desert (v 6, cf. 43:19; 43:3), return of the ransomed to Zion (v 10, cf. 51:11). Cf. also 18:7; 45:14.

48 "An Interpretation."

nant (35:10; 37:31, cf. 46:3), an important one to Isaiah of Jerusalem. Foremost is the use of the enigmatic sign-name for his son, Shearjashub, "a remnant returns". Given as a sign to the wavering Ahaz in the face of the Syro-Ephraimite crisis (7:3–9), its meaning was, to say the least, ambiguous. It was probably originally intended, as was the sign name Mahershalalhashbaz ("the spoil speeds, the prey hastes", 8:1–4), to assure Ahaz that if he had faith, his enemies would be reduced to a pitiful remnant. Yet the same tool of Yahweh (Assyria) could produce the demise of Judah as well, if no faith was exercised (7:9; 8:5–8). This is precisely what happened, so that Jerusalem is reduced to a pitiful remnant (1:8–9) or a smouldering stump (6:13). The sign names were double-edged oracles, that could result in judgement or salvation. As used by Isaiah, the word "remnant" is the essentially negative political concept of the people who are left after a military campaign. It is used not only to describe Judah (1:9, cf. 30:17), but also Assyria (10:19), Syria (17:3, 5f), Moab (15:9; 16:4); Keder (21:17) and the Philistines (14:30).

But though the message of a "remnant" may be bad news to a nation still intact (Amos 5:3), it can be good news to those that survive (Amos 5:15). This seems to be the thinking behind the redaction of Isaiah's oracles. In the enigmatic sign name Shearjashub they saw the promise of hope left to those who had survived God's terrible judgement. This is made clear by the midrash on that name found in 10:20–23. In v. 20 "him who smote them" now refers to Assyria, and not Yahweh (cf. 9:13). The message of hope is that "a remnant will return" (v.21, cf. 7:3). Though the Davidic dynasty has been destroyed, the "Mighty God" (v.21, cf. MT 9:6) will now be their king and deliverer.

In a series of other crucial passages, the "Babylonian" redactors continually repeat their hope in a surviving, returning remnant (4:2–6; 11:11–16; 27:12–13; 28:5–6. Cf. also 6:13). The destruction of Jerusalem is regarded as a cleansing, refining one, a full payment for sins (4:4, cf. 40:2). Now it may be that the ambiguity of the original sign name Shearjashub was sufficient justification for these redactors to impart new meaning into what they considered to be the vital "word of God".

But the link to Isaiah is stronger[49]. That Isaiah himself could hold out hope even amidst the disappointing events of 701 B.C. is clear from the oracle of future restoration through refining judgement found in 1:25–26. J. Jensen has convincingly demonstrated the pedagogical nature of Isaiah's prophecies of judgement by examining Isaiah's well-known connection with the wisdom tradition[50]. The sinful state of Judah is described as a lack of knowledge (1:3; 5:13; 6:9), and the promised future restoration is depicted in terms of the restoration of true judges and counsellors (1:25–26). Perhaps

---

49 Contra G. Fohrer, "Die Struktur der altestamentlichen Eschatologie," *Studien zur altestamentlichen Prophetie* (1949–1965) (BZAW 99. Berlin: A. Töpleman, 1967) 32–58.

50 "Weal and Woe in Isaiah: Consistency and Continuity," *CBQ* 43 (1981) 167–187.

the most significant feature is Isaiah's description of Assyria as Yahweh's "rod" and "staff" (10:5–15). In Proverbs, there is a whole series of texts which counsel the parent to *chastise* his son with a staff or rod in order to *save* him from death and give him wisdom (10:13; 13:24; 22:15; 23:13,14; 26:3; 29:15). When we remember that Isaiah depicts Yahweh as a father dealing with his foolish, rebellious children who shun instruction (1:2–3; 30:1,9), then it can be seen that the role of Assyria in God's judgement of his people is intended for the pedagogical purpose of correction, not destruction. This role finds further confirmation in the parable of the farmer in 28:23–29. The wisdom motif of instruction is clear (v.26), and the whole point of the parable is that punishment is not an end in itself. The farmer does not use a threshing sledge in harvesting his more fragile crops, but a *rod* and staff (v.27). The whole purpose of ploughing and harvesting is to produce fruit, not ruin it (vv. 24,28).

It is significant that the parable of the farmer ends with a reference to the plan of Yahweh (v.29), a universal theme that we noted earlier. Here is the theological justification for the *Nachgeschichte* of Isaiah's oracles of salvation as well as judgement. Even though Isaiah depicts Israel as a severely beaten child in the aftermath of the events of 701 B.C. (1:4–9), and even though he knew his own efforts ended in failure (6:9–10), could he not have hoped that Yahweh's rebellious children would yet "return" to him (1:25–26)? Perhaps this is why he recorded his oracles, in the hope that some future generation would recognize that "in returning and rest you shall be saved" (30:15).

Now it might be objected that there is still a fundamental difference between a conditional hope based on future repentance, and the unconditional promise of redemption that seems implicit in the "Babylonian" redaction. This objection goes to the heart of the relation between Isaiah of Jerusalem and 2 Isaiah, and will be considered in this context.

2.2.2. Second Isaiah (40–55)

The differentiation of the ministry of Isaiah of Jerusalem from that of the one now called "deutero" or "second" Isaiah is one of the assured results of modern scholarship. There are clear differences of language, style, concepts; and the change in historical setting demands that the oracles found in Isaiah 40–55 be placed in the period of the Exile[51]. Though there is widespread disagreement over the literary unity and structure of these oracles, it

---

51 The most telling piece of historical evidence is the mention of Cyrus (43:28; 45:1. Cf. 41:2, 25; 45:13; 46:11; 48:14). The issue is not one of "predictive prophecy," as conservatives love to argue, but of the *nature* of prophecy, even in its predictive mode. OT prophets may have predicted the future, but they always related it to the present. The message about Cyrus would have been meaningless to the eighth century audience of Isaiah of Jerusalem.

is almost universally agreed that they are the product of a single individual, most likely given in Babylon. The only portion often *not* assigned to second Isaiah is the so-called "Servant Songs" (42:1–4(7);49:1–6; 50:4–9; 52:13–53:12), and will not be brought into reckoning because of this lack of consensus.

The consensus on the authorship of "second" Isaiah, however, generates its own problems. If the oracles of the two "Isaiahs" can be differentiated, what was the reason for joining them in the first place? We have seen from the "Babylonian" redaction of Isaiah 1–39 that it could not have been accidental. Yet many of the motives suggested for this linkage seem less than adequate. Fohrer thinks that it was because Isaiah was considered a prophet *par excellence*, but evidence suggests that Micah was more popular[52]. J. Eaton's suggestion of a physically continuous "school" of Isaiah lacks historical plausibility. R.P. Carroll's suggestion that the motive was to reinterpret the "failed" prophecies of Isaiah does not really explain why anyone would bother[53]. Blenkinsopp suggests that the joining arose from the similar political situations of the eighth and sixth centuries, but this is hardly a sufficient cause. P.R. Ackroyd thinks it stems from the "presentation" of Isaiah as a prophet of salvation in an early collection of his oracles (1–12)[54]. But all the pre-exilic prophets were similarly reinterpreted, so that this alone does not seem sufficient. Perhaps the most fruitful suggestion is that of R.E. Clements, who points to the thematic and religious connections between the two[55]. Ironically this is the province of older scholarship in its argument for authenticity. Yet after dismissing any claims to identity of authorship, there is ample evidence to suggest a fundamental identity of religious perspective, so that the joining of the oracles may have been "designed to clarify and fill out the divine message given to Israel, especially Jerusalem"[56]. In other words, there may have been a conscious awareness and expansion of an Isaiah tradition.

Though no thoroughgoing comparison of the theologies of "first" and "second" Isaiah is possible here, a comparison of key themes is instructive. In particular, Isaiah's temple vision (Chapter 6) gives an outline of what J. Roberts calls a "theocentric vision" that unites the theology of the entire Isaianic corpus[57]. Though the prophecies of "third" Isaiah (55–66) will be dealt with more fully later, it will be convenient to include them here as well.

Isaiah's original vision emphasizes both Yahweh's incomparable holiness and power. His most characteristic designation of Yahweh is as the "Holy One" (usually "of Israel", 1:4; 5:19,24; 10:17,20; 12:16; 17:7; 29:19,23;

---

52 P.R. Ackroyd, "Isaiah i–xii: Presentation of a Prophet," *VT Supp* 29 (1977) 22–24. He cites Jer. 26:17–19.
53 *When Prophecy Failed* (London. SCM, 1979).
54 "Isaiah i–xii."
55 "The Unity of the Book of Isaiah," *Interp* 36 (1982) 117–129.
56 R.E. Clements, "Unity," 128.
57 J.J.M. Roberts, "Isaiah in Old Testament Theology," *Interp* 36 (1982) 130–143.

30:11,12,15; 31:1; 37:23), a title rarely found outside of the larger Isaianic corpus. It seems no accident that this holiness of Yahweh is the passion of second and third Isaiah as well, and that the same characteristic designation is used (40:25; 41:14,16,20; 43:3,14,15; 45:11; 47:4, 48:17; 49:7; 54:5, 55:5; 60:9,14).

The second feature of Isaiah's theocentric vision, Yahweh's incomparable power, is expressed in a number of related ways. Isaiah beholds his God seated on a heavenly throne and exalted by the cry of the seraphim that "the whole earth is full of his glory" (v.3). The exaltation of Yahweh is a direct claim to this unique sovereignty in history (2:11–19). The glory (כבד) of Yahweh (3:8; 10:16), the divine King (6:5; 33:22), is contrasted to the emphemeral, earthly glory of those who oppose him (10:3,18; 16:14; 17:4). This concern for the divine sovereignty and glory is continued in second and third Isaiah in a similar vein. Both affirm Yahweh's exclusive glory (40:5; 42:8,12; 48:11, 58:8; 59:19; 60:1,2; 66:18,19) and similarly name Yahweh as King (41:21; 43:15; 44:6) or depict him as exalted or enthroned (40:22; 57:15; 66:1). A unique addition to this theme of divine sovereignty, however, is second Isaiah's linkage of this concept with a doctrine of creation, a linkage that is repeated in third Isaiah. Yahweh is now the "Holy One, the creator of Israel, your King" (43:15). What is significant about this addition is not simply that Yahweh's power in the creation of the universe is affirmed (41:20; 45:12,18; 66:1–2), but that it is linked, or better, equated with his power in history (40:12–26; 45:7–13; 54:16). This creative power has implications for the election of Israel, as we shall see below.

Though the abstract, theocentric vision of Yahweh's holiness and power can be maintained roughly intact throughout the vicissitudes of history, the implications of that vision for the *people* must necessarily be adjusted to changing circumstances. If the vision given to Isaiah was to make any sense to second Isaiah and his followers, who had experienced the crushing blow of military defeat, loss of nationhood and cult, and exile in a foreign land, then that original vision would have to be reinterpreted or actualized to fit their current needs.

There certainly are things that can be reaffirmed in Isaiah's inaugural vision. Both Isaiahs recognize that a holy God demands a holy people. Perhaps more important is the mutal recognition of the inability of the people to live up to that demand, and its consequences. The people had ears but could not hear, eyes but could not see (6:9–10, cf. 42:18–20). Second Isaiah affirms that the fulfilment of Isaiah's prophecies of judgement by the events of 587 B.C. are the just result of Israel's sin, as he describes it in a lawsuit genre very similar to Isaiah's (43:26–28, cf. 1:18–20. See also 42: 23–25; 48:1–11; 50:1).

However, the real question that faced second Isaiah in the light of the judgement of the exile was not over its justice, but over its aftermath. Granted that Isaiah's vision was of the Holy One *of Israel*, what right did second Isaiah have to speak of the election of Israel after judgement? Had not God cast off his people?

Second Isaiah (and third) does affirm the further election of Israel, and in the same distinctive Zion terminology as Isaiah of Jerusalem (1:8,27; 3:16, 17; 8:18; 10:12,24,32; 14:32; 16:1; 18:7; 28:16; 29:8 *et al* cf. 40:9; 41:27; 46:13; 49: 14; 51:3,11,16; 52:1,2,7,8; 59:20; 60: 14; 62:1,11; 64:10; 66:8). How could he conceive of this? First of all, it is because he regarded the judgement of 587 B.C. as payment in full for Israel's past transgressions (40:2). More important, like first Isaiah, he regarded the goal of that judgement to be purification, not annihilation (48:10), the chastising of rebellious children (43:6; 45:10; cf. 1:24–26).

But does not second Isaiah's addition of oracles of salvation add an unconditional element that is foreign to the either/or tension of Isaiah's original oracles? Not at all. While it is certainly true that the oracles of salvation of second Isaiah are expressed in very strong predestinarian terms, this no more prejudices the role of human response than the divinely ordained negative response that was predicated of Isaiah's original commission (6:9–10). If second Isaiah does not preach repentance as did Isaiah of Jerusalem, it is a result of the conviction that justice has been satisfied, and not that human response is no longer necessary. If second Isaiah stresses the overwhelming power of Yahweh to accomplish his divine purpose or plan of salvation (44:26,28; 46:10,11), it is to create faith, not resignation to the divine inevitability, just as Isaiah of Jerusalem's stress on Yahweh's plan of judgement was meant to create faith through repentance, not despair (1:19,20).

Perhaps the most significant passage is Isaiah 55:6–9. Coming as a preface to the unqualified concluding assurance that Yahweh's purpose or plan would not fail to be accomplished (55:10,11), it paradoxically issues a conditional call to faith to "seek the Lord while he may be found" (v.6). Most important is how this faith is expressed: by repentance ("let the wicked forsake his way" v.7a) and faith ("let him *return* to the Lord" v.7c).

We can see, then, that second Isaiah's oracles can be regarded as a creative reinterpretation of the oracles of Isaiah. This is not to say that all of his material stems from Isaiah of Jerusalem, but that the basic concerns and motifs of Isaiah are caught up into a larger configuration. If a number of motifs such as condemnation of the cult and oracles of judgement are missing or de-emphasized, it is because of the changing *Sitz im Leben* and not a fundamental rejection of the tradition. That second Isaiah was keen to reinterpret what he could of Isaiah's oracles can be seen in his handling of the Davidic convenantal tradition. Though political realities would not allow him to simply repeat Isaiah's promises to the Davidic monarchy, he skillfully actualizes this tradition by "democratizing" it, and applying the Davidic promises to the entire nation (55:1–5)[58].

How does this consciousness of tradition relate to attribution? Paradoxic-

---

58 See O. Eissfeldt, "The Promises of Grace to David in Isaiah 55:1–5," *Israel's Prophetic Heritage*. Fest. Muilenburg. Edit. B.W. Anderson (London: SCM, 1962) 196–207.

ally, the oracles which give such eloquent witness to second Isaiah's creative personality at the same time conceal his identity. Only in Isaiah 40:6 do we have the possibility of a self-conscious prophetic call. That the pericope 40:1–11 takes the literary form of a prophetic call narrative has long been recognized[59]. It depicts the heavenly council in a fashion remarkably similar to that of Isaiah 6, especially in its emphasis on Yahweh's glory (40:6)[60]. Only the third section (vv 6–8) refers to a human messenger, and even here the evidence is ambiguous. In verse 6 the response to the voice crying is in the MT, Syriac, and Targum, "he said," while the LXX, Vulgate, and IQIsa read, "I said." Thus it is textually ambiguous whether this is an autobiographical reference to second Isaiah, or just a third person reference to someone (or something) else[61]. This ambiguity is heightened in the fourth section (vv 9–11), where the herald is most probably identified as personified Zion.

Even if it be granted that 40:6 contains a personal reference to second Isaiah, one still must ask why there are no historical or autobiographical details connected with his call. Westermann's suggestion that second Isaiah's anonymity was due to the overwhelming conviction that his oracles were the Word of Yahweh[62] fails to answer why the other, self-attributed oracles of the classical prophets could also be described as the "coming of the word of Yahweh" (e.g. Jer 11:1; Ezek 14:2; Hos 1:1). D. Petersen's suggestion that this ambiguity reflects the flux of the prophetic office divided from its monarchical patronage may have some value[63], but since other figures contemporary with and subsequent to second Isaiah continued to prophesy under their own name, it cannot be a sufficient cause.

We have already discussed the intimate connection of the oracles of second Isaiah with those of Isaiah of Jerusalem; a connection that can even be traced in the theme of the call narratives themselves (6:1–10; 40:1–11). Since the purpose of a call narrative is not strictly to give autobiographical details, but to claim authoritative status for the person's oracles, might not the ambiguous anonymity of second Isaiah have a deeper cause? That is, could the suppression of "prophet's" identity be due to an awareness of his part in a larger Isaiah tradition? If this were so, the "call narrative" of 40:1–11 would serve the dual purpose of both authorizing the message while making it clear that it was not independent of the larger whole.

That such a function is possible is further supported by the elements of "canon-consciousness" that we find in second Isaiah. That is, there is a strong awareness of authoritative tradition. Foremost among these is the admittedly enigmatic theme of "former/new things" (41:21–29; 42:6–9; 43:8–13;

---

59 See N. Habel, "Call Narrative," 314–316.
60 See F.M. Cross, "The Council of Yahweh in Second Isaiah," *JNES* 12 (1953) 274–277.
61 D. Petersen, *Late Israelite Prophecy,* 20, thinks IQIsa should be read as a qal feminine singular participle ("she said"), and refer to Zion (cf. v 9), a possibility.
62 *Isaiah 40–66* (Philadelphia: Westminster, 1969) 6–8.
63 *Late Israelite Prophecy,* 23.

44:6–8; 45:20–21; 46:8–11; 48:3–8,14–16). Attempts at finding a universal referent for the "former things" has met with signal failure[64]. A more helpful approach is to see the *use* to which this concept is put. Here we find ourselves returning to a central theme of Isaiah of Jerusalem: the sovereignty of Yahweh in history. Second Isaiah basically uses the theme "former/new things" as an argument from prophecy: if the things which Yahweh forefold through the prophets came true in the past, then by implication the future oracles of second Isaiah, the "new things" would come true as well. Though he does make reference to Yahweh's creative/redeeming acts in the past, the brunt of his argument is that even their current exile is part of Yahweh's overarching plan, a plan or "former thing" which was "declared of old" and now been brought to pass (48:1–11). Yet despite their rebelliousness and punishment, Yahweh did not make a full end, for the sake of his *glory* (v.11).

Since the key to second Isaiah's argument from prophecy is the ability to demonstrate Yahweh's sovereignty even in the midst of the defeat of exile (cf. also 42:23–25; 43:26–28; 50:1), then the obvious question is, Who was it that revealed this purpose of refining punishment (48:10) from "of old" (v 3)? Everything we have discussed so far points to Isaiah of *Jerusalem*. Given the clear identification of Isaiah's prophecies of judgement with the events of 587 B.C. in the "Babylonian" redaction of his oracles, and the thematic affinities of the two Isaiahs, not the least of which is the emphasis on Yahweh's sovereign power and glory, and plan for history (44:26; 46:10–11) how could second Isaiah have failed to have the original Isaiah in mind? This identification receives further confirmation by the shared concern for *witnesses* to Yahweh's revelation. Near the end of his ministry Isaiah of Jerusalem had his prophecies against Judah inscribed in a book, that it might be a "witness for ever" (30:8. Cf. also 8:1–2, 16). In his argument from prophecy, second Isaiah rejects the witnesses of false gods (44:9; Cf. 43:9), and declares that the validity of his argument is confirmed by the witness of Israel to the "things of old" which Yahweh has declared to them (44:8, cf. 43:10–12).

This "canon-consciousness" in second Isaiah is clearly an important element in his perspective on revelation and tradition. It hardly seems an accident that his entire work is bracketed by two references to the creative, enduring word of God (40:8; 55:10–11)[65]. Whether or not second Isaiah considered himself a prophet, in the light of the above discussion it is unlikely that he thought of himself as *independent* of the relevation given previously to Isaiah of Jerusalem. This is by far the most plausible explanation for the anonymity of his oracles. One can agree with B.S. Childs' agreement,

---

64 See von Rad, *Theology II,* 246–247; A. Bentzen, "On the Ideas of 'the Old' and 'the New' in Deutero-Isaiah," *StTh* 1 (1948–49) 183–187; C. Stuhlmueller, "'First and Last' and 'Yahweh-Creator' in Deutero-Isaiah," *CBQ* 29 (1967) 495–511; C.R. North, "The Former Things and the New Things in Deutero-Isaiah," *Studies in Old Testament Prophecy.* Fest. T.H. Robinson. Edit. H.H. Rowley (Edinburgh: T and T Clark, 1950) 111–126.
65 See W. Zimmerli, "Jahwes Wort bei Deuterojesaja," *VT* 32 (1982) 104–124.

"the question must be seriously raised if the material of Second Isaiah in fact ever circulated in Israel apart from its being connected to an earlier form of First Isaiah"[66]. If this is the case, then we have in second Isaiah the furtherance of *Vergegenwärtigung* in an entirely new mode: no longer the redactional alteration of original oracles or the addition of small sections for hermeneutical purposes, but now the semi-pseudonymous addition of a (literarily) separate work.

2.2.3 *Third Isaiah* (56—66)

We have already seen some of the ways in which "third" Isaiah joins with second Isaiah in picking up and developing traditional themes from Isaiah of Jerusalem. Now we need to demonstrate how this is in fact part of a larger process of *Vergegenwärtigung,* where not only the oracles of first Isaiah but also those of second Isaiah are combined in a further actualization. But first the title "third" Isaiah needs to be clarified. Though there have been a few who have maintained the unity of Isaiah 40—66[67], most have followed Duhm in positing a division of separate oracles for Chapters 56—66. As well as stylistic differences, these oracles display a clearly different, post-exilic *Sitz im Leben* from that of second Isaiah. Some have tried to attribute these oracles to the work of a single author[68], but the lack of cohesiveness in this section has led the majority of scholars to regard "third" Isaiah as a collection of multi-authored oracles. Scholars have long recognized that they must be the result of a series of reflections or reinterpretations of previous Isaianic material[69]. The problem was that the lack of historical references made it difficult to reconstruct their life setting.

A major breakthrough in this regard has been the recent work of Paul Hanson[70]. Building on O. Plöger's theory of the conflict of theocratic and eschatological groups in the second century[71], Hanson traces this conflict back to the very beginnings of Second Temple Judaism. Central for our concerns is his attribution of third Isaiah to a "visionary" band of second Isaiah's disciples, who are in conflict with a hierocratic Zadokite party over rival restora-

66 *Intro,* 329.
67 C.C. Torrey, *The Second Isaiah* (New York: Charles Scribner's Sons, 1928); J. Smart, *History and Theology in Second Isaiah* (Philadelphia: Westminster, 1965).
68 See especially K. Elliger, *Die Einheit des Tritojesaja* (Stuttgart: W. Kohlhammer, 1928); "Der Prophet Tritojesaja", *ZAW* 49 (1931) 112—141. Elliger thought third Isaiah to be a disciple of second Isaiah. Cf. *Deuterojesaja in seinem Verhältnis zu Tritojesaja* (Stuttgart: W. Kohlhammer, 1933).
69 See W. Zimmerli, "Zur Sprache Tritojesaja", *Gottes Offenbarung* (München: C. Kaiser, 1963) 217—233, reprinted from *SThU* 20 (1950) 110—122; D. Michel, "Zur Eigenart Tritojesajas", *ThViat* 10 (1965—66) 213—230.
70 P. Hanson, *The Dawn of Apocalyptic* (Philadelphia: Fortress, 1979) 32—208.
71 O. Plöger, *Theocracy and Eschatology* (Richmond: John Knox, 1968).

tion plans for post-exilic Jerusalem[72]. While Hanson's reconstruction has been rightly criticized as too linear, and his account of the polarization between visionary and hierocratic groups as too rigid[73], his account of how the "disciples" of second Isaiah adapt the oracles of their master to their new post-exilic situation is well founded and will form the basis of most of what follows.

Contrasted with the immediacy of second Isaiah's oracles (45:8; 51:5), the opening chapters of third Isaiah make it abundantly clear, that having return-ed to Jerusalem, the exiles are troubled by the lack of fulfilment of second Isaiah's glorious prophecies. This problem of delay is nowhere better express-ed than in 59:1: "Behold, the Lord's hand is not shortened, that it cannot save", an   affirmation of second Isaiah's rhetorical question (50:2). The "disciples" of second Isaiah[74] were unwilling to abandon his prophecies, but had to respond to the bleak conditions of the Return. The result is a further ac-tualization or *Vergegenwärtigung,* adapting the oracles of *both* Isaiahs. Thus we have the response to delay in 59:2 "but your iniquities have made a sep-aration between you and your god". Here we have a return to a fundamental theme of Isaiah of Jerusalem, implicit also in second Isaiah, that blessing was predicted on a spiritual "return" to Yahweh. Physical return to Zion was not enough. That a latent tradition of first Isaiah is being reactivated can be seen from 59:3, "For your hands are defiled with blood", an allusion to 1:15. Third Isaiah addresses the problem of delay by a marvellous synthesis of first Isaiah's emphasis on repentance and second Isaiah's promise of salvation. The best illustration of this is his actualization of the inaugural vision of second Isaiah (57:14; 62:10, cf. 40:3 f.). Whereas in second Isaiah the angelic mes-sengers are to "prepare the way" for Yahweh himself as he leads the people in a second Exodus from Babylon to Palestine, in third Isaiah the "way" is now spiritualized to depict the moral pilgrimage or return of the people to Yahweh. Physical return *with* Yahweh is now transformed to spiritual return *to* Yahweh[75].

This spiritualization of second Isaiah's Exodus motif is repeated in 58:8b, where instead of Yahweh's presence before and behind his people, we have said of the people, "your righteousness shall go before you, the glory of the Lord shall be your rearguard" (Cf. 52:12). It is important to notice in this same context (58:1–12) that this spiritualization of second Isaiah's vision by its linkage with first Isaiah is not just superficial moralizing. This actualization is used to address the specific problems or shortcomings of the community.

---

72 The visionaries take their restoration plan from second Isaiah, while the Zadokites rely on Ezekiel 40–48.

73 See especially the review of R.P. Carroll, "Twilight of Prophecy or Dawn of Apoc-alyptic?", *JSOT* 14 (1979) 3–35.

74 The term "disciples" does not necessarily imply a "school" initiated by second Isa-iah himself. It may well be so, but is not necessary for our purposes.

75 See W. Zimmerli, "Zur Sprache", 223–225; P. Hanson, *Dawn,* 69–70. For a further allusion to second Isaiah's vision, cf. 62:11; 40:10.

In particular, the sin which is an impediment to full restoration is a defiled and corrupt cult (Cf. 56:9—12). In 58:2—5 the use of a number of technical cultic terms makes it clear that third Isaiah regards the official restored cultus as apostate or illegitimate[76]. In a judgement oracle similar to Isaiah 1:10—17, third Isaiah returns to the earlier Isaianic emphasis on the superiority of moral obedience to mere ritual. This explains third Isaiah's repeated condemnation of cultic and social evils (e.g. 57—59) in terms similar to first Isaiah. This reliance on tradition in fact makes it difficult to determine if all of the accusations, such as the reference to fertility rites and child sacrifice (57:5—6), are concrete instances or, as is more likely, merely hyperbolic.

What exactly was the issue between the disciples of second Isaiah and the cult? Though Hanson's picture of the conflict of two rival, mutually exclusive restoration plans may be an oversimplification, there is no doubt that elements of the tradition of second Isaiah would have been unacceptable to a Zadokite priesthood. We already saw how the Davidic promises were applied by second Isaiah to all Israel (55:1— 5). Third Isaiah repeats this democratization of royal prerogatives (62: 3) and carries the process one step further. In a section replete with affirming references to the salvation oracles of second Isaiah (60—62)[77], third Isaiah specifically democratizes the cult (61:6). All Israel shall be called the "priests of Yahweh". And as if this were not scandal enough, it is made clear in an earlier oracle that even foreigners and eunuchs could have access to the cult (56:3—8; contrast Ezek 44:9; Lev 21:16f.; 22:10).

The only "first" person narratives in third Isaiah occur in this same central section which re-presents the restoration plan of second Isaiah, and these offer the possibility of a glimpse into the self-consciousness of his "disciples", especially in relation to their "mentor" (61:1—3; 62:1—12). The first of these (61:1—3) is unfortunately a controversial passage. The connection of this passage to the servant songs of second Isaiah has long been recognized. Indeed the opinion of many is that it is a servant song, and written by an earlier hand[78]. Others, however, regard this as a prophetic- "I", and straightforward evidence of the prophet's commission[79]. A resolution of the dilemma has been offered by P. Hanson[80]. Building on the observations of W. Zimmerli that the passage represents the earliest exegesis of the servant songs[81], ne notes that it plays a central, legitimizing role in the re-presentation of second Isaiah's plan of restoration in Chapters 60—62. The disciples of second

---

76 Hanson (*Dawn,* 109—110) cites דרש (cf. Am 5:4—6; Zeph 1:6; Isa 8:19; 31:1; Jer 21:2; Ezek 29:1, 3), משפטים (cf. Lev 26:46) and קרב (cf. Ezek 44: 15—16).

77 See Hanson, *Dawn,* 60—61.

78 D. Petersen, *Late Israelite Prophecy,* 24, cites W. Cannon, "Isaiah 61:1—3 as Ebed-Yahweh Poem," *ZAW* 6 (1926) 287.

79 Eg. Westermann, *Isaiah 40—66,* 366.

80 *Dawn,* 64—67.

81 "Zur Sprache," 226—228.

Isaiah thus combine elements of his servant and call traditions (cf. 40:9; 41:27; 49:8–13; 52:7) in order to justify or legitimize their further work. In other words, it is an expression of their "prophetic" consciousness, but at the same time an affirmation of their *dependence* on previous tradition. This is an expression of the conviction of a continuity of revelation that allows for the phenomenon of *Vergegenwärtigung*.

Perhaps just as important is the conviction that this actualization or furtherance of tradition could be carried out by a group as well as by an inspired individual. We cannot know whether Isaiah 61:1–3 was written by an individual or as the representative of a group, but we do know that a collective definition of the Servant and his mission is not without parallel (Cf. 49:3). That such a collective interpretation is intended here is made clear from the other "call" narrative, Isaiah 62:1–12. The free citation of second Isaiah's call narrative in 62:10–11 (cf. 40:3,10) once again asserts a fundamental continuity with his message. But the "first person" passage (62:1) reveals that that message has not yet been fulfilled, and the commission of "third" Isaiah is defined in terms of proclaiming that message until it be fulfilled. That "third" Isaiah is in fact a special group is seen in the central section (62:6–9). Here we have revealed the role of the "watchmen" (שמרים). The watchmen were sentinels who guarded the cities and warned of attack (1 Sam 14:16; 2 Sam 18:24–27; 2 Kgs 9:17–20; Psa 127:1; Cant 3:3 ; 5:7)[82]. The prophets used the image metaphorically, to refer to their own commission to guard Israel from evil (Ezek 3:17; 33:7, Jer 6:17; Hos 9:8; Isa 20:11–12). Two passages are of particular import in relation to 62:6–9. In the redacted oracles of first Isaiah, we have a reference to Isaiah setting up a "watchman" in a vision to await the coming destruction of Babylon (21:6–10). In verse 8 this figure takes on his own prophetic consciousness, by assuming a first person dialogue with Yahweh. A key element in this dialogue is *delay*. The sentinel serves long and arduous days and nights before his task is complete and the prophetic message of doom fulfilled. Though originally the "watchman" in this oracle may have been Isaiah himself (Cf. Ezek 33:1–7), it is easy to see how the disciples of second Isaiah could have interpreted the watchman's role as a delegated inheritor of the prophetic message, bound to watch for its fulfilment. That they did so is supported by reference to the second relevant passage, Isaiah 49:16. Here second Isaiah reassures a dispirited "Zion" that Yahweh has not forgotten her, and has Yahweh remark, "your walls are continually before me". Returning to Isaiah 62:6–9, we see that the themes of both of the above-mentioned passages are caught up in a new actualization, intended to express the commission of the disciples of second Isaiah. Yahweh has now set watchmen upon the walls of Jerusalem, who serve day and night without rest, bringing the Lord to remembrance lest he forget his promises, until the day he esta-

---

82 The root צ פ ה is more frequent than שמר, but there is no fundamental difference in meaning or use.

blishes Jerusalem (vv 6– 7). No clearer testimony to the consciousness of a
living prophetic tradition can be found in the prophetic corpus.

Yet it must also be said that tradition is handled much more rigidly
in third Isaiah than in second or first Isaiah. Third Isaiah is full of near
or complete citations from the other two works, and *Vergegenwärtigung*
often takes the form of a type of midrashic exegesis of *texts*[83], a feature that
becomes much more prominent in post-Exilic writings.

How fully the process of *Vergegenwärtigung* can lead is seen with the
reaction of the disciples to their rejection (63:16; 66:5) by the "blind watchmen" of the Zadokite leadership (56:10). After a hyperbolic condemnation
of the cult (65:1–7)[84], they further spiritualize the oracles of first and
second Isaiah (65:8–25). Once more judgement is promised, but this time
only to those who do not "seek" Yahweh (65: 1, cf. vv 8–16). The beatific
vision of restoration is now offered to "those who seek me" (v 10, cf. 33.9).
In other words, the remnant is redefined along spiritual lines, and no longer
includes all of those who returned from Babylon. By calling themselves
"servant" and "chosen" (vv 8–9, 13–15), these disciples claim to be the
true Israel (cf. 41:8,9, 42:1, 44:21, 45:4, 49:3).

The radical character of this actualization of this remnant theology is seen
by the juxtaposition of oracles of judgement and salvation in verses 13–16.
Second Isaiah (and the redactors of first Isaiah) saw the restoration of Zion as
the consequence of return *after* judgement, and was clearly tied to the events
of history. But third Isaiah envisions future salvation and judgement as simul-
taneous: a physical and historical impossibility. That these oracles have left
the realm of real history is most vividly expressed in the following verse
"For behold, I create new heavens and a new earth" (v. 17a). Here are the
roots of the two aeon doctrine so characteristic of apocalyptic eschatology.
Yet it must be emphasized that this deferment of hope to an apocalyptic
future is not regarded by third Isaiah as an abandonment of the promise of
first and second Isaiah. His vision of the future (vv 17–25) is full of allusions
and citations[85]. Foremost is his identification of Second Isaiah's "former/new
things" motif with his future vision (v. 17), and his reuse of first Isaiah's
metaphor of tranquility among beasts of prey (v.25, cf. 11:6–9). However,
in the hands of third Isaiah these metaphors previously used to illustrate
history now take on the character of a real programme for the new age.

It seems as though we have come a long way from the oracles of Isaiah
of Jerusalem, and indeed we have. In fact this does not even end the story,
for successive redactions continued to actualize third Isaiah's "apocalyptic"
vision, especially by highlighting its universal application, positive and negative, for the nations (see 66:22–23, chapters 24–27). But at least we have
seen that there is an inner logic and consistency to this development of the

---

83 See esp. D. Michel, "Zur Eigenart."
84 *Dawn*, 146–150.
85 See U. Mauser, "Isaiah 65:17–25," *Interp* 36 (1982) 181–186.

Isaiah tradition. It now remains to summarize our findings and consider their implications for literary attribution.

2.3 Summary

In our general introduction to the prophetic literature, we suggested that there were four elements of prophetic revelation which could radically alter the province of *geistiges Eigentum* and literary attribution: its nature as divinely inspired, unified (part of a larger whole), autonomous, and interpretive. It is just these features that are found in abundance in the Isaianic corpus. The consciousness of *inspiration* can be found throughout the tradition, and the central affirmation is given in terms of participation in the council of Yahweh (6:1–13, 40:1–11, cf. 61:1–3). This leads to the second element, the conviction of the *unified* will of Yahweh. Implicit in the idea of the council of Yahweh, this idea is made explicit by the frequent references to the "plan" of Yahweh for Israel and the nations (5:19, 8:10, 23:8–9, 44:26, 46:10–11). The *autonomous* nature of the Isaianic oracles is evident throughout the tradition. Isaiah of Jerusalem recorded his words for future generations (8:1, 16, 30:8), and second and third Isaiah regard the Word as both creative and effective (40:8, 55:11, 66:5). Finally, the prophetic revelation in the Isaiah tradition is frequently *interpretive,* a process that Isaiah himself encouraged with his use of double-edged sign names such as Shearjashub. Time and again we have seen the traditio-historical principle of *Vergegenwärtigung* in effect, as previous revelation was actualized to meet the needs of a new generation. Isaiah's oracles of judgement were re-applied to the destruction of Jerusalem by Babylon, and his hope of salvation was linked with second Isaiah's promise of return from exile. Third Isaiah caught up the oracles of both Isaiahs in a further actualization intended to cope with the disappointment and controversy of the post-exilic era, finally deferring hope to an apocalyptic future. Yet though these actualizations were radical at times, they were by no means arbitrary. There is a genuine sense of "canon-consciousness" in the development of the tradition. The "core" traditions appear to take on an increasingly inflexible nature, so that by the time we reach third Isaiah we often see actualization take the form of midrashic interpretations of *texts.*

How does this all apply to literary attribution? At first it should be recognized that no clear distinction can be made between anonymity and pseudonymity in the expansion of the tradition. The process of *Vergegenwärtigung* was carried on by the addition of a few words at the head of a collection (1:1, 2:1), or an interpretive phrase (23:13), the insertion of small oracles (4:2–6), or larger ones (13:1–14:24), the borrowing of material from other sources (36–39 = 2 Kgs 18–20), the addition of the unified literary work of a single author (40–55), and the addition of a large collection of multi-authored oracles (56–66). Which of these can be labelled anonymous? Pseudonymous? If the evidence that we have gathered from the self-consciousness of "second" and "third" Isaiah is any guide, the question is meaningless (40:1–11, 61:1–3, 62:1–12). These legitimizing "call" narratives serve to underscore both their participation in an ongoing revelation and their dependence on previous revelation. Their uncharacteristic anonymity highlights their claim to be part of *one* revelation and *one* tradition, a tradition whose clearly recognized head was Isaiah of Jerusalem. The anonymous/pseudonymous expansion of the Isaianic corpus is a recognition that Isaiah had become *part* of the tradition, and *the resultant literary attribution of that corpus must be regarded more as a claim to authoritative tradition by the participants in the process, and less a claim to actual authorship by Isaiah of Jerusalem.*

Chapter 3

Authorship, Revelation and Canon
in the Wisdom Tradition

In the previous chapter we discovered a characteristic "pattern" of tradition and revelation in the prophetic tradition. The nature of its oracles as inspired, unified or coherent, autonomous, and interpretive had a profound effect on the formation of the prophetic corpus and its literary attribution. It now remains to see if these features can be found outside of the prophetic tradition. In particular, it is important to examine the development of the Writings, the third and latest part of the Hebrew canon, since it is in this period that Greco-Roman influence comes to the fore. If this later Jewish literature proves resistant to the ethos of Greco-Roman literary attribution, and retains the features that we have previously discussed, then the foundation will be laid for extending our findings into the NT itself. Two main areas lie before us: the wisdom and apocalyptic traditions. This chapter will deal with the former.

As before, a selective approach will be utilized. First, the nature of the wisdom tradition in Israel will be examined, to set a context for understanding its writings. Second, the figure of Solomon will be examined to ascertain his historical role in this tradition, and the role of kingship generally. Third, the Solomonic wisdom corpus will be studied to reach an understanding of the function of literary attribution.

3.1 The Nature of Jewish Wisdom

Since the "pattern" of anonymity/pseudonymity that we isolated in the prophetic tradition was based on the relation of revelation and tradition, it is necessary to establish the authoritative and revelatory nature of the wisdom literature. Though the precise definition and development of Hebrew wisdom is a task too complex for treatment here[1], our stated objective can be achieved by examining wisdom's relation to creation, the Spirit, and prophecy.

---

1 For an introduction to the history and issues of wisdom research and further biblio-

When W. Zimmerli asserted that the authority of wisdom was based upon the personality of the wise man[2], he did so in the belief that Israelite wisdom was like Egyptian wisdom, and that both were fundamentally non-religious. This erroneous position was as much the result of a misunderstanding of Egyptian wisdom, as of Israelite[3]. H.H. Schmid suggests that this is because Egyptian wisdom (and Mesopotamian) never speaks of the gods (in the plural), but remains basically monotheistic and is bound up with the *creator* god alone[4]. This emphasis on creation was seen much earlier in Israelite wisdom, and several men were quick to focus on it as the key to the authority structure of Israelite wisdom. J.C. Rylaarsdam was one of the first to point out the fundamental correspondence of world view of prophet, priest, and wise, and indeed of all near Eastern culture[5]. Though rumblings were heard, it was several decades, however, until the force of this idea was felt by scholarship[6].

The foundation of Israelite wisdom was the belief in a Creator-God, whose nature guaranteed the structure of life (Prov 3:19–20; 8:22–31; Job 12:7–10; 28:23–27; Sir 1:4–10; 24:3,5,9; Wis 7:22–26; 8:1,6; 9:9). There could be no artificial distinction between secular and sacred. Even God's actions were part of the causality of the universe. This does not mean that

---

graphy, see J. Crenshaw, "Prolegomenon," *Studies in Ancient Israelite Wisdom* (NY: KTAV, 1976) 1–45; R.E. Clements, *A Century of Old Testament Study* (London: Lutterworth, 1976), esp. 110–112, 114; W. Baumagartner, "The Wisdom Literature," *The Old Testament and Modern Study. A Generation of Discovery and Research.* Edit. H.H. Rowley, (Oxford: Clarendon Press, 1951) 210–237; J.A. Emerton, "Wisdom," *Tradition and Interpretation.* Edit. G.W. Anderson (Oxford: Clarendon, 1979) 214–237; G. Fohrer, *TDNT* VII, 476–496; J.L. McKenzie, "Reflections on Wisdom," *JBL* 86 (1967) 1–9; R.E. Murphy, "Assumptions and Problems in Old Testament Wisdom Research," *CBQ* 29 (1967) 407–418; idem, "Wisdom-Theses and Hypotheses," *Israelite Wisdom. Theological and Literary Essays in Honour of Samuel Terrien.* Edit. J.G. Gammie et al. (Missoula: Scholars Press, 1978) 35–42; R.B.Y. Scott, "The Study of the Wisdom Literature," *Interp* 24 (1970) 20–45; G.T. Sheppard, *Wisdom as a Hermeneutical Construct* (BZAW) 151, Berlin: de Gruyter, 1980) 1–12; D.F. Morgan, *Wisdom in the Old Testament Traditions* (Oxford: Blackwell, 1981); J. Crenshaw, *Old Testament Wisdom: An Introduction* (Atlanta: John Knox, 1981).

2 "Concerning the Structure of Old Testament Wisdom," *Studies in Ancient Israelite Wisdom.* Edit. J. Crenshaw (NY: KTAV, 1976) 175–207.

3 Egyptian scholarship was then in its infancy.

4 *Wesen and Geschichte der Weisheit* (BZAW 101, Berlin: Töpelmann, 1966), 80–81. See also *Gerechtigkeit als Weltordnung* (Tübingen: Mohr 1968).

5 *Revelation in Jewish Wisdom* (Chicago: University Press, 1946) 14. "The core of the general cultural viewpoint held in common rests on the conviction that existence is fundamentally rational and moral. The divine rule, to whatever deity assigned, is held to be constant and intelligent. The divine order rewards those who discover and obey it; it punishes those who transgress it – life is morally interpreted."

6 See H. Ringgren, *Word and Wisdom* (Lund: Hakan Ohlssons Boktrycheri, 1947 127; H.H. Schmid, *Wesen,* 197; and H.-J. Hermission, *Studien zur israelitischen Sprüchweisheit* (Neukirchen-Vluyn: Neukirchener Verlag, 1968) 150–151.

there was any confusion between God and the world. But Hebrew epistemology was never broken down into the modern bifurcation of a separate, secular, absolute knowledge which operates independently from a religious "faith" knowledge. Reality could not be considered apart from Yahweh[7]. For this reason, wisdom is more than intellectual prowess. It is the ability or readiness to accommodate oneself to order, discipline, and to be in harmony with reality (spiritual and physical). This is the reason for the linkage of the "fear of the Lord" with wisdom (Prov 1:7; 9:10 ; 15:21–23; 18:1–7 *et al*) Wisdom is a theological concern. This is why foolishness can even be equated with atheism (Ps 14:1)[8] and the finding of wisdom equated with salvation (Prov 8:35). The authority of wisdom is the authority of God[9]. For this reason it is possible to speak of wisdom as revelation[10].

Another support for the authoritative and revelatory nature of wisdom can be seen in the increasing linkage of wisdom and Spirit in the wisdom tradition. The skill of craftsmen is attributed to the gift of Yahweh through the filling of the spirit of wisdom (Ex 31:1–5; 35:31–33). Skill in leadership, a wisdom trait, is also connected to the Spirit (Num 11:16–17; 27:18; Deut 34:9; Isa 11:2f; 1 Chr 12:18; Gen 41:38). The later wisdom tradition makes this linkage even stronger by the virtual equation of the Spirit and (hypostasized) Wisdom (Wis 1:7; 9:17; 11:20).

Though a full discussion of the development of this linkage is beyond the scope of this investigation, the key probably lies in the early association of wisdom and spirit as attributes of God which were of particular importance in his creation and sustenance of the world[11]. Thus wisdom and spirit came to be regarded as virtually equivalent in the functioning of creation (*spirit*, Jdt 16:14; Job 34:14; Ps 33:6; 104:30; *wisdom*, Prov 8:22–31; Sir 24:3–5; Wis 7:22; 8:1). Though in a few instances this increasing emphasis on wisdom as a divine gift through the Spirit led to the virtual equation of wisdom and oracular literature[12], for the most part the wisdom tradition maintained a creative synergism between the activity of God's Spirit and man's[13].

The question of the revelatory nature wisdom comes most strongly to the fore in its relation to prophecy. The wise man's הצע has often been contrasted to the prophetic דבר as a piece of non-revelatory advice compared to a divine pronouncement[14]. B. Gemster strongly refutes this contention[15]. In

---

7 G.von Rad, *Wisdom in Israel* (London: SCM, 1972) 17.

8 "Folly is practical atheism." *Ibid.*, 64.

9 See N. Phillips, "Authority in the Wisdom Admonitions," *ZAW* 93 (1981) 418–426; J. Crenshaw, "Prolegomenon," 26–35.

10 See R.B.Y. Scott, "Priesthood, Prophecy, Wisdom, and the Knowledge of God," *JBL* 80 (1961) 10–11.

11 See J.C. Rylaarsdam, *Revelation,* 99–122.

12 E.g. Sirach's identification of wisdom and law (Sir 24:23).

13 Rylaarsdam, *Revelation,* 106–107.

14 E.g. W. McKane, *Prophets and Wise Men* (London: SCM, 1965) 55–62; W. Zimmerli, "Structure."

15 "The Spiritual Structure of Biblical Aphoristic Wisdom. A Review of Recent Stand-

a study of יעץ and its derivatives, he notes that even in those passages where it might be interpreted as private counsel, there remains a strong sense of authority (Judg 19:30; 20:7; 2 Sam 15–17; 1 Kgs 12). Elsewhere it signifies not discussable advice but resolute decision (Isa 5:19, 14:24; 19:17; 44:24 *et al*). In a similar article on the role of the counsellor in Israel, P.A.H. de Boer isolates three pertinent characteristics:

1. The action of counselling is for the restoration or maintenance of life (i.e. salvation) (1 Kgs 1:11f; 2 Sam 16:20; Isa 1:26; 16:3; Prov 11:14; Dan 4:27).
2. A counsel is a decision which determines the future. It may be considered a synonym for an oracle, the word of the prophet or priest. True counsel is a decision in a difficult situation given by an authorized person, and is to be followed ("done") on penalty of death (2 Sam 16:23; Isa 47:13; Mic 4:9; Job 29:21–25; Prov 20:18; 24:6).
3. Counsellors form a special caste, and are afforded equal status to priest and prophet (2 Sam 15:12; Jer 18:18; Ezek 7:26)[16].

Though wisdom can be afforded a place in revelation on equal footing with prophecy, it must be admitted that the path of acceptance of wisdom revelation in Israel was a rocky one. Though both the creation theology of wisdom and the salvation-historical theology of prophecy had equal claims to ancient Israelite roots[17], the movements held each other at arm's length throughout the pre-exilic period. This is because of the fundamental tension between wisdom's approach to man as man (under a universal Creator) and the sacral approach to man as elect (convenanted Israelite). The need to reconcile these tensions during the threat to the national religious tradition posed by the exile may have led to the increasing "nationalization" of later wisdom, and its closer identification with covenant and law. The way this was done was to emphasize the "gift" or supernatural aspect of wisdom, with a subsequent de-emphasis of its more universal "natural" aspect.

Though the quality of immanence rather than transcendence results in an emphasis on "wisdom" rather than "word" in the wisdom writings[18], from our discussion above we can conclude that wisdom was regarded as revelation, whether attained by natural or supernatural means. This means that the same condition holds for wisdom as it does for prophecy in relation to *geistiges Eigentum*. Wisdom comes from Yahweh, and cannot be had apart from

---

points and Theories," *Adhuc Loquitur: Collected Essays of Dr. B. Gemser*. Edit. A.van Selms and A.S.van der Woude (Leiden: Brill, 1968) 144–149, reprinted in *Studies in Ancient Israelite Literature* (J. Crenshaw, edit.) 215–219. See also J. Crenshaw, "Excursus B; *ēsa* and *dabar:* The problem of Authority/Certitude in Wisdom and Prophetic Literature," *Prophetic Conflict* (BZAW 125. Berlin: de Gruyter, 1971) 116–123.

16 "The Counsellor," *Wisdom in Ancient Israel and in the Ancient Near East*. Fest. H.H. Rowley. Edit. M. Noth and D.W. Thomas (VT Supp 3, Leiden: Brill, 1960) esp. 43–56.

17 J.F. Priest, "Where is Wisdom to be Placed?" *JBR* (=*JAAR*) 31 (1963) 279.

18 R.B.Y. Scott, "Wisdom, Word, and Spirit. Revelation in the Wisdom Literature," *Interp* 2 (1948) 281–282. See also *The Way of Wisdom in the Old Testament* (New York: Macmillan, 1971) 134.

Him. Furthermore, since wisdom is founded on Yahweh's role as creator of a reliable world-order, wisdom is not only "divine", it is *unified* or *coherent.* There can only be one wisdom, though of course no human can hope to grasp it in its totality (Qoh 8:16–17). For this very same reason wisdom can be regarded as "independent" of the wise man, or *autonomous,* taking a life of its own. This idea is nowhere more dramatically displayed than in the hypostatization of Dame Wisdom (Prov 1–9; Wis 10–11). This universal and independent quality of wisdom gives it its resolutely traditional character as well (Job 15:17–18; Sir 8:9)[19]. Given wisdom's creationist commitment to discovering the physical and spiritual laws which govern life, it would be the epitome of foolishness to disregard the accumulated lore of the past. Wisdom writings are full of admonitions to receive instruction.

Yet oriental wisdom cannot be said to be "traditionalist" in the rigid *traditum* sense. An equally important aspect of wisdom was individual, contemporary experience. Since no human can exhaust wisdom, along with instruction there is a mutual emphasis on searching (Prov 18:17; 20:27; 25:2; 28:11, Qoh 1:13; 7:25; Job 5:27), observation (Prov 23:26; Qoh 8:9), and discernment (Prov 7:7; Job 6:30). Even traditional wisdom cannot be appropriated mechanistically, because at times it can be contradictory (Prov 26: 4–5). Everything has its time and its place (Qoh 3:1–8), so that wisdom cannot be simply appropriated, but must be *interpreted* for the contemporary situation (Prov 1:2–6; Qoh 11:9–10; Sir 18:26; 39:33–34). "Every matter has its time and way" and "the mind of the wise man will know the time and way" (Qoh 8:6a, 5b). This creative tension between the dual affirmation of the eternal validity of wisdom revelation and the continual need for contemporaneous re-application and expansion is precisely a statement of the principle of *Vergegenwärtigung* that we discovered in the prophetic tradition. How that principle is expressed in relation to authorship and the literary expression of biblical wisdom is now the focus of our concern.

3.2 King Solomon and the Wisdom Tradition

An important characteristic of the wisdom tradition is the authority it invests in its representatives, especially the king[20]. As the wise king *par excellence,* Solomon dominates biblical wisdom literature, and thus any study of authorship and tradition must use him as a focal point.

---

19 A. DePury, "Sagesse et Revelation dans l'Ancien Testament," *RThPh* 27 (1977) 12. See also H.H. Schmid, *Wesen,* 28, who notes that even Sirach, the only wisdom author, is still not an author in the modern sense. "Sirach, too, is determined by the 'discourse of the elders,' who (in their turn) have learned from their fathers (Sir 8:9)." He was thus the custodian of tradition.

20 See P.A.H. de Boer, "The Counselor"; J. Crenshaw, "Excursus," 122.

In Egyptian wisdom, the pharaoh was a divine being who maintained harmony and order in nature and society by upholding *ma'at,* the organizing principle of the cosmos[21]. Though there are significant differences between Israelite and Egyptian kingship ideologies[22], the role of the king in Israelite society is quite similar. A strong connection is made between the divine endowment of the king with wisdom and his convenantal responsibilities to lead and judge the people, and promote their welfare (2 Sam 14:20; 1 Kgs 3: 28; Prov 8:14–16; Mic 4:9). One of the qualifications of the Messiah/king is wisdom (Isa 9:6; 11:2; Jer 23:5). The harmony and prosperity of the kingdom are connected to the king's ability to promote justice (Ps 72). Wisdom is connected not only to Solomon, but to David (2 Sam 19:27), Hezekiah (Prov 25:1), and non-Israelite kings such as Lemuel (Prov 31:1)[23].

This representative or typical role of Near Eastern kingship should alert us to the possibility of a similar role in literary attribution. Egyptian wisdom literature is almost universally pseudonymous. Yet the concern with historical events and figures in other Israelite traditions may suggest that for Israelite wisdom, Solomonic attribution was not a mere literary device, but a conscious appeal to a stream of tradition that was regarded as historical.

The major source for the Solomonic origins of wisdom is the account of Solomon's reign found in 1 Kings 3–11. While all agree that the narrative contains pre-Deuteronomic material, there is no agreement on its distribution. In recent years the stress has been on the antiquity of material[24]. Scepticism over early dating should at least be tempered, since the narrative does not contain the miraculous and extraordinary features of later legendary accounts. Even the most generally accepted Deuteronomistic contribution (1 Kgs 11:41) gives evidence of the antiquity of the Solomonic wisdom tradition, since it is the custom of the Deuteronomist to summarize in a few words the contents of his sources, in this case the "book of the acts of Solomon"[25]. The editor of Kings gives no attention to the role of wisdom after Solomon, which shows that it is not his peculiar interest[26].

---

21 *ma'at* has been translated "truth, right, justice, basic order, world order." It stands over both gods and men. See A. Volten, "Der Begriff der Maat in der ägyptischen Weisheittexten, *Les Saggesses due Proch-Orient Ancien* (Colloque de Strasbourg, 1962. Paris: Presses Universitaires de France, 1963) 73–101: H.H. Schmid, *Wesen,* 17–24; H. Gese, *Lehre und Wirklichkeit in der alten Weisheit* (Tübingen: Mohr, 1958) 11–21 (N.V.)

22 Particularly the Egyptian ideas of divine kingship and submission of the gods to *ma'at* would have been anathema to Israelite Yahwism.

23 See further N. Porteous, "Royal Wisdom," *Wisdom in Israel and in the Ancient Near East* (Edit. M. Noth and D.W. Thomas, VT Supp 3) 247–261.

24 R. Whybray, *The Intellectual Tradition in the Old Testament* (BZAW 135, Berlin: DeGruyter, 1974) 92, see also J. Liver, "The Book of the Acts of Solomon," *Bib* 48 (1967) 75–101.

25 R. Whybray, *Intellectual Tradition,* 92–93. He cites especially 1 Kgs 16:5,20,27; 22:39. Cf also 1 Kgs 22:46; 2 Kgs 13:8,12; 14:15,28; 20:20; 21:17.

26 Further see B. Porten, "The Structure and Theme of the Solomon Narrative (1 Kings 3–11)," *HUCA* 38 (1967) 114–116.

Perhaps the most important pericope of the narrative is the account of Solomon's dream at Gibeon (3:4–15). Though the hand of the Deuteronomist is evident, a number of features testify to its essential antiquity. Noth observes that the setting of the pre-Israelite sanctuary at Gibeon is something that could never be attributed to the Deuteronomist, and the fact that it was not altered testifies to the tradition's long established antiquity and importance[27]. The theme of incubation (seeking a dream/revelation at a shrine) is also a well established ancient Near Eastern practice[28]. A possible objection to the account's antiquity is the emphasis on wisdom as a divine gift, which, it is argued, can only come from the later theologizing tendency of post-exilic wisdom[29]. Yet the divine source of wisdom is an idea with ancient roots, and as Noth points out, the crucial difference in this account is the nature of the wisdom represented. Unlike later "supernatural" or revealed wisdom, the emphasis here is on the human aspect of wisdom. It is a (divinely given) human ability, given in the same manner as riches[30]. Thus the Gibeon account can serve as vital testimony to the antiquity (if not historical veracity) of the linkage of Solomon and wisdom.

The sole reference to Solomon's literary activities outside of the literature attributed to him lies in 1 Kings 4:29–34 (MT 5:9–14). The corruption and displacement of the text has added to the difficulty of assessing its place in the history of tradition. The strongest proponent of its antiquity is A. Alt, who connects the nature wisdom of the account with the *Listenwissenschaft* or encyclopaedic listing of natural phenomenon common to the wisdom literature of the ancient Near East[31]. The relationship of this nature wisdom to the use of proverbs and songs, however, is problematic. Yet if a post-Deuteronomic redactor had wanted to insert a reference to Solomon's legendary wisdom and literary efforts, it seems unlikely that he would have used such an uncommon type, rather than the better known *Erfahrungsweisheit* that Proverbs associates with Solomon. The lack of Deuteronomic editing is also no sure guide to dating[32]. The preservation of the tension in 1 Kgs 5:9–14 (MT) may be a testimony to the great age and strength of the tradition. Yet it must be admitted that this pericope offers very uncertain evidence for determining Solomon's literary participation in wisdom origins.

The titles in Proverbs 10:1; 25:1 are the only other biblical references to Solomon's literary activity. Though much of the material in the collections

27 M. Noth, "Die Bewährung von Salomos 'Gottlicher Weisheit'," *Wisdom in Israel and the Ancient Near East* (Edit M. Noth and D.W. Thomas, VT Supp 3) 227.

28 J. Gray, *I and II Kings* (London: SCM, 1964) 120.

29 E.g. E. Würthwein, *Das Erste Buch der Könige*, 1–16 (Göttingen: Vandenhoeck and Ruprecht, 1977) 48.

30 M. Noth, "Bewährung," 233–234.

31 A. Alt, "Die Weisheit Salomos," *ThLZ* 76 (1951) 139–144, reprinted in *Kleine Schriften zur Geschichte des Volks Israel,* II (Munchen: C.H. Beck, 1953) 90–99.

32 Contra R.B.Y. Scott, "Solomon and the Beginnings of Wisdom in Israel," *Wisdom in Israel and the Ancient Near East* (Edit. M. Noth and D.W. Thomas, VT Supp 3) 267–272.

they head is pre-exilic, the actual superscriptions may not be. Even if they are, the titles are no sure witness of literary origins, since the phrase "proverbs of Solomon" may designate nothing more than a designation of a type of proverb (like a Miltonic ode) or locate it in a certain era (like Elizabethan poetry)[33]. The reference to the men of Hezekiah (25:1), however, shows that literary wisdom was present at the royal court at least this far back, and may serve as supplementary evidence for the anitquity of the belief in Solomon's link with wisdom.

On the face of it, there must be some historical basis for the linkage of wisdom and Solomon. The answer most likely lies in the organization that Solomon provided to it. Solomon's close ties with Egypt[34], witnessed by his marriage to Pharaoh's daughter, may have afforded him the opportunity to organize Israel's diverse wisdom traditions, borrowing from the Egyptian model. The absolutely unique linkage of Solomon to wisdom in the literature of Israel may serve as testimony that, during the reign of Solomon, wisdom as a *national* tradition was formed, and thus Solomon can be regarded as the father of wisdom in Israel. Solomon's personal investment, especially in terms of literature, is more open to question. What is important for our study interest is to see the great antiquity and historical probability of the belief that Solomon was the founder of a national wisdom tradition. This means that the (perceived) historical origins of Israelite wisdom ought to play a role in literary attribution. This is the phenomenon to which we now turn.

3.3 Authorship and Authority in the Solomonic Wisdom Corpus

3.3.1 *Proverbs*

Since we cannot isolate original Solomonic material in Proverbs as we did with the oracles of Isaiah, a different approach must be used. This leads us to observe the structure of the book, and the meaning and relation of the superscriptions. Two are attributed to Solomon (1:1 ; 10:1), one to the court scribes of Hezekiah who were working from a Solomonic text (25:1), two to non-Israelite writers (Agur, 30:1 ; and Lemuel, 31:1) ; and two to unknown wise men (22:17 ; 24:23). These superscriptions suggest that each of these units or collections had their own process of tradition[35]. The question arises,

---

33 *Ibid.*, 272–273.

34 See A. Malamat, "The Kingdom of David and Solomon in its Contact with Egypt and Aram Naharaim," *BA* 21 (1958) 97.

35 G. von Rad, *Wisdom,* 15, n.1. P. Skehan's suggestion, "A Single Editor for the Whole Book of Proverbs," *CBQ* 10 (1948) 15–26, that the units and their super-

is there any overarching unity to Proverbs, or is it merely a list of unrelated collections? The answer is that there is a definite unifying structure to the book, and this structure embodies the linkage of the process of *Vergegen-wärtigung* with that of authorship.

Scholars had long suspected a connection between the structure of Proverbs and that of Egyptian didactic literature[36]. It was left to C. Bauer-Kayatz to specify the Egyptian connection, by demonstrating that Proverbs 1–7 is patterned on the genre of Egyptian Instruction[37]. Kayatz notes that most Egyptian Instructions begin with a prologue that give brief information about the author and recipients, and an infinitival list of the programmatic goals of the Instruction, and concludes that Proverbs 1:1–7 functions similarly[38]. In fact, the prologue can be seen as an introduction or thesis summary of the entire book of Proverbs. Debate has long continued over the nature of Proverbs 1–9. The "hypostasis" of wisdom that it contains points to a post-exilic origin, yet many have been unwilling to concede that there are no features of early wisdom included. Others have been willing to posit a radical series of redactions in the collection to explain its diverse nature[39]. A simpler and yet more profound solution can be found in the suggestion that the prologue and first collection attempt to bring a harmonizing perspective to the disparate elements of wisdom in the whole book. Kayatz points to two distinctives within the prologue and first collection which go beyond the pattern of the Egyptian Instruction. First is its application to every man, rather than any narrow vocational elite, and second, it lifts up a unique integrating theme of principle: "the fear of the Lord"[40].

The prologue and first collection can be regarded as an attempt to actualize and synthesize the various layers of the wisdom tradition. At the heart of this is the Hebrew understanding of revelation and the *nachleben* or re-use of wisdom.

> ... the introduction (Prov 1:2–6) exemplifies how an Israelite is able to include the wisdom of Ahiqar, Amenemope, and others within the framework of his Yahwistic belief. He did not see any obstacle in the fact that a proverb was a product of human insight or even a borrowing (if he was even aware of the latter). He did not share our theological presuppositions about revelation, or the "sacred", or the "profane". No matter what striking similarities may be adduced between the Old Testament wisdom and extrabiblical literature, Israel's wisdom was founded, or at least expressed, within a people in covenant with Yahweh[41].

---

scriptions are the creation of a single author is too fanciful and contrived. He thinks they are organized around the numerical value of the names Solomon, Hezekiah, etc.

36 See P. Humbert, *Recherches sur les sources égyptiennes de la littérature sapientiale d'Israel* (Neuchâtel: Secretariat de l'Universite, 1929) 63–64.

37 *Studien zu Proverbien 1–9* (Neukirchen-Vluyn: Neukirchener Verlag, 1966).

38 *Ibid.*, 24. She cites and quotes from the Instructions of Pitahhotep, Cheti, and Amenomope.

39 R.N. Whybray, *Wisdom in Proverbs* (London: SCM, 1965) 11–32.

40 *Studien zu Proverbien 1–9*, 26.

41 R.E. Murphy, "The Interpretation of Old Testament Wisdom Literature", *Interp*

The role of the superscription to the first collection (1:1), then, takes on great importance. It is certainly intended for the book as a whole. Yet the obvious reference to other authors in the other collections means that no modern understanding of authorship can be intended. The use of the name of Solomon should not, however, be regarded as a mere literary device. The dynamics for Solomonic attribution are the same as found in our study of prophetic tradition. In the process of tradition history, the various layers of tradition are harmonized, supplemented, actualized, and the literary work that finally evolves is attributed to the figure who stands at its head. *Far more than a literary form (Egyptian or otherwise), the attribution of Proverbs to Solomon is a theological claim to an authoritative tradition, a distinctive Israelite wisdom tradition which began to take national form in the reign of Solomon*[42].

3.3.2 *Canticles*

The question might be raised whether Canticles or the Song of Songs can be regarded as either a wisdom book or as Solomonic in any fashion other than through simple misattribution. The answer to that question in fact serves as the key to resolving the problem of the book's chequered history of interpretation[43]. As is well known, as early as the first century (A.D.) the literal interpretation of Canticles was abandoned in favour of an allegorical, "prophetic" reading of the text. For Jews the relation of bride and groom became symbolic of Israel and Yahweh ; for the Christians it was the Church and Christ. This interpretation lasted until the nineteenth century, when Canticles came to be regarded as a drama of two or three characters, to be performed during wedding celebrations. The difficulty of adapting the text to such a production has led most current scholars to abandon this approach, and to return to a literal interpretation, characterizing Canticles as an essentially secular celebration of human love. Yet this approach raises serious problems about its function in the canon.

An understanding of the role of Solomon in the book's attribution helps to resolve these difficulties. As N. Gottwald points out, it is a matter of question whether אֲשֶׁר לִשְׁלֹמֹה (1:1) signifies actual authorship, since it can also denote *possession* ("belonging to Solomon"), *dedication* ("in honour of

---

23 (1969) 298; see also B.S. Childs, *Introduction to the Old Testament as Scripture* (London: SCM, 1979) 557.

42 Childs', *ibid.*, 551–2, points out another crucial function of Solomonic attribution. It serves to guard against wisdom being submerged in the sacral and historical traditions of Israel. It testifies to an autonomous form of tradition and revelation, parallel to the Law and Prophets, that has equal claim to legitimacy and antiquity.

43 For the history of interpretation, see H.H. Rowley, "The Interpretation of the Song of Songs", *The Servant of the Lord and other Essays on the Old Testament* (Oxford: Blackwell, 1965[2]) 195–245; R.E. Murphy, "Towards a Commentary on the Song of Songs", *CBQ* 39 (1977) 482–496.

Solomon"), *style* ("in the fashion of Solomon"), or *subject matter* ("concerning Solomon")[44]. In any case, the long form of the relative shows the ascription to be editorial, and later than the original composition[45].

The name of Solomon only occurs six times in the body of the work. The first and last two are figurative allusions to Solomon's wealth (1:5; 8: 11–12), and cannot be connected to any claim of authorship. There are three references which identify the lover as a "king" (1:4,12; 7:5), but no personal identification is made. It is *only* in Chapter 3 that we have a clear depiction of Solomon in the role of groom (vv. 7, 9, 11). R. Gordis notes that the elements of this pericope are hard to reconcile to the rural setting found elsewhere in Canticles, and suggests that we have here a song composed on the occasion of one of the Solomon's marriages to a foreign princess (cf. Ps 45)[46].

Apart from the question of Chapter 3 dating to Solomon's era, the contrasts of settings and literary divergences of the entire book have led the majority of scholars to regard it as an anthology of diverse love songs with a long history, rather than a unified literary work. This means that we must look for any editorial elements within the body of the work that might give some hermeneutical direction for the work's overall purpose. Here is where Canticles 8:6–7 plays such a crucial role. In contrast to the rest of the book, these verses consider "love" in the abstract. Form critically they have a close affinity with the *mashal* or proverbial saying[47]. This link to wisdom methodology, coupled with the allusions and references to Solomon, suggest that these diverse love songs were collected and used by a wisdom scribe (or scribes) to reflect on the mystery of love.

The wisdom writings demonstrate a marked concern about human sexuality and marriage (Prov 5-15; 7:5–27; 9:13–18; 31:10–31; Sir 26:1–4 ;36: 21–26). One of the great riddles to the wise was "the way of a man with a maiden" (Prov 30:19)[48]. Therefore whatever the origin of the diverse materials in Canticles, it is clear that in their present state they are intended to be read in a sapiential context. It is for this reason that the modern designation of the work as a secular "celebration of human love" is inappropriate. As J.-P. Audet points out, Jewish antiquity never personifies or glorifies *love,* but it does personify and glorify *wisdom*[49]. This is not to denigrate human sexuality, but to place it clearly within the context of the divine

---

44 "Song of Songs", *IDB* IV, 420.

45 The short form is used elsewhere without exception. *Ibid.*

46 "The Song of Songs", *Poets, Prophets, and Sages. Essays in Biblical Interpretation* (Bloomington, Indiana: University Press, 1971) 365–368, reprinted from *Mordecai M. Kaplan Jubilee Volume* (Jewish Theological Seminary of America, 1959).

47 M. Sadgrove, "The Song of Songs as Wisdom Literature", *Studia Biblica* I (1978) 245. See Qoh 12:13 for a similar moralizing summary.

48 For further parallels between Canticles and the wisdom literature, see Sadgrove, *ibid.,* 248, n.4.

49 "Le Sens du Cantique des Cantiques", *RB* 62 (1955) 213–215.

order of creation. A "secular" reading of Canticles introduces a modern distinction that would have been repugnant to the wise of Israel.

It is the sapiential context that helps us to understand the role of Solomon in Canticles. The references and allusions to him reinforce the hermeneutical intent of the editors that the book be read as *wisdom*[50]. That this intent was fulfilled can be seen through the universal positioning of Canticles among the wisdom writings. The choice of Solomon was governed by both *form* and *content*. Not only was Solomon uniquely associated with the genre of wisdom writing (1 Kgs 4:32), the reputation of his wealth and marriages also lent itself to the concern of Canticles (Chap. 3), a connection that may have been facilitated by the possible Solomonic dating of this song. That the "attribution" of Canticles to Solomon could not have been regarded as strictly a literary statement can be seen by 8:11–12, where the bridegroom *addresses* Solomon. This is a phenomenon similar to what we found in Proverbs, and indicates that *attribution was regarded more as a claim to authoritative tradition than as a statement of literary origins*.

3.3.3 *Qoheleth*

Although a full discussion of the critical problems involved in the study of Qoheleth lies beyond the scope of this work, it is necessary to survey these considerations to set the context of interpretation of this difficult book. No scholars would defend the work as coming from the time of Solomon, but the dating still falls over a period of several centuries, anywhere from the early post-exilic period down to its mention by the Qumran sect. It is generally dated 300–200 B.C. on the basis of language, but the lack of historical referents within the text make any further specification difficult[51]. The unity of the book has also been vigorously debated, and decisions about its disunity have often occasioned theories of multiple authorship. Though no clear consensus has been reached regarding the structure of the book, it is now generally agreed to be the work of one person, with at least two additional redactors[52]. Redactions is limited for the most part to the prologue (1:1–12) and the epilogue 12:8–14).

---

50 B.S. Childs, *Intro,* 579.
51 For a full discussion, see B.S. Childs, *ibid.,* 582; A. Lauha, *Kohelet* (Neukirchen-Vluyn: Neukirchener Verlag, 1978) 1–3; H.W. Hertzberg, *Der Prediger* (Gütersloh G. Mohn, 1963) 42–52; R. Gordis, *Koheleth, the Man and his World* (New York: Jewish Theological Seminary of America, 1955[2]) 63–68.
52 For full discussion of the unity and structure, see J.A. Loader, *Polar Structures in the Book of Qoheleth* (BZAW 152, Berlin: de Gruyter, 1979); B.S. Childs, *Intro,* 582; A. Lauha, *Kohelet,* 4–7; R. Gordis, *Koheleth,* 69–74; H.W. Hertzberg, *Prediger,* 35–42; A. Wright, "The Riddle of the Sphinx: The Structure of the Book of Qoheleth," *CBQ* 30 (1968) 313–334; W. Zimmerli, "Das Buch Kohelet-Traktat oder Sentenzensammlung?" *VT* 24 (1974) 221–230.

Though the question of Solomonic authorship of Qoheleth is no longer a live one, there is still a great deal of doubt over whether to regard the book as pseudepigraphic. M. Hengel conveys this perplexity by describing it as "semi-pseudonymous"[53]. The enigmatic quality of the book is portrayed best in its little understood title, "Qoheleth"[54]. The designation is the active feminine participle of the root קהל. The perfect form does not appear in the OT, but the noun means "assembly, congregation"[55]. Thus the title may mean "one who assembles a company or congregation." The feminine participial form is best explained as an occupational designation that has become a proper noun[56]. This usage is confirmed by the appearance of the title within the body of the letter with the article (7:27; 12:8), which indicates it was used as some sort of office. In the context of the wisdom movement, the term or title could designate some sort of teacher who gathers a group of pupils or disciples around him, or who may even instruct the people at large. This was certainly the case with Qoheleth (12:9). In the light of this, Scott's rendering of the name as "Teacher" may be the closest to its original meaning[57].

Although it seems clear that the name "Qoheleth" itself is not a pseudonym, the introduction to the book (1:16–2:12) does raise the question of an assumed identity most likely that of King Solomon. The difficulty in assessing the intent behind this portrayal is engendered by the fact that nowhere is the name Solomon used[58], and even the whole fiction or portrayal of kingship is dropped after the second chapter. Indeed, in the body of the book Qoheleth shows by his attitude and perspective that he is not a king (4:13,16; 5:7–9; 8:2–4; 10:4,20).

Some have claimed that no real portrayal of kingship is being made. Levez reinterprets מלך of 1:12 as "head of a school"[59]; similarly W.F. Albright renders it "counsellor"[60]. Ginsberg suggests that it means "property holder"[61]. All these attempts to divert the meaning of "kingship" in 1:12 falter

53 *Judaism and Hellenism*, Vol. I (London: SCM, 1974) 129.
54 "Ecclesiastes" is from the Vulgate, which is merely a transliteration of the LXX Ἐκκλησιαστής. We get our distorted English translation "Preacher" because of Luther's rendering of the Vulgate as "Prediger."
55 *BDB* 874.
56 Cf. similar participles, Ezra 2:55 and Neh 7:57 "office of scribe"; Ezra 2:57 and Neh 7:59 "office of gazelle tender."
57 *The Way of Wisdom*, 175. For further discussion, see the bibliography on the title listed by A. Lauha, *Kohelet*, 29.
58 1:1b "son of David, king in Jerusalem," the clearest reference to Solomon, is most universally agreed to be the work of a later redactor, who probably thought the author *was* Solomon. See A. Lauha, *Kohelet*, 29.
59 As cited by O. Eissfeldt, *The Old Testament. An Introduction* (Oxford: Blackwell, 1966) 493.
60 "Some Canaaite-Phoenician Sources of Hebrew Wisdom," *Wisdom in Israel and in the Ancient Near East* (Edit. M. Noth and D.W. Thomas, VT Supp 3) 15, n.2.
61 "The Structure and Content of the Book of Koheleth," *Wisdom in Israel and the Ancient Near East* (Edit. M. Noth and D.W. Thomas, VT Supp 3) 148–149.

because the fiction and portrayal of kingship is broader than the etymology of one word. O. Loretz tries to address this broader perspective by admitting a type of literary device, or theatrical "Ich-Erzählung". It is not fictitious autobiography, but merely stems from the traditional linkage of kingship and wisdom. The idea is that if the king can lay title to "wise", then the wise can lay title to "king"[62]. Though this is a creative suggestion, Loretz can find little support for his view, except in late Jewish writings[63].

Most writers agree that a king, and more specifically Solomon, is intentionally portrayed in the introduction of Qoheleth. J.A. Loader points out that the work alludes to specific features of the life and work of Solomon. Thus both he and Qoheleth are wise men *par excellence* (cf. I Kgs 4:29ff, Qoh 1:13–17); extremely rich (cf. I Kgs 4:21–28; Qoh 2:7–10); the owners of cattle and gardens (cf. I Chr 27:27–31; Qoh 2:4–7); lord over many slaves (cf. I Kgs 10:5; Qoh 2:7); and having many musicians (cf. I Chr 25; II Chr 5:12–13; Qoh 2:8)[64]. What literary device would permit this fiction? Many suggest a connection to Egyptian wisdom literature, the royal instructions or testaments[65]. This is not to say that the entire book is to be considered a royal testament. Since the form is limited to the first two chapters, it may be that Qoheleth just used it to make his point, and then dropped it.

The most important question is not the source of the literary device the author used, or how extensively it was used, but why he used it. It is generally agreed that the central theme of Qoheleth, "All is vanity" (1:2 *et al*) is directed towards criticizing an overly optimistic and mechanistic doctrine of retribution[66]. The historical development of Israelite religion toward a more personal religious view point (because of the weakening or loss of the cultic institutions) led to a dissatisfaction with the simpler casuistic wisdom of Proverbs. The heightening of individualsim made the problem of theodicy an acute one, and later wisdom focuses on this concern (Job, Qoheleth, Wisdom of Solomon). The choice of the figure of Solomon was a natural one, because no more effective critic of *Vergeltungsdogma* could be had than the wisest and richest king in Israel's history[67]. If the doctrine could be criticized from the perspective of the one who externally most closely seems to embody it, then the lie would be given to the simplistic positions of Qoheleth's day.

Is the use of Solomon merely a literary device, however? No. The choice

---

62 *Qohelet und die Alte Orient* (Freiburg: Herder, 1964) 149–166.
63 He cites b Sanh 102b; b Sabb 156a; b Ber 62a; b Git 64a. *Ibid.,* 150.
64 *Polar Structures,* 19.
65 See P. Humbert, *Recherches;* M. Hengel, *Judaism,* 129; J.C. Rylaarsdam, *Revelation,* 13: G. von Rad, *Wisdom,* 226; A. Lauha, *Kohelet,* 2; O. Eissfeldt, *Intro,* 499; J.A. Loader, *Polar Structures,* 19–20; K. Galling, "Kohelet-Studien," *ZAW* 50 (1932) 298–299.
66 It is generally accepted that Israel held a concept of an effective power inherent in the nature of creation. The laws of the universe specified that a casual relationship existed between good deeds and blessings, bad deeds and tragedy. See K. Koch, "Gibt es ein Vergeltungsdogma im Alten Testament?" *ZThK* 52 (1955) 1–42.
67 M. Hengel, *Judaism,* 130.

of Solomon by Qoheleth is also a deliberate attempt to place his work firmly in the context of the Solomonic wisdom tradition. The place of Qoheleth within the Hebrew tradition has often been hotly debated. Heinrich Heine has called the work, "Das Hohelied der Skepsis", while Franz Delitzsch has called it, "Das Hohelied der Gottesfurcht"[68]. Though it has often been popular to speak of Qoheleth's "heterodoxy"[69], there are strong reasons for regarding him as keeping within the framework of the biblical wisdom tradition, albeit at the radical edge[70]. This "radical orthodoxy" of Qoheleth is demonstrated when we see that the criticism or corrective that he makes appeals directly to an early and essential element of Hebrew wisdom. As M. Noth has demonstrated[71], both the wisdom of Solomon and his riches are free, gracious gifts of the sovereign God, according to the account in 1 Kings. There is no inherent connection between the two. This means that the source of Qoheleth's corrective was the historic Solomon wisdom tradition itself. The preservation of God's sovereign freedom above the world that he had created had always been an essential distinctive of Hebrew wisdom. It was this distinctive that Qoheleth sought to preserve, under the authority of Solomon. Here is an example of *Vergegenwärtigung,* the actualization of a tradition to meet the needs of a new generation.

> ... by his speaking in the guise of Solomon, whose own history now formed part of the community's common memory, his attack on wisdom was assigned an authoritative role as the final reflections of Solomon. As the source of Israel's wisdom, his words serve as an official corrective from within the wisdom tradition itself[72].

The presence of Qoheleth in the canon is evidence of a community decision that it was a legitimate expression of the biblical wisdom tradition. Though its acceptance was undoubtedly facilitated by its attribution to Solomon, it is naive to think that a simple linkage with the name Solomon was enough to achieve a work's recognition. Indeed, the record of dispute over the book is testimony to the critical sifting process of the community[73]. Yet the rapid acceptance of the book, despite misgivings, shows the success of its actualization of the biblical tradition[74].

---

68 A. Lauha, *Kohelet,* 22.

69 See for example, R.B. Salters, "Qoheleth and the Canon", *ET* 86 (1975) 341.

70 See R.N. Whybray, "Conservatisme et Radicalisme Dans Qohelet", *Sagesse et Religion* (Collogue de Strasbourg, 1976. Paris: Presses Universitaires de France, 1979) 3–81.

71 "Die Bewährung".

72 B.S. Childs, *Intro,* 584.

73 R.B.Y. Scott, *Ecclesiastes,* 194; A. Lauha, *Kohelet,* 20–21.

74 Its presence in Qumran Cave 4 (150 B.C.) shows that it must have achieved some sort of authoritative status quite rapidly. Reference is often made to its "orthodox redaction" (Qoh 12:13–14) as a factor in its acceptance. This may be granted, but certainly not as a crucial factor. See however the well reasoned suggestion of G. Sheppard, "The Epilogue to Qoheleth as Theological Commentary", *CBQ* 39 (1977) 182–189, that the epilogue to Qoheleth is not an orthodox redaction, but a thematicizing of not only Qoheleth, but the whole wisdom corpus. As such it can be seen as an indicator of a nascent canon of wisdom writings.

How, then, are we to regard the use of authorship in the book of Qoheleth? Certainly we can affirm that it embodies that same principles that we have discovered elsewhere. Authorship is more concerned with authoritative tradition than literary origins. Yet we can go beyond this. With the book of Qoheleth we can see the full birth of the genre of canonical pseudepigrapha. Unlike the books of Proverbs and Canticles, or the works of the prophets, Qoheleth is not a collection of material of varying ages, some likely authentic; but is the totally independent work of a creative individual. Though making claim to the same tradition process of *Vergegenwärtigung*, it is not a redaction or supplementation, but an entirely new work issued under the authority of another. If this is not the essence of pseudonymity, what is? Those (usually conservative) scholars who argue that the pesudonymity of Qoheleth is only a literary device, not seriously undertaken and transparent to all[75], have serious difficulty reconciling this view to the fact that the book was immediately and almost universally received as Solomon's. Its pseudonymity is only "transparent" to a modern critic. The objection that if Qoheleth had intended to be identified as Solomon, he would have signed his name as in other pseudepigrapha, misses the point. We have already witnessed the ambiguous indifference that the wisdom tradition displays toward literary attribution in Proverbs and Canticles. It is unrealistic to expect Qoheleth to act otherwise. Even the later Wisdom of Solomon displays the same ambiguity of attribution (see below).

The study of Qoheleth reveals one more important facet in understanding the rise of canonical pseudepigraphy. As we note in our study of the prophetic tradition, there always exists a fundamental difficulty in trying to understand the nature of the redactors of the biblical writings: what kind of men they were, how they regarded their task. This is because they always obscure their presence in the text. Yet in the epilogue to Qoheleth, we may get a glimpse into this process, at least for a certain time and element of Israel's history. As we have seen, the author or "Qoheleth" may be regarded as carrying on the biblical process of *Vergegenwärtigung,* though in a radically different form. Yet as a true "redactor", Qoheleth obscures his own identity in his work of reinterpreting the Solomonic wisdom tradition. In the epilogue to his book, though, we have what might be called a "redaction of the redactor" (a grossly distorted usage, it must be admitted). That is, in Qoheleth 12:9—11 we have the addition of later material from a person who is at least an admirer, and most likely a pupil, of Qoheleth. Though the pupil/redactor obscures his own identity, he does give important information concerning the life and thought of Qoheleth, as well as a justification for his work[76]. It

---

75 See Joyce Baldwin, "Is There Pseudonymity in the Old Testament?" *Themelios* 4 (1978) 8.

76 Or commendation. Some would deny that it is apologetic in nature, but merely written to commend the work. See A. Lauha, *Koheleth,* 220. Others feel that its work is defensive, an indication of the swift controversy it aroused. See H.W. Hertzberg, *Prediger,* 219—220.

is these observations that give us important insights into the process of *Vergegenwärtigung*.

The first information we receive is that "Qoheleth" was a wise man (12: 9), who stands in a line of succession of wise men (12:11). This may sound like stating the obvious, yet it is an important indicator that at least in post-exilic Israel there were classes of men specially devoted to wisdom and its preservation, particularly in literary form (12:9, 10). Moreover, this unself-conscious identification of Qoheleth as a wise man without reference to the guise of Solomon shows that this type of literary fiction must have been an accepted practice within his circle.

The mention of Qoheleth's teaching ministry (12:9) directed to all the people, shows that he was not a private philosopher, but had a community concern. This supports the translation of his enigmatic title as "Teacher". Evidently his was a critical task, sifting the rich material of wisdom and giving it literary form, yet with a concern to present the truth without distortion (12:9, 10). What is given is an (admittedly ideal) picture of the anonymous handling of tradition, not far different from what has been inferred.

The rationale for such handling of traditional material can be found in the cryptic phrasing of verse eleven: "The sayings of the wise are sharp as goads, like nails driven home ;they lead the assembled people, for they come from one shepherd." (NEB). The latter half of the verse is difficult to trans-late, and the NEB above preserves some of the ambiguity inherent in the text since it is hard to know if the "they" refers to a group of wise men or their teaching. The Hebrew text contains not a pronoun but the phrase, אספת בעלי[77]. There are two major interpretations of this phrase, dependent on the identification of its referent ("words", or "the wise") and the corres-ponding meaning of אספת ("collection", *Sammlung;* or "assembly", *Ver-sammlung*)[78]. If "words (of the wise)" and (אספת) בעלי are parallel, then אספת means "collection", i.e. a collection of proverbs or wisdom say-ings. בעלי , "lords", would then have to refer to the individual sayings in the collection[79]. The difficulty with this translation is that בעל cannot de-signate a small part of a whole, and normally serves as a designation for living beings (cf. Qoh 10:11, 20)[80]. The second interpretation reads אספת as "as-semblies". בעלי would refer to the leaders of the assemblies. This reading is more likely, since it fits the context of certain wise men leading the people

---

77 LXX: οἱ παρὰ τῶν συνθεμάτων ; Vulgate: magistrorum consiluum ; Peshetta: "masters of the threshold"; Targum: "masters of the Sanhedrin". Cited by C.F. Whitley, *Koheleth,* 103.

78 A. Lauha, *Kohelet,* 219–220; *BDB,* 127.

79 So Hertzberg, *Prediger,* 218–219. He also cites Odeberg, Midrasch, and Bentzen in support.

80 Hertzberg counters the latter objection by citing Isa 41:15, where בעל is used of a threshing sledge. But even here the usage may be governed by its connection with living beings, for Israel is to be *made* a living threshing sledge. *Prediger,* 219. The "lords" could refer to the dominant or ruling thoughts of the collection, but this is unlikely since it destroys the parallelism to "words."

or their school (*Lehrmeister*). The difficulty in this view is that it eliminates the parallelism to "words of the wise". A. Lauha feels this is no problem, however, because the early corruption of the text suggests that the phrase "lords of the assemblies" was not originally connected to the first part of the sentence (as the Masoretic text now has it), but to the last part. In this case the redactor would have taken the thought of a proverb ("the words of the wise are like goads and like driven nails") and more closely defined it. That is, the honoured *Lehrmeister* are authoritative not because of individual intellectual brilliance, but because they are authorized or "come from" (נהנ) "one shepherd"[81]. This seems the most plausible translation and interpretation.

The identification of the "one shepherd" has also been problematic. Many identifications have been made, such as Moses and even Aristotle[82]! Yet only three have any major plausibility. The first is that it refers to Qoheleth, as the head of a school[83]. This is unlikely, since Qoheleth is probably included in the phrases, "leaders of the assembly" and "words of the wise". A second suggestion is that it means Solomon, or at least a king. This is possible, since the image of the king as shepherd is known in the OT. But the image of kingship has been studiously avoided in this passage, and since Qoheleth is clearly identified as a wisdom teacher and not as Solomon, it is less likely. The third alternative, most commonly adopted, is that "one shepherd" refers to God[84]. This is the usual designation (Ps 23:1; 80:1; 95: 7; Isa 40:11; Ezek 34:12). This interpretation best fits it with the purpose of the redactor.

Er schenkt nicht nur dem Selbstwert von Kohelets literarischen Schaffen Anerkennung, sondern hebt besonders hervor, dass Kohelet ein Werkzeug Gottes war, um die Menschen aufzumuntern und zu leiten. Gott rüstet den Weisen mit einem Charisma aus, das ihn zum Lehramt befähigt[85].

It is important to note how strong an evidence this verse gives for a concept of an ongoing process of revelation through tradition, at least as it applies to biblical wisdom. Whether בעלי אספה is identified as collections of wisdom sayings or leaders of assemblies, and whether the "one shepherd" is identified as Solomon or God, this verse cannot fail to be read as an affirmation of the unity of God's revelation in the tradition process. Certainly no case should or could be built on the basis of this one difficult verse. Yet it serves as a more direct confirmation of what has been inferred in all our study of the process of tradition. That it occurs in the epilogue to Qoheleth

---

81 A Lauha, *Kohelet*, 219–220.
82 D.S. Margoliouth, "The Prologue of Ecclesiastes," *Exp* 8 (1911) 467.
83 O. Eissfeldt, *Intro*, 493.
84 G.A. Barton, *Ecclesiastes*; H.W. Hertzberg, 219; A. Lauha, *Kohelet*, 220.
85 H.W. Hertzberg, *Prediger*, makes a similar point, "Gott als der *eine* Hirte wird damit als der letzte und eigentliche Autor der Weisheit angesehen. Dann aber will der Satz *hier* noch besonders hervorheben, dass auch die Qoh-Spruchsammlung eine von Gott gegebene ist."

is particularly important for our understanding of the development of canonical pseudepigraphy, for *what we may infer is a commonly held view of revelation through tradition is now being used to justify the creation of an independent pseudonymous literary work as the Word of God.*

3.3.4 *The Wisdom of Solomon*

When we turn to the next "Solomonic" work, the Wisdom of Solomon, we see that the phenomenon discovered in Qoheleth is repeated. This is particularly significant, since the origin of this work brings us close to NT times. Furthermore, since the work was not everywhere received, it may give us some clues as to the forces involved in judging the process of tradition and literary attribution.

The Wisdom of Solomon will be regarded here as a literary unity[86]. The book's original language is Greek, and it is dated anywhere from 220 B.C. to A.D. 50. It is almost universally regarded as having arisen in a Hellenistic Jewish milieu, probably Alexandria.

Insight into the nature of Wisdom of Solomon's authorship is necessarily contingent upon an understanding of its purpose and structure. As implied from the history of debate over its unity, this has long been a source of contention. Among older scholarship, the alleged negative references to Qoheleth found in Wisdom 2 led to the theory that the book was written as a rebuttal of the skepticism of Qoheleth[87]. A variation of this theme was that Wisdom was not written to counteract Qoheleth, but rather the misinterpretation and misuse of it by Alexandrian hedonists[88]. The literary allusions were more apparent than real, however, and the decisive refutation of this theory came from the work of P.W. Skehan[89].

Other theories about Wisdom try to trace its function to Alexandrian culture. Thus, for example, B. Mack suggests that the book is essentially a re-

---

86 See D. Winston, *The Wisdom of Solomon* (Garden City, New York: Doubleday, 1979) 9–14, for an historical survey of opinion. He cites the arguments of J. Reese as decisive. See J. Reese, "Plan and Structure in the Book of Wisdom," *CBQ* 27 (1965) 391–399; *idem, Hellenistic Influence on the Book of Wisdom and its Consequences* (Rome: Biblical Institute Press, 1970) 122–145. More recently, D. Georgi, *Weisheit Salomos* (Gutersloh: Mohn, 1980) 394, argues for it as the product of a school.

87 See for example, G.A. Barton, *Ecclesiastes,* 57–58; A.T.S. Goodrick, *The Book of Wisdom* (London: Rivingtons, 1913) 23–31.

88 See for example, G.L. Grimm, *Das Buch der Weisheit* (Leipzig: Hirzel, 1860) 29–30.

89 See "The Literary Relationship of the Book of Wisdom to Earlier Wisdom Writings," *Studies in Israelite Poetry and Wisdom* (Washington: Catholic Biblical Association of America, 1971) 213–236. This is an abbreviated version of his 1930 unpublished doctoral dissertation. Skehan demonstrates that if anything Wisdom is dependent on *Job.*

formulation of the Egyptian Isis myth[90]. These suggestions confuse form with intent, and have not been widely received. Recent scholarship has come to realize that despite its Greek language and Alexandrian milieu, Wisdom is basically a Hebrew work, rooted in the OT[91]. Yet attempts to fit it into biblical forms, such as midrash, have proved inadequate[92].

The most viable and comprehensive understanding of the structure and purpose of Wisdom has come from the work of J. Reese. He maintains that the book is divided into four main divisions, using smaller literary genres, while the whole book is governed by the genre of *logos protreptikos,* or protreptic[93]. This is a genre that developed in the classical Greek period, and remained popular throughout the hellenistic and imperial period. It was a union of philosophy and rhetoric, an exhortatory discourse designed to commend a philosophy of life[94]. According to Reese, all the qualities displayed in the book of Wisdom are part of this genre: "a positive and even apologetic attitude about the control of the universe, a firm position against opposing philosophies of life, and the deliberate display of a wide range of knowledge"[95]. Since this form was particularly used in an academic setting, Reese feels that the work is an address to Hellenistic Jewish students. The writer of Wisdom is trying to help them in their confrontation with Hellenism, to be neither overwhelmed by it nor to reject its positive contributions. This more narrow focus, in my opinion, ought not to eliminate other purposes for the book, including an appeal for the conversion of apostates and even interested Greeks. The focus certainly does remain, however, on the Jewish community.

The next question one must ask is how the use of the figure of Solomon fits into the literary structure and purpose of the book. The Solomonic "autobiography" is found in Chapters 6–9. While the name of Solomon is not used, it is clearly a first-person account of his experiences, real and imagined, as well as his supposed reflections on the nature of wisdom (cf. 7:7–14 and 1 Kgs 3:4–15; 7:17–22 and 1 Kgs 4:33–34 ; 8:11 and 1 Kgs 3:16–28). Though scholars had always suspected a polemical use of the figure of Solomon[96], it was only J. Reese's study that identified the literary form and function of·the passage[97]. Reese, as well as others, feels that the figure of the king can only be understood against the background of Hellenistic king-

90 *Logos and Sophia* (Göttingen: Vandenhoeck and Ruprecht, 1973) 90–95.
91 See M. Hadas, "Wisdom of Solomon," *IDB* IV, 862; C. Larcher, *Études sur le Livre de la Sagesse* (Paris: Gabalda, 1969(·85–103, 181–236.
92 J. Reese, *Hellenistic Influence*, 90–91.
93 *Ibid.,* 117 ff. See also D. Winston, *Wisdom,* 18. Winston says that F. Focke, *Die Entstehung der Weisheit Salomos* (Göttingen, 1913) 86, had already suggested this.
94 J. Reese, *Hellenistic Influence,* 117, 118. He cites for a treatment of this genre in Greek literature, Theodore C. Burgess, "Epideictic Literature," *Studies in Classical Philology* 3 (1902) 89–261.
95 *Ibid.*
96 For example, Wisdom's "Solomon" versus that of the Alexandrian hedonistic, or versus that of Qoheleth.
97 *Hellenistic Influence,* 72–77; 102–130.

ship ideology, particularly as it finds expression in the literary form of Hellenistic kingship tracts[98].

> (The author's) presentation must be understood against the background of the widespread anthropological speculation of religious inspiration devoted to elaborating the kingly ideal in the hellenistic world from the time of Alexander the Great. Formulated in the new literary genre of tracts "On Kingship"; this speculation played an important educative and propaganda role in the various kingdoms that sprang up in the Greek-speaking world after the death of Alexander. Originally, these tracts were written by philosophers to provide prudent pedagogical advice for the reigning monarch or heir apparent. But soon productions of this genre became the ordinary vehicle for tracing the moral ideals of Hellenism in the form of a mirror for the wise and benevolent king[99].

This literary usage of kingship is not without precedent or parallels in other Jewish writings. The banquet scene in the Letter of Aristeas is commonly held to be dependent on the genre of kingship tracts[100]. Likewise, Philo in his *Life of Moses* portrays Moses as an ideal Hellentistic king.

However, though both Aristeas and the Wisdom of Solomon resemble kingship tracts in content or theme, they are not formally kingship tracts, either as a whole or in their relevant parts. J. Reese feels that Wisdom 6:12–16, 21–10:21 can be identified as a distinct literary genre, based on an analysis of its elements and purpose. He notes that the list of encyclopaedic knowledge, the attributes of personified Wisdom which reflects Isis aretologies, the moral and intellectual qualities of the kingship ideology, and the international frame of reference can all be explained as an attempt to synthesize the positive elements of Hellenistic philosophy and Alexandrian religious sentiment with Hebrew wisdom, under the rubric of the wise king Solomon[101]. The literary form or genre that the author uses can be defined as ἀπορία or "problem".

> Because the Sage was striving to produce a constructive synthesis in the "book of Wisdom proper" (6:12–16,21 – 10:21); it belongs to the area of "problem" literature, not in the narrow biblical sense of a work that questions traditional values, but in the tradition of Greek philosophical speculation. *His aim is not to challenge the data of the Bible, but rather to penetrate its lesson and adapt it for a new generation* (italics mine). He finds an appropriate genre in hellenistic scholastic tradition, namely the ἀπορία, "problem". This literary form developed out of attempts of philosophers such as Aristotle to answer questions of logic or moral conduct. It was a form of writing popular in the scholastic world during the first century B.C., pre-

---

98 *Ibid.,* 72–77; H. Duesberg and D. Fransen, *Les Scribes Inspirés* (Maredsous: Editions de Mardesous, 1966) 755–780; D. Winston, *Wisdom,* 63ff.

99 *Hellenistic Influence,* 72–73. See E.R. Goodenough, "The Political Philosophy of Hellenistic Kingship", *Yale Classical Studies* 1 (1928) 52–102. This genre would explain the address to the rulers in Wisdom as a mere rhetorical device. The writer did not even have to have a pagan audience in mind.

100 J.J. Lewis, "The Table-Talk Section in the Letter of Aristeas", *NTS* 13 (1966) 53–56; G. Zuntz, "Aristeas Studies I: The Seven Banquets", *JSSt* 4 (1959) 21–36; O. Murray, "Aristeas and Ptolemaic Kingship", *JThS* n.s. 18 (1967) 337–371.

101 *Hellenistic Influence,* 107. See also T. Finan, "Hellenistic Humanism in the Book of Wisdom", *IThQ* 27 (1960) 30–78.

cisely because its "religious dogmatism" was favourable to this form of investigation. Scholarly discussion of historical and religious problems was part of the educational program prevailing in Alexandria[102].

This combination of new literary forms and a desire to actualize old tradition to a new situation is by now recognized as a common expression of the principle of *Vergegenwärtigung,* though it must be admitted that the scope of the actualization and synthesis in the Wisdom of Solomon dwarfs any previous attempts. How, then, does the figure of Solomon relate to the authorship and authority of this writing, and to its place in the canon? As was noted, the name of Solomon does not appear in the book, though unlike Qoheleth there is no question that the identification is intended. This omission of name can be traced to the genre of protreptic, which always deals with persons as types, and thus proper names are omitted[103]. It would be a mistake to regard the use of Solomon as merely a type, however[104]. The choice of Solomon can also be regarded as a conscious attempt to root itself in the tradition of Hebrew wisdom, and to claim its authority as well. As in the case of Qoheleth, the relationship of this claim to the actual attribution of the book is an ambiguous one, and tells us that even at this late date, and in the midst of a Hellenistic culture, the spirit of *geistiges Eigentum* had not permeated Jewish religious writings.

The reception of the Wisdom of Solomon by various communities testifies that its claim to tradition and authority were not universally received. Indeed, the book was only used and transmitted in Christian circles[105]. Its rejection from the Jewish canon was probably based on a number of factors. No doubt its Greek language was a serious barrier. It certainly precluded any chance that it would be accepted as a work of Solomon. More seriously, though, the work was also likely rejected because it went far beyond the bounds of the biblical wisdom tradition. Its radical attempt at a rapprochement between the worlds of Hellenism and Judaism was simply too sweeping to be able to make universal appeal to the various communities in Israel, particularly in a period when nationalist feeling ran so high. The epilogue to Qoheleth, with its prohibition of more books, may also have been a factor.

The book was widely adopted in Christian circles, though its attribution to Solomon got a mixed reception. Most of the early church fathers ascribed it to Solomon (Clement of Alexandria, Tertullian, Origen, Cyprian)[106]. Jerome

---

102 *Ibid.,* 107–108. He notes that this form would have been recognized by all, since all boys in Alexandria were educated by this method.

103 *Ibid.,* 76, 117–119. This is not only true for Solomon, but for the other heroes of Israel's faith mentioned in Chap. 10 of Wisdom.

104 D. Winston, *Wisdom,* 139, makes this point against Reese. It is unfair, however, because Reese himself contrasts the non-historical allegorizing of Philo with Wisdom's grounding in history.

105 R.M. Grant, "The Book of Wisdom at Alexandria. Reflections on the History of the Canon and Theology", *StPatr* VII, 462.

106 As cited by W.O.E. Oesterley, *An Introduction to the Books of the Apocrypha* (London: SPCK, 1935) 196.

believed it to be falsely ascribed, a fact reflected in the omission of the name of Solomon from its title in the Vulgate. What is of particular importance is that doubts concerning its authorship did not preclude the book's usefulness and acceptance. Thus Eusebius regards the use of Solomon as a literary device (Praep. Evang. vii. 12). The Muratorian fragment goes even further. It both recognizes the book and acknowledges its pseudepigraphic origins, stating that it was "written by the friends of Solomon in his honour" (line 70). The Peshitta MSS 12a1 gives this extended superscription to the book: "The Book of the Great Wisdom of Solomon, the son of David; of which there is a doubt, whether another Wise Man of the Hebrews wrote it in a prophetic spirit, putting it in the name of Solomon, and it was (so) received"[107]. This evidence of Wisdom's acceptance despite its literary origins gives testimony to the receptiveness of the Christian community to pseudonymous writings[108]. The main criterion seemed to be content, not authorship (in the modern sense).

The canonical reception (acceptance *or* rejection) of the Wisdom of Solomon shows how tenuous is the distinction between a "valid" actualization of tradition and an "invalid" one. Ultimately it is the community that decides, and yet for this period of history the question comes to the fore: which community? The history of Wisdom's reception is just part of the larger story of the sectarian Judaism of this era. Since the development of a canon is a question of self-identity, it is inevitable that disagreement over the authority of certain writings would also be reflected in the actual separation of Judaism into various (more or less distinct) groupings. Thus is is no accident that Qumran, for instance, not only had a different attitude toward the cult than the Jerusalem hierarchy, but that this was also reflected by their possession of a distinctive corpus of writings, some shared with Judaism at large, many not. The actualization of tradition, literary attribution, and the formation of a canon are thus all caught up in the larger question of the legitimization and self-definition of a socio-religious group, often over against another or others. Whether or not a certain writing, such as Wisdom of Solomon, was a "legitimate" actualization of the Solomonic tradition is a religious value judgement that depends on one's adherence to certain religious groupings, both then and now. The important thing to note is that this "canonical" decision should in no way be confused with a *literary* decision about the validity of the pesudonymous attribution of tradition. The reception of the Wisdom of Solomon by the early Christian community shows that an acceptance· of the growth of tradition, including the use of pseudonymity, was still very much alive among the group that concerns us most: the Jewish sect that was later to be called the Christian Church. *The attribution of the Wisdom of Solomon, accepted or not, was a claim to authoritative tradition, not primarily a statement of literary origins.*

---

107 *Ibid.*

108 Indeed, by its portrayal of Solomon's writing as an "open letter" to rulers, it may have helped pave the way for epistolary pseudonymity.

3.3.5 *The Psalms of Solomon*

There are good grounds for believing that the Solomonic attribution of the Psalms of Solomon comes from a later hand, and thus could technically be called mis attribution rather than pseudonymity. However, an investigation into the ethos of this work might still prove instructive. It is a matter of some debate whether these Psalms are the work of one person or several. At the very least they are the work of one generation, since the clear allusions to Pompey (2:2, 6, 30–33:8:16–24) and other references to Hasmonean rule (e.g. 17:8) place the writings in the period from 70–40 B.C. Though the original language was probably Hebrew, our extant versions are now in Syriac and Greek.

The identity of the person or group responsible is difficult to isolate with precision. Older scholarship loved to depict the writing as a Pharisaic protest against the Saduccean control of the cult, but the current trend is to reject any distinctive Pharisaic elements, and simply to regard the writing as the work of one of the numerous anonymous eschatological groups in Palestine of that era[109]. The purpose of the document, however, is more clear. These Psalms are an obvious protest against what they regard as a defiled cult (1:9; 2:3; 8:13; *et al*) and an illegitimate (non-Davidic) monarchy (17:5–8)[110]. They are also psalms of lament and hope. They regard the odious occupation of the Romans as a just punishment for the sins of their leaders (2:1–7; 8:16). Yet the death of Pompey (2:30–33) brought hope that God would vindicate the righteous of the land whom the author of the Psalms represented (e.g. 17,18).

It is this overarching concern with the problem of theodicy that probably explains the Psalms of Solomon's special "sapiential" character. Though they preserve many genres from the canonical Psalms, they are not as distinct, and the work as a whole is more highly reflective (e.g. PssSol 10). They could be characterized as wisdom psalms[111].

It is in this context that the attribution of Psalms of Solomon should be considered. There is no direct allusion to king Solomon in the text, and the superscriptions are later additions that were added as part of their use in the ceremony of worship, as their connection with musical instructions implies

---

109 See esp. J. O'Dell, "The Religious Background of the Psalms of Solomon (Re-evaluated in the light of the Qumran texts)", *RdQ* 3 (1961–62) 241–257. The most recent work however marks a shift back in direction. J. Schüpphaus, *Die Psalmen Salomos* (Leiden: Brill, 1977) regards the Psalms as *early* Pharisiac. See esp. pp. 1–20.

110 From Aristobulus I (104 B.C.) onward the Hasmoneans claimed the title of king, until Pompey deposed Aristobulus II.

111 See J. Mowinckel, "Psalms and Wisdom", *Wisdom in Israel and in the Ancient Near East* (Edit. M. Noth and D.W. Thomas, VTSupp 3) 205–224, esp. 219–222; H.L. Jansen, *Die spätjüdische Psalmendichtung, ihr Entstehungskreis und ihr "Sitz im Leben"* (Oslo, 1936) (N.V.).

(e.g. PssSol 15)[112]. It is frequently suggested that these superscriptions and the later attribution of the entire work to Solomon are the result of the "closure" of the Davidic Psalter[113]. Solomon was deemed as an esteemed alternative who could help secure the acceptance of the work. This essentially negative approach has two weaknesses. First, the inviolability of a "Davidic" canon is questionable at this period (e.g. 11QPs[a] 151). Second, this approach labours under the assumption that psalms had to be ascribed to famous figures of the past to be received as authoritative. But the Hodayoth of Qumran put the lie to this. The ascription of the Psalms of Solomon to Solomon, particularly if by a later hand, ought not to be regarded as an appeal for authority, but as a recognition of it.

The attribution of these Psalms, then, should be approached from a positive perspective. Having achieved a level of authority in expressing the hopes and aspirations of a beleaguered community, what prompted the community to attribute them to Solomon? Their sapiential character is an obvious answer. Since Solomon was regarded as a writer of wisdom songs *par excellence* (1 Kgs 5:12), and songs of a similar nature were attributed to him even within the Davidic Psalter (72, 127), the attribution was a logical choice[114].

The reasons for attribution may go even deeper, relying on content as well as form. As mentioned earlier, an overarching concern of the Psalms of Solomon is the problem of suffering. It is significant that the very first psalm has personified Zion repudiating a *Vergeltungsdogma*. She had interpreted her prosperity as an indicator of the piety of her children, but now recognized this was not the case (1:3–7). Nickelsburg thinks that this chapter may have been written as an introduction to the whole collection[115]. If this is so, then the central message is thematicized in terms similar to what we find in Qoheleth. The wealth and prestige of the Hasmonean dynasty had been used as a sign of its legitimacy. But the author(s) of the Psalms of Solomon replies that there is no inherent connection between wealth and righteousness, wealth and wisdom in rule. Here we remember the strong linkage of kingship and wisdom, the king being responsible to establish the divine justice or order in society. This motif plays a strong part in the Solomon legend (1 Kgs 3:28; 10:9; Ps 72). What better way to expose the illegitimacy of the Hasmoneans and to assure the righteous hope for justice than by speaking in forms and figures that reflect upon the royal wisdom traditions of Solomon?

---

112 J. Schüpphaus, *Die Psalmen Salomos*, 151–153.

113 E.g. A.M. Denis, *Introduction Aux Pseudépigraphes Grecs D'Ancien Testament* (Leiden : Brill, 1970) 63; J. Schüpphaus, *Die Psalmen Salomos*, 153; Eissfeldt, *Intro.* 612–613.

114 H.E. Ryle and M.R. James, *Psalms of the Pharisees, commonly called The Psalms of Solomon* (Cambridge: University Press, 1891) lxi, also point to the possible resemblance of certain passages to the style of Proverbs (4:4–6; 5:15–20; 6:1–3; 9:5–9; 14:1–3; 16:7–15; 18:12–14). G. Nickelsburg, *Jewish Literature Between the Bible and the Mishnah* (London: SCM, 1981) 204, also thinks that PssSol 2:34–39 is reminiscent of Wis 1–6.

115 *Ibid.*

Support for this association can be seen in the messianic psalms that are certainly intended as a concluding message of hope (PssSol 17,18). In contrast to the priestly emphasis of Qumran, the future messianic figure in the Psalms of Solomon is a *king*, son of David (17:5, 23). His paramount virtue is a divinely given wisdom (17:25,31,40,42; 18:8), enabling him to judge the people and establish righteousness (17:28–29,31,33,41,45–48; 18:8–10). He will subdue foreign nations and make them serve Zion (17:27,32,34). He will once again make Jerusalem the centre of a holy cult of Yahweh 17:32, 33). Yet still he is a man, a vassal-king, aware that Yahweh is his God (17:28, 42) and indeed the true King (17:38, cf. v.51). What figure in Israel's history could serve as a paradigm for such a future king? The answer is surely *Solomon*, son of David, builder of temple, wisest and most powerful King of Israel[116].

Now this is not to assert that the original author intended this identification to be made. We simply do not know. But the sort of ambiguity that we met with in the king figures of Qoheleth and Wisdom of Solomon ought to caution us against dismissing the possibility too easily. The lack of identification may have been precisely to avoid the crass expectation of a Solomon *redivivus*, since the future king will be a "greater Solomon", refusing to trust in horse and rider (PssSol 17:37, cf. 1 Kgs 10:28–29) and "pure from sin" (PssSol 17:41, cf. 1 Kgs 11:4). At the very least the affinities of this messianic figure with the traditions of Solomon make it quite likely that the attribution of the Psalms of Solomon, whether by the author(s) or by a later hand, was a natural one, according to both form and content. *This traditional, theological undergirding of the work's literary attribution makes it possible to assert that whenever it took place, the Solomonic attribution was more of an assertion of authoritative tradition than a statement of literary origins.*

3.3.6 *Excursus: Other Solomonic Literature*

The treatment above by no means exhausts the number of writings attributed to Solomon. The figure of Solomon has inspired more apocryphal stories and writings than perhaps any other figure in antiquity, not only in Jewish culture but in many others as well[117]. Though there are many later Solomonic writings[118], we have been concerned to investigate the Jewish writings of the pre-Christian or NT era. There remains only two writings

---

116 See Ryle and James, *Psalms of Solomon*, lv.

117 For a treatment of the legends concerning Solomon, see L. Ginzberg, *The Legends of the Jews*, Vol IV, VI (notes) (Philadelphia: Jewish Publication Society of America, 1911); St. J. Seymour, *Tales of King Solomon* (London: Oxford Press, 1924); G. Salzberger, *Die Salomosage in der semitischen Literatur* (Berlin: 1907) (N.V.).

118 For a list of these and their texts, see J.H. Charlesworth, *The Pseudepigrapha and Modern Research with a Supplement* (Missoula: Scholars Press, 1981) 199 ff.

which might fit these criteria: The Odes of Solomon and The Testament of Solomon.

Originally composed in Syriac, the Odes of Solomon were written somewhere between A.D. 75–125 in Syria, probably in or near Edessa[119]. Now clear of suspicion of gnostic origins[120], they are the product of a Jewish-Christian community with strong links to Qumran and the Johannine writings[121]. Though the abundant evidence of inspiration in these Odes are of great value in the study of NT prophecy[122], they are of marginal value in our investigation of Solomonic attribution. The Odes might well be called the "Odes of the Risen Christ", since they are full of such prophetic "I"-sayings (8:8–19; 10:4–6; 17:6–16; 22:1–12; 28:9–20; 31:6–13; 36:3–8; 41:8–10; 42:2–30). Indeed, B.W. Bacon suggests that they were originally called the "Odes of the Lord's Rest" (26:3)[123]. It is more likely that they were anonymous.

The likelihood of the Solomonic attribution being original is very small. Nothing in the work alludes to him[124]. The earliest testimonies to Solomonic authorship are the third century Pistis Sophia and Bodmer Papyrus XI (G)[125]. The most likely cause of the Solomonic attribution was through its textual juxtaposition with the Psalms of Solomon[126]. Its Jewish character may have

119 See J.H. Charlesworth, "Odes of Solomon" *IDBS* 637–638; J.Quasten, "The Odes of Solomon", *Patrology I* (Utrecht-Antwerp: Spectrum, 1962) 160–168; J. de Zwaan, "The Eddessene Origin of the Odes of Solomon", *Quantulacumque. Fest. K. Lake.* Edit. R.P. Casey (London: Christophers, 1937) 285–302 (N.V.); R.M. Grant, "The Odes of Solomon and the Church of Antioch", *JBL* 63 (1944) 377 (N.V.).

120 See J.H. Charlesworth, "The Odes of Solomon – Not Gnostic", *CBQ* 31 (1969) 357–369.

121 See A.F.J. Klijn, "The Influence of Jewish Theology on the Odes of Solomon and the Acts of Thomas", *Aspects du judéo-christianisme* (Colloque de Strasborg, 1964. Paris: Presses universitaires de France, 1965) 167–177, with discussion 177–179; H. Chadwick, "Some Reflections on the Character and Theology of the Odes of Solomon", *Kyriakan I. Fest. J. Quasten.* Edit. P. Granfield and J.A. Jungmann Münster: Aschendorff, 1970) 266–270; J.H. Charlesworth, "Qumran, John, and the Odes of Solomon", *John and Qumran.* Edit. J.H. Charlesworth (London: Chapman, 1972) 107–136; J.H. Charlesworth and R.A. Culpepper, "The Odes of Solomon and the Gospel of John", *CBQ* 35 (1973) 298–322; J. Carmignac, "Un qumrânien converti au christianisme: l'auteur des Odes de Solomon", *Qumran-Probleme.* Edit. H. Bardtke (Berlin: Akademie, 1963) 75–108.

122 See D. Aune, "The Odes of Solomon and Early Christian Prophecy", *NTS* 28 (1982) 435–460; M. Lattke, "The Apocryphal Odes of Solomon and New Testament Writings", *ZNW* 73 (1982) 294–301.

123 "The Odes of the Lord's Rest", *Exp* 1 (1911) 193–209. (N.V.).

124 The connection of the "crown" of 1:1f with Cant 3:11 is strained. See J.H. Bernard, *The Odes of Solomon* (Cambridge: University Press, 1912) 45–46.

125 For a full discussion of relevant texts and quotations, see J.H. Charlesworth, *The Odes of Solomon* (Missoula: Scholars Press, 1977); J. Quasten, *Patrology I*, 161–162; J.R. Harris, *The Odes and Psalms of Solomon* (Cambridge: University Press, 1909) 22–35.

126 See J.H. Bernard, *Odes*, 14–15.

helped this association. The Odes of Solomon are thus an example of mistaken or misattribution, and are of little value for our investigation.

The Testament of Solomon appears to offer as little support. Written originally in Greek, the work dates from the third century A.D., though it may have incorporated an earlier (first century A.D.) Jewish work[127]. The work is of great interest for studying the relation of wisdom and apocalyptic, since its preoccupation with Solomon's power over demons probably stems from the mantic wisdom similar to apocalyptic writings (e.g. Daniel), and is probably traceable to Babylonian influence[128]. Though we have evidence that Solomon's wisdom was connected to exorcism in the first century A.D. (Josephus, Ant viii.2.5), the late and composite nature of the present Testament of Solomon makes it impossible to judge the role of tradition and attribution in the earlier work. One suspects, however, that it would be similar to what we have already discovered.

3.4 Summary

Though the structure and content of Hebrew wisdom is radically different from that of prophecy, and though its openness to foreign influence is unquestionable, it is highly significant that in terms of the relationship of revelation and tradition, the same pattern or features recur. Like prophecy, wisdom has a *divine* source (Prov 1:7; Job 28:28; Ps 111:10) made more explicit by its linkage with the Spirit (Num 11:16–17; 27:18; Deut 34:9; Isa 11:2; 1 Chr 12:18; Wis 1:7; 9:17; 11:20; PssSol 18:8). Its message is *unified* or *coherent* as well, based on the divine order in creation (Prov 3:19–20; 8:22–31; Job 12:7–10 . 28:23–27; Sir 1:4–10; 24:3,5,9; Wis 7:22–26; 8:1,6; 9:9). The proverbial nature of wisdom demonstrates its *autonomous* nature, but the most radical expression of this is without doubt the later hypostatization of wisdom (Prov 1–9; Wis 10–11). Finally wisdom is *interpretive,* a skill that depends not only on the reception of a *traditum,* but on its creative application to contemporary life (Prov 1:2–6; Qoh 8:5–6; 11:9–10; Sir 18:26; 39:33–34).

In investigating the role of Solomon in the history of Israel's wisdom traditions (1 Kgs 3–11) we saw that there is reason to believe that he did play a foundational role. At the very least, the Solomon legends fit in very well with the role of kingship in wisdom, to promote the divine justice and order

---

127 For Greek text and discussion of origins, see C.C. McCown, *The Testament of Solomon* (Leipzig: Hinrichs, 1922) (N.V.). For an older English translation and discussion, see F.C. Conybeare, "The Testament of Solomon", *JQR* 11 (1899) 1–45; see also D.C. Dulling's introduction in Charlesworth, *OT Pseudepigrapha I,* 935–959.

128 See S. Giverson, "Salomon und die Dämonen", *Essays on the Nag Hammadi Texts in honour of Alexander Böhlig.* Edit. M. Krause (Leidon: Brill, 1972) 16–21; L. Ginzberg, *Legends* IV, 149–154.

in society (Ps 72). Yet when it came to literary attribution in the Solomonic corpus we discovered a profoundly ambiguous indifference toward a rigid identification with Solomon (cf. Prov 1:1; 22:17; 24:23 ;30:1; 31:1; Cant 1:1; 8:11–12 ;Qoh 1:1; 12 ;12:9–10; Wis 6–9; PssSol 17–18). What seems to be more important is the use of elements of the Solomonic tradition to underscore a *theological* point. Proverbs attempts to nationalize and synthesize diverse wisdom material under the rubric of Solomon, who may in fact have initiated the process. Canticles uses the Solomonic tradition to interpret the phenomenon of human love. Qoheleth addresses the problem of theodicy and combats a mechanistic *Vergeltungsdogma* by recourse to the life of the wise king. Wisdom of Solomon helps the Jews of Alexandria enter into dialogue with the wisdom of Hellenism by allowing Solomon to commend his way of life and thought. Even the Psalms of Solomon expressed its messianic hope in terms paradigmatic of Israel's wisest and most powerful king. All these demonstrate the principle of *Vergegenwärtigung*.

It is for this reason that the characterization of pseudonymity in the wisdom literature as a search for additional authority is misleading[129]. The use of Solomon's name was a *claim* to authoritative tradition, not an additional appeal, made to bolster the author's own creative efforts. Of course, not all would accept that claim, as the history of the Wisdom of Solomon demonstrates. But it is necessary to differentiate between a *canonical decision*, which determines if a work is regarded as a valid actualization of a tradition, and a *literary-critical decision*, which determines if pseudonymous attribution is acceptable under any circumstances. *It is this distinction which allows us to conclude that even when the move is made from collective works such as Proverbs to the fully independent works such as Qoheleth and Wisdom of Solomon, attribution in the wisdom tradition is primarily an assertion of authoritative tradition, not a statement of literary origins.*

---

129 E.G. M. Noth, "Die Bewährung", 232.

Chapter 4

Authorship, Revelation and Canon
in the Apocalyptic Tradition

It is now time to examine the second of the extra- and post-prophetic traditions, that of apocalyptic, which is crucial for two reasons. First, its writings are almost universally pseudonymous. Second, though the extent of its influence has been hotly debated, no one can deny that the apocalyptic tradition forms a major bridge or link between the Testaments. If the continuity of the principles of literary attribution between apocalyptic and the previous traditions can be demonstrated, then a major case can be made for extending our findings into the NT itself.

In keeping with our established methodology, not all the relevant documents will be discussed in detail. After a general discussion of the nature of apocalyptic in which certain principles will be suggested, these principles will be tested by a more detailed examination of the Daniel and Enoch traditions.

4.1 The Nature of Apocalyptic

Though no comprehensive treatment can be given of the thought and literature of Jewish apocalypticism[1], it is necessary to note the long-standing debate over apocalyptic origins. Though the majority of scholars, past and present, have seen the roots of apocalyptic in OT prophecy[2], there are a number of features in apocalyptic, such as the "scientific" interest in astrology

---

1 See J.M. Schmidt, *Die jüdische Apokalyptik. Die Geschichte ihrer Erforschung von den Anfängen bis zu den Textfunden von Qumran* (Neukirchen: Verlag des Erziehungsvereins, 1969); K. Koch, *The Rediscovery of Apocalyptic.* (London: SCM, 1972); J. Barr, "Jewish Apocalyptic in Recent Scholarly Study," *BJRL* 58 (1975) 9–35; F.M. Cross, "New Directions in the Study of Apocalyptic," *JTC* 6 (1969) 157–165; E.W. Nicholson, "Apocalyptic," *Tradition and Interpretation.* Edit. G. W. Anderson (Oxford: Claredon, 1979) 189–213; M.A. Knibb, "Prophecy and the Emergence of the Jewish Apocalypses," *Israel's Prophetic Tradition.* Fest P.R. Ackroyd. Edit. R. Coggins *et al* (Cambridge: University Press, 1982) 155–180.
2 See especially S.B. Frost, *Old Testament Apocalyptic* (London: Epworth, 1952); H.H. Rowley, *The Relevance of Apocalyptic* (London: Lutterworth, 1955[2]); D.J.

(1 En 72–82), cosmogony (Jub 2:2ff; 4 Ezra 6:38ff; 2 En 24–33) and history (Dan 8–12; 8–12; 1 En 85–90; 4 Ezra 11–12,; 2 Bar 36–40; 53–74), often expressed by *Listenwissenschaft*[3], that cannot be explained by such an appeal. Though most have rightly rejected G. von Rad's idea that wisdom (not prophecy) is the true origin of apocalyptic[4], more recent scholarship has recognized its influence[5]. Especially significant has been the affinity demonstrated between mantic wisdom and apocalyptic[6]. The function of mantic wise men was to divine the secrets of the future by various relevatory methods, including the interpretation of dreams, omens, oracles, and stars (Gen 41:8; Esth 1:13; Isa 44:25; 47:10–13; Jer 50:35f; Deut 2:2; 4:4f; 5: 7,11), a function similar to the apocalyptic seer (cf. Gen 41: Dan 2). Mantic wisdom was prominent in Mesopotamia, and it seems no accident that Daniel is trained in the art of the Chaldeans (Dan 1:17–20).

A number of other features could be cited to demonstrated the possible influence of later wisdom upon apocalyptic, such as their similarities in cosmologies[7], or attitudes toward time[8]. Wisdom *Gattungen* such as parables (1 En 45:1; 58:1) and ethical admonitions (TLevi 13; 1 En 82:2–4) are evident in the literature[9], and both traditions share the linkage of wisdom and righteousness (Dan 12:10; 1 En 99:10; 4 Ezra 13:54,55; 2 Bar 38:2,3; TLevi 13:1–6. Cf. Prov 9:9; Qoh 9:1; Job 28:28; Sir 19:20)[10]. Once freed from the either/or debate of the prophetic/wisdom origins of apocalyptic, one is able to appreciate apocalypticism as a multi-faceted, multi-cultural phenomenon of the Ancient Near East. Especially important are the studies of J.Z. Smith, who argues persuasively for apocalypticism as a scribal phenomenon[11].

Russell, *The Method and Message of Jewish Apocalyptic* (London: SCM, 1964); P. Hanson, *The Dawn of Apocalyptic* (Philadelphia: Fortress, 1979).

3 See M.E. Stone, "Lists of Revealed Things in the Apocalyptic Literature," *Magnalia Dei: The Mighty Acts of God.* Fest. G.E. Wright. Edit. F.M. Cross *et al* (Garden City, NY: Doubleday, 1976) 414–452.

4 See G. von Rad, *Wisdom in Israel* (London: SCM, 1972) 263–282. The most extensive refutation is P. Osten-Sacken, *Die Apokalyptic in ihrem Verhaltnis zur Prophetie und Weisheit* (Munchen: Kaiser, 1969).

5 See C. Rowland, *The Open Heaven* (London: SPCK, 1982).

6 See H.-P. Muller, "Mantische Weisheit und Apokalyptik," *Congress Volume: Uppsala 1971.* Edit. A. Anderson *et al* (VT Supp 22, Leiden: Brill, 1972) 268–293; "חכם 3. Mantic Wisdom," *TDOT IV,* 376–378.

7 See J.J. Collins, "Cosmos and Salvation: Jewish Wisdom and Apocalyptic in the Hellenistic Age," *HR* 17(1977) 121–142.

8 See S.J. de Vries, "Observations on Quantitative and Qualitative Time in Wisdom and Apocalyptic," *Israelite Wisdom.* Fest. S. Terrien. Edit. J.G. Gammie *et al* (Missoula: Scholars, 1978) 263–276.

9 See further R.A. Coughenour, *Enoch and Wisdom* (Ph.D., Case Western Reserve University, 1972); *idem,* "The Wisdom Stance of Enoch's Redactor," *JSJ* 13 (1982) 47–55.

10 See M. Hengel *Judaism and Hellenism, I* (London: SCM, 1974) 207–208; J.G. Gammie, "Spatial and Ethical Daulism in Jewish Wisdom and Apocalyptic Literature," *JBL* 93 (1974) 356–385.

11 "A Pearl of Great Price and a Cargo of Yams: A Study in Situational Incongruity," *HR* 16 (1976) 1–19; "Wisdom and Apocalyptic," *Religious Syncretism in Anti-*

The learned character of apocalyptic, however, should not be exaggerated. The chief value of recognizing it lies in the light it sheds on the *form* of the literature more than its *content*. That is, though apocalyptic subject matter draws most heavily on OT prophetic themes, this is in itself no indication of the self-consciousness of the groups which produced the literature. Here is where wisdom terminology plays such a crucial role. The four major Jewish apocalypses or cycles of apocalypses (Daniel, 1 Enoch, 4 Ezra, 2 Baruch) from the central era of apocalypticism (200 B.C. – A.D. 100) all give evidence of a scribal or "wisdom" *Sitz im Leben*.

Four features are of particular importance. First, the heroes are never called prophets or called to prophesy[12]. Rather they are clearly designated as "scribes" or "wise men". Daniel is "skillful in all wisdom" (Dan 1:4; cf. 1:17,20; 2:23; 5:11,12,14). Enoch is a "scribe of righteousness" (1 En 12:4), a "writer of all the signs of wisdom" (1 En 92:1; cf. 37:4; Jub 4:17f.). Ezra is a "scribe of the knowledge of the Most High" (4 Ezra 14:50 (Syr); cf. 14:40; 4:22; 5:22). Baruch prays, "I did not depart from your wisdom" (2 Bar 38:4; cf. 50:1).

Second, the intended audience of the apocalypses, the community of the elect or righteous in the end time, is frequently characterized as "wise". In Daniel, by remaining faithful in the great tribulation in the end time, "those who are wise shall shine like the brightness of the firmament" (Dan 12:3; cf.11:33,35) and "those who are wise shall understand" (12:10) the words he has written. Enoch concludes his work by promising a great mystery, that his writings will be given "to the righteous and wise" (1 En 104:12; cf. 93:9–10) and promises that the elect will receive perfect wisdom in the new age (5:8; cf. 32:3,7). God instructs Ezra to give his seventy apocalyptic books "to the wise among your people" (4 Ezra 14:47; cf. 8:51–52; 12:38; 14:13,26). Speaking of God's plan, Baruch counsels, "everyone who will understand will be wise at that time" (2 Bar 28:1; cf. 14:5; 44:14; 48:23–24; 51:3–7).

Third, the wise community of the end time (or its leaders) have a redemptive role to play by sharing the seer's message with those for whom it was intended. Daniel promises that even during the terrible persecution of the end, "those among the people who are wise will make many understand" (Dan 11:33; cf. 12:3). Having mysteriously preserved his message for the wise of the end time, Enoch encourages them to share it with the children of the earth: "Reveal it to them with your wisdom, for you are their guides" (1 En 105:1; cf. 82:2–3; 104:12). Ezra is more circumspect, under instruction that "some things you shall make public, and some you shall deliver in secret to the wise" (4 Ezra 14:26). The public writings are the Law, but Ezra's apocalyptic works are reserved for the wise (4 Ezra 14:45–46). When Baruch's followers lament the loss of their "Shepherd" when he announces his imminent death, Baruch reassures them, "If you look upon the Law and are intent upon wisdom, then the lamp will not be wanting and the shepherd will not give way and the fountain will not dry up" (2 Bar 77:15–16; cf. 13:3–5; 46:4–6).

Fourth, the message of the seer is characterized as wisdom. When Daniel receives his interpretation of dream visions, he thanks Yahweh for giving him wisdom (Dan 2:20–23; cf. 9:22), and seals his book for only the wise to understand (Dan (12:4,9). Enoch calls his message a "vision of wisdom" (1 En 37:1; cf. 82:2–3; 92:1). Ezra calls his secret books, "the spring of understanding, the fountain of wisdom, and the river of knowledge" (4 Ezra 14:47; cf. 8:4). The problem of theodicy (the destruction of Jerusalem)

---

quity. Edit. B.A. Pearson (Missoula: Scholars, 1975) 131–156, reprinted in *Map is Not Territory* (Leiden: Brill, 1978) 67–87.

12 Only two extant Jewish apocalypses of this era are attributed to prophetic figures, the Apocryphon of Ezekiel and the Apocalypse of Zephaniah, and their fragmentary nature make it difficult to ascertain the nature of their attribution and the *Sitz im Leben* of their production. The Apocalypse of Elijah is probably misattributed. The (Syriac) Apocalypse of Baruch probably comes the closest to styling its hero as a prophet, using the expression, "the Word of the Lord came (to Baruch)" in two instances (2 Bar 1:1; 10:1).

which Baruch attempts to resolve is described as the problem of discovering "the beginning and end of (God's) wisdom" (2 Bar 14:9; cf. 51:3,7)[13].

The above features clearly show that at least a significant portion of the Jewish apocalypses were produced by learned, scribal groups[14]. Whatever their historical identity,
it is clear that they related to their literary works and their pseudonyms not in terms of
prophecy, but in terms of wisdom. One must then ask how this affects their understanding of revelation and literary attribution.

The idea of regarding apocalyptic literature as revelatory still requires
some justification, for the old opinion that the apocalyptists were crude
"epigonists" or imitators of ancient prophecy still persists in some quarters.
For this reason some regard the references to visions, auditions, and other
forms of revelation in the apocalyptic literature to be mere literary devices[15].
Yet without denying the literary character of apocalyptic accounts, there
remains evidence of genuine psychical experience[16]. Even when the apocalyptists give obvious evidence of the "rational" treatment of material, we must
take with the utmost seriousness their conviction that they were communicating authoritative, divine information[17]. Yet recognizing this raises another
problem: the question of the so-called "cessation" of prophecy or the "loss"
of the Spirit after the time of Ezra, a widespread if not universal doctrine in
Judaism from 200 B.C. onward[18]. How could the apocalyptists have revelatory experiences if they felt that prophecy had ceased? The answer has to
lie in how they regarded those experiences.

Apocalyptic revelation cannot be understood apart from the fundamental
problem that it addresses, that of *Weltverständnis*[19]. Apocalyptic shares

---

13 Baruch frequently identifies the Law with wisdom (e.g. 48:24; 51:4), but does not
   limit it to this. See esp. 54:18; 59:4–11.
14 Further, see M.A. Knibb, "Apocalyptic and Wisdom in 4 Ezra," *JSJ* 13 (1982)
   56–74.
15 E.g. W.R. Murdock, "History and Revelation in Jewish Apocalypticism," *Interp* 21
   (1967) 181–183.
16 See D.S. Russell, *Method*, 164–173; M. Hengel, *Judaism*, I, 207; C. Rowland, "The
   Visions of God in Apocalyptic Literature", *JSJ* 10 (1979) 137–154; *idem, Open
   Heaven*, 214–247; M.E. Stone, "Apocalyptic – Vision or Hallucination?", *Milla-wa
   Milla* 14 (1974) 47–56; S. Niditch, "The Visionary", *Ideal Figures in Ancient
   Judaism*. Edit. J.J. Collins and G.W.E. Nickelsburg (Chico, California: Scholars
   Press, 1980) 153–163; A. Wilder, "The Rhetoric of Ancient and Modern Apocalyptic", *Interp* 25 (1971) 446.
17 Even the prophets stylized their accounts. Cf. K. Freer, *A Study of Vision Reports
   in Biblical Literature* (Ph.D., Yale University, 1975); F. Horst, "Die Versionschil-
   derungen der alttestamentlichen Propheten", *EvTh* 20 (1960) 193–205.
18 1 Macc 4:46; 9:27; 14:41; 2 Bar 85:3; Josephus, *Apion* 1:8. For rabbinic evidence,
   see R. Meyer, "προφήτης", *TDNT* VI, 816–819. For full treatment, see T. Willi,
   "Das Erlöschen des Geistes", *Jud* 28 (1972) 110–116; R. Leivestad, "Das Dogma
   von der Prophetlosen Zeit", *NTS* 19 (1973) 288–299; D. Aune, "The Use of
   ΠΡΟΦΗΤΗΣ in Josephus", *JBL* 101 (1982) 419–421.
19 See U. Luck, "Das Weltverständnis in der jüdischen Apokalyptik dargestellt am
   ätheopischen Henoch und am 2 Esdra", *ZThK* 73 (1976) 283–305.

with classical wisdom the belief that the (God-given) structure of the cosmos ought to guarantee "justice" or the proper functioning of human life and society. However, the increasing subjugation and dislocation of Judaism during the Babylonian, Persian, and Hellenistic period meant that this world-view became more and more "out of synchronization" with the harsh realities of life. It is hard to believe in Yahweh and his divine order when your world is in chaos. Classical wisdom was content to live with this tension, regarding Yahweh's ways as inscrutable (Job 38–42; Prov 30:1–4; Qoh 8: 16–17; Sir 3:21–24). Apocalyptic, however, tried to resolve the tension by an appeal to "higher wisdom"[20]. That is, it claimed to explain the "true" state of world affairs by appealing to a knowledge of the hidden affairs of heaven (Dan 2:20–23)[21]. Unsurprisingly the means of attaining this "higher wisdom" are precisely those methods regarded as impossible by classical wisdom. To the question of Proverbs, "Who has ascended to heaven and come down? " (30:4), Enoch and other heroes of the apocalyptists would reply "I have!" (e.g. 1 En 14:8)[22]. It is no wonder that the esoteric lore that is revealed is sometimes expressed in almost the same categories to which classical wisdom denied access, such as the storehouse of the wind and hail (1 En 18:1–4; 41:3–4; cf. Job 28:25–26; 38:22–30), or the movement of the heavenly luminaries (1 En 72–82; cf. Job 38:31–33).

Many of the distinctive features of apocalyptic can be explained by this appeal to higher wisdom. Historical reviews, including *vaticinia ex eventu* (Dan 7–11; 1 En 85–90,93; 4 Ezra 11–12; 2 Bar 53,56–74) can be seen as an affirmation of a higher purpose in history, unseen by human eye, and not, as is so often stated, merely a crass attempt to gain credibility for the author's other prophecies[23]. The lists of cosmic phenomenon do not reflect a morbid interest in esoteric lore for its own sake, but an attempt to affirm that even in the midst of untold anxieties on earth the stability of the cosmos continues and offers hope for the future.

This shift to a heavenly reality in order to address the problem of *Weltverständnis* was not without precedent. As we saw in Chapter 2, many of the OT prophets believed in the unseen plan of Yahweh, which had been revealed to them in the heavenly council (Amos 3:7; Isa 6:1–13; 40:1–11; Ezek 1–3; Jer 23:18–20; Zech 3:7; cf. 1 Kgs 22:19–23). No doubt the apocalyptists

---

20 See M. Hengel, "Excursus Four: 'Higher wisdom through revelation' as a characteristic of religion in late antiquity", *Judaism* I, 210–218, also 250–251.

21 Apocalyptic literature in fact affirms the classical wisdom doctrine of Yahweh's inscrutability in very similar terms (2 Bar 14:8–11; 4 Ezra 4:10–11), but does so in the context of Yahweh's breaking the impasse through a gracious divine revelation (Cf. 2 Bar 15:3–4; 4 Ezra 14:22ff).

22 The two main vehicles of apocalyptic revelation are the dream/vision and the heavenly journey, though, as the verse cited illustrates, it is not always easy to distinguish them. (Nor may it have been for the seer. Cf. 2 Cor 12:1–4). The essential idea is that the seer is given access to the divine reality, which C. Rowland captures magnificently in the title of his book, *The Open Heaven*.

23 See E. Osswald, "Zum problem der vaticinia ex eventu", *ZAW* 75 (1963) 27–44.

built on these prophetic origins. Yet their portrayal of divine determinism goes beyond anything found in the classical prophets (ApAb 22; AsMos 12: 4–5; 4 Ezra 6:1–6; 2 Bar 48:1–9; cf. 1 QS 3:15–17), and displays features that may well be attributed to wisdom thinking. This determinism is not only volitional, that is, determined in the mind of God; it is also cosmological, written in the very structure of the cosmos (1 En 14–36).

One of the most characteristic expressions of this overarching divine reality or plan is the theme of the heavenly books. Though found in other literature, it nowhere receives the force and depth of treatment as in apocalyptic. There seem to be five essential types, though with some not inconsiderable overlap. One of the most familiar is the Book of Life (Dan 12:1; Jub 30:22; 36:10; ApZeph 3:7; 9:2; 1 En 47:3; 104:1; 108:3; cf. Exod 32: 32–33; Isa 4:3; 1 QM 12:2–3; 4 Q Dib Ham; Luke 10:20; Phil 4:3; Rev 3: 5; 13:8; 17:8; 20:12,15; 21:27)[24]. This is a record of God's elect. Also familiar is the Book of Deeds, also referred to as a book of judgement (Dan 7:10; Jub 5:13,14; 16:9; 19:9; 24:33; 28:6; 30:19–23; 39:6–7; 1 En 81:4; 89:62–65,70–71,76–77; 90:17–20; 97:6; 98:7–8; 104:7; 4 Ezra 6:20; 2 Bar 24:1; ApZeph 3:6; 7:1ff; T Ab(A) 12; 2 En 19:5; 50:1; 52:15; cf. Mal 3:16; Rev 20:12; Pirke Aboth 2:1). This is a record of all the deeds of mankind, good or evil, which is to be used as a basis of judgement. The third type might be called the Book of Nature (Ps 139:14–16; 1 QH 1:24; 1QS 10:6,8, 11)[25]. This book is only alluded to, and it is difficult to know whether it was pictured as a separate book containing the laws of nature, or if the references simply imply that the cosmos is a "book" that can be "read" by astrology, divination, etc. The fourth type might be called the Book of Law or Doctrine (Jub 3:10,31; 4:5,32; 6:17,28–31,35; 16:3,29–30; 28:6; 30:9; 32:10,15,28; 33:10; 49:8; 50:13). Found only in Jubilees, it is identified with both the Law of Moses and the sectarian *halakah* that accompanies it (no distinction is made between the two). Since this type of book often promises judgement, it could be confused with the Book of Deeds. But there is a distinction to be made between a record of deeds used as a basis of judgement, and a law that promises judgement if it is broken. There are also definite links between the Book of Law and the Book of Nature, since a great deal of the sectarian *halakah* is bound up with its cultic calendar based on the solar year (Jub 1:1–5). The Book of Law also has an important link to the fifth type, the Book of Fate, since prophecy is part of the Torah (Jub 16:3). The Book of Fate, or as Daniel calls it, the Book of Truth, is perhaps the most important for our understanding of apocalyptic eschatology (Dan 10:21; Jub 16:9?; 23:32; 24:33?; 31:32; 32:21–22; 1 En 81:1–2; 93:1–3;

---

24 Talmudic references are cited by S.M. Paul, "Heavenly Tablets and the Book of Life", *JANESCU* 5 (1973) 350–351.

25 Ps 139:16 may refer to another type, the Book of Fate, depending on the rendering of גלמי (cf. NEB, JB). See M. Dahood, "The Value of Ugaritic for Textual Criticism", *Bib* 40 (1959) 168–169, who offers a plausible solution.

103:2–3; 106:19 ;108:7,10 ; TLevi 5:4; 2 En 53:2–3; cf. Rev 5:1ff)[26.] The Book of Fate records the divine plan for the entire course of world history, and thus can easily be regarded as the conceptual source of apocalyptic historical reviews and prophecies concerning the end. Many scholars feel that this thinking was influenced by the Tablets of Fate or Destiny in Babylonian astral religion[27]. A strong parallel is the Babylonian tablets' association of nature and the order of existence[28], and the further association of these tablets and heavenly wisdom[29]. Yet crucial differences in the function of the Babylonian tablets and their relation to deity (they were a type of magical amulet, giving power over gods and men alike) rule out direct borrowing.

The significance of the widespread attestation to heavenly books in apocalyptic literature should not be underestimated[30]. Here we have a commonly held belief that all of the matters relating to physical and spiritual life, the cosmos and history, are contained in *written form* in heaven. Taking the prophetic idea of the counsel of Yahweh one step further, in apocalyptic revelation *unified becomes uniform, coherent becomes comprehensive.* Unlike the prophet, the apocalyptic seer has access to the *whole* counsel of Yahweh, for *all time.* This heavenly wisdom, especially as it is expressed in the form of eternal books, likewise demonstrates the *autonomous* quality of apocalyptic revelation. Not only does it take on a life of its own after it is spoken by the seer – it is sometimes regarded as having a life of its own before it is ever revealed to him! (E.g. 1 En 81:1–7; 93:1–3, where Enoch's revelation is described as recounting or transcribing from the heavenly

---

26 Several fragments from Qumran also refer to deterministic heavenly tablets which convey fate or truth. See A. Dupont-Sommer, *The Essene Writings From Qumran* (Oxford: Blackwell, 1961) 326; J.M. Allegro, "Some Unpublished Fragments of Pseudepigraphical Literature from Qumran's Fourth Cave", *ALUOS* 4 (1962–63) 3. The cases of Jub 16:9; 24:33 illustrate the difficulty of classifying these books since they could easily be classified as books of fate (since they predict an end), deeds (since they note sin) or law (since they assure that disobedience to law will be punished). This difficulty reminds us of the danger of making distinctions that may not been drawn so sharply in antiquity.

27 H.L. Jansen, *Die Henochgestalt: Eine vergleichende religionsgeschichtliche Untersuchung* (Oslo: J. Dybwad, 1939) 46–47,68,75; G. Widengren, *The Ascension of the Apostle and the Heavenly Book* (Uppsala: Lundquist, 1950) 7–21; A.Y. Collins, *The Combat Myth in the Book of Revelation* (Missoula: Scholars Press, 1976) 212–216; L. Koep, *Das himmlische Buch in Antike und Christentum* (Bonn: P. Hanstein, 1952) 19–22.

28 When Zu stole the tablets, "The norms were suspended". See "The Myth of Zu", OB version 2:1 (*ANET,* 111); Assyrian version 3:90f. (*ANET,* 113). Similarly, the victory of Marduk and his possession of the tablets is followed by creation. See "Enuma Elish", 4:120–5:66 (*ANET,* 67–68).

29 They are even called the "tablets of wisdom". See G. Widengren, *Ascension,* 10.

30 As well as the literature cited above, see F. Nötscher, "Himmlische Bücher und Schicksalglaube in Qumran", *RdQ* 1 (1959), 405–411, reprinted in *Von Alten Zum Neuen Testament* (Bonn: Nönner Biblische Beiträge, 1962) 72–79; D.S. Russell, *Method,* 107–108; M. Hengel, *Judaism,* I, 200–201; E. Rau, *Kosmologie, Eschatologie und die Lehrautorität Henochs* (Hamburg: Schultze, 1974) 312–379.

books). The comprehensive scope of apocalyptic revelation also makes it easy to justify the "re-application" of the seer's message, since his apprehension of the *whole* counsel of Yahweh would have meant that his message was directed to *every* generation, especially the end one[31].

But one might well ask how this rigid and comprehensive approach to revelation could facilitate the growth of tradition, since the ancient seer was regarded as having "seen it all"? To "see it all" is not, however, the same as explaining it all, as the relationship of the growth of rabbinic oral law to the doctrine of eternal Torah will testify[32]. This is why it is important to understand the *interpretative* nature of apocalyptic revelation.

Apocalyptic revelation can be described as inspired interpretation, as witnessed by the predominance of dreams and visions in the literature. The use of dreams and their interpretation can be traced well back into the history of Israel and the Near East[33], though the history of its reception in Israel is checkered (Cf. Num 12:6; Deut 13:2–6; Jer 23:25–32). In any case, already in the OT dreams can be regarded as revelatory, yet unlike the "word" of classical prophecy, they are often symbolic and require interpretation. In the Near East, dreams were interpreted in three ways: by an intuitional understanding of the symbols, by a comparison with the precedent of other dream interpretations, and by further revelation through a dream or vision[34]. The last method is particularly significant, since it denotes an essentially *secondary* revelation to explain the meaning of a *primary* revelation.

Even more important is the fact that this peculiar capacity to receive "interpretive revelations" is linked with wisdom in at least one stratum of the OT (Gen 41:39–40), and with a reliance upon the God of Israel, who alone has sovereign control of history (Gen 41:25–32) and is able to give interpretations of his revelation (Gen 40:8). It hardly seems an accident that the apocalyptic hero Daniel is portrayed in exactly the same role. As a highly skilled wise man (Dan 1:17), he is able to interpret Nebuchadnezzar's dream (Dan 2) when the Chaldeans cannot, because Daniel's God is the only one who is able to reveal it. He alone controls history (Dan 2:20–23).

---

31 Yet only the generation of the end may have been able to *understand* it, as the theme of "sealing" suggests (Dan 12:9). But this may not have been a universal theme in apocalyptic, since 2 Baruch seems to think that there will always be a few wise shepherds among the people (46:4–5).

32 Thus the accumulated lore of oral law, which in the first instance is attributable to specific rabbinic pronouncements, is traced back to Moses' revelation on Sinai (Pirke Aboth 1:1ff). Both oral and written law were foreseen by him. See Russell, *Method*, 83–84; R. Meyer, "προφήτης", 817.

33 For the NE background, see A.L. Oppenheim, "The Interpretation of Dreams in the Ancient Near East", *TAPhS* 46 (1956) 179–255. For Israel, see E. Ehrlich, *Der Traum im Alten Testament* (BZAW 73. Berlin: Töpelmann, 1953); W. Richter, "Traum und Traumdeutung im Alten Testament", *BZ* 7 (1963) 202–220; S. Zeitlin, "Dreams and their Interpretation from the Biblical Period to the Tannaitic Time: An Historical Survey", *JQR* 66 (1975) 1–18.

34 A.L. Oppenheim, "Interpretation", 219–221.

A major development of Daniel, however, is that this revelatory wisdom of interpretation is not limited to dreams. It also applies to visions (Dan 7:1; 8:1; 10:1)[35], and even to the interpretation of *scripture* (Dan 9:1ff; cf. 5: 5ff). How is this hermeneutical jump made? The answer is found in the concept of *raz* or "mystery" linked with interpretation in both Daniel and the Qumran texts.

In the OT, *raz* only occurs in Daniel (2:18,19,27,29,30,47; 4:6 MT)[36], all in connection with Nebuchadnezzar's dreams and Daniel's *pesher* or interpretation. The dream is a secret or mystery that belongs to God, and its interpretation must be "discovered" or "revealed" (גלה, 2:19,29,30,47 bis). However, it is not just any secret, but an eschatological secret concerning God's purpose in the consummation of this age (Dan 2:37–45; 4:20–27; cf. 7:17–26). The Qumran texts are full of references to God's mystery (*raz*), especially in the Hymn Scroll (e.g. 1 QH 1:21; 2:13; 4:28; 5:36; 7:27 *et al*). These texts do not limit the mystery to dreams, but are keen to apply it to all aspects of revelation, including God's presence in the structure of the cosmos (1 QH 1). "Mystery" is thus just another expression of the problem of *Weltverständnis* which we discussed above. It is significant that at Qumran as well as in Daniel the *pesher* or interpretation of mysteries is linked to *wisdom* (1 QS 11:3,6,18–19; 1 QH 1:19–21; cf. Qoh 8:1). The writings of Qumran also make clear how Daniel could shift from dream interpretation to scripture, for the Commentaries show that the *raz* included the previous revelation of scripture (see 1 Qp Hab 7:4–5). In other words, just as the primary revelation of dreams requires a secondary interpretive revelation, so do other forms of revelation, including visions and scripture. This stress on the enigmatic nature of (primary) revelation is not without precedent, having its roots in late prophecy[37]. Nor is the theme of secondary, revelatory interpretation absent from the literature of the rabbis[38]. Thus it comes as no surprise when an examination of the principles of dream interpretation in the OT, apocalyptic, and rabbinic writings shows that they are virtually identical to the principles of the *pesharim* of scripture, especially the prophets[39].

How does this relate to the growth of apocalyptic tradition? As we discussed earlier, the heroes of the major apocalypses are regarded as scribes and wise men, not prophets (Dan 1:4,17,20; 2:23; 5:11,12,14; 1 En 12:4;

---

35 Dan 7:1 shows that no strong distinction is made between dreams and visions. This is true of other apocalypses as well. Cf. 4 Ezra 11:1; 12:8; 2 Bar 36:1.

36 Though cf. Isa 24:16, a corrupt text.

37 E.g. Ezekiel 39 portrays the mysteries of the future as hidden in older prophecies, and proto-Zechariah (1:7–6:8) needs an angel to interpret the visions given to him by the Lord.

38 The revelatory *bath qol* was sometimes used to settle halakic disputes. Some rabbis used dreams and interpretation as a source of revelation (b Ber 55a–57; Lam Rab 14–18) and even used a dream to interpret scripture (b Ber 56a). As cited by S. Niditch, "The Visionary", 163.

39 See A. Finkel, "The pesher of Dreams and Scriptures", *RdQ* 4 (1963–64) 357–370.

37:4; 92:1; 4 Ezra 14:40,50; 2 Bar 38:4; 50:1). Their function is not to prophesy, but to interpret God's (mysterious) revelation, whether in the cosmos or in scripture. This is why their message is not characterized as prophecy, but as wisdom (Dan 2:20–23; 9:22; 12:4,9; 1 En 37:1; 82:2–3; 92:1; 4 Ezra 14:47; 2 Bar 14:9; 51:3,7). Returning to the dilemma posed earlier, we asked how the apocalyptists could affirm the doctrine of the cessation of prophecy while continuing to record the fruits of revelatory experiences? The answer lies in the different perception of prophetic and apocalyptic inspiration. Though both traditions may share many of the same pneumatic and literary forms, and, as we shall see, both share the same concern of *Vergegenwärtigung* that leads to the reinterpretation of traditional material, there is one crucial difference:

> Herein lies the difference, that interpretation within the bounds of OT prophecy appears itself as prophecy, while within apocalyptic it appears differently. Prophetic interpretation is interpretation in the prophetic spirit; apocalyptic interpretation is interpretation in the spirit of interpretation[40].

For this reason, I. Willi-Plein suggests that the thesis of T. Willi ("Das Erlöschen des Geistes") needs to be modified: "Only the spirit of prophecy has ceased, not the spirit as such"[41]. Though references to the Spirit are rare in the apocalypses and Qumran (undoubtedly because of its connection with prophecy), those that do occur show a clear connection between the Spirit and their interpretive revelations. In preparing to share his accumulated lore with his gathered children in testamentary fashion, Enoch remarks, "the spirit is poured over me so that I may show you everything that shall happen to you forever" (91:1). Ezra prays, "send the Holy Spirit to me" (4 Ezra 14:22) in order that he might not only restore the lost books of Moses, but also seventy secret books for the wise, and God answers with a drink giving wisdom (14:40). Daniel's interpretative wisdom is attributed to "the spirit of the holy gods" (Dan 4:8,18; 5:11,12,14).

The link of the Spirit to a revelation that is characterized by sapiential terminology ("understanding", "knowledge", "insight", "wisdom", etc.) demonstrates important links between the pneumatologies of the apocalyptic and wisdom traditions, no matter how differently it is expressed. We discussed in Chapter 3 the links between Spirit and wisdom, particularly in the late wisdom writings. It is especially significant that this linkage was directed toward the wisdom interpretation of the primary revelation of Law and Prophets (Sir 39:1–11).

Scholars have long noted that the choices of pseudonyms in apocalyptic literature are not arbitary, and there appears to be a conscious effort to build on a specific tradition, as in the prophets[42]. Thus, for example, The Apoca-

---

40 I. Willi-Plein, "Das Geheimnis der Apokalyptik", *VT* 27 (1977) 62–81. (my translation)

41 *Ibid.* (my translation). See also M. Hengel, *Judaism* I, 206.

42 E.g. D.S. Russell, *Method*, 109–117; M.E. Stone, "Apocalyptic", 55; C. Rowland, *Open Heaven*, 62–63.

lypse of Abraham builds on the tradition of Genesis 15; and 1 Enoch on Genesis 5:21–24. The historical role of Baruch and Ezra in the problems of Jerusalem's fall in 587 B.C. made them logical choices to address the similar problems of A.D. 70. The problem has been how to explain the revelatory connection between the (perceived) founder of the tradition and his later followers. The spirit of interpretation of (higher) wisdom provides the key. As we discussed earlier, the message of the ancient seer was directed to a special group, the wise (Dan 11:33,35; 12:3,10; 1 En 5:8; 32:3,7; 93:9–10; 104:12; 4 Ezra 14:13,26,47; 2 Bar 14:5; 28:1; 44:14; 48:23–24; 51:3–7). The point of contact between the apocalyptists and their pseudonyms is wisdom. It is given to these later, learned scribes to understand and interpret God's mysteries, just as it was given to the ancient seer whom they follow.

Though the pseudonymous form of the apocalypses makes it difficult for the apocalyptists to express their conviction for a continued or shared revelatory wisdom with the ancient seer (a situation similar to the prophetic writings), there is one feature which makes this apparent. We already saw the *pseudonymous* Daniel's participation in the revelation of God's mysteries (Dan 2:23,28–29). In the *anonymous* literature of Qumran, the author can freely proclaim his *own* inspired wisdom and insight into God's mysteries (1 QS 11:3,6; 1 QH 1:21; 14:12–13; 16:6–7). A comprehensive picture of the scope and nature of this revelation is found in Chapter 12 of the Hymns (1 QH 12). In the midst of a description of the mystery of God's sovereign control over nature (12:1–11a) and the course of history (12:13b–18), the poet accounts for his inspiration:

> And I, gifted with understanding, I have known Thee, O my God, because of the Spirit (12) that Thou hast put in me; and I have heard what is certain according to Thy marvellous secret because of Thy holy Spirit. (13) Thou hast (o)pened Knowledge in the midst of me concerning the Mystery of Thine understanding .... (1 QH 11b–13a)

That the apocalyptists shared a similar perspective on inspiration with Qumran is seen by the linkage of this inspired wisdom to a special dispensation of the End Time. Thus the full meaning of prophetic mysteries is only available to the end generation, especially through the Teacher of Righteousness (1 QpHap 7:1–5). This same feature is preserved by the apocalyptists by addressing the seer's message to the wise of the End Time (see above), who will not only see but be able to make others understand (Dan 11:33; 12:3; 1 En 82:2–3; 104:12; 105:1; 2 Bar 13:3–5; 46:4–6; 77:15–16). This belief probably lies behind the theme of "hiding" or "sealing" of the apocalypses (Dan 8:26; 12:4,9; 1 En 104:10–13; 4 Ezra 14:38,42–47; AsMos 1:17–18). Rather than a simple literary ruse to cover the recent origin of the writings, it was likely an expression of the conviction that only the last generation (the author's own) was able to "break" the seal of the mystery of God's working and plan[43].

---

43 See I. Gruenwald, "Knowledge and Vision", *Israel Oriental Studies* 3 (1973) 72.

However, because *perfect* wisdom was reserved for the New Age (1 En 5:8; cf. 1 Cor 13:12), apocalyptic revelation could never be considered perfect or complete. This is why 4 Ezra can totally and openly change the interpretation of the fourth Kingdom of Daniel ("But it was not explained to him as I now explain or have explained it to you", 12:12). Similarly the book of Daniel contains several revised accounts of the time of the end (7: 25; 8:14; 9:27; 12:7,11,12)[44]. In other words, if the conviction of a shared revelatory wisdom made *Vergegenwärtigung* in the apocalyptic tradition possible, the perception of its imperfect or incomplete nature made it necessary. Thus although the ancient seer (unlike the prophetic tradition) was regarded as having spoken directly to the needs of the "future" generation, the imperfect understanding of that generation would require further elaboration and interpretation of that vision as the End approached[45].

From the above discussion we have seen that, despite some radical differences, there is a "pattern" in the relationship of revelation and tradition in apocalyptic which is similar to that of prophecy and wisdom and ought to have similar effects on the perception of *geistiges Eigentum* and literary attribution. It remains to demonstrate this in a closer investigation of the Daniel and Enoch traditions. Before doing so, however, it might be instructive to take note of one other feature of apocalyptic revelation that may have a bearing on literary attribution.

It will be remembered that the autonomous and unified (if not uniform) nature of apocalyptic revelation was demonstrated by a treatment of the theme of the "heavenly books" in the discussion above. At times there appears to be more than just a formal connection between the heavenly books as a source of information and the apocalyptic writings themselves. Jubilees *equates* the Law of Moses with the heavenly book (3:10), and the midrashic construction of the book suggests that this *includes* Jubilees itself. Enoch's account of transcribing from the heavenly books (1 En 93:1,3) could easily lead one to believe that his work and they were virtually the same. The presence in heaven of *literature* that *may* at times have been equated with the writings of the seers (or *vice versa*) makes it at least possible that the apocalyptist thought that heavenly copies existed of their hero's works. In this case it might be possible to "recover" them by revelation.

We do in fact have some evidence to suggest that they believed this. In 4 Ezra 14 we have the story of Ezra the scribe "reproducing" the Torah of

---

44 See H. Burgmann, "Die vier Endzeittermine in Danielbuch", *ZAW* 86 (1974) 542–550.

45 Though the interpretive revelation of apocalyptic is often portrayed as the result of visionary or ecstatic experience (e.g. Dan 9:21–23), it must not be forgotten that underlying this is an intense "rational" study of tradition (Dan 9:1). No clear line can be drawn between "rational" (using certain hermeneutical principles) and "inspired" insight. Thus Josephus (*War*, 2:159) connects the visionary ability of the Essene seers to the fact that from early youth they are devoted students of the scriptures.

Moses and the Prophets which had been lost during the Exile, through divine dictation characterized as higher wisdom (14:40). It is significant that his own (secret) works were produced in the same fashion (14:26,44—47), leaving open the possibility that they could be reproduced as well[46]. Tertullian shows that this belief was not restricted to a small sect or applied only to the Law and Prophets, for in his treatise *On Female Dress* (I.3) he defends the canonicity of 1 Enoch by remarking that even if it had been lost in the deluge, Noah could have restored it in a manner similar to Ezra's restoring the Law and Prophets. Perhaps the clearest theological "justification" for such reproduction is found in Daniel 2. In this passage which forms the thematic core of the whole book, Daniel is able not only to interpret the dream of Nebuchadnezzar, but also to *reproduce* it. Indeed, far from being an incidental embellishment, this is a central feature of the narrative. The proof that Daniel is a follower of the one true God, and that his interpretation is true (for anyone can offer an interpretation) is the fact that he is able to reproduce God's message to Nebuchadnezzar.

The evidence above indicates that it is at least possible that, in some instances, the pseudonymous books of the apocalyptists (or parts of them) were not only regarded as stemming from the ancient seer in terms of a continuity of *tradition,* but were also regarded as inspired *reproductions* of his works. This conclusion is not necessary, however, to justify the use of pseudonymous attribution. Faithful tradition is enough, as Tertullian relates (above). We have already demonstrated how the structure of apocalyptic allows for the growth of tradition. It now remains to demonstrate that growth and its relation to literary attribution.

4.2 The Daniel Tradition

If the book of Daniel had not been included in both the Jewish and Christian canons, we might have been able to dismiss the pseudonymous apocalypses as aberrations from "mainstream" Judaism. But its inclusion forces us to account for it, and makes it an obvious choice for investigating the role of revelation and tradition in literary attribution.

4.2.1 *The Figure of Daniel*

The question of Daniel's identity is not one that can be easily solved by focusing on the testimony of one book (Dan 1:3—6). Though the canonical

---

46 The story of Jeremiah re-dictating his lost scroll to Baruch (Jer 36) may have been regarded in a similar manner by the apocalyptists.

book of Daniel is obviously the most prominent, the LXX additions to Daniel (Susanna, Bel and the Dragon, The Prayer of Azariah, The Song of the Three Young Men) and the fragments of another Daniel apocalypse at Qumran (4 Qp Dan) demonstrate that there was a large cycle of Daniel traditions. The attribution of visionary material to Daniel continued well into the Middle Ages[47].

The name Daniel is common enough in the OT. In 1 Chronicles 3:1 there is a Daniel, son of David and Abigal. Ezra 8:2 (cf. Neh 10:7) refers to a priest of that name who returns from the Exile. This could possibly be our Daniel, though it is difficult to understand how such a prominent figure should receive such slight treatment. Ezekiel speaks of a Dan'el, renowned for his piety and wisdom (14:14,20). Ezekiel's Dan'el may have some connection with the Dn'il of the Ugaritic Legend of Aqhat (see A.V. 4–8), *ANET* 151), who is depicted as a judge and defender of orphans and widows. This connection may be strengthened by Jubilees 4:20, where the legendary wisdom figure Enoch marries Edni, the daughter of Dan'el.

Though some have tried to trace a linear development in these various Daniel legends[48], the evidence is too fragmentary to establish any principled relationships. Unfortunately, there is not much hope of establishing the historicity of the figure of the canonical apocalypse. There may well have been a young wise man who distinguished himself among the Babylonian exiles, but there is no way of confirming this. What is important for our purposes is that Daniel is regarded as an historical figure of the Exile by the apocalypse, whatever the possibility of lost legendary accretions or origins. This means that the use of his name ought to be more than just a literary device, as we shall see.

4.2.2 *The Court Tales of Daniel (1–6)*

The sixth century date of Daniel has been under question ever since the neo-Platonist Porphyry (third century A.D.) accurately placed the writing in the time of Antiochus IV Epiphanes, and except among a few conservative scholars[49] this position has won the day. The arguments are based on exter-

---

47 See F. Macler, "Les Apocalypses Apocryphes de Daniel", *RHR (=AMG)* 33 (1896) 37–53, 163–176, 288–319 (N.V.).

48 See H.-P. Müller, "Magisch-mantische Weisheit und die Gestalt Daniels", *UF* 1 (1969) 89–94; J. Day, "The Daniel of Ugarit and Ezekiel and the Hero of the Book of Daniel", *VT* 30 (1980) 174–184. *Contra*, see H.H.P. Dressler, "The Identification of the Ugaritic Dnil with the Daniel of Ezekiel", *VT* 29 (1979) 152–161; J.J. Collins, *The Apocalyptic Vision of Daniel* (Missoula: Scholars, 1977) 23.

49 See E.J. Young, *The Prophecy of Daniel* (Grand Rapids: Eerdmans, 1953); R.K. Harrison, *Introduction to the Old Testament* (London: Tyndale, 1969) 1110–1127; J. Baldwin, *Daniel* (Leicester: Intervarsity, 1978).

nal witnesses (none before the second century), language[50], the internal witness of the historical reviews (7–12), and general theological development[51].

However, the second century dating of the present Daniel does not exclude the possibility of an earlier date for portions of it. Recent scholarship has identified Chapters 1–6 as previously collected court tales which, as do those of Esther, stem from the Eastern Diaspora, and were designed to encourage the exiles about the possibility of success in a foreign context[52]. There are a number of important features in these tales, some of which have already been mentioned in our discussion on the nature of apocalyptic revelation. Daniel and his companions were wise men, serving in the typical Near Eastern role as royal counsellors, and trained in all forms of wisdom, including the learning of the Chaldeans, noted for their divinatory skills (1:4). Daniel is particularly skilled in dream and vision interpretation (1:17). The focal point of the collection is the tale about Nebuchadnezzar's dream in Chapter 2. He requests his wise men to tell him its contents as well as interpretation (2:1–6), information which they protest can only come from "the gods" (2:11). Daniel succeeds where the foreigners fail, because "there is in heaven a God who reveals secrets" (2:28a; cf. 2:47) and He is Yahweh, God of Daniel and source of all wisdom (2:20–30). This leads even Nebuchadnezzar to proclaim him "God of gods and Lord of Kings" (2:47). The wisdom of Daniel and his friends is "ten-times" better than their foreign counterparts (1:10) because it comes not from human skill (2:27,30), but from faithful adherence to Yahwism.

Unfortunately, there is little we can say about the historical identity of the group that composed and/or collected these wisdom tales. The setting and function of the tales surely suggests a Diaspora provenance, and the character of the material shows that it must have been some sort of wisdom group[53]. In any case, here we have evidence of a virile Yahwism, not afraid to adopt the forms and methods of foreign cultures and "demythologize" them, putting them to the service of its faith[54]. The date of origins of these

---

50 Though see K.A. Kitchen, "The Aramaic of Daniel", *Notes on Some Problems in The Book of Daniel* (London: Tyndale, 1965) 31–79; R. Vasholtz, "Qumran and the Dating of Daniel", *JETS* 21 (1978) 315–321.

51 For a full survey of scholarly research on Daniel, see W. Baumgartner, "Ein Vierteljahrhundert Danielforschung", *ThR* 11 (1939) 59–83, 125–144, 201–228; J.C.H. Lebram, "Perspectiven der gegenwärtigen Danielforschung", *JSJ* 5 (1974) 1–33.

52 See W.L. Humphreys, "A Life-Style for Diaspora: A Study of the Tales of Esther and Daniel", *JBL* 92 (1973) 211–223; S. Niditch and R. Doran, "The Success Story of the Wise Courtier: A Formal Approach", *JBL* 96 (1977) 179–193; W. Towner, "The Poetic Passages of Daniel 1–6", *CBQ* 31 (1969) 317–326; J.J. Collins, "The Court Tales in Daniel and the Development of Apocalyptic", *JBL* 94 (1975) 218–234; *idem. Vision.*

53 G. Dautzenburg suggests that the inclusion of the three companions in the narrative reflects a school of wisdom scribes (2:18,23,36). *Urchristliche Prophetie* (Stuttgart: Kohlhammer, 1975) 47.

54 Though there was opposition to the mantic activities represented in Daniel through-

tales is open to surmise. A third or fourth century date might be suggested, but there is nothing to preclude that some of the material might be earlier, even going back to the events they describe. The collection, however, would be much later. As it stands it is a literary unity, woven around the alleged chronology of Daniel's career.

4.2.3 *The Apocalypse of Daniel (7–12)*

While Daniel 1–6 is variously described as midrash, *hagadoth,* or court tales, the absolute consensus is that the literary and theological elements of Daniel 7–12 make it an apocalypse. Yet there is near equal consensus that the two units are closely related. In fact, the apocalypse can be regarded as an elaboration or reinterpretation of the court tales, especially Chapter 2.

The role of Chapter 7 is pivotal in this regard, as its similarities with Chapter 2 show. Both show Daniel receiving a revelation in a similar manner, the dream or night vision (2:19; 7:1–2,13) which includes both symbol and interpretation. The content is also similar, since the four kingdom schema is preserved (2:31–45; 7:2–8). Though Daniel 7 uses beast imagery from a different source[55], the majority of scholars identify the referents as the same as Chapter 2: Babylon, Media, Persia, and Greece. Likewise, they both envision a divine intervention into history at the end of the fourth kingdom (2:34–35; 7:9–14), in order to set up God's immutable and unending kingdom (2:44; 7:14,18,27). Though the agents of Yahweh's intervention are differently identified (or symbolized) as a stone cut "by no human hand" (2:34,45) or as the "Son of Man" (7:13), their use as collective symbols for the kingdom and/or its peoples (2:44; 7:18) is quite similar.

The similarities between Daniel 2 and 7 have led some to suggest that they are part of a larger (pre-Maccabean) unit, and that the references to Antiochus Epiphanes (7:8, 11a, 20b,21,22,24b,25) are later interpretive interpolations[56]. Even if this were so, this would suffice to show how the acutaliza-

---

out Israel's history, it seems to be directed toward false belief rather than false practice (Deut 13:2–6; Jer 23:25–32). Note that after a long polemic against it, Sirach admits that the situation is altered entirely when Yahweh is behind it (Sir 34:1–8).

55 For the sources of the beast imagery, see J.J. Collins, *Vision,* 95–122; M. Delcor,. "Les sources du chapitre VII de Daniel", *VT* 18 (1968) 290–312; T. Wittstruck, "The Influence of Treaty Imagery on the Beast Imagery of Daniel 7", *JBL* 97 (1978) 100–102. A. Hartman and A. DiLella suggest that the use of the strange verb דקק "to crush to pieces" (7:7, 19, 23) in regard to the animais and their prey may be explained by literary borrowing from 2:34,40,44f ("smashing" of metals). *The Book of Daniel* (Garden City: Doubleday, 1978) 208.

56 E.g. Hartman and DiLella, *ibid.,* 156. A. Lenglet marshalls a further argument, demonstrating that Chapters 2–7 have a symmetrical arrangement: four kingdoms (2 & 7), miraculous deliverances (3 & 6), contrasts of two Gentile kings (4 & 5). See "La structure littéraire de Dan 2–7", *Bib* 53 (1972) 169–190. The Aramaic

tion of earlier Daniel material occurs, applying an ancient schema to a new *Sitz im Leben*. Yet the *differences* of Chapter 7 from Chapter 2 show that the actualization is rather larger in scope. The four kingdom schemas of Daniel 2 and 7 have a rather different function[57]. Chapter 2 is not written to condemn any kingdom. Nebuchadnezzar is even described as a "head of gold". Yet Chapter 7 describes these kingdoms as monsters rising out of chaos. Likewise the framework for Chapter 2 is not salvation-history. Israel is barely alluded to in 2:44. Yet this is the clear thrust of Chapter 7 (vv 18,27). This stress on the persecution and vindication of God's elect in Chapter 7 also accounts for the urgency of its climax: the crushing of a blasphemous revolt against God (7:25), rather than the final dissolution of the fourth kingdom through internal weaknesses (inter-marriage, 2:43).

This is why the references to Antiochus ought not to be regarded as superficial additions, but as an integral part of the interpretive framework. In his attempt to annihilate Judaism, Antiochus had ruled out any chance for the religious rapprochement which Daniel 2 had suggested was possible with foreign monarchs. Rather then abandon these traditions, however, the author of the apocalypse reinterpreted them. By not acknowledging Yahweh as sovereign in history as did Nebuchadnezzar (2:46–47; cf. 5:34–37), Antiochus speaks "words against the Most High" and thinks "to change the times and the law" (7:25), a direct threat to Yahweh's sovereign lordship (cf. 2:21 "He changes times and seasons; he removes kings and sets up kings"). For this reason Yahweh will remove him (7:26–27). The author places this interpretive development within the framework of Chapter 2 by further elaboration of the last kingdom. Described as feet in Chapter 2, presumably with ten toes, the kingdom becomes a nameless beast with ten horns in Chapter 7 (v.7), and out of these ten (Hellenistic) kings comes one horn, Antiochus (7:8).

Thus the whole focus of Chapter 7 is to reinterpret Chapter 2 in light of a new *Sitz im Leben*, the terrible persecution of the mid-second century. The author recognizes the value of Chapter 2 and its emphasis on Yahweh's sovereign lordship, but *the message needs to be further interpreted*. This is the principle of *Vergegenwärtigung* which we have seen active throughout Jewish tradition, and it is in fact the *raison d'etre* for the entire apocalypse. Rather than serving as an isolated unit, Chapter 7 is a hermeneutical bridge that helps to make the transition between the tales and the apocalypse. It re-initiates the chronological cycle of the tales: Nebuchadnezzar/Belshazzar (7:1; 8:1), Darius (9:1), Cyrus (10:1)[58]. By so doing it helps the pseudonymous seer take a "closer

---

of Dan 7 also links it to Chapters 2–6. Both language and symmetry, however, can be redactional devices. See below.

57 See esp. J.J. Collins, *Vision*, 12–13.

58 As Collins, *ibid.*, 13–14 remarks, this shows that Dan 7 is to be placed with 8–12, not 1–6. Yet the writing of Chapter 7 in Aramaic shows that the apocalypse is meant as an extension of Chapters 2–7. The translation of Chapter 1 into Hebrew may have served the same purpose.

look" at the key features of the Daniel tradition (Chapter 2), and make his initial application to his own era (Chapter 7)[59]. Having established his hermeneutical connections and guidelines, the author is then free to further elaborate his own era, using a wide variety of supplementary materials. This is exactly the pattern in Chapters 8–12.

Chapter 8 picks up the theme of the kingdoms again, but this time with different beast imagery. However, because Chapter 7 has already set the context, Chapter 8 can move quickly to its own era after lightly touching on the Media/Persian empires. Its real concern is to elaborate on the final symbol of Chapter 7 (cf. 8:9 and 7:24; 8:11,24 and 7:25), though this should again be seen as reaching ultimately back to Chapter 2. Thus 8:25 reaffirms that the final kingdom will be broken "by no human hand" (cf. 2:34,45), and its concern for the length of time (8:14) can be seen as reaching beyond 7:25 back to 2:21. The media of revelation is also tied to the tales, since an angel or "holy one" gives the interpretive revelation (8:13, cf. 4:13,23).

Chapter 9 is also concerned with the question of the "times" (cf. 8:14; 7:25; 2:21), but now brings in additional material from Jeremiah to address the issue, the prophecy of seventy years (Jer 25:11–14; 29:10). The setting of the vision (9:1) is just at the end of the Babylonian era and the beginning of the Median period, i.e. just when Jeremiah's prophecy should have been realized. The treatment of Jeremiah shows a "canon-consciousness" that meant that this earlier revelation could not be discarded, but had to be reinterpreted to fit the time of the Maccabean author. In other words, some way of addressing the problem of the delay of the (eschatological) end had to be found. Given the hermeneutics of apocalyptic revelation as inspired interpretation, the solution is not a surprising one. After demonstrating his devotion to Yahweh in a manner similar to the Daniel of the tales (prayer, fasting, and confession, 9:3–4a,20. Cf. 1:8; 6:10), the Daniel of the apocalypse is accepted as a "favoured man" (9:23; cf. 6:21–22), and shown that the proper interpretation is that *seventy weeks of years* (490) was intended, thus bringing the time of the end down to the Maccabean era, specifically to the time of Antiochus IV (9:27).

After briefly touching upon the Persian empire, the author returns to an even more detailed *vaticinium ex eventu* of the last kingdom in Chapters 10–12. There are a number of elements that reveal the ethos of the author. In 10:21 we have mentioned the heavenly books, specifically the Book of Truth (cf. Book of Deeds, 7:10; Book of Life, 12:1), which is clearly the source of Daniel's interpretive revelation, his ability to see God's purpose more accurately. A. Lacocque makes the interesting suggestion that this might be related to the "books" of scripture (i.e. Jeremiah) which Daniel reads in 9:1[60]. In any case the author is able to reinterpret traditions (from

---

59 Note how the author of 4 Ezra (11:1; 12:11) reinterprets Daniel's fourth kingdom again, this time identifying it as Rome. Thus the original revelation cannot be mistaken, but its interpretation may be.

60 *The Book of Daniel* (London: SPCK, 1979) 179–180, 204.

Daniel 1–6, Jeremiah, etc.) because of his access to "higher wisdom" (9:22). That this message is regarded as wisdom is also seen by the mention of the *maskilim,* the elect of the end for whom the message is intended (11:33,35; 12:3,10; cf. 1 QS 1:1; 3:13; 9:12), obviously reflective of the author's own community. It is they who are able to unseal the mystery and reveal the content of Daniel's visions and interpretations (12:10).

4.2.4 *Attribution in Daniel*

As we have seen, Daniel 1–6 represents an earlier collection of anonymous tales from the Diaspora, while Daniel 7–12 is a pseudonymous creation of Maccabean times in a Palestinian setting. The force behind the creation and addition of the apocalypse is one that we have met time and again in our study of Jewish tradition: *Vergegenwärtigung*. This is made possible by three shared perspectives. First, the author and his community could identify with Daniel and his companions, for both were *maskilim* (1:4; 11:33). Second, they share a similar message and purpose: the affirmation of God's sovereignty in history and the encouragement of the faithful (2:21; 11:36b). Third, they share a similar approach to revelation as inspired interpretation.

By structuring the apocalypse around the four-kingdom schema of Chapter 2, and recapitulating the chronological sequence of the tales, the author of the apocalypse creates a large "pesher" of the anonymous tales[61]. His conviction of the continuity of revelation and tradition means that his own identity was not significant. Put more positively, *the attribution of the book of Daniel is primarily a claim to authoritative tradition, not a statement of literary origins.*

4.3 The Enoch Tradition

No apocalyptic literature apart from Daniel has had more influence on Judaism and Christianity than the works of the Enoch tradition. Besides the book of 1 Enoch, itself a cycle of apocalypses[62], we also have extant 2 Enoch (Slavonic) and 3 Enoch (Hebrew). Nor does this exhaust the number

---

61 A. Szöernyi, "Das Buch Daniel, ein kanoniserter pescher?" *Congress Volume, Geneva 1965* (VTSupp 15. Leiden: Brill, 1966) 278–294, makes a similar point, but posits a pre-Maccabean *Urtext* in *all* the Chapters (1–12) that is highly unlikely.

62 Scholars almost universally accept a five-fold division of separate "books": 1. Book of Watchers (1–36), 2. Book of Parables (37–71) 3. Astronomical Book (72–82), 4. Book of Dreams (83–90), 5. Epistle of Enoch (91–105). This does not deny that independent blocks of material are encorporated within these divi-

of Enochic pseudepigrapha. J.T. Milik argues for a Book of Giants isolated from Qumran fragments as originally part of the cycle of 1 Enoch[63]. P. Grelot thinks he has isolated another Enoch source in 4 Q MessAram[64], and J. Greenfield and M. Stone posit two others[65]. However, the fragmentary and hypothetical nature of these latter sources, and the composite and late dating of 2 Enoch and 3 Enoch make them unsuitable for our study. Thus we will limit ourselves to the growth of 1 Enoch (minus the additions from the Book of Noah, Chapters 106–108).

4.3.1 *The Figure of Enoch*

The legend of Enoch's righteousness or communion with God and his unique translation to heaven, the two elements of Genesis 5:21–24, provided a spark that turned into a raging fire of speculative interest by the second century B.C. One of the first major studies of this legend, that of H.L. Jansen[66], sought its origin in Mesopotamian mythology, and many have followed his lead[67]. According to this approach, Enoch, the seventh after Adam, was modelled after the wise, seventh antediluvian Mesopotamian monarch Emmeduranki, the initiator of civilization, as well as on other wisdom figures, such as Xisouthros, transmitter of antediluvian wisdom by means of books which survived the Flood, and Nabu, scribe in charge of the Tablets of Fate, who records human deeds and their destinies. As we shall see, these parallels are more than superficial to Jewish Enoch traditions, and some sort of influence must be posited, direct or indirect.

By the Hellenistic era the legend of Enoch's exemplary wisdom and piety was well established. Sirach 44:16 (49:14) cites him as an example of wisdom (Hebrew) or repentance (Greek)[68]. Wisdom of Solomon 4:10–15 alludes to Enoch's translation, its purpose being the preservation of his purity. Philo regards Enoch as a patron of ecstatic, "otherwordly" wisdom, in contrast to the wordly wisdom of Abraham[69]. Jubilees is by far the most fruitful

---

sions. Critical considerations such as dating, text, etc. in the study below will essentially follow that of G.W.E. Nickelsburg, *Jewish Literature Between the Bible and the Mishnah* (London: SCM, 1981).

63 *The Books of Enoch: Aramaic Fragments of Qumran Cave 4* (Oxford: Clarendon, 1976) 298–339.

64 "Hénoch et ses écritures", *RB* 82 (1975) 488–498.

65 "The Enochic Pentateuch and the Date of the Similitudes", *HThR* 70 (1977) 64.

66 *Die Henochgestalt.*

67 See P. Grelot, "La légende d'Hénoch dans les apocryphes et dans le Bible: Son origine et signification", *RSR* 46 (1958) 5–26, 181–210; *idem,* "La géographie mythique d'Hénoch et ses sources orientales", *RB* 65 (1958) 33–69; R. Borger, "Die Beschwörungsserie bīt mēseri und die Himmelfahrt Henochs", *JNES* 33 (1974) 183–196 (N.V.).

68 See D. Lührmann, "Henoch und die Metanoia", *ZNW* 66 (1975) 103–116.

69 *On The Change of Names,* 34–40.

source of traditions outside of the Enoch literature (Jub 4:15–26; 5:1–10; 7:20–29; 10:1–17; 21:10). J.C. Vanderkam gives a convenient outline of its material:

A. Enoch During His 365 Years
   1. The first wise man (4:17)
   2. The first author, writing by revelation:
     a. astronomical/calendrical works (4:17,18; cf. 4:21)
     b. a cosmological work (4:21)
     c. a testimony (4:18,19)
     d. halakot (7:38–39; 21:10)
   3. A visionary (4:18,19,21)
   4. A husband and father (4:20)
   5. An associate of the angels for 500 years (4:21)
   6. One who testified to the watchers (4:22)
A. Enoch After His Translation
   1. Resident of the garden of Eden (4:23–24)
   2. Recorder and judge of human actions until the judgement (4:24; cf. 10:17)
   3. A priest in the mountain temple (4:25–26)[70].

The witness of Jubilees and others gives clear evidence of a complex Enoch tradition in Judaism, both oral and written. Though the present state of research is not mature enough to be able to write a history of the tradition, we should be able to demonstrate how the writers and redactors of 1 Enoch used the traditions found in Genesis 5 and Jubilees and applied them to their own *Sitz im Leben*.

4.3.2. *The Astronomical Book (1 Enoch 72–82)*

The third century (B.C.) Astronomical Book, or Book of the Heavenly Luminaries, is the oldest section of 1 Enoch and a prime example of the heavenly journey type of apocalypse. Enoch is taken up on a tour of the heavens by the angel Uriel, where he observes "everything" (80:1). Yet the book's efforts to demonstrate (with incredible tedium) the regularity and order of the universe is not intended solely as an exercise in esoteric astronomical lore, but is directed toward salvation-historical concerns: proper cultic practice (82:4–5). The astronomical configurations are based on the 364 day solar calendar which we find in Jubilees and Qumran (1 En 82:6), thus giving further evidence of an ancient sectarian dispute. According to the Astronomical Book, the world of the eschatological end (the author's own time) is "out of syncronization" with the cosmic order because of the Jerusalem hierarchy's dependence on a lunar rather than a solar cultic calendar (80:2ff; 82:5). Rather than a minor debate, this calendric difference meant that the required feasts and sacrifices were being offered on the wrong

70 "Enoch Traditions in Jubilees and Other Second-Century Sources", *SBL 1978 Seminar Papers,* I. Edit. P.J. Achtemeier (Missoula: Scholars Press, 1978) 241.

days, and thus *Israel had abandoned the Law.* This was the reason for her subjugation and misfortune, and could not be corrected until the proper cult was restored (82:7–8).

This imputation of a sectarian calendric dispute to the Enoch tradition may be older than the Astronomical Book (cf. Jub 4:17,18), but in any case it is easy to see how the connection was made. As one who "walked with God" (Gen 5:24), and who had read the heavenly books (1 En 81:1–2), Enoch would have been in a position to know the "true" divine order of the universe (82:7–8). As such, he would have been keen to transmit this "higher wisdom" (82:2) for the benefit of all who desire righteously to obey God's ordinances, especially the wise generation of the end (81:6; 82:1–3), who would share this salvific message with others. Here we have a prime example of the actualization of an ancient tradition. Because of their solidarity with the wise and righteous Enoch, the author and his community are able to address the problems of theodicy and the cult by an appeal to his authoritative tradition.

4.3.3 *The Book of Watchers (1 Enoch 1–36)*

Composed of even older units, the third century (B.C.) Book of Watchers is one of the oldest Jewish apocalypses, and is divided in three parts: the introduction (1–5), the story of the Watchers and Enoch's intercession (6–16), and the account of Enoch's heavenly journey (17–36).

As in the Astronomical Book, Enoch's complete heavenly knowledge (1:2a) is intended for the elect of the last generation (1:3ff). Likewise the contrast of the order of nature (2:1–5:3) and the disorder of the wicked suggest that the "law of the Lord" (5:4) may include the (calendric) laws of nature[71]. Disobedience will not go unpunished (5:5–6), and the elect will live in total cosmological harmony (5:7–9), made possible by the wisdom that will be given to them (5:8).

The second section (6–16) is divided into two parts: the sin of the Watchers (6–11) and the intercession of Enoch (12–16). Chapters 6–11 are an independent midrashic expansion on Genesis 6:1–4[72]. Why was it incorporated into the Enoch tradition? The onomastica of the angel lists reflect a wisdom interest compatible with the Enoch legend, but more important, the story of the Watchers serves two vital purposes. As an etiological argument, it gives an additional explanation to the problem of theodicy by tracing the origin of evil to cosmic rebellion[73]. As a paradigmatic argument, it offers a

---

71 J.J. Collins, "The Apocalyptic Technique: Setting and Function in the Book of Watchers", *CBQ* 44 (1982) 96.

72 Actually it contains *two* independent traditions, the Azazel and Semyaza myths.

73 See P.D. Hanson, "Rebellion in Heaven, Azazel, and Euhemeristic Heroes in 1 Enoch 6–11", *JBL* 96 (1977) 195–233; G.W.E. Nickelsburg, "Apocalyptic and

typology of evil, and serves as a vehicle for the concerns of the redactor's *Sitz im Leben,* such as the issue of purity[74].

This paradigmatic value of the story of the Watchers is further revealed in its linkage with Enoch's role as intercessor (savior/judge), a long-standing tradition that may possibly be traced back to Mesopotamian influence (cf. Jub 4:22–26)[75]. It is instructive to note the wisdom shades of Enoch's role. He is a "scribe of righteousness" (12:4; 15:1; cf. 92:1), who carries the written petition of the Watchers to heaven (13:6). The reply he returns is also in written form, "the book of the words of righteousness" (14:1), proclaiming God's judgement. Most important, Enoch's role as intercessor/judge is determined by his God-given capacity for wisdom, *a capacity that is shared in some degree with other men* (14:2–3). This paradigmatic, intercessory role provides the key to the actualization of these traditions:

> Why did Enoch and the Flood hold such fascination for apocalyptic writers in the later Persian and early Hellenistic period? Undoubtedly they were struck by this combination of factors: a wise and just man (Enoch) living in a generation of iniquity, or before it, knowing of the approaching terrible end of the wicked. The Flood as the first End was of extreme interest to apocalyptic writers because it was interpreted typologically of the approaching final End. Enoch played a role similar to the one assigned by these writers to the Just who will remain in the generation before the End, an idea well-known from the writings of Qumran[76].

In other words, here we have a creative combination and actualization of traditions in order to address the needs of a current generation, not only to explain the cause of their suffering, but through their patron Enoch to encourage them to play a similar redemptive role in ending it, because of their shared capacity (in kind, though not degree) for wisdom. The final section of the book, Enoch's heavenly journey (17–36), is only loosely tied to the story of the Watchers, but it serves a vital function as well. The lengthy tour of the cosmos is meant to demonstrate that the message of judgement/salvation which has been given to Enoch and his followers are already realities imprinted in the cosmos, awaiting fulfillment on earth (27:1–4), and are not dependent on human power, but God's (36:4).

Myth in I Enoch 6–11", *JBL* 96 (1977) 383–405; J.J. Collins, "Apocalyptic Technique"; *idem,* "Methodological Issues in the Study of I Enoch: Reflections on the Articles of P.D. Hanson and G.W.E. Nickelsburg", *SBL 1978 Seminar Papers,* I. Edit. P.J. Achtemeier, (Missoula: Scholars Press, 1978) 315–322; D. Dimant, "I Enoch 6–11: A Methodological Perspective", *idem,* 323–339; C.A. Newsom, "The Development of I Enoch 6–19: Cosmology and Judgment", *CBQ* 42 (1980) 310–329.

74 See D.W. Suter, "Fallen Angel, Fallen Priest: The Problem of Family Purity in I Enoch 6–16", *HUCA* 50 (1979) 115–135.

75 See H.L. Jansen, *Die Henochgestalt,* 8–9.

76 D. Dimant, "I Enoch 6–11", 330.

4.3.4 *The Book of Dreams (1 Enoch 83–90)*

The third oldest book of 1 Enoch (160 B.C.) differs significantly in its mode of revelation, its dream/vision format being more like Daniel. The book contains two visions. The first vision (83–84) is a warning of God's approaching judgement in the Flood. Encouraged by his grandfather Mahalalel (83:8), Enoch intercedes with God that a righteous remnant might be spared, but confirms judgement for the rest (84:5–6). Thus we have made explicit the implicit analogies of the Book of Watchers. Enoch's role as cosmic mediator (between the Watchers and God) is now overtly expanded to that of earthly mediator as well (between men and God).

The second vision (85–90), often called the Animal Apocalypse, serves to extend this schema into world history, and therefore make Enoch's role toward his own generation applicable for "the generations of the world" (83:10), as the testamentary framework of both visions implies (83:1; 85; 1–2). Thus a succession of animals symbolically parade the history of God's dealings with men, up to the Maccabean revolt and the events of the author's own day, in order to demonstrate God's sovereign control of history. Reflecting earlier traditions, the sufferings of Israel are traced to two origins: their own disobedience (89:32–33), and the overzealousness of their angelic shepherds (89:65). But judgement would be accomplished and the elect redeemed (90:20–39). This message of judgement/salvation is linked to the first vision (90:24), and thus the author/redactor of these traditions accomplishes his task of further actualizing Enoch's paradigmatic role as intercessor in a crucial time of history, intent on proclaiming God's sovereign wisdom (84:3).

4.3.5 *The Epistle of Enoch (1 Enoch 91–105)*

The early second century (B.C.) Epistle or Admonitions of Enoch is styled on the form of an Aramaic letter[77], providing an example of epistolary pseudepigraphy two centuries before the NT. It too contains earlier, independent material, notably the Apocalypse of Weeks (93:1–10; 91:11–17)[78] Like the Animal Apocalypse in the Book of Dreams (85–90), this Apocalypse of Weeks is incorporated into the large context of a testamentary address, not only for Enoch's children (91:1ff), but for "the latter generations which uphold uprightness and peace" (92:1). Thus it is meant to make Enoch's paradigmatic role and message relevant for the author's own time. This is forcefully communicated by its linkage of Enoch and the final generation. Enoch is the seventh born in the first week, a time of righteousness (93:3). In the final,

---

77 J.T. Milik, *Books of Enoch*, 51–52.

78 See F. Dexinger, *Henoch's Zehnwochenapokalypse und offene Problems der Apokalyptikforschung* (Leiden: Brill, 1977).

seventh week, a righteous remnant of Israel will similarly be given sevenfold or complete wisdom (93:10; cf. 91:10)[79], i.e. the author's own community[80].

This wisdom connection to Enoch is important to bear in mind, since the Epistle is replete with prophetic forms and material, as G.W.E. Nickelsburg has demonstrated[81]. But as Nickelsburg freely admits, Enoch is not styled as a prophet, and the redaction gives clear evidence of a "wisdom circle"[82]. Thus Enoch is characterized as a scribe (92:1)[83], whose access to heaven, the words of angels, and the heavenly books (93:2) makes his message a "complete wisdom teaching" (92:1, Knibb translation), given to the elect who are wise (98:9; 104:12). This message is redemptive (99:10), and is entrusted to the latter day wise to share with their generation (100:6ff; 105: 1-2), as Enoch did with his.

This message, of course, is none other than the Epistle of Enoch, though it may be intended to include the *entire* Enochic corpus, and possibly Torah as well (104:11-13). This would be in keeping with both 4 Ezra and 2 Baruch, whose own concluding portions include references to both their own works and the Law as part of God's message for the wise (4 Ezra 14; 2 Baruch 77). Here we have then, a well developed sense of "canon-consciousness", where traditions are now taking authoritative literary form. This makes it all the more crucial to note that the author's attempt to actualize the Enochic traditions in the Epistle is set in the context of a dispute over authoritative interpretation, probably over Torah (104:6-11). Sinners are those who alter "the word of truth" (104:9,10 marg.), and "write out my Scriptures on the basis of their own words" (104:10). But the faithful "righteous and wise" through a process regarded as a "mystery" will receive an undiluted version they can treasure as wisdom (104:11-13). This undoubtedly includes the "commentary" of Enoch, for he relates earlier "For I know this mystery; I have read the tablets of heaven and have seen the holy writings, and I have understood the writing in them; and they are inscribed concerning you" (103:2).

The production and (possible) consolidation of the Enochic writings, then, must be viewed as part of the "canonical process", the formation of a community's self-identity, often over against others. Taken in this perspective, *it is of fundamental importance to notice that true doctrine is defined in*

---

79 M. Knibb, *The Ethiopic Book of Enoch* (Oxford: Clarendon, 1978) 225 translates the Ethiopic in 93:10 as "teaching". The Aramaic reads "wisdom and knowledge" (חכמה מדע). See J.T. Milik, *Books of Enoch*, 265-267. The Aramaic also includes a reference to the "missionary" activity of this remnant, "for witnesses to righteousness".

80 See G.W.E. Nickelsburg, "The Epistle of Enoch and the Qumran Literature", *JJS* 33 (1982) 343.

81 "The Apocalyptic Message of I Enoch 92-105", *CBQ* 39 (1977) 309-328.

82 *Ibid.*, 326-328. See also R. Coughenour, "The Woe Oracles in Ethiopic Enoch", *JSJ* 9 (1978) 192-197.

83 The Ethiopic and Aramaic diverge, but the import is the same. See J.T. Milik, *Books of Enoch*, 260-263.

terms of the faithful understanding and transmission of God's revelation to Enoch, while false doctrine is defined as the distortion and production of unfaithful books. In other words, authorship or attribution is inseparably tied to authoritative tradition.

4.3.6 The Book of Parables (1 Enoch 37–71)

The Book of Parables or Similitudes are by far the latest part of 1 Enoch. Its dating and provenance have been hotly debated because of the Son of Man references and their relation to NT christology. However, a pre-Christian dating is not necessary for our purposes. The majority of scholars regard the Parables as a Jewish work stemming from the (late) first century (A.D.), thus they will provide evidence contemporaneous with the composition of the NT.

The book is divided into three sections or parables (38–44; 45–57; 58–71). The use of this designation shows its wisdom orientation, but its description as a "vision of wisdom" makes it a very different type from that of Proverbs, and thus the literary genre is best described as an apocalypse[84]. According to D.W. Suter, the technique of the book is to make a *māšāl* or comparison between two related phenomena: the fate of the righteous/wicked, and the pattern of the cosmos/eschaton[85]. This appeal to "higher wisdom" is one familiar to us now, and it is no accident that the designation parable occurs elsewhere as well (1 En 1:2–3; 93:1,3 Aram.).

The Book of Parables reveals a similar *Sitz im Leben*. The message is characterized as a "vision" or "words" of wisdom (37:1–2), intended not only for Enoch's generation but succeeding ones (37:3). The message is made possible by the Lord of Spirit's extraordinary gift of wisdom to Enoch (37: 4). This wisdom could find no reception among men, so now it resides in heaven (42:1–2), where in the eschaton the elect shall partake of it (48:1). This perspective carries over into the Book of Parables' most distinctive material, the role of the Son of Man. His existence and purpose is revealed to the righteous only by revelation of the "wisdom of the Lord of Spirits" (48: 7). The fruit of his ministry will be an outpouring of wisdom and the revelation of the "mysteries" of righteousness (49:1–2), because of his being indwelt by "the spirit of wisdom" (49:3). These messianic features have obvious links with the prophecies of Isaiah (cf. Isa 11:2).

The question of the role and nature of the Son of Man is a debate far too complex for treatment here. It might, however, be suggestive to relate his

---

84 D.W. Suter, "Māšāl in the Similitudes of Enoch", *JBL* 100 (1981) 193–212, reversing a position taken earlier in *Tradition and Composition in the Parables of Enoch* (Missoula: Scholars, 1979).

85 "Māšāl". He notes that the three parables are held together by the recapitulation of a six-fold pattern: 1. the vision of the heavenly court, 2. the secrets of the heavens, 3. the kingdom, how it is divided, 4. the deeds of mankind, how they are weighed in the balance, 5. the dwelling of the righteous, 6. the lot of the sinners.

identity to the redaction of the work. D.W. Suter had pointed out that with the exception of 1 Enoch 64:1–68:1, the name of Enoch is confined to the editorial material surrounding the main parables (37:1; 39:1–2a; 60:1; 69:29), and that even 64:1–68:1 is an editorial composition to unite the collection[86]. This would mean that much of the material in the Book of Parables, particularly in regard to the Son of Man, may have been anonymously independent. Why would this material be identified with Enoch? Suter suggests that 64:1–68:1 is a midrash on Isaiah 24:17–23, which in turn builds on the Flood narrative of Genesis[87]. If this is so, then it may be that the redactor made a connection between the messianic prophecies of Isaiah and the person and work of Enoch. This would explain the explicit identification of Enoch as the Son of Man (71:14), which cannot be expurgated from the text as R.H. Charles attempted. In other words, the linkage of this messianic material with Enoch's name can possibly be understood as a further actualization of the Enoch tradition. The wisdom features of this future figure may have suggested to the redactor that not only was the wise Enoch the originator of the message of salvation/judgement in the eschaton, *he was also the means of carrying it out*. This, of course, is only a hypothesis which requires a great deal more substantiation[88]. In any case, the addition of the Son of Man material (whether or not he is identified with Enoch) can be regarded as another effort to supplement and clarify the traditions of Enoch.

4.3.7 *Attribution in 1 Enoch*

We have seen some of the ways in which the minimal "core" tradition of Genesis 5:21–24 has been elaborated in a series of apocalyptic actualizations that results in the corpus of 1 Enoch. While it is hard to believe that such an elaborate edifice can be built on such a small foundation, there is an inner logic to the growth of this tradition. In particular, the identification of Enoch with antediluvian wisdom and righteousness made it possible for the learned apocalyptists to perceive their understanding of history and the cosmos as his.

Indeed, the traditional connection with Enoch is not only demonstrated in the growth and redaction of the individual books of 1 Enoch, it may well be involved in the redaction and collection of the whole. It has long been

---

86 *Tradition*, 136–144.
87 *Ibid.*, 2,57–61. Cf. 1 En 54:1–56:4.
88 See further J.J. Collins, "The Heavenly Representative: The 'Son of Man' in the Similitudes of Enoch", *Ideal Figures in Ancient Judaism*. Edit. J.J. Collins and G.W.E. Nickelsburg (Chico: Scholars Press, 1980) 111–133; E. Sjöberg, "Henoch als der Menschensohn", *Der Menschensohn im äthiopischen Henochbuch* (Lund: Gleerup, 1946) 147–189; A. Caquot, "Remarques sur les chap. 70 et 71 du livre étheopien d'Hénoch", *Apocalpyses et Théologie de l'Espérance. Congrès de Toulouse, 1975*. Edit. L. Monloubou (Paris: Éditions du Cerf, 1977) 111–122.

suggested that the five-fold nature of 1 Enoch was indicative of its organization as a "pentateuch" along the lines of Moses' work[89], but the lack of any clear parallels made this explanation unsatisfactory. In a recent article D. Dimant makes the much more plausible suggestion that the work was organized around the traditional chronology of Enoch's career[90]. Dimant notes that Jubilees 4:16–25, working from Genesis 5:21–24, divides Enoch's career into three distinct phases:

1. His activities before his marriage and the birth of Methuselah, 65 years. Cf. Gen 5:21; Jub 4:16–19.
2. His sojourn with the angels for a period of six jubilees (300 years, i.e. 6 x 50). Cf. Gen 5:22 "walked with God" 4 Q 227; Jub 4:20–22.
3. His final rapture from among men into Paradise, and his activities there. Cf. Gen 5:24 "he was not, for God took him"; Jub 4:23–25[91].

These phases are reproduced in 1 Enoch. The Book of Watchers covers events in the first (1 En 1–5; cf. Jub 4:19) and second (1 En 6–36; cf. Jub 4:21–22) periods of Enoch's career. The Astronomical Book (72–82) continues the second, heavenly journey phase, and concludes his life on earth (81–82). The Book of Dreams (83–90), though it records events from Enoch's first phase, before he learned to write or was married (83:2; cf. Jub 4:20), has a setting as a *testament* to his son Methuselah, and this also marks the end of his earthly life, the division between the second and third phase[92]. This accords with the ending of the Astromomical Book (81–82). The Epistle of Enoch (91–105) continues the testamentary form. Finally, the Appendix on Noah (106–108), not covered in our investigation, records events after Enoch's earthly life, i.e. from the third phase of his career, in heaven (cf. Jub 4:23–25). The only book not to fit into the chronological sequence is the Book of Parables, but its composite nature and absence from Qumran have led most scholars to regard it as not forming part of the original collection. If this is so, then even the organization of the original books of 1 Enoch may have been guided by the tradition of Jubilees[93] and Genesis.

Whatever the final form of the corpus, we have seen how the tradents of Enoch's tradition experienced a sense of continuity in terms of a revelation charactered as wisdom (5:8; 14:2–3; 37:3; 48:7; 93:10; 98:9; 104:11–13; 105:1–2) which allowed them to further actualize that tradition and to attribute the result to the figure who stood at its head. Moreover, in 104:6–11 we found that literary attribution was inseparably tied to the issue of

---

89 See G.H. Dix, "The Enochic Pentateuch", *JThS* 27 (1925) 29–42.
90 "The biography of Enoch and the books of Enoch", *VT* 33 (1983) 14–29.
91 *Ibid.* Adapted from 18–21.
92 4 Q 227 and Jub 4:21ff only allude to this return after the 300 year sojourn in heaven, but it only makes sense that he cannot be taken to heaven a final time if he does not first return to earth. 1 Enoch 81:5–6 makes this explicit. D. Dimant, "The biography", 22–23.
93 This is not to say that 1 Enoch is literally dependent on Jubilees, only the tradition it preserves.

authoritative interpretation. Therefore we can conclude with confidence that both in the parts and the whole, *attribution in 1 Enoch is primarily a claim to authoritative tradition, not a statement of literary origins.*

4.4 Summary

We have found that the four elements or "pattern" which we isolated in the prophetic and wisdom traditions and which radically hindered the province of *geistiges Eigentum* and literary attribution are also present in the apocalyptic tradition. Despite the widespread belief in the cessation of the prophetic spirit in their era, the apocalyptists were able to continue to write *inspired* writings because of their perception of revelation as inspired interpretation or wisdom. Thus their heroes are generally not prophets but wise men or scribes (Dan 1:4; 1 En 12:4; 4 Ezra 14:40,50; 2 Bar 38:4) whose message is characterized as (higher or revealed) wisdom (Dan 9:22; 1 En 37:1–2; 4 Ezra 14:47; 2 Bar 14:9). Likewise the recipients of this message (the apocalyptists) are called wise (Dan 12:10; 1 En 104:12; 4 Ezra 14:47; 2 Bar 28:1), who are commissioned to share its redemptive message (Dan 11:33; 1 En 105:1–2; 2 Bar 77:15–16). Thus the apocalyptists identify with their heroes in terms of the spirit of wisdom (1 En 91:1; Dan 4:8; 4 Ezra 14:22) of which they also partake because of their proximity to the eschaton (1 En 5:8; cf. 1 QH 12; 1 QpHab 7:4–5) and thus can break the seal of hidden mysteries (Dan 12:4,9; 1 En 104:10–13; 4 Ezra 14:38; As Mos 1:17–18).

The strong determinism of apocalyptic (ApAb 22; As Mos 12:4–5; 4 Ezra 6:1–6; 2 Bar 48:1–9) expressed in its historical reviews (Dan 7–11; 1 En 85–90,93; 4 Ezra 11–12; 2 Bar 53,56–74) also demonstrates its *unified* or *coherent* nature. Indeed, this element becomes so strong that in the theme of the heavenly books (e.g. Book of Fate or Truth: Dan 10:21; Jub 23:32; 1 En 81:1–2; 93:1–3; TLevi 5:4; 2 En 53:2–3) we have recorded in heaven the total course of existence which make unified become uniform, and coherent become comprehensive, so that the ancient seer is believed (unlike the prophets) to have received the whole counsel of God for all generations. These books also testify to the *autonomous* nature of that revelation, so much so that as well as having a life of its own after it is given to the seer, in some cases it seems to have an independent life *before* it is given to him (1 En 81:1–7; 93:1–3).

Apocalyptic revelation is also interpretive, and for this reason is resolutely traditional. In its quest for a solution to the problem of theodicy or *Weltverständnis*, the disruption of their religious world-view caused by successive foreign dominations, these men rejected the counsel of classic wisdom that God's ways were inscrutable (Prov 30:4), and sought to "boldly go where no man has gone before" (cf. 1 En 14:8), i.e. to penetrate the mysteries of heaven and discover what was the "real" state of affairs (Dan 2:20–23; 2 Bar 14).

One ought to assume that a perceived continuity of revelation and tradition would result in the further growth of tradition through *Vergegenwärtigung.* This is what we found in Daniel and 1 Enoch. The "apocalypse" of Daniel (7–12) reinterprets the earlier "court tales" (1–6) by recapitulating their chronology and actualizing the four kingdom schema of Chapter 2, thus addressing the terrible suffering under Antiochus IV. 1 Enoch contains several centuries of growth. The Astronomical Book (72–82) uses the Enoch legend to address an ancient calendric dispute. The Book of Watchers (1–36) links an ancient midrash on Genesis 6:1–4 to Enoch's role as intercessor to create a paradigm appropriate for the trouble times of the End. The Book of Dreams (83–90) makes this paradigm more explicit. The Book of Parables (37–71) seems to raise the role of Enoch to a new level, making him the instrument of fulfillment of his own future visions by linking him with the enigmatic Son of Man. The Epistle of Enoch (91–105) strengthens the link between Enoch and the last generation by its testamentary discourse.

The link that the Epistle of Enoch makes between the pseudonym and the hidden authors is particularly important, because it is expressed in the "canonical" terms of authoritative tradition (104:10–13). These verses reveal that the production of this literature is inseparably tied to the question of a community's self-identity and its understanding or proper interpretation of its "scriptures", and false interpretation is characterized as the falsification of literature. In other words, attribution cannot be separated from the issue of interpretation. It is doubly interesting, then, to compare the canonical reception of 1 Enoch and Daniel. Why was Daniel accepted into both the Jewish and Christian canon, and 1 Enoch was not? [94] The answer is not that the pseudonymous origins of Enoch were discovered, while those of Daniel were not. Tertullian shows that people were willing to believe 1 Enoch came from Enoch (*On Female Dress,* I.3). The answer certainly does not lie in the prestige of the name. Scholars frequently attribute apocalyptic pseueonymity to the attempt to gain a work's acceptance through attachment to a famous name, yet they have a hard time explaining how a book named after an obscure figure of the Exile was accepted, and that named after the famous Enoch of antiquity was not. The truth is that the criterion for judgement was *content,* not authorship. Daniel is almost unique among the apocalypses for its lack of sectarian concern. On the other hand, the 364 day solar calendar in 1 Enoch would alone be enough to ensure its rejection by the Jerusalem hierarchy and later Pharasaic Rabbinism. This fact only serves to confirm the conclusion, that *in the apocalyptic tradition, attribution is primarily a claim to authoritative tradition, not a statement of literary origins.*

---

94 1 Enoch was highly respected in some Christian communities, and thus it probably was "canonical" for some time. Cf. Jude 14.

Chapter 5

Pseudonymity in the New Testament

5.1 Summary of Jewish Background Studies

We have now surveyed three major Jewish "streams of tradition" that may have a bearing on attribution in the NT. This certainly does not exhaust all the relevant data. In particular, a further investigation of the pre-A.D. 70 rabbinic material would be most interesting, but the form and tradition critical efforts necessary to isolate and study such a tradition are simply beyond the scope of this investigation. Even within the context of the traditions which we have studied, it was not possible to study every document. Rather, "typical" literature was chosen to illustrate features isolated in a more general discussion. Nevertheless, our investigation has been sufficiently broad and deep enough to demonstrate that, despite the wide diversity of the prophetic, wisdom, and apocalyptic traditions, there was a similar "pattern" in the relationship of revelation and tradition which also resulted in a common approach to literary attribution. Naturally the purpose of this chapter is to compare our findings with the writings of the NT, to see if we can discover a repetition of this pattern and approach. If so, then we can claim to have established a major paradigm for understanding NT anonymity/pseudonymity.

Before we turn to the NT, it would be helpful to summarize our findings:

1. The fundamental assumption of all these traditions is that they are expressive of *divine* revelation. They are not abstract philosophical or literary works, but religious literature produced in the service of Yahwism. The prophet speaks, "Thus says Yahweh" (e.g. Isa 43:1). Wisdom has a divine source (Prov 1:7; Job 28:28), and is even linked with the Spirit (Wis 1:7; 9:17; PssSol 18:18). The apocalypticists are not epigonists, but recognize in their heroes a divine "higher" wisdom (1 En 91:1; Dan 4:8; 4 Ezra 14:22) which they can share (Dan 12:10; 1 En 104: 12; 4 Ezra 14:47; 2 Bar 28:1) because of their proximity to the eschaton (1 En 5:8; cf. 1 QH 12; 1 Qp Hab 7:4–5). Though the methods of obtaining their information vary greatly (not all are oracular), they all agree that their truth is expressive of a divine, not human *Geist*.

2. The nature of the revelation presented in these traditions is *unified* or *coherent*. The rigid Yahwism of Israel meant that if a truth was divine, it also had to be expressive of the unified or coherent mind and purpose of the one God Yahweh. Prophecy speaks in terms of the council of Yahweh (Isa 6:1–3; 40:1–11) or his plan (Isa 5:19; 8:10; 44:26; 46:10–11). Wisdom operates on the basis of the divine order of creation (Prov 3:19–20; 8:22–31; Job 12:7–10; Sir 1:4–10;

Wis 7:22–26). Apocalyptic is rigidly deterministic (ApAb 22; AsMos 12:4–5; 4 Ezra 6:1–6; 2 Bar 48:1–9). This does not mean that revelation was necessarily uniform or comprehensive, i.e. that all truth was perceivable for all time (though apocalyptic approaches this). Rather it means that there was a consistency and continuity to revelation that allowed all truth and all eras to be related.

3. In these traditions divine revelation is also regarded as *autonomous,* or having a life of its own. This is not to deny its roots in history or origins in the minds of individuals, but to affirm that it has a relevancy beyond the life of the individual and the historical moment. Thus Isaiah had recorded his oracles for future generations (Isa 8:1,16; 30:8), and later generations recognized the effective, creative power of the prophetic word (Isa 40:8; 55:11; 66:5). Wisdom's creationist approach is by its very nature universalist, and its autonomous nature is dramatically expressed in the hypostatization of Dame Wisdom (Prov 1–9; Wis 10–11). An equally dramatic motif in apocalyptic is the heavenly books, containing the entire record of history and the cosmos (e.g. Book of Fate or Truth, Dan 10:21; Jub 23:32; 1 En 81:1–2; 93:1–3; TLevi 5:4). Indeed in a few instances this apocalyptic revelation in the form of heavenly books seems to be autonomous *before* it is transcribed by the apocalyptic hero (1 En 81:1–7; 93:1–3), leaving open the possibility of heavenly copies of revelatory works which might be reproduced (Dan 2; 4 Ezra 14).

4. Revelation in these traditions is also *interpretive.* Divine truth was never something communicated in terms of abstract, universal propositions, but had to be both perceived and applied in historical context. The many symbolic acts and names (e.g. Shearjashub, Isa 7) used by the prophets shows the enigmatic nature of prophecy, whereby the prophet not only interprets the will of Yahweh for the moment, but does so in terms that invite further interpretation. Wisdom invites men to search for and discern the ways of wisdom (Prov 7:7; 18:17; Qoh 1:13; 7:25; Job 5:27; 6:30). Yet such "universal" principles cannot be applied indiscriminately, since they can be contradictory (cf. Prov 26:4,5). Historical time and context need to be "interpreted" (Prov 1:2–6; Qoh 3:1–8; 11:9–10; Sir 18:26; 39:33–34). Apocalyptic is concerned with the problem of *Weltverständnis,* discerning the mysteries of God in history (Dan 2:18,19,27,29,30,47; 4:6 MT; cf. 2 Bar 14; 1 QH 1:21, 2:13 *et al*) by higher, interpretive wisdom (1 En 91:1; Dan 4:8; 4 Ezra 14:22).

5. The combination of the elements of revelation as divine, unified or coherent, autonomous, and interpretive places revelation in a unique relationship to tradition. Rather than the simple repetition of a static *traditum*, the freezing of revelation in space and time, tradition becomes a living process, whereby the older elements are caught up into a new actualization and made a fresh word of Yahweh to a new *Sitz im Leben. Vergegenwärtigung* takes place on many levels and in many ways, but there seems to be three basic categories.

   a. *textual* – Actualization does occur in terms of the reinterpretation of texts or oracles. This takes place frequently in 3 Isaiah (cf. 57:14; 62:10; 40:3f; also 65:17–25; 11:6–9) Cf. also Daniel 2 and 7.

   b. *contextual or thematic* – This is where the earlier tradition provides not so much the text as the context of actualization, making it possible. A prime example is 2 Isaiah, whose message would seem to be totally opposite to that of Isaiah, but in fact cannot be understood apart from him and from the movement of history. The figure of Qoheleth might provide a similar phenomenon.

   c. *configurational* – Here is where the most sweeping actualization often take place. It might be said that the process of tradition often has a "gravitational" effect, drawing to itself independent, free-floating traditions that have no inherent connection with it. This is the supplemental aspect of *Vergegenwärtigung,* drawing upon independent traditions in order to address topics or issues not treated by the original tradition. Efforts are then made to place these (formerly independent) traditions into a harmonic configuration with the original. 2 Isaiah makes use of creation and exodus typologies. Wisdom of Solomon and Sirach sapientialize the historical traditions of Israel. Daniel (9) appeals to the prophecies of Jeremiah to discern the time of the end. The Book of Watchers (1 En 1–36) uses the Azazel myth to highligh the mediatorial role of Enoch and his followers. The Book of Parables (1 En 37–71) relates the messianic motif of the Son of Man to Enoch's predictions of the end, going so far as to equate the two figures.

6. The stream of tradition of *Vergegenwärtigung* was not, however, an amorphous entity which could take any shape or direction. There is an increasing level of *"canon-consciousness"* in the growth of tradition, as core traditions become increasingly inflexible, particularly in the move towards authoritative texts. Since these traditions served as the focus of identity of religious groupings in Israel, any sweeping alteration at the core level would be regarded as a threat to the community foundations. Growth took place at the edges. Thus Jewish tradition must be seen as the fruit of the dialectic between the conservative forces of "canon" or the crystalization of tradition and the expansive force of *Vergegenwärtigung*, or contemporization of tradition.

7. This dialectical relationship between stability and adaptability, "canon-consciousness" and *Vergegenwärtigung*, explains the puzzling combination of concern for origins with a lack of concern for *geistiges Eigentum* in the modern sense. The ancient figures were "canonized", i.e. *part* of the authoritative core traditions, standing at their head. Material could be added to the tradition, but its origins were irreplaceable. This is probably why 2 Isaiah expresses his call in the same terms as Isaiah of Jerusalem, but does not identify himself (Isa 40:1–6; cf. Isa 6). Similarly, this explains the paradoxical way in which the Solomonic literature is attributed to Solomon, while at the same time making no attempt to hide other hands (Cf. Cant 1:1; 8:11–12; Prov 1:1; 22:17; 24:23; 30:1; 31:1; Qoh 1: 1, 12; 12:9–10). This link of attribution with authority is no better expressed than by the Epistle of Enoch (1 En 104:6–13), where false interpretation is depicted as forgery, and correct interpretation is depicted as the faithful transmission and production of literary works. *Therefore we can conclude that in the prophetic, wisdom, and apocalyptic traditions, literary attribution is primarily an assertion of authoritative tradition, not literary origins*[1].

Before applying these results of our background study to the NT, two words of caution need to be given. First, the "pattern" we established is not a rigid rule for what has to take place, but a general reconstruction of what historically *did* take place, and is therefore more descriptive than regulative. Care needs to be taken, then, not to apply it too rigidly. Second, the "pattern" was isolated in order to understand pseudonymity, not to try to prove or disprove it. *This "pattern" cannot be used as a primary literary-critical tool for discovering the pseudonymous origins of Jewish or Christian literature*[2].

In this regard, it must be stressed that the aim of this chapter, as in our background studies, is not to prove or disprove pseudonymous origins. Obviously choices will need to be made over the authenticity of the literature

---

1 Another element frequently found in these traditions is the presence of "schools" or elite groups (e.g. the "watchmen" of Isaiah 62:6 or *maskilim* of Daniel 11:35), but this is not a necessary condition.

2 The absence of the pattern may possibly be used as a secondary argument for authenticity.

under discussion, and mention will be made of the standard arguments, but the purpose of what follows is to discover the "why" of NT pseudonymity, not the "if".

5.2 The Nature of NT Revelation and the Jesus Tradition

It is admittedly quite audacious to attempt a treatment of the pheno-menon of revelation in the NT as some sort of monolithic, uniform entity. That we do so is not in order to make light of the differences between Jesus and the Church, or between churches, or indeed between various roles in the churches. Indeed, the titling of this section as "NT Revelation" rather than "NT Prophecy" is in recognition of the fact that the charismatic experience of Jesus and the earliest church cannot be limited to the latter designation. However, our study of Jewish traditions has shown that despite widely varying outlooks, methods, and purposes, they share a number of important attitudes toward revelation and tradition that could make it possible to talk about the features of Jewish or OT revelation. Since this investigation is ad-dressed to the world of NT scholarship, it will not be necessary to examine the more familiar NT phenomenon in such detail, and thus what follows will be more illustrative than investigative.

Whatever the differences, Christianity begins with Jesus of Nazareth, and there is no question that in Jesus we have a person who speaks and acts from an inspired or revelatory perspective. Whatever more he was or is, Jesus functioned as a prophet[3]. He had a reputation as a prophet (Mark 6:15 par; 8:28 pars; 14:65 par; cf. Matt 21:11,46; Luke 7:16,39; 24:19), performed symbolic acts like a prophet (e.g. Temple Cleansing, Mark 11:15–19 pars), had ecstatic experiences (Luke 10:18), and demonstrated prophetic insight or clairvoyance (Mark 2:5,8 pars ;9:33 ff.; 10:21 pars ; Luke 6:8; 9:47; 11: 17; 19:15; Matt 12:25 par; John 2:24f; 4:17 ff). Jesus compared his minis-try with that of the prophets (Mark 6:4f par; Luke 13:33; cf. Matt 23:31– 36 par; 23:37 ff par), and thought of himself as commissioned or "sent" from God (Matt 10:40 par; 15:24). He attributes the power to the Spirit or "finger" of God (Matt 12:28; Luke 11:20), and by his warning against blas-pheming the Spirit makes it clear that to reject his message is to reject the Spirit who inspired it (Mark 3:28–30 pars). Thus his audience recognizes that he speaks from a position of *divine* authority (Mark 1:27 parr; 6:2 par). His words are not his own.

The key to Jesus' self-consciousness lies in his recognition that in his person and proclamation, the eschatological kingdom of God was present,

---

3 See D. Hill, *New Testament Prophecy* (London: Marshall, Morgan, and Scott, 1979) 48–69; J.D.G. Dunn, *Jesus and the Spirit* (London: SCM, 1975) 11–92.

breaking in upon men. His message that the kingdom "is at hand" (ἤγγικεν, Mark 1:15 *et al*) is the reason for this fresh outburst of the prophetic spirit, characteristic of the eschaton. This eschatological orientation also explains another feature of Jesus' teaching: it is *interpretive*. However authoritative and unmediated his teaching, it is ultimately directed toward the "scriptures", the religious traditions of Israel. No matter how radical his approach to the Law (e.g. Matt 5:21–48), his ministry has to be understood in the context of fulfillment, the coming of God's promised kingdom (Luke 6:20–26; Matt 5:2–11; cf. Matt 5:17–20; Luke 4:16–21).

It is precisely this sense of the inbreaking power of the eschaton that forms the bridge between the charismatic experience of Jesus and that of the early church[4]. Thus Acts depicts the experience of Pentecost as the fulfillment of Joel 2:28–32 (Acts 2:17,18)[5]. The possession of the Spirit is the characteristic sign of the church (Acts 2:38; 4:31; 10:46; 19:6; Rom 5:5; 8:1 ff; 8:9,14 ;1 Cor 1:4–9; 6:9–11; 12:13; 2 Cor 1:21f; 3 ;Gal 3:1–5 ;4:6f; Col 2:11 ff; 1 Thess 1:5f), and that Spirit is the source of *all* her ministries (Rom 12:4–8; 1 Cor 12:4–31; Eph 4:4–12). Though Acts portrays all Christians as "prophets" in the sense of the universal presence of eschatological power, it also recognizes that there are specific Christians who practice the gift of prophecy on a more regular basis (11:27–30; 13:1; 15:32; 21:1–14). This accords with practice in the Pauline churches (1 Cor 12:10, 29). Nevertheless, prophecy is given supreme importance in all the churches (1 Cor 14:1; 1 Thess 5:19–21; Rom 12:3–8; OdesSol 8:1–7; Hermas, *Mand* xi ;Did 10–13)[6].

As with Jesus, prophecy and/or revelation in the church is not only regarded as *divine*, but is also by nature *interpretive*. The early church freely interpreted the Hebrew scriptures in the light of Christ (Matt 2:23; 27:9f; Acts 1:20; 4:11; Rom 12:9; 1 Cor 15:54 ff; Eph 4:8). It is particularly important to note that this process not only includes text plus interpretation (Matt 1:23; 2:6,15,18,23 *et al*), but also includes the blending of texts and interpretation (1 Cor 2:6–16; Gal 4:21–5:1; 2 Pet 3:5–13 *et al*). The supreme example of this blending is the book of Revelation, which has nearly 500 allusions to the OT but not a single quotation. This "expository" function seems to be a part of both NT prophecy and teaching, and makes it hard at times to distinguish them. Thus, for example, J.D.G. Dunn regards Stephen's lengthy midrash in Acts 6:14; 7:1–53 as an example of charismatic teaching[7], while D. Hill regards it as a prime example of prophetic ex-

---

4 This is the central message of J.D.G. Dunn's classic study, above.
5 Cf. Numbers Rabbah on Num 11:17.
6 See J. Reiling, "Prophecy, the Spirit and the Church", *Prophetic Vocation in the New Testament and Today*. Edit. J. Panagopoulos (NTSupp 45. Leiden: Brill, 1977) 58–76; E. Boring, *Sayings of the Risen Jesus* (Cambridge: University Press, 1982) 22–136; G. Dautzenberg, *Urchristliche Prophetie* (Stuttgart: Kohlhammer, 1975); U. Müller, *Prophetie und Predigt im Neuen Testament* (Gütersloh: Mohn, 1975); and the studies of Hill and Dunn, above.
7 *Jesus*, 185–186.

hortation[8]. It seems no accident that in this very passage there is the linkage of wisdom and spirit (Acts 6:10; cf. 1 Cor 12:8; Col 1:9; Eph 1:17), and it would be well to remember that not only was the renewal of prophecy expected in the eschaton, but also perfect wisdom (e.g. 1 En 5:8). Thus teaching is a charism as well (1 Cor 14:6,26; Rom 12:7; Eph 4:11), and is often closely associated with prophecy (1 Cor 12:28; 14:19,31; Rom 12:6–7; Eph 4:11; Acts 13:1; Rev 2:20; John 14:26; Did 11:10; 13:1–2; 15:1–2)[9]. A distinction can be made between the two, but it probably consists more of a difference of (oracular) emphasis rather than essence.

Neither Jesus nor the early church could have used the Jewish scriptures as they did if they had not been convinced that this previous revelation was both *autonomous* (a living word of God) and *unified* or *coherent*, capable of unfolding new meaning and relevance to their own day. One cannot speak of fulfillment unless there is an overarching plan of Yahweh. None would dispute that this was the thinking behind their methodology. The more pressing question is how the words of *Jesus* were regarded and treated by the first Christians. Here is where form, redaction, and tradition criticism has played such a valuable, if controversial, role.

There is no question that the early church considered Jesus to be divinely inspired. The fact that his words were preserved orally for over three decades after his death shows that from the beginning his teaching had taken on an *autonomous*, living quality which continued to be a source of religious identity for the primitive community. However, when we compare the *written* expression of that Jesus tradition in the Synoptics and John, we find significant differences in the way it is preserved and portrayed. The debate which has raged ever since the rise of historical criticism is over the nature and extent of this transformation. The issue is complicated further by a unique feature of Christian revelation: the identification of the Spirit as the Spirit of Jesus (Acts 16:7; Rom 8:9; Gal 4:6; Phil 1:19; cf. John 14:16). This is predicated on the belief in Jesus' resurrection and exaltation, so that a revelation of God/the Spirit becomes a revelation of Christ (cf. Rev 1:1–2; 1:10; 2:11). The result of this is that Christian prophetic speech could take the "I-form" familiar to us in the OT, but now be attributed to the risen Christ, not Yahweh. Two prime examples are the letters to the churches in Revelation 2–3 and the speeches in the Odes of Solomon (8:8–21; 10:4–6; 17:6–15; 22:1–12; 28:8–19; 31:6–13; 36:3–8; 41:8–10; 42:3–10). Odes of Solomon 42:6 offers a succinct theological justification of these prophecies: "Then I arose and am with them, And I will speak by their mouths". Words

---

8 *NT Prophecy*, 99–100.

9 See further E. Earle Ellis, "The Role of the Christian Prophet in Acts", *Apostolic History and the Gospel*. Fest. F.F. Bruce, Edit. W. Gasque and R.P. Martin (Exeter: Paternoster, 1970) 55–67; D. Hill, "Christian Prophets as Teachers or Instructors in the Church", *Prophetic Vocation in the New Testament and Today*. Edit. J. Panagopolous (NTSupp 45. Leiden: Brill, 1977) 108–130; D.H. Greeven, "Propheten, Leherer, Vorsteher bei Paulus" *ZNW* 44 (1952–53) 1–43.

of the risen Christ may also be 'behind the "sentences of holy law" that we find in the epistolary literature (e.g. 1 Cor 3:17; 14:38; 16:22a; Gal 1:9)[10]. The problem arises when we turn to the gospel record. The question is whether (and how much) the material we have recorded has its source in prophetic "words of the Risen Christ", as opposed to the words (or voice) of the historical Jesus. The "fluid tradition school", epitomized by R. Bultmann[11], thinks that no distinction was made between pre- and post-Easter sayings. In fact, *all* the words of Jesus, even the pre-Easter ones, were regarded as sayings of the risen Christ by the early Christians. This allows for a sweeping transformation of the Jesus tradition. The "controlled tradition school", epitomized by M. Dibelius[12], violently disagrees, arguing that the church clearly distinguished between pre- and post-Easter sayings, though occasionally a few might be confused (e.g. Matt 10:5; 18:20; Luke 11:49–51).

Though the issue of prophetic "I"-sayings is a crucial one for the historical reconstruction of the life and teaching of Jesus[13], the resolution of this issue is less important for this investigation. Even the presence of "I"-sayings outside of the gospel framework shows that the earliest Christians regarded the revelation of Jesus/Christ as *unified* or *coherent*, that is, part of a larger whole which could be expanded by further interpretation and revelation. Thus when we turn to the formation of the gospel tradition, the issue really is more one of form and emphasis than of essence. That Jesus' teaching or revelation was interpreted for the various life-settings of the church is clear from the variety we find in the four gospels. Though there may be grounds for thinking that some thematic *Vergegenwärtigung* (in the Spirit or context of Jesus) or "I"-sayings may have found their way into the gospel record, it is more likely that the predominant form of *Vergegenwärtigung* in the gospels is textual, that is, the expansion and interpretation of words and events in the life of the historical Jesus. Certainly the manifold evidence of interpretive redactional activity shows that the expansion of the Jesus tradition cannot be solely (and probably not even primarily) attributed to the oracular activity of Christian prophets, but must also be seen as part of the early Church's (charismatic) teaching activity (see R. Riesner, *Jesus als Lehrer*, Tubingen: Mohr, 1981).

---

10 See E. Käsemann, "Sentences of Holy Law in the New Testament", *New Testament Questions of Today* (London: SCM, 1969) 66–81; but *contra*, K. Berger, "Zu den sogennanten Sätzen heiligen Rechts", *NTS* 17 (1970–71) 10–40.

11 See *The History of the Synoptic Tradition* (New York: Harper and Row, 1963). The terms are from M.E. Boring, *Sayings*, 1–14.

12 See *From Tradition to Gospel* (New York: Scribners, 1935).

13 See further J.D.G. Dunn, "Prophetic 'I'-Sayings and the Jesus Traditon: The Importance of Testing Prophetic Utterances Within Early Christianity", *NTS* 24 (1977–78) 175–198; M.E. Boring, "Christian Prophecy and the Sayings of Jesus: The State of the Question", *NTS* 29 (1983) 104–112; D. Hill, "On the Evidence for the Creative Role of Christian Prophets", *NTS* 20 (1974) 262–274; *idem*, *NT Prophecy*, 160–185.

Lest this discussion flounder on generalities, it would be helpful to demonstrate the growth of tradition or *Vergegenwärtigung* in the Gospel of John. No where is this better displayed than in its use of the ἐγώ εἰμι formula, which is less a sign of prophetic speech ("I"-sayings) than it is a christological confession, which highlights the purpose of the gospel (20:31). Though the motif does occur a few times in the Synoptics (Mark 6:50 par; 13:6 par; 14: 62 par) and may well be a part of the historical words of Jesus, the frequency of its use in John (26 times on the lips of Jesus) shows that John has seized upon it as a theological tool. He was probably motivated by the connection with the א ה י נ א formula predicated of Yahweh in the OT (Gen 28:13, 15; Exod 3:14; 6:2,9; 20:1–5; Lev 17–26; Isa 45:5,6,18,21,22; 46:9; Hos 13:14; Ezek 20:5; Joel 2:27; Ps 81:11). Thus he makes the ἐγώ εἰμι a prime vehicle for confessing the deity of Christ[14]. His more characteristic use of the formula is in combination with a metaphor: bread of life or living bread (6: 35,48,51), light of the world (8:12), door of the sheep (10:7,9), good shepherd (10:11,14), resurrection and life (11:25), way, truth, and life (14:6), vine (15:1,5). Since the context of John's Bread of Life Discourse (6:22–59) is one of the few portions of John which has parallels to the Synoptic record, it would be helpful to see how John (or the Johannine school) treats the Jesus tradition in this chapter[15].

Chapter 6 of John preserves three central incidents from the life of Jesus that are also linked in the Synoptic gospels, and form the climax to Jesus' Galilean ministry: The feeding of the multitude (6:1–14; cf. Matt 14:13–21; 15:32–38; Mark 6:30–44; 8:1–10; Luke 9:10–17), Jesus walking on the sea (6:15–21; cf. Matt 14:22–32; Mark 6:45–52), and Peter's confession (6:66–71; cf. Mark 8:27–9:1; Matt 16:13–28; Luke 9:18–27). Sandwiched between these is the Bread of Life Discourse (6:22–65), which, as we shall see, may preserve some further Jesus *logia,* but is mainly intended as an interpretive discourse or midrash that ties these incidents together and leads up to Peter's confession.

---

14 E. Schweizer (and Bultmann following him) argues for the primacy of Mandaean influence, but this position has met increasing rejection. See *Ego Eimi* (Göttingen: Vandenhoeck, 1939) (N.V.). For a full treatment of the issues, see D. Daube, "The 'I Am" of the Messianic Presence", *The New Testament and Rabbinic Judaism* (London: Athlone, 1956) 325–329; S. Schulz, *Komposition und Herkunft der Johannischen Reden* (Stuttgart: Kohlhammer, 1960) 70–131; H. Zimmermann, "Das absolute ἐγώ εἰμι als die neutestamentliche Offenbarungsformel", *BZ* 4 (1960) 54–69, 266–276; R. Schnackenburg, "Excursus 8: The Origin and Meaning of the ἐγώ εἰμι Formula", *The Gospel According to St. John, II* (New York: Seabury, 1980) 79–89; R.E. Brown, "Appendix IV: EGO EIMI – 'I AM'", *The Gospel According to John I–XII* (New York: Doubleday, 1966) 533–538; A. Feuillet, "Les *Ego eimi* christologiques du quatrième évangile", *RSR* 54 (1966) 5–22, 213–240.

15 It is almost universally recognized that the gospel of John exhibits a number of redactional levels (e.g. Brown isolates five). Since this survey is only meant to be illustrative, no concerted effort will be made to distinguish these levels, but only to show where "John" builds upon a core layer of Jesus tradition.

Though the question of John's relation to the Synoptics is a thorny one that cannot be dealt with here, either John (if he is using one or more of the Synoptics) or the independent tradition which he is using not only uses the framework found in the Synoptics, but shapes the theological traditions found in them in order to anticipate themes found later in the Bread of Life Discourse. R. Schnackenburg notes six elements in the feeding pericope that are later "exegeted" by the discourse.

1. The masterful, purposeful action of Jesus, producing a *sign* (6:10 12; cf. 6:26, 30).
2. The association of the feeding with bread and the Passover, giving a manna typology (6:4–5; cf. 6:31 -32).
3. The mention of the mountain (6:3, 15) and the "prophet who is to come" (6: 14), recalling the figure of Moses (cf. 6.32; Deut 18:15).
4. The gift of bread satisfies all (6:11–12; cf. 6:33,54).
5. Jesus gave thanks (εὐχαριστήσας) and distributed the bread, a latent eucharistic motif (6:11; cf. 6:23,52–58).
6. The blindness of the crowd, physically sated (6:12) but spiritually unaware, who want to make him king (6:15), not understanding the sign (cf. 6:26,42,52)[16].

John preserves just the sparest details of the incident on the sea of Galilee, yet even this may well be in keeping with his theological intent. What we are left with is simply the divine epiphany (6:20). The signification of Jesus' divine status (ἐγώ εἰμι) and helping presence (μὴ φοβεῖσθε) helps bridge the gap between physical sign (6:1–15) and spiritual meaning (6:22–65) by giving the reader a glimpse of Jesus' true origins, thus anticipating what is to follow.

Though many would dispute the unity of the Bread of Life Discourse (see n.15), there is no question that the entire section revolves around the midrash introduced at 6:31[17]. Though some might wish to argue that the core of the midrash goes back to Jesus[18], it is more likely that the "seam" occurs at 6:30, since it is difficult to explain why the crowd would demand a sign that Jesus had already performed, unless the verse is regarded as an editorial introduction to the midrash proper. This is not to say that the midrash is an intrusion into the account, or violates the record of Jesus' teaching as found in 6:25–29. Indeed, as we shall see, the whole intent is to further interpret this record (and the incidents that *it* refers to) for the church of John's day.

There is no reason to doubt that 6:25–29 gives a faithful account of an incident in the life of Jesus. Though the language is Johannine, the dialogue fits well into the aftermath of the feeding account. The expectation of a messianic reproduction of the miracle of the manna was current among the

16 *John, II,* 10.
17 See esp. P. Borger, "Observations on the Midrashic Character of John 6", *ZNW* 54 (1963) 232–240; *idem, Bread From Heaven* (NTSupp 10. Leiden: Brill, 1965).
18 E.g. R.E. Brown, *John, I,* 278 ff.

Jews[19], and the reaction of the crowds (6:14,26) was one that might be expected. Both Mark (8:11–21) and Matthew (16:1–12) record that Jesus contrasted the spiritual meaning of the feeding incident with the blindness of those who focus on the demand for a physical sign, though in this case it is the Pharisees, not the crowd. And like John this contrast of physical/spiritual in relation to the feeding of the multitude serves to highlight the insight of faith in Peter's confession, which immediately follows all three accounts (John 6:69; Mark 8:29; Matt 16:16). Even the refusal of a sign (Mark 8:12 par) is not a contradiction of John 6:26, because in Johannine terminology a (true) sign is precisely something spiritual rather than merely external, so the intent is the same. This is not meant to imply, however, that the discourse about the bread and leaven in the Synoptics and the account in John 6:25–29 are parallel. Their similarities in thought argue for the authenticity of the Johannine tradition, but do not require that they are variants of the same incident.

The central thrust of the incident (6:25–29) is both soteriological and christological. Whereas the crowd wanted physical food which they associated with physical deliverance, Jesus points them to a spiritual "food which endures to eternal life" (v.27; cf. 4:14). Even more important, it is Jesus who gives this food, and to receive it one must exercise belief in him (v.29).

It is the nature of interpretation to make explicit what is implicit, and this is the function of the midrash which begins in v.31. Whether the tradition comes from John or another source is unimportant. The OT citation is not precise; it could refer to a number of passages (cf. Exod 16:14 MT; Num 11: 9; Ps 77:24 MT; Neh 9:15; Wis 16:20). In any case it spells out the manna typology implicit in the feeding incident, and gives an interpretation which exhibits the developed self-consciousness of these Christians, particularly over against Judaism. Thus in verse 32 it is "not Moses", but the "Father" who "is giving" (not "gave") the "true bread" (not manna). In other words, the focal point of salvation-history has shifted from past to present, physical to spiritual, and particular (Jewish) to universal. The crescendo of the midrash reaches its peak in the *combination* of christology and soteriology of the great "I AM" of verse 35: "I am the bread of life" (cf. v.20). In the confession of the early church, Jesus not only *gives* the bread of life (v.27), he *is* the bread of life, Jesus is what he gives. Once again the proclaimer becomes the proclaimed in a vivid actualization of Jesus' teaching. Just how developed is this christology can be seen by verse 40, where it is no longer the Father, but the Son, who will raise up the faithful on the last day.

The context of this actualization, at least as it is found in John, is made clear from 6:41–51. The rift between the church and Judaism had become so wide that Jesus' opponents are simply called "the Jews" (v.41). The argument over Jesus' origins, always apparent (v.42; cf. Luke 4:22; Mark 6:3 par), had now reached fever pitch. The Jews are upbraided for their lack of faith, their

---

19 See Midrash Rabbah on Qoh 1:9; 2 Bar 29:8.

"murmuring" which recalls the attitude of their fathers in the wilderness (v. 43, cf. Exod 16; Ps 106:24–25). Once again the manna typology is spelled out, in order to make clear that the real issue is one of spiritual, not physical origins. Just as the crowd could not see the spiritual reality behind the physical loaves (6:26), so the Jewish opponents of the church cannot perceive the true identity of Jesus of Nazareth (6:42).

A further actualization is given in verses 51c–59. This "eucharistic" pericope is often regarded as an addition to the narrative, and the history of its exegesis is marked by bitter controversy[20]. Space will not allow for a discussion of whether its eucharistic motif is in harmony with, or fundamentally opposed to, the "spiritual" interpretation of the bread of life in the previous passages[21]. In any case, in the mind of the author of these verses there is a connection between the two. In a further actualization of the bread of life motif, the author answers the question how it is that one can "eat" the bread of life, i.e. how the life of Christ is mediated, and does this by giving a graphic portrayal of the Eucharist. The mention of the synagogue (v.59) may indicate that this question was also part of the church's apologetic encounter with Judaism, but it is also possible that the strong emphasis on the corporeality of the Eucharist (v.55) may be a reaction to gnostic or docetic elements within the community which had rejected the sacrament and the physical death it implied (cf. 1:14). The succeeding pericope (6:60–65) shows that there were problems within as well as without the christian community, though its emphasis on spiritual reality (v.63) *may* indicate that it was written before the eucharistic pericope was added. Whatever the precise *Sitz im Leben,* we can see that the author is clearly trying to relate the teaching of Jesus to the sacramental ministry of the church.

We have now seen how John and his community have taken elements of the Jesus tradition, some shared with the Synoptics, others not, and by both shaping that tradition and expanding it with the lengthy Bread of Life Discourse, have achieved a vital restatement or actualization of that tradition, addressing the crucial needs of the church of their day. Foremost among their technique was the use of the ἐγώ εἰμι formula (6:20,35,41,48,51), which encapsuled the church's confession that in Jesus they saw the reality of God himself, and with him found life. Thus it is no accident that the discourse finds its climax in the confession of Peter "You are (σύ εἶ) the Holy One of God" (6:69), who alone has "the words of eternal life" (6:68).

No doubt the scale of the actualization that we find in John will be disturbing to some. Yet if we compare it to documents in the OT such as Isaiah, we find that this type of development is not unusual. It must also be remarked that John is by far the most theologically developed of the gospels, no doubt partly due to its longer gestation. It comes as no surprise that the

---

20 See the discussion and bibliography listed in R. Schnackenburg, *John, II,* 56–69.
21 On the issue of sacramentalism/anti-sacramentalism in John's gospel, see R. Brown, *John; I,* cxi–cxiv.

most developed of the gospels also has the most theologically articulate justification of that development, the Paraclete passages in John (14:15–13; 15: 26–27; 16:4–15; cf. 1 John 2:27; 4:2f,6; 5:6–10)[22]. It is most important to note that the role of the Paraclete is not only to conserve Jesus' words ("bring to your remembrance", 14:26) but to *interpret* them as well ("teach you all things", 14:26; cf. 16:13–15). James Dunn remarks,

> The dialectic of the Johannine concept of revelation is summed up in that one word, ἀναγγελεῖ. For it can have the force of '*re*-announce', '*re*-proclaim'; but in 16:13 as in 14:25 it must include some idea of new information, new revelation (cf Isa 42:9; 44:7; 46:10), even if that new revelation is in effect drawn out of the old by way of reinterpretation. In this word, as in these passages as a whole, both present interpretation and interpretation of the past are bound up together *in the dynamic of creative religious experience*[23].

Other examples of *Vergegenwärtigung* in the Jesus tradition could be cited. The parables, for instance, have undergone a long history of tradition[24]. Even in those few instances where the teachings of Jesus are preserved in the Pauline literature, we see a clear pattern of development[25]. The examples from the Bread of Life Discourse are enough, however, to demonstrate the nature and extent of the process. From what we have examined it is easy to see a clear parallel with the pattern we found in our investigation of the Jewish background. *The divinely inspired, autonomous, unified or coherent, and interpretive nature of NT revelation is directly responsible for the growth of the Jesus tradition in a manner similar to what we found in the Jewish scriptures.* This similarity of process also explains another feature of the gospel accounts: their anonymity. Why do none of the gospel writers identify themselves, though at least in some cases (Luke 1:1–4; John 21:24) they are well known to their readers? Because it is the gospel of *Jesus Christ* (Mark 1:1), and no other attribution is needed. Once again attribution is linked with (authoritative) tradition. And how was it decided what form of the tradition was authoritative, what actualization was valid and what was not? Once again we must have recourse to the religious communities themselves (Matt 7:15–20; 1 Thess 5:19–21; 1 Cor 2:6–16; 12–14; 1 John 4:1–2; Rev 2:2; Did 11:8–12). The gospels, like so much of the OT literature, are the fruit of a dialectic encounter between the conservative forces of "canon" and the expansive forces of *Vergegenwärtigung,* the need to preserve core traditions and at the same time make them relevant to new situations.

---

22 See R.E. Brown, "The Paraclete in the Fourth Gospel", *NTS* 13 (1966–67) 113–132; M.E. Boring, "The Influence of Christian Prophecy on the Johannine Portrayal of the Paraclete and Jesus", *NTS* 25 (1978–79) 113–123.

23 *Jesus,* 352.

24 For an extensive bibliography and history of interpretation of the parables, see W.S. Kissinger, *The Parables of Jesus* (Metuchen: Scarecrow, 1979).

25 See D.L. Dungan, *The Sayings of Jesus in the Churches of Paul* (Oxford: Blackwell, 1971), especially his treatment of the divorce sayings, 81–135.

The obvious question is whether this relationship between revelation and tradition can be extended to other parts of the NT. Having traced this Jewish pattern into the core of Christian beliefs about Jesus, is it possible to explain the formation of the rest of the NT in terms of the isolation of other, "apostolic" (in the broad sense) traditions? While the rise, scope, and definition of the apostolate is an issue far too complex for a complete treatment here[26], it is easily affirmed that among the primitive Christian communities there arose a type of leader called "apostle" (not limited to the Twelve, see Acts 14:14; Gal 1:19; Rom 16:7; 1 Cor 15:7), and that this type of leadership became quickly, if not immediately, supremely authoritative ("first apostles", 1 Cor 12:8; cf. 14:37–38; Eph 2:20; 3:5; 4:11; 1 Thess 2:6; 2 Pet 3:2; Rev 18:20; Luke 6:13; Acts 1:2; 15:6,22; 16:4 *et al*). This authority was probably connected with their role in the origins of these communities. This would explain the linkage of these figures to the guardianship of the religious traditions which formed the communities' identity ("apostles' teaching", Acts 2:42; cf. 4:33; Jude 17; 2 Thess 2:15; 1 Cor 7:10; 9:14; 11:2,23; 15:3; Phil 4:9). It is important to note that apostleship is a charismatic phenomenon, as is prophecy and teaching (1 Cor 12:8; Eph 4:11; cf. Acts 2:43). In fact, the apostles incorporate the revelatory features of prophecy and teaching in their ministries (Acts 13:1; 11:26; 15:35; 18:11; 20:20; 28:31; 2 Cor 12:12; 2 Pet 3:2; Jude 17; 1 Tim 2:7; 2 Tim 1:11)[27].

Since the early Christian communities seem to have afforded a distinctive role to certain "apostolic" figures, and tied its authoritative traditions to them in a way unparalleled by other tradents, then it may be possible to speak of individual "apostolic" traditions, *if in certain cases the stamp of an individual's personality and teaching is so strong that it becomes part of the tradition itself*. It is to this possibility that we turn, by examining those documents where the problem of pseudonymity most strongly comes to the fore: the deutero-Pauline and Petrine epistles.

---

26 See C.K. Barrett, "The Apostles in and after the New Testament", *SEÅ* 21 (1956) 30–49; *idem*, *The Signs of an Apostle* (London: Epworth, 1970); *idem*, "Shaliah and Apostle", *Donum Gentilicium*. Fest. D. Daube. Edit. E. Bammel *et al*. (Oxford: Clarendon, 1978) 88–102; F. Hahn, "Der Apostolat im Urchristentum. Seine Eigenart und seine Voraussetzungen", *KuD* 20 (1974) 54–77; J.A. Kirk, "Apostleship Since Rengstorf: Towards a Synthesis", *NTS* 21 (1975) 249–264; R. Schnackenburg, "Apostles Before and During Paul's Time", *Apostolic History and the Gospel*. Fest. F.F. Bruce, Edit. W. Gasque and R.P. Martin, (Grand Rapids: Eerdmans, 1971) 287–303; *idem*, "Apostolicity: the Present Position of Studies", *OiC* 6 (1970) 243–273.

27 This is not to agree with the simplistic position of W. Grudem, *The Gift of Prophecy in I Corinthians* (Washington: University Press of America, 1982) that the NT apostles are equivalent to OT prophets, because their prophecies do not have to be sifted like those of the lesser congregational prophets. This is a misunderstanding of both OT and NT prophets, since *all* prophecies are sifted by the various communities. Did Paul have no opposition? The authority (and revelatory experience) of the apostles is different only in degree, not kind.

5.3 The Pauline Tradition

There is no question that Paul identified himself as an apostle (Rom 1:1; 1 Cor 1:1; 2 Cor 1:1; Gal 1:1 *et al*), and that he was generally recognized as such by his communities. His ministry was a charismatic one, for though he never calls himself a prophet, his self-designation as *servant* (Rom 1:1; Gal 1: 10; Phil 1:1; cf. 2 Kgs 9:7; 17:13,23; Ezra 9:11; Jer 7:25; 25:4; Zech 1:6) and the prophetic overtones of his call (Gal 1:15—16; Acts 9:1—19; 22:3— 21; 26:12—23; 1 Cor 15:8; cf. Isa 49:1—6; Jer 1:4—5) make it clear that Paul regarded himself as an agent of God's revelation[28].

An even more important feature of Paul's "apostolic" ministry is its uniquely personal nature. Paul identifies his election with a special task in the divine economy — the promotion of a law-free gospel to the Gentiles (Gal 1: 16; 2:7). Even though Acts qualifies the picture somewhat by inaugurating the Gentile mission with Peter and Cornelius (10:1—11:18), it, too, recognizes that Paul is pre-eminently the apostle to the Gentiles by virtue of his call (9:15; 22:21; 26:16—18). This consciousness of a unique ministry explains why Paul can at the same time affirm his continuity with the Jerusalem kerygma (Gal 2:2) and nevertheless call his message "my Gospel" (Rom 2:16; 16:25; 1 Thess 1:5; 2 Thess 2:14; 2 Cor 3:3; cf. 2 Tim 2:8). Though no "disciples" of Paul are mentioned in his letters (cf. Acts 9:25), Paul does maintain a type of patriarchal authority over his converts[29]. "For though you have countless guides in Christ, you do not have many fathers. For· I became your father in Christ Jesus through the gospel" (1 Cor 4:15). Here is an indissoluble bond between Paul and the community's origins. As father to his churches, Paul becomes the paradigm for his gospel. This is why Paul's characteristic exhortation to churches that he has founded is to "be imitators of me" (1 Thess 2:11—15a; 2 Thess 3:6—9; Phil 3:15—17; 1 Cor 4: 14—16; 10:31—11:1; Gal 4:12), while to other churches (not founded by him) he urges imitation of God the Father or Christ (Rom 15:7; Col 3:13; cf. Eph 5:1)[30]. *In other words, in the case of Paul and his churches, the apostolic gospel (authoritative tradition) is inextricably bound up with the person of Paul himself. Paul is the embodiment of his tradition, and there is little difference between imitating Paul and preserving his tradition (2 Thess 3:6—7; cf. 2:15; 1 Cor 11:2).*

An even more remarkable feature of the personalization of the Pauline tradition is that it even extends to a characteristic *form* of communication.

---

28 See further M. Ashcroft, "Paul's Understanding of Apostleship", *RExp* 55 (1958) 406—408; J.M. Myers and E.D. Freed, "Is Paul Also Among the Prophets?", *Interp* 20 (1966) 40—53.

29 E.g. τέκνον for Onesimus (Phlm 10), Timothy (1 Cor 4:17; cf. 1 Tim 1:2); τέκνα for the Galatians (Gal 4:19) and the Corinthians (1 Cor 4:14; 2 Cor 6:13).

30 See D.M. Stanley, "'Become imitators of me': The Pauline Conception of Apostolic Tradition", *Bib* 40 (1959) 859—877.

R.W. Funk has written a classic study on how Paul communicates his traditional authority[31]. The ideal was oral, face to face communication, the unmediated transmission of tradition through the (actual) apostolic presence (Rom 1:11; 15:23 ff, 29 ;Phlm 22; 1 Cor 4:19; 16:7; 2 Cor 12:14; 1 Thess 2:17; Phil 2:24; Gal 4:20). Yet human limitations place restrictions on this method, and Paul had to find other means to mediate his apostolic authority. He did this by using emissaries, the most prominent of whom were Timothy (1 Thess 3:1–6; 1 Cor 4:17; 16:10–11; Phil 2:19–23) and Titus (2 Cor 8: 16–23; 12:18). "Therefore I sent to you Timothy, my beloved and faithful child in the Lord, to remind you of my ways in Christ, as I teach them everywhere in every church" (1 Cor 4:17).

Yet even emissaries are limited by space and time, and could not ensure the continuity of the apostolic presence in such a far-flung mission. Once spoken, no matter how faithfully, the apostolic word is dissipated. It is no doubt for this reason that Paul resorted to the form of communication most associated with him: the apostolic letter. Paul took the form of ancient letters and adapted it to apostolic speech, thereby creating a new *Gattung*[32] He clearly intended the letters he wrote to be a substitute for his apostolic presence, or better, a mediation of his apostolic presence (Rom 15:15; Phlm 21; 1 Cor 4:14 ;2 Cor 13:10). This is why Paul can write to the Corinthians and say that though absent in body he is present in spirit, because his letter conveys his apostolic pronouncement of judgement on an incestuous member of the congregation (1 Cor 5:3–5; cf. 4:14).

Though A. Deissmann at the beginning of the century did a service to scholarship by stressing the occasional nature of Paul's writings[33], the studies of Funk and others have demonstrated that his views were an over-reaction[34]. Paul certainly did not think that he was writing "scripture" for a (closed) canon, but it is a mistake to dismiss his writings as ephemeral. "His letters are *occasional*, but not *casual*. And they are not *private,* but *personal; authoritative* and not simply products of the moment"[35]. In other words, Paul realized that he was communicating authoritative tradition by his letter form, and in so doing, helped to sow the seeds of a "canon-consciousness" that could make it possible for a later generation to identify and build upon a distinctive Pauline tradition.

To demonstrate that they did so is our next task. The two main bodies of

---

31 "The Apostolic Parousia: Form and Significance", *Christian History and Interpretation*. Fest. J. Knox. Edit. W.R. Farmer *et al.* (Cambridge: University Press, 1967) 249–268.
32 See K. Berger, "Apostelbrief und apostolische Rede. Zum Formular frühchristlichen Briefe", *ZNW* 65 (1974) 190–231; J.L. White, "Saint Paul and Apostolic Letter Tradition", *CBQ* 45 (1983) 433–444.
33 *Light From the Ancient East* (London: Hodder and Stoughton, 1910) 217ff.
34 For an excellent account of and response to Deissmann's theories, see W. Doty, "The Classification of Epistolary Literature", *CBQ* 31 (1969) 183–199.
35 J.C. Beker, "Contingency and Coherence in the Letters of Paul", *USQR* 33 (1978) 141.

NT literature that will be studied are Ephesians and the Pastorals. Although some would want to include Colossians and 2 Thessalonians among the deutero-Paulines, the arguments are so contested that it would not be methodologically sound to assume, as we will do with Ephesians and the Pastorals, that their pseudonymity is a foregone conclusion.

Though some lines of chronological development will be traced in the growth of pseudonymity, the first work to be treated will be the Pastorals. This is because, although they are not chronologically the first pseudonymous NT documents, they often serve as both a cornerstone for the presence of epistolary pseudonymity, as well as the focus of objections to it. Thus if pseudonymity can be explained in the Pastorals, its presence elsewhere should be correspondingly more easily explained.

5.3.1 *The Pastorals*

5.3.1.1 *The Problem of the Pastorals*

Ever since the advent of literary-critical investigations, the authenticity of the Pastorals has been placed in doubt[36]. Though today the large majority of scholars would designate them as pseudonymous in part or whole, there remains a significant minority of support for authenticity that cannot be dismissed as crank or hopelessly out of touch[37]. There are significant objections to the pseudonymity of the Pastorals, but, as we shall see, those objections are more theological than literary-critical.

The arguments over authenticity are external, historical, literary and theological. As for external testimony, the evidence is inconclusive, though the Pastorals do not appear in the earliest Pauline canon[38].

The historical argument is two-fold. First, the places, events and names found in the Pastorals do not fit with the chronology of Acts and the genuine Paulines[39]. Even supporters of authenticity agree that they conflict, but seek

---

36 As well as standard introductions and commentaries, for a detailed summary of scholarly opinion, see P. Trummer, *Die Paulustradition der Pastoralbriefe* (Frankfurt: P. Lang, 1978) 19–56; E. Ellis, "The Authorship of the Pastorals. A Resume and Assessment of Current Trends", *EvQ* 32 (1960) 151–161; P. Rogers, "The Pastoral Epistles as Deutero-Pauline", *IThQ* 45 (1978) 248–260.

37 Supporters of inauthenticity include H.J. Holtzmann, M. Dibelius, P. Vielhauer, R. Bultmann, G. Bornkamm, E. Käsemann, E. Schweizer, O. Knoch, B. Easton, C.K. Barrett, P.N. Harrison, A.Q. Morton. Supporters of authenticity include C. Spicq, J. Jeremias, B. Reicke, O. Roller, H. Schlier, J.N.D. Kelly, D. Guthrie, J.A.T. Robinson, B. Weiss, A. Schlatter, W. Michaelis, G. Holtz.

38 Of Marcion, For the history of the canonization of the Pastorals, see F. Weniger, *Die Pastoralbriefe in der Kanongeschichte zur Zeit der Patristik* (Diss., Wein, 1964).

39 P. Rogers, "Pastoral", 250. Compare: (1 Tim 1:3 and Acts 19:22; 20:1); (Titus 1:5 and Acts 27:8); (2 Tim 2:9; 4:6 and Acts 28:30ff.). See also M. Dibelius and H. Conzelmann, *The Pastoral Epistles* (Philadelphia: Fortress Press, 1972) 15–16, 126–127, 152–154.

to resolve it by the fragile hypothesis of a release and second Pauline imprisonment subsequent to Acts[40]. Second, the development of church organization in the Pastorals is too complex to have occurred during the life of Paul. While defenders of authenticity have rightly objected to the extreme form of the argument, that a second century monarchical episcopate is found in the Pastorals, there is still no question that the Pastorals display an emphasis on church structure unknown in the genuine Paulines[41].

The literary argument revolves around the differences of language and style between the Pastorals and the undisputed Paulines[42]. While it must be conceded that early attempts at this argument were hindered by flawed methodology[43], later refinements still demonstrated a significant difference between the Pastorals and other Paulines, while maintaining a unique homogeneity in the Pastoral corpus itself[44]. In the face of this, defenders of authenticity have resorted to arguments regarding the versatility of Paul[45], his advanced age and special circumstances, and most especially, the theory of a different secretary[46]. While it must be admitted that Paul indeed used secre-

---

40 For the evidence of Paul's possible release and travel to Spain, see J.B. Lightfoot, *Biblical Essays* (London: Macmillan, 1893) 421ff.; also conveniently summarized by J. McRay, "The Authorship of the Pastoral Epistles", *RestQ* 7 (1963) 12, n.87; also L. Pharigo, "Paul's Life After the Close of Acts" *JBL* 70 (1951) 277–284. The weakness of the theory is that even if Paul was released, his supposed activity was in Spain, not Asia Minor, as the Pastorals require.

41 For arguments that church order does not require late dating of the Pastorals, see J. Jeremias, "Zur Datierung der Pastoralbriefe", *ZNW* 52 (1961) 101–104; J.P. Meier, "*Presbyteros* in the Pastoral Epistles", *CBQ* 35 (1973) 323–345.

42 The earliest proponent of this argument was P.N. Harrison, *The Problem of the Pastoral Epistles* (London: Oxford University Press, 1921); revised in *Paulines and Pastorals* (London: Villiers, 1964). Later work using statistics and computer techniques was A.Q. Morton, and J. McLeman, *Paul, the man and the myth: a study in the authorship of Greek prose* (London: Hodder and Stoughton, 1966).

43 For criticism of Harrison's criterion of *hapax* per page of text, see. W. Michaelis, "Pastoralbriefe und Wortstatistik", *ZNW* 28 (1929) 69–76; F.R.M. Hitchcock, "Tests for the Pastorals", *JThS* 30 (1929) 272–279; B.M. Metzger, "A Reconsideration of Certain Arguments Against the Pauline Authorship of the Pastorals" *ET* 70 (1958) 91–94. For the criticism of Morton's technique, particularly his dependency on the frequency of connectives such as καί, see esp. P.F. Johnson, "The Use of Statistics in the Analysis of the Characteristics of Pauline Writers", *NTS* 20 (1973–74) 92–100. More generally on the use of statistics, see J.J. O'Rourke, "Some Considerations about Attempts at Statistical Analysis of the Pauline Corpus", *CBQ* 35 (1973) 483–490.

44 K. Grayston and G. Herdan, "The Authorship of the Pastorals in the Light of Statistical Linguistics", *NTS* 6 (1959) 1–15. Even J.N.D. Kelly accepts the difference in style, language. *A Commentary on the Pastoral Epistles* (London: Black, 1963) 21–27.

45 H. Chadwick, "All Things to All Men", *NTS* 1 (1954–55) 261–275.

46 Major support for this theory comes from O. Roller's work, *Das Formular der paulinischen Briefe* (Stuttgart: W. Kohlhammer, 1933). See also G.J. Bahr, "Paul and Letter Writing in the First Century", *CBQ* 28 (1966) 465–477; *idem,* "The Subscriptions in the Pauline Letters", *JBL* 87 (1968) 27–41.

taries for the recording of at least some of his letters (Rom 16:22, 2 Thess 3: 17; 1 Cor 16:21; Gal 6:11; Col 4:18; Phlm 19), the continuity of style in the genuine Paulines shows that either Paul must have used the *same* secretary throughout the course of his life, *except* for the Pastorals (an unlikely possibility), or more likely, that Paul's secretaries had little influence on the style and content of his letters. If the latter is true, recourse to a secretary hypothesis for the Pastorals requires an involvement of the secretary in the composition of the letters that is unparalleled elsewhere, and thus is not a "secretary" hypothesis at all[47].

The theological argument is admitted by all to weigh most heavily against authenticity. Serious differences exist between Paul and the Pastorals in the areas of soteriology, ecclesiology and ethics[48]. Space unfortunately, does not permit even an outline of these differences. Many will be raised in what follows below, however, as we investigate how the Pastorals adapt Pauline tradition to a new *Sitz im Leben*.

A final inconsistency that points to the pseudonymous origins of the Pastorals also highlights the problems that this involves. In 1 Timothy 2:7 we find "Paul" using an oath ("I am telling the truth; I am not lying") to affirm his diverse calling and authority. This is probably modelled on Romans 9: 1[49]. But unlike Romans, where the oath is given to people who do not know Paul personally, here it is given to *Timothy*, Paul's "true child in the faith" (1:2), who would have no reason to doubt Paul's call and authority! This reveals the real underlying problem of the Pastorals: the continuance of Paul's

---

47 Jeremias admits this, in effect, when he says that the secretary must have had a freer hand than normal. *Die Briefe an Timotheus und Titus* (Göttingen: Vandenhoeck and Ruprecht, 1975) 9–10. For criticism of Bahr (n.46), see A. Bandstra, "Paul, the Letter Writer", *CTJ* 3 (1968) 176–180. P. Dornier, *Les Épîtres pastorales* (Paris: Gabalda, 1969) 25, tries to escape this dilemma by positing a secretary *and* a radical redactor, a theory born of desperation. Many have attributed the Pastorals to Luke, serving as either Paul's secretary: redacting them, or writing them "for" him, perhaps posthumously. See A. Feuillet, "La doctrine des Épîtres Pastorales et leur affinités avec l'oeuvre lucanienne", *Revue Thomiste* (Toulouse) 78 (1978) 181–225; G. Querdray, "La doctrine des Épîtres pastorales, leur affinités avec l'oeuvre lucanienne. Remarques nouvelles. *EeV* 88 (1978) 631–638; A. Strobel, "Schreiben des Lukas? Zum sprachlichen Problem der Pastoralbriefe", *NTS* 15 (1969) 191–210; C.F.D. Moule, "The Problem of the Pastoral Epistles: A Reappraisal", *BJRL* 47 (1965) 430–452; J.D. Quinn, "The Last Volume of Luke: the Relation of Luke-Acts to the Pastoral Epistles", *Perspectives on Luke-Acts.* Edit. C.H. Talbert (Edinburgh: T. and T. Clark, 1978) 62–75; S.G. Wilson, *Luke and the Pastoral Epistles* (London: SPCK, 1979). It must be said that the parallels in the Pastorals to Luke are no greater than those to Paul, and thus there is no firm foundation to this theory. See esp. in criticism, I.H. Marshall (Review of S.G. Wilson), *JSNT* 10 (1981) 69–74; N. Brox, "Lukas als Verfasser der Pastoralbriefe", *JAC* 13 (1970) 62–77.

48 P. Rogers, "Pastoral", 252–258; C.F.D. Moule, "Problem", 432–437. Examples are a different attitude towards the law (1 Tim 1:8ff.) and a different usage of Pauline themes like "faith" and "in Christ" (1 Tim 2:13; 2 Tim 1:1). See J.A. Allen, "The 'In-Christ' Formula in the Pastoral Epistles", *NTS* 10 (1963) 115–121.

49 R.F. Collins, "The Image of Paul in the Pastorals", *LTP* 31 (1975) 154.

authority for a later era. But it also underlines the fundamental problem of the pseudonymous presentation of that authority, for "I am not lying" illustrates the difficulty of affirming the truth of Paul's authority and teaching by using a technique that involves deception.

In the final analysis, it is this problem that actually determines why many people choose for or against the authenticity of the Pastorals. The various arguments can be given more or less weight, but the key difficulty is not with the evidence, but with the technique. The Pastorals are unique among the NT pseudepigrapha in their thoroughly epistolary style, and the fact that they are issued as a threefold corpus. Though some might be able to accept some sort of general treatise as a tribute to the apostle, even if issued in his name, the volume of personal details and emotional displays seem to go beyond all propriety. J.N.D. Kelly remarks,

> It is one thing to publish under the name of Paul or some other apostle a treatise, whether in the form of a letter or something else, which the author sincerely believes to express the great man's teaching, or which he even believes to have been disclosed to him by the self-same Spirit which used the great man as his mouthpiece. It is quite another thing to fabricate for it a detailed framework of concrete personal allusions, reminiscences and messages, not to mention outburst of intensely personal feeling, which one knows to be pure fiction but which one puts together with the object of creating an air of versimilitude[50].

Nor is this objection felt only by those who support authenticity. Dibelius/Conzelmann regard the *persönliche Notizen* as the strongest basis for an argument for authenticity, and state that whoever argues otherwise *must* provide an explanation for their inclusion[51]. A popular explanation of older scholarship was the fragment hypothesis, given classic expression by P.N. Harrison[52]. In this theory, fragments (consisting of the personal information and emotional passages) of genuine Pauline letters were incorporated into a larger literary work by a pseudonymous author or disciple. The lack of textual evidence or seams of redaction, plus the difficulty in envisaging historic-

---

50 *Pastoral Epistles,* 33. Similarly, F. Torm, *Die Psychologie der Pseudonymität in Hinblick auf die Literatur des Urchristentums* (Gütersloh, 1932), reprinted in *Pseudepigraphie in der heidnischen und jüdisch - christlichen Antike.* Edit. N. Brox (Darmstadt: Wissenschaftliche Buchgesellschaft, 1977) 146 (52) remarks, "Es scheint mir, dass diese Auffassung der Briefe, sie seien ein mit ethischen Zwecken und mit rafinierter Berechnung erdichtetes Drama in drei Akten, uns eine Verfasserpersönlichkeit vorführt, die psychologisch nicht fassbar ist. Ein so sonderbarer Mensch hat niemals gelebt." See also C.F.D. Moule, "Problem", 446–448; B. Reicke, "Chronologie der Pastoralbriefe", *ThLZ* 101 (1976) 81–94.

51 "Excursus: Information About Persons", *Pastoral Epistles,* 127.

52 *Problem,* 87–135. He later revised his theory of five fragments to three. See "Important Hypothesis Reconsidered: III. Authorship of the Pastoral Epistles", *ET* 67 (1955–56) 80; *Paulines,* 106–128. See also C.K. Barrett, *The Pastoral Epistles* (Oxford: Clarendon Press, 1963) 10–12; A.T. Hanson, *The Pastoral Letters* (Cambridge: University Press, 1966) 10–14; later retracted in "The Domestication of Paul: A Study in the Development of Early Christian Theology", *BJRL* 63 (1981) 402–418.

ally how the scraps could have been collected and edited, have meant the rejection of this theory even by conservative scholars keen to preserve a Pauline core[53].

How can the explicit epistolary pseudonymity of the Pastorals be explained? Are the only options authenticity or forgery? What follows below will be an attempt to demonstrate how even the personal information of the Pastorals fits into our overall pattern of pseudonymity in Jewish and Christian tradition.

5.3.1.2 *Paul and His Followers in the Pastorals*

The question which needs to be answered regarding the personal information of the Pastorals is, Why did the author feel the need to identify so strongly with Paul and his associates? The solution is hinted at by noting two peculiar features of the corpus[54]. First, there is an overwhelming emphasis on tradition both in its proper preservation (orthodoxy) and its proper expression (orthopraxy). Characteristic of this concern is the use of the terms ὑγιαίνειν, ὑγιής, "to be sound", "sound", which occur nowhere else in the NT. "Sound teaching" (1 Tim 1:10; 2 Tim 4:3; Titus 1:9; 2:1), "sound words" (1 Tim 6:3; 2 Tim 1:13), "sound in faith" (Titus 1:13; 2:2), and "sound speech" (Titus 2:8) indicate a danger of *un*sound teaching, a fact that is confirmed by the mention of "other teaching" (1 Tim 1:3) in a distinctively negative vein. That the concern is not only with proper belief, but also with proper behaviour is seen both in the negative results gained by false teaching (1 Tim 1:4; 6:3–5; cf. 2 Tim 3:2–9; Titus 1:10–16) and in the fastidious emphasis on proper conduct among those entrusted with proper teaching (1 Tim 3:1–13; 4:6–12; 6:2–5; Titus 1:5–9).

With this emphasis on the purity of tradition comes an increasing objectification of it as well. Thus in the Pastorals "faith"(πίστις) is used preponderantly in terms of "*the* faith" i.e. orthodox belief, rather than Paul's characteristic designation of πίστις as "trust"[55]. An equally important objectifying word is παραθήκη, "deposit", "entrusted goods" (1 Tim 6:20; 2 Tim 1:12, 14). This term seems more restricted than "faith" or "teaching", and is prob-

---

53 J.N.D. Kelly, *Pastoral Epistles,* 29; C.F.D. Moule, "Problem", 448.

54 As pointed out by J. Zmijewski, "Die Pastoralbriefe als pseudepigraphische Schriften - Beschreibung, Erklärung, Bewertung", *Studien zum Neuen Testament und seiner Umwelt* (Linz) 4 (1979) 103ff.

55 Conservatives point out that Paul uses faith in terms of orthodoxy as well (Rom 16:17; Gal 1:23; Eph 4:5; Phil 1:27; Col 2:7) and that the Pastorals also display a concept of faith as trust (1 Tim 1:5,14; 2:15; 2 Tim 1:5; 3:15). See E. Ellis, "The Problem of Authorship: First and Second Timothy", *RExp* 56 (1959) 352–353. This is true, but the *characteristic* usage remains the exact opposite between Paul and the Pastorals.

ably to be regarded as the gospel, the basic kerygmatic tradition (cf. 2 Tim 1: 10–14) which lies at the core of Pauline tradition[56].

The second peculiar feature of the Pastorals, besides its emphasis on the purity of tradition, is the absolute value that is placed on the authority of Paul and his apostolate. Paul is *the* apostle to the Gentiles, *par excellence* (1 Tim 2:7; 2 Tim 2:8–10). There are no other apostles even mentioned. This exclusive focus on Paul demonstrates that behind the Pastorals was a community whose identity was exclusively created and sustained by the figure of Paul. For them, Paul was not only a bearer of the proper tradition, but *part* of the tradition itself.

This twofold emphasis of the Pastorals on the purity of tradition and the linkage of that tradition with the figure of Paul provides the hermeneutical key for the pseudepigraphal techniques used. For it represents a similar approach (in manner, if not degree) to that of the genuine Paulines, and can be regarded as a legitimate attempt to extrapolate this approach to a post-Pauline community. Since for this community the gospel was pre-eminently *Paul's* gospel (2 Tim 2:8; cf. 1 Tim 1:11), its purity could only be maintained by re-enforcing the image of the apostle as well as his words. Pauline tradition had to be expressed in Pauline images: "be imitators of me".

This hermeneutical key is confirmed where we examine how the fundamental concerns of orthodoxy and orthopraxy are addressed by the Pastorals. In both cases it is the figure of the apostle as a foundational example that is used. The most significant indication of this is the use of ὑποτύπωσις, "prototype", "masterplan", "outline", which occurs only twice in the NT. Both occur in the Pastorals, and both are used of Paul, once in regard to his personal experience of the gospel (1 Tim 1:16) and once in regard to his teaching or doctrine (2 Tim 1:13). The meaning and implications of each will be discussed below.

The first usage of ὑποτύπωσις is in the context of Paul's conversion and experience of God's grace (1 Tim 1:12–17). In this paradigmatic account, Paul is regarded not only as *a* sinner, but *the* sinner, "the foremost of sinners" (1:15b). This is obviously patterned on 1 Corinthians 15:9f, but the thrust has been radically altered. Rather than an expression of humility of call in comparison with the other apostles as in 1 Corinthians, here Paul becomes a paradigm of the sinner: the worst possible case. Earlier commentators often regarded this as an overzealous attempt to portray Paul's humility, but the device is much more significant. It is meant to portray Paul as an archetypal sinner, in order that his experience of grace might be archetypal as well. This is precisely what is stated in 1:16b,c "that in me, as the foremost (of sinners), Jesus Christ might display his perfect patience for an example (ὑποτύπωσιν) to those who were to believe in him for eternal life." Actually, the RSV trans-

---

56 G. Lohfink, "Die Normativität der Amtvorstellungen in den Pastoralbriefen", *ThQ* 157 (1977) 95–97. *Contra,* K. Wegenast, *Verständnis,* who thinks that it stands for the entire Pauline teaching. But the fact that *Paul* receives the παραθήκη rules this out (2 Tim 1:12).

lation of ὑποτύπωσιν as "example" misses the force of both the passage and the compounding preposition[57]. The prefix added to τύπος gives the special idea of "a form outlined as the basis of further work"[58]. Dibelius/Conzelmann suggest "proto-type"[59], but even this fails to render the idea of normativity. Perhaps "archetype" is best, for the intent is that in both degradation before conversion and experience of grace after, Paul serves as an outline or standard for all his communities. His life as ὑποτύπωσις establishes the parameters of legitimate Christian experience[60].

This emphasis is not antithetical to what we know from the Paulines, but represents only an extrapolation. In Philippians 3:17 and 2 Thessalonians 3:9, Paul presents himself as an example (τύπος) to the community, and this is further linked in both cases to the verb μιμέομαι. But in the Pastorals Paul becomes *the* example, or outline (ὑποτύπωσις), an essential part of the tradition itself. It is this paradigmatic value of Paul's experience that leads to the use of much of the personal information in the Pastorals. Note that immediately after the account of Paul's conversion and its promotion as archtype (1 Tim 1:12–17), comes the charge to Timothy to follow this pattern (1: 18f). Even more significant is the information about Hymenaeus and Alexander (1:20), who serve as negative illustrations of the failure to follow the Pauline example. This indicates that in the Pastorals information, not only about Paul, but also about his associates (good or evil), is given not primarily for its historical or occasional value (or for verisimilitude), but for its paradigmatic, theological value. The personal information has a typological intent[61]. This is not to make a judgement, however, regarding the historical value of this information. A great deal may be accurate[62]. The point is the *use* which the author makes of the information at his disposal.

---

57 Kelly's translation as "illustration", *Pastoral Epistles,* 55 also misses the meaning.

58 E.K. Lee, "Words Denoting 'Pattern' in the New Testament", *NTS* 8 (1962) 170.

59 *Pastoral Epistles,* 30.

60 But it does not of course, express Christian experience in its totality. This is where the fundamental idea of outline comes in "... in light of the original meaning of the word, it is possible to argue that the μακροθυμία shown in Paul's case should be regarded as an outline of God's dealing with men, which would be later filled up and coloured with the rich variety of expressions of God's mercy as the gospel spread throughout the world". Lee, "Words", See further R. Collins, "Image", 165–172; P. Trummer, *Paulustradition,* 116–120.

61 See N. Brox, "Zu den persönlichen Notizen der Pastoralbriefe", *BZ* 13 (1969) 76–94; P. Trummer, *Paulustradition,* 132–141.

62 Dibelius/Conzelmann, *Pastoral Epistles,* 127–128, thinks the Pastorals may well have had access to accurate traditional material, and at times may even be used to "correct" Acts. C. Maurer "Eine Textvariante erklärt die Entstehung der Pastoralbriefe", *ThLZ* 3 (1947), 321–337, attempts to demonstrate that nearly all of the information in the Pastorals can be drawn from a naive reading of Acts and the Paulines. The most balanced judgement is given by N. Brox, "Notizen", 86; "Der Umstand, dass in den besprochen wie auch in anderen Texten einige der erwähnte Namen auch anderworts (in Paulusbriefen und in der Apostelgeschichte) begegnen, berichtet zu der ohnehin naheliegenden Vermutung, dass nicht lauter 'Erfindungen' aneinandergereiht, sondern vorhandene Personen - und Situationsüberlieferungen".

The typological intent of the Pastorals is demonstrated not only in the account of Paul's conversion, but also in the use of Paul as a paradigm of discipleship. Thus in 2 Timothy 1:8–12 we are given a picture of Paul's suffering for the sake of the gospel (cf. 4:6ff.). That this experience is intended as an "outline" is indicated by its introduction: "Be not ashamed ... share in suffering for the gospel". Similar to 1 Timothy 1:12–17, this model of suffering is linked to Paul's election as a special servant of God's grace (2 Tim 1: 11–12). Likewise the illustration of Pauline discipleship results in a charge to Timothy to follow in his steps (2:1ff.). And once again, this use of personal information in a typological fashion is not limited to Paul, but is also applied to his associates (2 Tim 1:15–18). The rejection of Paul by "all Asia", especially Phygelus and Hermogenes, can be regarded as a rejection of the Pauline model of discipleship. Similarly, the mention of Onesiphorus, who was "not ashamed of my chains" (1:16) is a clear illustration of the acceptance of that model. The same typological function can be attributed to the personal information of 2 Timothy 4:10ff., which follows on the heels of a further mention of Paul's sufferings (4:6f) and another charge to Timothy (4:1ff.). Thus we are left with pictures of the desertion of Demas, "in love with this present world" (4:10), as well as a list of Paul's faithful associates, which would arouse all sorts of meaningful recollections. All in all, there is victory promised to all who will stay the course, as had Paul (2 Tim 2:10–13; 4:8, 17–18).

If the first stage of ὑποτύπωσις illustruates how the author of the Pastorals incorporated the traditions of Paul's Christian experiences in order to express a concern for orthopraxy, the second usage has a similar function in regard to the concern for orthodoxy, with a parallel shift to the traditions of Paul's teaching (2 Tim 1:13). It is no accident that the second occurrence of ὑποτύπωσις, this time identified with Paul's teaching, actually takes place at the conclusion of the paradigmatic passage concerning Paul's model of discipleship, which we discussed above (2 Tim 1:8–12). For in actuality orthodoxy and orthopraxy cannot be separated, and are not in either Paul or the Pastorals. In 2 Thessalonians 3:9, Paul as τύπος is not only concerned with moral examples but is linked with binding tradition (3:6) and authoritative direction as well (3:10ff.). In Romans 6:17, which may well serve as the model for 2 Timothy 1:13, we have τύπον διδαχῆς, "standard of teaching". The idea is of a mould to which Christians conform, and thus expresses the idea of both proper belief *and* practice[63].

The difference, however, between the Pastorals and Paul is that, as we saw with his ethical example, the τύπος now becomes ὑποτύπωσις. Whereas in Paul the standard or example was linked with general apostolic (i.e. Christian) tradition, in 2 Timothy 1:13 is "the ὑποτύπωσις of sound words *which you heard from me*". Once again, Paul (in his teaching this time) becomes *the* type, or archetype of the community's traditions, and therefore

---

63 E.K. Lee, "Words", 169f.

the foundation of its identity. Just as Paul's life as ὑποτύπωσις serves to establish the parameters of legitimate Christian experience, so his words serve to establish the parameters of legitimate Christian teaching[64].

The proof of this paradigmatic function of Paul's teaching is found in the two major passages which we have already discussed (1 Tim 1:12ff.; 2 Tim 1:8ff.). In both we have linked with the use of ὑποτύπωσις the designation of Paul as διδάσκαλος, a title he never takes in the Paulines (1 Tim 2:7; 2 Tim 1:11)[65]. Similarly, in the Pastorals, διδασκαλία is the normative concept, while in Paul it is διδαχή. In Romans 6:17 and 16:17, Paul uses διδαχή to refer to a "standard of teaching", a clear expression of orthodoxy, but as we discussed above, it is general Christian tradition, not Pauline doctrine. Likewise, though a part of Paul's function was teaching (1 Cor 4:17b), his teaching is not to be differentiated from that of other apostles. (Though his relationship may be. Cf. 1 Cor 1:12; 4:14). But in the Pastorals, Paul is not *a* teacher or one who teaches, but *the* teacher. This may be the reason for the switch to διδασκαλία, for διδαχή is connected philologically with the more general διδασκω, "to teach", while διδασκαλία is connected philologically with the more specific, titular διδάσκαλος "teacher"[66]. A further indication of the distinctive outline of Paul's teaching tradition is its linkage in these two pericopes to his special election, particularly to the Gentiles (1 Tim 2:7; 2 Tim 1:11), and the special charge that is given to Timothy to imitate or hold fast to this pattern (1 Tim 1:18ff.; 2 Tim 1:13–14; 2:1ff.).

The archetypical approach to Pauline teaching explains once again the typological technique used in the Pastorals, not only with reference to personal information about Paul, but others as well. Many of those figures that we have already discussed could as easily have been subsumed under the headings of typical or antitypical representatives of sound teaching as well as of sound ethics, since there is no rigid distinction made between orthodoxy and orthopraxy. Perhaps the figures of Hymenaeus and Philetus (2 Tim 1:17f.), which were not mentioned above, are most illustrative of the danger of false teaching, for they had departed from an orthodox understanding of the resurrection[67].

---

64 But is does not, of course, express Christian teaching in its totality. E.K. Lee "Words", 170, says that the fundamental force of the metaphor is that of architecture. Paul has created the overall design, but it is up to Timothy and others to build the building. This fits in exactly with the principle of *Vergegenwärtigung.*

65 The unique title κῆρυξ also occurs in both verses. R. Collins, "Image", 152–153, argues that this title, and the phrase "knowledge of the truth" (1 Tim 2:4; 2 Tim 2:25; 3:7; Titus 1.1; cf. 1QH 10:20,29) are influenced by the thinking and terminology of Qumran, and signifies that Paul was regarded in a similar fashion to the Teacher of Righteousness. If so, this would further strengthen the case of Paul as *the* pattern.

66 G. Lohfink, "Paulinische", 97–98.

67 For a detailed attempt to expound the personal information and relate it to the *Sitz im Leben* of the post-Pauline author and his community, see N. Brox, "Notizen", and P. Trummer, *Paulustradition*, 116–132.

Because Paul had become such a part of the community-creating tradition of the Pastorals, due to his own unique personal relationship which he fostered in his genuine letters (e.g. 1 Cor 4:14–15), any restatement or *Vergegenwärtigung* of that tradition had to take place in personal terms, indeed more personal than in the general run of pseudonymous literature. *Paul's characteristic emphasis on "imitation" of the apostle by his children in the faith is the underlying reason for the detailed information about Paul and his associates that we find in the Pastorals. Authoritative tradition and the person of Paul cannot be separated.*

But the issue in the Pastorals is not over *Paul's* authority. Even the "false teachers" it opposes may well have accepted Paul as the authoritative, apostolic interpreter of the Jesus traditions that we find in the genuine Paulines. The real question is, Who interprets Paul? We have seen that in the Pastorals Paul has ceased to be merely *a* bearer and *a* teacher (interpreter) of tradition, and has become *the* bearer and *the* teacher, and thus part of the tradition itself (i.e. Jesus tradition + Pauline interpretation = Pauline tradition). The problem that arises in the post-Pauline community is, Who can serve as authoritative interpreters of Paul? Here is where the figures of Timothy and Titus enter, as the author of the Pastorals seeks to resolve the problem out of the Pauline tradition itself.

As we saw above, it was often the custom of Paul to send delegates to represent him and his teaching, and the two most prominent figures were Timothy and Titus, who enjoyed a special relationship to Paul. This special relationship could easily have been interpreted by later communities to be one of conversion by Paul, especially in the case of Timothy (1 Cor 4:14, 17). This is certainly indicated by the Pastorals, where Timothy and Titus are regarded as Paul's "children" (1 Tim 1:2; 2 Tim 1:2; Titus 1:4). In other words, the most effective representatives of Paul are those who owe their spiritual life to him, and it is this identification with Timothy and Titus as the recipients of a community-creating Pauline tradition that leads the author of the Pastorals to focus on them as authoritative interpreters of Paul.

Here we have the reason for the so-called "double pseudonymity" of the Pastorals[68], i.e. not only of authorship, but also of recipients. For not only is Paul regarded as part of the tradition, but also his representatives. If in Paul we have the archetype ($\dot{\upsilon}\pi \sigma \tau \dot{\upsilon} \pi \omega \sigma \iota \varsigma$), then in his legitimate representatives we should have the type ($\tau \dot{\upsilon} \pi \sigma \varsigma$) of Pauline Christian, and this is exactly the designation of Timothy and Titus in the Pastorals (1 Tim 4:12; Titus 2:7). That these figures are meant to be regarded as authoritative interpreters of Paul in contrast to the "false" interpreters threatening the community of the Pastorals is seen by the designation of Timothy as $\delta \dot{\sigma} \kappa \iota \mu \sigma \varsigma$, "approved", (2 Tim 1:15) and the false teachers as $\dot{\alpha} \delta \dot{\sigma} \kappa \iota \mu \sigma \iota$, "unapproved" (2 Tim 3:8;

---

68 W. Stenger, "Timotheus und Titus als literarische Gestalten (Beobachtungen zur Form und Funktion der Pastoralbriefe)", *Kairos* 16 (1974) 253; see also N. Brox, "Notizen", 88–91.

Tit 1:16). In Pauline tradition, their task was to "remind you of my (Paul's) ways in Christ" (1 Cor 4:17b). This is precisely their role in the Pastorals (ὑπομί'μνῃσκε; 2 Tim 2:14 ; Titus 3:1)[69]. Perhaps the most characteristic designation of the Pauline tradition that they are to hand on is simply ταῦτα (RSV, "these instructions", 1 Tim 3:14; 4:6,11; 5:7; 2 Tim 2:14; Titus 2: 15; 3:8)[70]. The fundamental mode of ministry for Timothy and Titus in the Pastorals is teaching (1 Tim 4:11,13,16; 6:2 ; 2 Tim 4:2; Titus 2:1,7), as we saw it was for Paul (cf. 1 Tim 2:7 ; 2 Tim 1:11).

The task of Paul's representatives, or authoritative interpreters, is not only to reproduce Pauline doctrine, but also to "reincarnate" the Pauline life-style or model of discipleship. This is the reason for the intensely personal advice given to Timothy and Titus by Paul in the Pastorals. Timothy in particular is reminded of his observance of both Paul's teaching and conduct (2 Tim 3: 10), and encouraged to reproduce it, particularly in the midst of persecution and suffering (2 Tim 1:8)[71]. The figures of Timothy and Titus, then, are presented as ideal representatives of Pauline tradition, and are intended by the author of the Pastorals as models (τύποι) for authoritative representatives in his own community. As such, Timothy and Titus as τύποι reincarnate the Pauline ὑποτύπωσις in both teaching and conduct: 1 Timothy 4:12. "an example in speech and conduct"; Titus 2:7, "a model of good deeds, and in your teaching show integrity". The personal information about Timothy and Titus, and the advice given them, can be seen as a direct result of the needs of the church leaders of the community behind the Pastorals.

Helpful as the "models" of Timothy and Titus might be to the community behind the Pastorals in depicting the nature of authoritative representatives of Paul, it still does not address the problem of who in fact can lay claim to that authority. Paul chose Timothy and Titus, and thus demonstrated that continuity with his tradition was possible in his absence, through representatives. But Paul was no longer around to do any more choosing. What gave the post-Pauline community the right to further represent Paul?

To address this problem, the author of the Pastorals focuses on the nature of the election of Timothy (since no tradition about Titus was available). Though there is generally a scarcity of references to the Spirit in the Pastorals, here they become of paramount importance. As we discussed above, the Pauline ὑποτύπωσις was directly linked to his special election by God (1 Tim 1: 12ff.; 2 Tim 2:8ff.), and in direct connection with this we also have Paul's charge to Timothy to be an authentic representative of Pauline ethics and teaching (1 Tim 2:18f.; 2 Tim 1:8, 13–14). However, in these *same* contexts

---

69 See also "exhort" (1 Tim 1:3; 2 Tim 4:2; Titus 2:15); "rebuke" (1 Tim 5:20; 2 Tim 4:2); "prove" (1 Tim 6:20; 2 Tim 1:14); "pass on" (Titus 3:8).

70 "The demonstrative *tauta* is used by the author of the Pastorals to indicate that Paul's disciple is "faithful to transmit his teaching to the church." R. Collins, "Image", 159–160.

71 See L.T. Johnson, "II Timothy and the Polemic Against False Teachers: A Re-examination", *Journal of Religious Studies* 6/7 (1978/1979) 12.

the author of the Pastorals makes clear that it is not merely Paul's human choice that determines Timothy's representative role. For Timothy as well it is pre-eminently the choice of God through the Spirit. Paul charges Timothy "in accordance with the prophetic utterances which pointed to you" (1 Tim 1:18b; cf. 4:14), and urges him to "rekindle the gift of God ... the Spirit of power" (2 Tim 1:6,7; cf. 1 Tim 4:14) connected with his ordination[72]. It is the Spirit that is responsible for the election of Pauline representatives such as Timothy. It is also the Spirit which enables the representative to carry out his task, the same Spirit which elected and sustained Paul. Thus after Paul entrusts Timothy with his ὑποτύπωσις, he remarks, "guard the truth that has been entrusted to you by the Holy Spirit *who dwells within us*" (2 Tim 1:14). *Here we have a clear statement of the unity of revelation and interpretation that allows for a continuity of tradition,* just as we discovered in our background studies.

Yet again, the problem is how one connects the divine election of one individual (Timothy) to the ongoing representatives of Paul in the post-Pauline communities? The key lies in the comparison of two passages which have long served to illustrate the internal inconsistencies of the Pastorals. In 1 Timothy 4:14, Timothy's gift of the Spirit and ordination to his vocation comes about when the council of elders lay their hands on him. Yet in 2 Timothy 1:6, this same gift and laying on of hands is accomplished by Paul. Rather than a sign of the author's ineptness, this is an important theological affirmation about the continuity of tradition through representative figures. For it asserts that the ratification of the divine (Spirit) election of Pauline representatives took place not only through the instrumentality of Paul, but also through the instrumentality of a church hierarchy or council. *The implication is that although Paul is gone, the Spirit and the church leaders remain, and thus the continuity of authoritative interpreters of Paul can be maintained*[73]. Whether this thinking is in line with authentic Pauline teaching is a question which leads into the minefield of "early Catholicism", and cannot be discussed at length here[74]. At least it needs to be said that the Pastorals have not replaced the Spirit with office[75]. The office of teaching is still a Spirit inspired office (cf. Acts 20:28), not so much conferred as confirmed by the church hierarchy[76]. Likewise this type of confirmation by elders took place in Paul's own election to ministry (Acts 13:1–3; Gal 2:2).

---

72 See also 2 Timothy 1:9 "Who saved *us* and called *us* with a holy calling", which in the context implies a specific role for each.

73 But note it is the Spirit of teaching that remains. The Spirit of apostleship is gone, thus the continuity with Paul is stressed in terms of teaching.

74 See J.H. Elliott, "A Catholic Gospel: Reflections on 'Early Catholicism' in the New Testament", *CBQ* 31 (1969) 312–323; I.H. Marshall, "'Early Catholicism' in the New Testament", *New Dimensions in the New Testament Study.* Edit. R. Longenecker and M. Tenney (Grand Rapids: Zondervan, 1974) 217–231; J.D.G. Dunn, *Unity and Diversity,* 461–478.

75 *Contra* J.D.G. Dunn, *Jesus,* 347–349.

76 The succession that the Pastorals portray from Paul onwards is thus not primarily

It is this perceived continuity of revelation and tradition expressed in the teaching office of Pauline representatives that lies at the core of the church order promoted by the Pastorals. The author regards the church leaders (and himself) as standing in an authoritative, unbroken line of interpreters stretching back to Paul himself, *a development which Paul himself sanctioned.* This can be seen most explicitly in 2 Timothy 2:2. After Paul described his special election and reception of the παραθήκη(2 Tim 1:12), and it is further handed on to Timothy (1:14), the next step is for Timothy to ensure the continuity of tradition. "What you have heard from me before many witnesses entrust (παράθου) to faithful men who will be able to teach others also." Indeed, the whole structure of the Pastorals revolves around the two Pauline representatives of Timothy and Titus establishing a continuity of Pauline tradition through the church order (1 Tim 4:6; Titus 1:5)[77].

Most instructive is the nature of that church order. Once again we have the two-fold emphasis on proper conduct and proper teaching, particularly amongst the leadership. A bishop must be both above reproach (ἀνεπίλημπτον, 1 Tim 3:2) or blameless (ἀνέγκλητον, Titus 1:7), and "an apt teacher" (1 Tim 3:2), "able to give instruction in sound doctrine" (Titus 1:9). Similarly, an elder must be "blameless" (Titus 1:6), and "labour in preaching and teaching" (1 Tim 5:17). Even deacons must "hold the mystery of the faith", and be "blameless" (1 Tim 3:9, 10). In other words, the church offices in the Pastorals are to reflect the ὑποτύπωσις of Paul and the τύποι of Timothy and Titus, in both orthodoxy and orthopraxy. They are the further models of Pauline life and teaching for the church, the *Vergegenwärtigung* of Paul through his representatives, by virtue of their divine call.

5.3.1.3 *Vergegenwärtigung and Pauline Tradition in the Pastorals*

We have seen above how the Pastorals represent an advanced "canon-consciousness" in regard to Pauline tradition, so that even the literary form and its attendant *personalia* become part of the pseudepigraphic framework. But it also needs to be affirmed that despite this increasing rigidity there is still a fundamental continuity with the process of tradition which we found in earlier Jewish works and the Jesus tradition. This point can be missed even by those scholars who are conscious of the Pauline tradition in the Pastorals. Thus, for example, P. Trummer objects to H. Hergermann's comparison of tradition formation in the Pastorals and Synoptics, because Jesus was never

---

one of office, but of teaching or tradition. G. Lohfink, "Paulinische", 104–105; W. Stenger, "Timotheus", 253.

77 For an argument for the continuity of development from the helpers and disciples of the apostles to the church offices, see E. Berbuir, "Die Herausbildung der kirchlichen Ämter von Gehilfen und Nachfolgern der Apostel", *WiWei* 36 (1973) 110–128.

an author, as was Paul[78]. Once again Trummer demonstrates the confusion of form with intent, for he forgets that both Jesus and Paul were regarded as the founders of distinctive traditions, whether those traditions were oral or written. As we saw in previous chapters, the literary expression of pseudonymity is not central to its underlying motive: the actualization of tradition.

There is no denying that tradition in the Pastorals has become more of a fixed entity, which is evident not only in its regard for Paul and his letters, but also in the formal character of its drawing upon anonymous tradition' (e.g. "faithful is the word"; 1 Tim 1:15; 3:1; 4:9; 2 Tim 2:11; Titus 3:8). But as we have seen from our discussion above, the author of the Pastorals still uses great freedom and creativity in weaving together Pauline and other traditional material in a conscious effort to actualize Pauline tradition[79]. It is for this reason that efforts to denigrate the Pastorals as un-Pauline, and ascribe to them a basically non-Pauline understanding of tradition, are misguided.

The leading proponent of this position is K. Wegenast[80], using the works of E. Käsemann as his hermeneutical frame of reference. He contrasts the freedom that Paul has with tradition with the formality of the Pastorals. Paul is no servant of tradition, but of the κύριος; while for the Pastorals the *Lehrautorität* has taken the place of the Lord[81]. Wegenast traces this change to the rise of gnostic heresy, and a different concept of tradition. His essential thesis is that the Pastorals (and Colossians, Ephesians) have adopted the "gnostic" idea of tradition as doctrine handed down from Paul and used it against them. But this view is based on a philosophical *a priori* that the gospel that Paul preached had in fact no propositional content, but consisted of a non-cognitive existential encounter with the "Word"[82]. Since Paul cannot be the source of any kind of *traditum,* this idea must be traced to somewhere else, like the gnostics. But as we have seen, the Pastorals based their own idea of ὑποτύπωσις of Pauline doctrine (2 Tim 1:13) on the τύπος διδαχῆς (Rom 6:17) of Christian tradition that Paul appeals to in his own letters. This means that the Pastorals find their concept of tradition in Paul himself, not elsewhere. If the Pastorals emphasize the *traditum* more than the *traditio*, this is a question of emphasis, not origin, and is still in keeping with tradition formation we find elsewhere in Judaism.

This criticism of Wegenast is important because he is illustrative of the kind of thinking that has led to such a devaluation of the Pastorals. In order to "save" Paul, one has had to jettison the Pastorals, and in so doing cut it off from its Jewish origins. Nowhere is this more evident than in the consid-

---

78 *Paulustradition,* 88. See H. Hegermann, "Der geschichtliche Ort der Pastoralbriefe", *Theologische Versuche,* II. Edit. J. Rogge and G. Schille (Berlin: Evangelische Verlagsanstalt, 1970) 47–64.

79 See further N. Brox, *Die Pastoralbriefe* (Regensburg: F. Pustet, 1969[4]) 68–69.

80 *Verständnis.*

81 *Ibid.,* 165–166.

82 *Ibid.,* 40.

eration of pseudonymity in the Pastorals. A classic illustration of this is the thesis on Pauline pseudonymity by D. Penny:

> The thesis to be tested is that the Pastorals, by wedding an essentially non-Pauline expression of Christianity to a strong image of Paul, want to make a polemical statement about Paul and the interpretation of his letters, viz. they want to make Paul into a clear witness for the emerging 'Catholic' Christianity and to forestall the gnosticizing interpretation of his letters[83].

The basic thrust of Penny's thesis is that there is no real tradition connection between the Pastorals and Paul, and no real attempt to develop and apply his theology. Indeed, in their polemical encounter, the gnostics come off as more virtuous than the Pastorals, since the gnostics actually regard Paul as their authority, while the author of the Pastorals is only using him as a foil for his own ideas!

As we have seen in earlier chapters, one cannot deny an element of polemic in Jewish pseudepigraphy. Penny rightly identifies the pseudonymity of the Pastorals as "a polemical weapon in the controversy over the correct interpretation of Paul"[84]. What he cannot answer from his perspective is, Why would the author of the Pastorals bother, if Paul did not serve as some sort of authority figure for him? Penny's acceptance of the philosophical *a priori* discussed above has led him by necessity to create a radical disjuncture between the Pastorals and Paul. The methodological result is that when Penny is forced to come to terms with the great amount of Pauline material in the Pastorals he must argue for negligible Pauline influence in a fashion that has to be regarded as special pleading.

Though Dr. Penny's approach is no worse than that of many modern scholars, two examples cited from his thesis can be used to prove what he and others try to deny. For example, on page 119 he recognizes that the right of support of elders (1 Tim 5:17–18) probably depends on Paul's teaching (1 Cor 9:6–18). But he discounts this by saying that the Pastorals claim the right absolutely, and never mention the fact that Paul relinquished his rights. But this proves nothing. In 1 Corinthians 9:15–18 Paul mentions the reason for relinquishing his rights: so that there might be an element of "freewill" in his service that was lacking in the irresistible grace of his election. Obviously this is not something that could have been made a general principle in the Pastorals. What *does* temper this right to renumeration is the appeal to a godly contentment (1 Tim 6:6), a teaching that can easily be predicted on the life and teaching of Paul (Phil 4:11). We can see, then, a careful attempt to apply Pauline tradition *to a new Sitz im Leben.*

A second example is on page 110ff. of Penny's thesis. He acknowledges that 2 Timothy 1:9 and Titus 3:5,7 reproduce the language of the Pauline doctrine of justification, but again discounts it by noting that the focus of

---

83 *The Pseudo-Pauline Letters of the First Two Centuries* (Ph.D., Emory University, 1980).
84 *Ibid.,* 143.

concern is now "works" in general, not the works of the law. Again this proves nothing. There is no question that in the post-Pauline church the issue of circumcision was no longer a live one. But this does not preclude a wider application of the Pauline idea, particularly if there was a danger of some incipient gnosticism that implied that salvation was by some other means than grace. Rather than the "imitation of Pauline language as part of the pseudepigraphic framework" (113), this is a serious attempt to relate Paul to a later time (cf. on Eph 2:8–9, below).

This is not to say that everything in the Pastorals has its source in Paul. We have already demonstrated that there are thematic and configurational forms of *Vergegenwärtigung,* and there is no need to deny that the Pastorals make use of other sources of tradition. Indeed, there is no need to deny that when using Paul, the Pastorals sometimes stress those things which he does not. *Vergegenwärtigung* is not mere reproduction, but an attempt to reinterpret a core tradition for a new, and often different *Sitz im Leben*[85]. Who is to say what Paul would have done in the church at the beginning of the second century? Whatever one's personal opinion of the matter, this is a value judgement that should not affect how we understand the process and motivation of Pauline tradition in the Pastorals. At least it can be cautioned that the Pastorals may be more sensitive to the nuances of Pauline thought than much of modern scholarship, which because of so many preconceptions about Paul is unable or unwilling to hear the voice of an ancient interpreter[86].

5.3.1.4 *Canon and the Literary Shape of the Pastorals*

We have already seen how the literary technique of personal information in the Pastorals is not just a ploy to gain verisimilitude, but is tied to a "canon consciousness" of the personal nature of the Pauline tradition itself. These features had become *part* of the tradition. It is this process of the crystallization of the elements of tradition that may serve as a key to the final problem of pseudonymity in the Pastorals: its literary shape as a three-fold corpus.

The three-fold nature of the Pastorals has long been a bone of contention with supporters of authenticity[87]. Why would a pseudepigrapher go to all the trouble of writing three letters, when one would do? The content of the Pastorals is usually given as an answer: 1 Timothy is for established churches, 2 Timothy is a farewell address, and Titus is for new churches. While this is true, it scarcely seems enough justification. A more fruitful suggestion has

---

85 For a form critical analysis of the references to the opponents in the Pasorals, see R.J. Karris, "The Background and Significance of the Polemic of the Pastoral Epistles," *JBL* (1973) 549–564.

86 For detailed treatment of Pauline tradition in the Pastorals, see P. Trummer, *Paulustradition,* 173–240.

87 E.g. J.N.D. Kelly, *Pastoral Epistles,* 31: F. Torm, *Psychologie.*

been made by A.E. Barnett[88]. He observes that the Pastorals never circulated separately, but as a collection, and suggests that this idea of a collection that constitutes the Pastorals is based on its dependence on a Pauline collection, or in our terms, *on a Pauline "canon"* (not in the closed sense).

Now it must be admitted that there is no consensus whatever as to exactly how and when the transition was made from Paul's occasional writings to the preservation, delimitation, and use of them as scripture or canon in the closed sense. But whether as the result of the effects of a single individual[89] or as the result of a gradual association[90], virtually all scholars affirm the presence of a Pauline collection at or about the turn of the century. Leaving aside such NT documents as Ephesians and Hebrews, 1 Clement shows a knowledge of at least three of Paul's letters (35:5f; 36:2f; 47:1–3; 49:5); Ignatius (S m 1:1; Eph 12:2;18:1;Rom 5:1) and Polycarp (Phil 3:2) allude to several more. 2 Peter 3:15f (A.D. 125–135) refers to a Pauline collection, and later, of course, Marcion (around A.D. 150) actually publishes a ten member Pauline canon. Since the Pastorals allude to most if not all of Paul's letters, and their life setting best fits with the period shortly after the turn of the century, there is ample reason to believe that when the Pastorals were written there existed a collection of Paul's letters which had achieved some sort of authoritative status.

The literary shape of the Pastorals as a multi-volume work, then, may be due to an awareness that Pauline tradition was being increasingly identified with a body of literature. The multiple nature of the Pastoral corpus would then be a reflection that *even a Pauline "canon" had become part of the tradition.* W. Doty makes an observation on the order of the Pastorals that sheds further light on this "canon-consciousness". He contends that the content and syntax indicate that the letters were meant to be read sequentially, in the order of Titus, 1 Timothy, 2 Timothy[91]. This is in fact the order

---

88 *Paul Becomes a Literary Influence* (Chicago: University Press, 1941) 251; See also P. Trummer, "Corpus Paulinum - Corpus Pastorale", *Paulus in dem neutestamentlichen Spätschriften.* Edit. K. Kertelge (Freiburg: Herder, 1981) 122–145.

89 See E.J. Goodspeed, *An Introduction to the New Testament* (Chicago: University of Chicago Press, 1937); J. Knox, *Marcion and the New Testament* (Chicago: University of Chicago Press, 1942); C.L. Mitton, *The Formation of the Pauline Corpus of Letters* (London: Epworth, 1955); W. Schmithals, "On the Composition and Earliest Collection of the Major Epistles of Paul," *Paul and the Gnostics* (Nashville: Abingdon, 1972) 239–274.

90 So K. Lake, P.N. Harrison, A. Harnack, G. Zuntz *et al.* See further H. Gamble, "The Redaction of the Pauline Letters and the Formation of the Pauline Corpus", *JBL* 94 (1975) 403–418; A. Sand, "Überlieferung und Sammlung der Paulusbriefe", *Paulus in den neutestamentlichen Spätschriften.* Edit. K. Kertelge (Freiburg: Herder, 1981) 11–23; H.-M. Schenke, "Das Weiterwirken des Paulus und die Pflege seines Erbes durch die Paulus-Schule", *NTS* 21 (1974–75) 505–518, reprinted with additional bibliography in *Einleitung in die Schriften des Neuen Testaments,* I. Edit. H.-M. Schenke and K.M. Fischer (Gütersloh: Mohn, 1978) 233–247.

91 "Classification", 192–198. He cites the lengthy introduction of Titus 1:1–4; the

that is found in the Muratorian Canon. The appropriateness of this order is that it places 2 Timothy at the end of a supplementary Pauline canon, as his last will and testament. This gives the order of the Pastorals not only a logical progression, but a theological one as well.

Scholars have long been aware of the testamentary character of 2 Timothy, especially chapters 3 and 4, though they have often disagreed on the specific features of the genre[92]. But since testaments can be regarded as the literary expression of either oral or written tradition, the genre itself gives no indication that it was written as part of a larger Pauline "canon", The question is, within this "testament" of Paul in 2 Timothy are there any indications that it regards Paul's previous writings in a "canonical" sense, i.e. as authoritative?

The answer is Yes, though it lies in a less commonly accepted interpretation of an exceedingly well-known verse: 2 Timothy 3:16. In light of the above, it is quite possible that γραφή in 3:16 refers to a Pauline "canon" as well as the Jewish scriptures. This does not depend on either rendering πᾶσα as predicative or attributive, though the more likely predicative rendering[93], "every God-inspired scripture" (NEB) fits in better with the idea of Paul's (inspired) writings being profitable as well. The great majority of scholars hold that γραφή refers only to the Jewish scriptures. Their chief reason is that this is the universal referent in the LXX and earlier parts of the NT. But this is in fact because γραφή was linked with the idea of *canon*. This is clearly

---

repetition and redaction of the content of Titus in 1 Timothy; the abrupt conclusion of 1 Timothy and its merging into 2 Timothy.

92 See J. Munck, "Discours d'adieu dans le Nouveau Testament et dans la littérature biblique", *Aux Sources de la tradition chrétienne.* Fest. M. Goguel (Neuchâtel: Delachaux and Niesttle, 1950) 155–170; E. Stauffer, *New Testament Theology* (New York: Macmillan, 1955) 344–347; O. Knoch, *Die "Testamente" des Petrus und Paulus* (Stuttgart: KBW Verlag, 1973) 44–64; K. Baltzer, *The Covenant Formulary in Old Testament, Jewish and Early Christian Literature* (Oxford: Blackwell, 1971) 141–163; and A. Kolenkow, "The Genre Testament and Forecasts of the Future in the Hellenistic Jewish Milieu", *JSJ* 6 (1975) 57–71, as cited by J. Neyrey, *The Form and Background of the Polemic in 2 Peter* (Ph.D., Yale, 1977) 101, cf. 99–105. L.T. Johnson, "II Timothy", argues that 2 Timothy is not testamentary, but is in the form of personal paraenesis comparable with the works of Ps. Isocrates, Epicitetus, and Lucian. Though his work is undoubtedly useful to illuminate some of the background to 2 Timothy, none of the Hellenistic examples he cites are in the form of first person letters. They all use *other* men as examples, not themselves. Though unquestionably 2 Timothy serves a paraenetic purpose, its form remains as testament. For the most thoroughgoing form critical analysis of Jewish testamentary literature, see E. von Nordheim, *Die Lehre von Alten I: Das Testamente als Literaturgattung im Judentum der Hellenistisch - römischen Zeit* (Leiden: E.J. Brill, 1980). He makes the crucial point that though a definite *Gattung,* it does not need to be a separate literary work.

93 So C.K. Barrett, *Pastoral Epistles,* 114; Dibelius/Conzelmann, *Pastoral Epistles,* 120; J.N.D. Kelly, *Pastoral Epistles,* 202–203; A.T. Hanson, *Studies in the Pastoral Epistles* (London: SPCK, 1968) 43–44; J.W. Roberts, "Every Scripture Inspired by God", *RestQ* 5 (1961) 33–37; *idem,* "Note on the adjective after πᾶς in 2 Tim 3,16", *ET* 76 (1964) 359.

illustrated by 2 Peter 3:16, which mentions with Paul's letters the "other scriptures". If Paul's letters were to attain an authoritative status similar to the Jewish scriptures, they would be called γραφή as well. This is what took place in 2 Peter only a decade or two later, and there is much reason to believe in its occurence in 2 Timothy 3:16.

This interpretation is supported by both the context and the emphasis of the Pastorals elsewhere. γραφή of verse 16 must be related to ιερα γράμματα of verse 15. But verse 15 refers not just to the Jewish scriptures, but to Christian catechetical instruction, "how from childhood you have been acquainted with the sacred writings which are able to instruct you for salvation through faith in Christ Jesus". This echoes 2 Timothy 1:5, where the "sincere faith" of Timothy's mother and grandmother had also become Timothy's (cf. Acts 16). As we saw above, this personal information probably served as a point of identification for second and third generation Christians with Timothy, who became Christians within rather than from outside the community. If this is so, then verse 15 (and verse 16) must refer to something more than the Jewish scriptures, i.e. Christian teaching. And since the community tradition was focused on Paul, it is likely that at least Pauline instruction is intended. This is clear from the prior context (3:10–14). It opens with Paul admonishing Timothy, "you have observed my teaching, my conduct", and concludes with a charge very similar to the ὑποτύπωσις and παραθήκη charges of 1:13–14: "But as for you, continue in what you have learned and firmly believed, knowing from whom you learned it". 2 Timothy 3:16, then, can be regarded as an affirmation that the Pauline writings, as part of the inspired scriptures, are normative for church order and practice.

This interpretation also fits well with the use of the Jewish scriptures in the Pastorals, for if verse 16 was simply commending the authority of the Jewish scriptures, it would seem strange since the rest of the Pastorals infrequently uses them. Only 1 Timothy 5:18 is a direct quote, and even this is peculiar. After the citation λέγει γὰρ ἡ γραφή, we have a composite of Deuteronomy 25:4 and a Jesus *logion* "the labourer deserves his wages" (cf. Matt 10:10; Luke 10:7). Now this must mean that something besides the Jewish scriptures is regarded as scripture, either one of the canonical gospels or Q. It also may be a reference to Paul's writings, since Deuteronomy 25:4 is also a citation by Paul (1 Cor 9:9)[94]. At least it warns us that a rigid interpretation of γραφή in 2 Timothy 3:16 as only the Jewish scriptures goes against the grain of intent in the Pastorals.

If within the testamentary elements of the Pastorals we find evidence that the author regarded Paul's letters as scripture, then the implication is that the Pastorals were intended to supplement that "canon", or at least reflect it. In other words, if the Pastorals in their process of *Vergegenwärtigung* are to

---

94 C. Nielson, "Scripture in the Pastoral Epistles", *Perspectives in Religious Studies* (Macon, Georgia) 7 (1980) 17. But Neilson goes too far, and asserts that the Pastorals give evidence of a proto-Marcionite *rejection* of the OT.

make a claim to authoritative tradition, they must not only be pseudonymous, but "canonical" as well. They must reflect the literary and canonical
shape of Paul's corpus of letters, because that shape had become part of that
tradition.

The fundamental problem of the Pastorals is one that is met with in every
piece of pseudonymous literature we have discussed so far: how to actualize a
tradition after the (perceived) founder of that tradition is gone. But there are
unique features of the Pastorals that are due to the unique personalization of
that tradition by Paul himself. It is not enough to have a restatement of Pauline
tradition. *What is needed is an extension of the apostolic presence itself* into
the post-apostolic period. The way that this was achieved was by the characteristic methods used by Paul as a substitute, or better, mediation of his apostolic presence: the apostolic representative, and the apostolic letter.

This is most clearly seen in the other "testamentary" elements of the Pastorals: 1 Timothy 3:14–15; 4:13. Here it is not a question of Paul's dying,
but his absence – yet the connection between the two is obvious, and lay in
the mind of the author as well. There was no obviously testamentary features
in Paul's actual writings, but there was the problem of delay: "I am hoping
to come to you soon, but I am writing these instructions to you so that, if
I'm delayed, you may know how one ought to behave in the household of
God" (1 Tim 3:14–15a; cf. Rom 1:13; 15:22; 1 Cor 16:7; 2 Cor 1:15ff.; 1
Thess 2:17; Gal 4:20). W. Stenger has demonstrated the clear connection this
has with the "apostolic parousia" form in Paul[95], as delineated by Funk.
Aware of Paul's own use of his writings (Rom 15:15; Phlm 21; 1 Cor 4:14; 2
Cor 13:10; 1 Thess 5:27; Col 4:16) and his representatives Timothy and
Titus (1 Cor 4:17; 2 Cor 8:16–17), the author of the Pastorals elevates these
to "canonical" status: "Till I come, attend to the public reading of scripture,
to preaching, to teaching" (1 Tim 4:13). Not only so, but in making his claim
to authoritative tradition, he places his own work among this Pauline
"canon". J. Zmijewski is right when he says that the Pastorals are doing more
than asserting what Paul *would* have said *were* he present. The Pastorals are
in fact the presence and word of Paul[96].

And not only is Paul present in the literature of the Pastorals. He is present
in his representatives as well. This explains a unique feature of the Pastorals:
that they are addressed to Pauline co-workers, not churches. This is a theological assertion that apart from the Pauline literary corpus, there could be no
more direct word from Paul. From now on Pauline tradition and interpretation were in the hands of his legitimate representatives, who would mediate
his apostolic presence. In this regard, the suggestion of P. Trummer that the
testamentary genre of 2 Timothy may be intended not only to actualize the
Pauline tradition, but to conclude it, is perhaps close to target[97]. J.D. Quinn

95 "Timotheus", 255–259.
96 "Die Pastoralbriefe", 112–113.
97 *Paulustradition*, 246.

notes that the testamentary Epistle of Enoch ends the five-fold Enochic "Pentateuch" (1 Enoch), and that the last nine chapters of 2 Baruch are in the form of a testamentary letter[98]. Given the recognition of a Pauline literary body of tradition by the Pastorals, perhaps regarded as "scripture", it is certainly feasible that in offering his own supplementary corpus, the author was in effect writing a literary "conclusion" for the Pauline "canon". His intent was not necessarily to end the actualization of Pauline tradition, but only its literary expression. From henceforth any further *Vergegenwärtigung* must take place under the supervision of the "approved" leadership of the church, Paul's official interpreters.

It is this limitation and charge that may well be behind one of the closing images of the Pastorals: 2 Timothy 4:13. Though long a bastion of arguments for authenticity, this verse in fact has a peculiar ring that makes it difficult to reconcile with Paul's method elsewhere, as recognized by C. Spicq[99]. The resolution of the problem comes in determining the literary/theological motif that it presents. P. Trummer has demonstrated that the basic theme of this verse is *"apostolischer Selbstgenugsamkeit"*[100]. When we realize that this verse comes at the end of a long testamentary section, intended not just for Timothy but for all of Paul's authentic representatives (2 Tim 4:8b), it becomes a parting example to all who would seek to embody the Pauline ὑποτύπωσις. 2 Timothy 4:13a portrays the apostolic self-sufficiency in mode of life (orthopraxy). This is a repetition of the theme of 1 Timothy 6:6–10, the kind of lifestyle expected of a Pauline representative. The answer is godliness with αὐταρκεία (1 Tim 6:6). This is a clear actualization of Pauline teaching, using himself as an example (αὐτάρκης, Phil 4:11). Similarly in Acts 20:33, another testamentary depiction of Paul, we have on record Paul's statement that he did not want anyone else's money or clothes for himself. This same sort of "self-sufficiency" is enjoined in the Pastorals: "but if we have food and clothing, with these we shall be content" (1 Tim 6:8). When Paul requests his cloak, then (2 Tim 4:13a), it is a final reminder to all who would represent him what sort of archetype they must follow.

Similarly, in 4:13b,c we meet with the other aspect of the Pauline ὑποτύπωσις, self-sufficiency in sound teaching (orthodoxy). Though we cannot know exactly what the author of the Pastorals meant to represent by the "books" and "parchments", at the very least it is a reference to a corpus of literature, and thus is further evidence of a "canon-consciousness" that he portrays or extends back into the life of Paul himself. By so doing he is re-

---

98 "Last Volume", 68–69. He also cites the Epistle of Jeremiah as an appendix to the LXX collection of Jeremiah, Lamentations and Baruch. Of course the Epistle of Enoch did not in fact end the growth of Enoch literature (e.g. 2 Enoch, 3 Enoch). The *intent*, however, may still have been there.

99 "Pèlerine et vêtements (A propos de II Tim IV, 13 et Act XX, 33)", *Mélanges E. Tisserant* (Cità de Vaticans: Bibliotheca apostolica vaticana, 1964) 389–417.

100 *Paulustradition*, 78–86. See also "Mantel und Schriften (2 Tim 4,13). Zur Interpretation einer persönlichen Notiz in den Pastoralbriefe", *BZ* 18 (1974) 193–207.

minding the leaders of his church of the documents which serve as the foundation of their community. The parting message that the Pastorals give in their characteristic personal form is that even to the end of his life, all the apostle needed was his cloak and collection of writings, the basic necessities and the "scriptures", and this is all his representatives need for their task as well (cf. Mark 6:7–13 pars).

Whether or not the author of the Pastorals had such a developed sense of "canon" that he actually wanted to close the door on further writings, there is at least little doubt that the literary content and shape of the Pastorals is due to an overwhelming "canon-consciousness" of the characteristic expression of Pauline tradition. In other words, we have seen that the Pastorals take up many elements from Paul's writings (and from an oral tradition about him as well), and in the same characteristic personal and literary manner actualize this material for their own generation. Furthermore, we saw that the pressing need for this actualization was a crisis over authority: who were to be "approved" interpreters of Paul. *Therefore it is with confidence that we can conclude that in the Pastorals, attribution is primarily an assertion of authoritative tradition, not of literary origins.*

5.3.2. Ephesians

5.3.2.1 The Problem of Ephesians

What H. Cadbury has called "The Dilemma of Ephesians"[101] has continued to the present day. Though it may be said that a majority of recent scholarship holds it to be inauthentic, there is no real force in an argument from head-counting, and very many responsible and serious scholars maintain its authenticity[102]. But in a fashion similar in kind if not to degree to

---

101 *NTS* 5 (1959) 91–102.
102 See the standard commentaries and introductions for positions, esp. M. Barth for authenticity. Further for authenticity, see J.N. Sanders, "The Case for the Pauline Authorship", *Studies in Ephesians*. Edit. F.L. Cross (London: A.R. Mowbray, 1956) 9–20; E. Percy, *Die Probleme der Kolosser - und Epheserbriefe* (Lund: Gleerup, 1946); *idem*, "Zu den Problemen des Kolosser - und Epheserbrief" (reply to Käsemann), *ZNW* 43 (1950–51) 178–194; R. Brown, "Ephesians Among the Letters of Paul", *RExp* 60 (1963) 373–379; L. Cerfaux, "En faveur de l'authenticité des épîtres de la captivité. Homogénéité doctrinale entre Éphesiens et les grandes épîtres", *Littérature et théologie pauliniennes*. No edit (Bruges: Desclée de Brouwer, 1960) 60–71; A. van Roon, *The Authenticity of Ephesians* (Leiden: E.J. Brill, 1974); G. Caird, *Paul's Letters From Prison* (Oxford: University Press, 1976) 11–29; J.B. Polhill, "An Introduction to Ephesians", *RExp* 76 (1979) 465–479. Against authenticity, see further C.L. Mitton, *The Epistle to the Ephesians. Its Authorship, Origin and Purpose* (Oxford: Clarendon Press, 1951); *idem*, "The Authorship of the Epistle to the Ephesians", *ET* 67 (1955–56) 195–198: D.E. Nineham, "The Case Against the Pauline Authorship", *Studies in Ephesians*

the arguments over the Pastorals, the evaluation of the evidence is often determined by theological rather than literary critical considerations.

It is generally agreed that the external evidence gives no support to an argument against authenticity. The major arguments are in the areas of vocabulary and style, historical setting, doctrine, and the relationship of Ephesians to Colossians.

The stylistic and lexical arguments point out that there is a significant difference between Ephesians and the rest of the Paulines. Ephesians contains 90 words that do not occur elsewhere in Paul. This difference is compounded when it is realized that many of these words replace more customary Pauline words or phrases, such as *diabolos* for Satan, and "in the heavenlies" for heaven. There is quite a difference in style as well. Ephesians has long, unwieldy sentences, a great many genitival constructions and linkage of synonyms, an excessive use of the preposition ἐν, and a general lack of common Pauline particles and prepositions. Defenders of authenticity have minimized these differences, resorting to the familiar explanations of co-authorship, secretaries, and changing *Sitz im Leben*. While it is in fact true that no one would want to build an entire case for inauthenticity on this argument, the differences are real and not easily explained away.

A much more weighty argument lies in the historical setting of Ephesians. Though the general nature of the letter prevents one from establishing specific historical allusions, the letter as a whole reflects a later, probably post-Pauline life setting. The central Pauline issue of inclusion of the Gentiles is long over. Indeed, if anything it is the Jews who now are in danger of exclusion. There is likewise a decided lack of emphasis on the imminent parousia. The doctrine is there (1:4; 4:30; 5:5; 6:13), but 3:21 makes it clear that the author expected to be around for a long time. The eschatology of Ephesians is "realized" to a degree not matched by the other Paulines[103].

Another substantial argument against authenticity lies in the area of doctrinal differences. Though ἐκκλησία for Paul means a local congregation, in Ephesians it always designates a universal body. The apostles and prophets are called "holy" (3:5), a veneration which seems unlikely on the lips of Paul. Similarly, the θεμέλιος imagery of the church is now based on the apostles (2:20) rather than Christ himself (1 Cor 3:3). In general there is a strong

---

(see above) 21–35; P.N. Harrison, "The Author of Ephesians", *StEv*, II, 595–604; E.J. Goodspeed, *The Meaning of Ephesians* (Chicago: University of Chicago Press, 1956); E. Schweizer, "Zur Frage der Echtheit des Kolosser- und Epheserbriefe", *ZNW* 47 (1956) 287; J.A. Allan, "The 'In Christ', Formula in Ephesians", *NTS* 5 (1958–59) 54–62; E. Käsemann, "Probleme der Kolosser und Epheserbriefe" (review of Percy), *Gnomen* 21 (1949) 342–347; R. Martin, "An Epistle in Search of a Life Setting", *ET* 79 (1968) 296–302. A helpful survey of literature to 1968 is found in J.C. Kirby, *Ephesians, Baptism, and Pentecost* (London: SPCK, 1968) 3–56.

103 R. Martin, "An Epistle", 301, cites C. Masson *L'Epître aux Ephesiens* (1953) 199, on Eph 4:15, "... Already united to Christ as the body to the head, the Church grows towards Christ; she no longer waits for Him to come to her."

ecclesiological stamp to the theology of Ephesians which represents a significant development beyond Paul.

The strongest argument against authenticity is the dependence of Ephesians upon Colossians. Even defenders of authenticity for the most part admit the priority of Colossians[104]. The question, however, lies in the nature of the relationship. About one third of the words in Colossians appear in Ephesians, but only 6:21f (Col 4:7) reveals any sustained sequence of similarity that points to literary borrowing. Defenders of authenticity explain this by saying that both letters were written by Paul in a very short space of time[105]. This explains the similar ideas without the direct literary borrowing. This would make a great deal of sense except for a fundamental flaw. As C.L. Mitton has demonstrated, Ephesians uses many of the words which it borrows from Colossians, such as μυστήριον and οἰκονομία, in a fundamentally different sense[106]. While it is likely that an author will reuse ideas within a short period of time, it is highly unlikely that he would change the meaning of so many in an equally short period. Even E. Percy recognizes this difficulty, and in attempting to answer it must deal with no less than twenty-five of what he calls "striking differences"[107]. The most logical explanation of the relationship of Ephesians to Colossians is that the author was so steeped in the literature and thought of Paul that he had no need to actually copy passages from a text. This explanation is strengthened by the fact that Ephesians has more fragmentary correspondence with the other Paulines than any other Pauline writings including Colossians[108].

Though one might quibble with certain of the arguments against authenticity above, and though it may be freely admitted that the force of evidence is not so decisive as the Pastorals, it does seem likely that these arguments carry the day. The real problem, however, is not in the evidence itself. No amount of evidence will prove decisive in the face of more fundamental objections. Thus it is instructive to note the three reasons that E. Percy gives for maintaining the Pauline authorship of Ephesians[109].

The first objection is that so much of the letter is fundamentally Pauline. While this should of course be true of an authentic letter of Paul, this is not the force of his objection. When he says, "der Verfasser ..., wenn er ein an-

---

104 Exceptions are J. Coutts, "The Relationship of Ephesians and Colossians", *NTS* 4 (1957–58) 201–207; possibly A. van Roon, *Authenticity*, 413–437. (He actually argues that both depend on an Ur-text or outline).

105 E.g. J.B. Polhill, "The Relationship Between Ephesians and Colossians", RExp 70 (1973) 439–450.

106 *Ephesians*, 84–86; "Authorship", 196. See also Kümmel, *Intro.*, 359–360.

107 *Probleme*, 379–418.

108 van Roon, *Authenticity*, 432ff., admits this, but tries to explain it away by reference to common catechetical tradition. For parallels between Ephesians, Colossians and the rest of the Paulines, see E.J. Goodspeed, *The Key to Ephesians* (Chicago: University Press, 1956) 1–75 (English text); and C.L. Mitton, *Ephesians*, 279–315 (Greek text).

109 As cited by Mitton, "Authorship", 196–197.

derer als der Apostel selbst ist, mit seinem Paulusverständnis in der ganzen nachpaulinischen christlichen Literatur vor Luther ganz allein stehen dürfte"[110], he is expressing an underlying assumption of many who oppose the idea of canonical pseudepigrapha: if an author writes a pseudonymous writing, he cannot be very bright[111]. This follows from a picture of the pseudonymous author as an "imitator" or epigonist, incapable of his own ideas. Not only is this image denied by certain brilliant figures in Jewish pesudepigraphy (2 Isaiah, Qoheleth), it is denied by the very basis of Jewish pseudepigraphy itself. It was precisely the purpose of the author to be in touch with the thoughts of his pseudonym: not just to "imitate" him, but to think his thoughts after him. If many pseudonymous authors were less than successful in the attempt, this is in itself no criterion for determining whether it was possible in any given instance.

The second objection is even more basic, that in 3:1ff. we have an explicit claim to Pauline authorship. As Mitton remarks, this represents an importation of modern literary values into a field where it is most inappropriate[112]. In our own investigation we have already demonstrated that the use of authorship can be a claim to authoritative tradition, and the specific role of the verses that Percy mentions will be discussed further below.

The third objection that Percy raises is a valid one. He remarks, "Es fehlt nämlich im Eph. jegliche Spur irgendeines besonderen Zweck, das es hätte begreiflich machen können, dass ein Christ der nachpaulinischen Zeit diesen Brief unter dem Namen des Apostels geschrieben hätte"[113]. Though one can disagree that no occasion *can* be found, it is true that some reason *needs* to be found for the pseudonymity of Ephesians. Of course, as H. Cadbury points out, it is incumbent on both sides of the authenticity issue to suggest a reason for its writing[114]. Before we can discuss the pseudonymity of Ephesians, then, we need to establish the problems that gave rise to it.

5.3.2.2 *The Occasion and Purpose of Ephesians*

The search for the occasion of Ephesians is greatly complicated by the fact that there are virtually no personal greetings or historical referents in the letter, apart from the references to Paul himself and Tychichus as the letter

---

110 *Probleme*, 356.
111 This is the force of J.N. Sanders argument, "The Case for", 19.
112 "Authorship", 197.
113 *Probleme*, 443.
114 "Dilemma", 96. Also R. Martin, "An Epistle", 297, who remarks that a description of Ephesians by defenders of authenticity as "a spiritual testament of Paul to the church" (J.N. Sanders), "a meditation on great Christian themes" (D. Guthrie) or "the quintessence of Paulinism" (F.F. Bruce) is inadequate. It leaves Ephesians without any specific historical occasion, which is without precedent among Paul's letters.

bearer, both part of the pseudepigraphical framework. The readers are Gentile (2:11), but that is about all we know. They have no first-hand knowledge of Paul (1:15; 3:2), but even this may be due to borrowing from the framework of Colossians. Some would question whether Ephesians is really a letter, but its epistolary form is well defined. This, of course, has no real bearings on whether the letter was actually "sent", or just "discovered" and shared with those who needed to hear its message. The praescript, ἐν Ἐφέσῳ, is no help either, since scholars are in virtually total agreement that this is not original[115]. There the agreement ends, for suggestions as to what really belongs there are as numerous as the publications which deal with it[116].

The only real option for determining the occasion of Ephesians lies in an examination of the themes and content of the letter. One peculiar feature is the strong contrast of "we" and "you" in the first two chapters. The most obvious explanation is that the author is identifying himself (as Paul) with Judaism. But the real question is, Why?

Goodspeed thinks that this is just a part of the framework of pseudonymity, and that the writer is a Gentile who slips and reveals his identity at 2:3[117]. There he identifies himself with his Gentile past by remarking, "we all once lived in the passions of our flesh". The *real* purpose of Ephesians is to introduce a newly formed collection of Paul's writings (spurred by a reading of Acts), a collection that is alluded to in 3:3f.[118]. Though this theory has had strong support in the past[119], it founders on three points. There is no evidence that Ephesians ever stood at the head of a Pauline canon, the priority of Acts to Ephesians is problematic, and Ephesians does not read like an introduction or summary. As for 2:3, this need not be read as the slip of a Gentile. In Galatians 4:9f., Paul refers to Judaizing as a return to the "weak and beggarly elemental spirits", and this type of thinking may well have promoted the author of Ephesians to identify pre-Christian Judaism in the same fashion, "like the rest of mankind" (Eph 2:3d).

Another suggestion for the purpose of the "we-you" formula of Ephesians is the so-called liturgical theory. Noting the paraenetic material relating to neo-

---

115 Both external and internal evidence are against it. It is not included in B, ℵ, 1793, or p[46], and it is inconsistent with the statement within the text that Paul has never seen the recipients (1:15; 3:2), since Paul was well-known at Ephesus.

116 Suggestions include "Laodicea" (after Marcion), "Asia", "one and faithful", as well as the unfounded "blank space" theory in support of Ephesians as an encyclical letter. See R. Batey, "The Destination of Ephesians", *JBL* 82 (1963) 101; J.P. Wilson, "Note on the Textual Problem of Ephesians 1:1", *ET* 60 (1948–49) 225–226; M. Santer, "The Texts of Ephesians I.1", *NTS* 15 (1969) 247–248; G. Zuntz, *The Text of the Epistles* (London: Oxford University Press, 1953) 228; n.1; A. Lindemann, "Bemerkungen zu den Addressaten und zum Anlass des Epheserbriefes", *ZNW* 67 (1976) 235–251; W. Kümmel, *Intro.*, 352–356; A. van Roon, *Authenticity*, 72–85; P.N. Harrison, "Ephesians", 602–604.

117 Goodspeed, *Key*, v.

118 See *Meaning*, 1–75.

119 Esp. A.E. Barnett, C.L. Mitton, W.L. Knox.

phytes in Ephesians, it has been suggested that the "letter" is really part of one or several baptismal homilies and/or liturgies, either by Paul or someone else[120]. The problem is that any "baptismal" references are most insubstantial, and much of the letter is simply too complex and diverse to be fitted into such a scheme.

H. Chadwick has done a service in pointing out the backward-looking nature of the "we-you" section, that is, its concern to trace back Christian foundations[121]. He tries to explain this by referring to crisis of identity among Gentile churches. In a culture that loved antiquity and based truth on age, the Gentile church had to explain how such a new phenomenon such as Christianity could be true. The apologetic answer of Ephesians was to demonstrate the great antiquity of Christianity through its Jewish roots, and by placing both Christ and the church in the sphere of eternity (the "heavenlies"). The value of Chadwick's thesis is that it demonstrates that Ephesians can be written for a specific occasion or situation but it does not have to be restricted to a local one. It is a "weite geistige Krise"[122]. But though the proof of its antiquity was in fact a feature of Judaism in its apologetic encounter with paganism, this does not seem to be the moving factor in Ephesians. Apologetic literature is not this subtle, and the recipients do not seem threatened by any outside criticism in this regard. The concern of the author is not so much with the antiquity of the Christian faith as its Jewishness. That the author's interest in Judaism lies beyond a mere platform for the sake of apologetic is shown by the numerous contacts that Ephesians has with the language and thought of Qumran[123]. In light of this it is likely that he was in fact a Jew.

It must also be said, however, that this interest of the author in Judaism and the relation of Jews and Gentiles is more theological than practical. That is, there is no evidence of any actual conflict between Jewish and Gentile Christian groups. The most basic conflict of Paul's day, the inclusion of the Gentiles without circumcision or the law, seems past and forgotten. This is shown by the failure to mention works of the law in the restatement of Paul's doctrine of justification (2:8–9). Indeed, the recipients need to be reminded that there was a time when they stood outside God's grace and covenant (2: 12). Though hostility is mentioned (2:14), it seems to reflect more an attitude or state of mind on the part of the recipients. It is unlikely that they had any substantial contact with Jewish Christians. This is shown by the author's

---

120 R.A. Wilson, "'We', and 'You' in the Epistle to the Ephesians", *StEv*, II, 676–680; J.C. Kirby, *Ephesians.*

121 "Die Absicht des Epheserbrief", *ZNW* (1960) 143–153.

122 *Ibid.,* 152.

123 See K.G. Kuhn, "The Epistle to the Ephesians in Light of the Qumran Texts", *Paul and Qumran.* Edit. J. Murphy - O'Connor (London: G. Chapman, 1968) 115– 131. But the use of household codes and familiarity with Hellenistic thought make it unlikely that he was a Palestinian Jew. For further bibliography on Ephesians and Qumran, see M. Barth, *Ephesians,* I (New York: Doubleday, 1974) 405–406.

need to "instruct" them in the basic attitudes of pre-Christian Judaism[124]. This does not mean, however, that their attitude was one of benign neglect, or that Judaism had no place in their thinking. The hostility motif (2:14,16) indicates conscious ill will on their part[125].

How could this state of affairs have come about? Certainly the seeds of conflict are present in Judaism itself, in the bitter invective that its rival groups hurled at each other (e.g. Qumran). The gospel tradition is full of similar invective. The Pharisees and other religious leaders are roundly condemned[126]. By the time of John (and Acts) "the Jews" has become a general term for the enemies of Jesus (5:18; 6:41; 8:57ff.; 10:31). Perhaps because of a desire to distance itself from a Judaism that had increasingly deteriorating relations with Rome, the Lukan writings seek to exonerate the Romans and thus place even more blame on the Jews for the death of Jesus. The rejection of Jesus by the Jews came more and more to be regarded as a forfeiture of their divine privileges. "Therefore I tell you, the kingdom of God will be taken away from you and given to a nation producing the fruits of it." (Matt 21:43).

Anti-semitism could have grown among the Pauline mission as well. The havoc caused by the Judaizers would certainly have caused a great deal of ill will, and the invective that Paul pours out against them (e.g. Gal 5:12) could easily have spilled over by his followers into a general attitude toward Judaism. Even Paul's writings could easily be interpreted to mean that the Gentile church *was* Israel as opposed to part of it (together with the Jews). J. Munck demonstrates how Paul's citation of Isaiah 54:1 in Galatians 4:27 is used by later church writers to exult over the growth of the Gentile church in contrast to the stagnation of the Jewish church, the implication being that the *Gentiles* are the child of Sarah[127].

---

124 For instance, they are reminded of the circumcision issue (2:11) "at one time you Gentiles in the flesh, called the uncircumcision by what is called the circumcision". Even the terminology seems foreign to them. W. Kümmel, *Intro.*, 364, rightly rejects W. Grundmann's suggestion in "Die NHΠΙΟΙ in der urchristlichen ·Paränese", *NTS* 5 (19 58–59) 194, n.1, that behind Ephesians is tension caused by migrating Jewish Christians fleeing from the Jewish wars. Similarly unconvincing is D.C. Smith, "The Ephesian Heresy and the Origin of the Epistle to the Ephesians", *Ohio Journal of Religious Studies* 5 (1977) 78–103, who argues that the problem stems from Gentile converts to a speculative variety of Judaism, who later become Christians and continue to stir up arrogance toward mainline Judaism.

125 For this reason A. Lindemann's conclusions ("Bemerkungen") are too negative. Since he cannot detect any trace of actual conflict between Jewish and Gentile elements in Ephesians, he maintains that the author is not Jewish, and the entire discussion of Jew/Gentile relations has nothing to do with racial relations or salvation-history, but is just a theological foil or literary technique to address the problem of disunity within an entirely Gentile church.

126 J. Munck, "Israel and the Gentiles in the New Testament", *JThS* 2 (1951) 13, cites from Matthew: "evil and faithless generation" (12:39; 16:4; 17:17), "hardening of hearts" (13:13–17), "den of thieves" (21:13), "woe" (21:23).

127 *Ibid.*, 14. He cites 2 Clem 2:1–3; Justin, Apol 53:5; Clement of Alex, Protr 9:2f.; Strom ii 28.

There were three ways in which the Gentiles began to supplant Jewish Christians[128]. First, as was seen, they took over the gospel traditions, and regarded Jesus' work as essentially directed to the Gentiles. Second, the Gentile church took over the Jewish scriptures as its Bible. Now this was done from the beginning, but in the later stages it ceased to be a Jewish book. Even the OT promises could be seen as made to (Gentile) Christians, not Jews[129]. Third, a separate tack from the first two stages was to separate the gospel tradition and Gentile Christianity from Judaism and the Jewish scriptures.

This came to classic expression in the gnosticism of Marcion, but its roots are much earlier. Doubly significant is that among such groups the predominant authority figure is Paul and his writings.

With this historical understanding of the rise of anti-Semitism in the early church, particularly among the Pauline communities, it becomes possible to regard the "we-you" section of Ephesians in a clearer light. Käsemann remarks, "The letter betrays its historical setting precisely here. What Paul mentioned hypothetically in Romans 11:17ff. has happened here: Jewish Christianity is pushed aside and despised by the steadily growing Gentile Christianity"[130]. This explains the predominant use of συν compounds in these chapters. The author is reminding the Gentiles that they *share* in salvation with Jewish believers. It is not that they need reminding that they are recipients of the OT promises, but that they are partners with the Jews in those promises. So the tables are turned, and "Paul", who had defended the right of Gentiles to be Gentiles in the church, now supports the right of Jews to be Jews (cf. 1 Cor 7:17ff.). Since the problem had arisen among his communities, and may well have used his writings as supports for their beliefs, it was incumbent upon "Paul" to correct the situation, by an application or reinterpretation of Pauline theology to the problem of the day.

It must be said, however, that the fundamental concern of the author does not lie in the theoretical level. He is concerned not merely with attitudes, but actions, and knows that this distortion of theological perception has had in fact many consequences, not limited to Gentile/Jewish relations. This is shown by the fact that the "we-you" section is really only part of a larger theme of unity. that expresses itself in a number of different ways in Ephesians. Throughout the letter there is evidence that the community is rife with problems of division and abberant behaviour. There is concern that some are lapsing into a pre-Christian moral state (4:17ff.). There are also signs of division, not only among church members (4,2,3), but also insinuating itself into the marriage relationship (5:21–33).

---

128 *Ibid.,* 14–15.
129 *Ibid.* He cites Epist Barnabas 13:1: "Let us now see whether this people (the Christian church) or the first people (the Jews) receive the inheritance, and whether the covenant is intended for us or for them".
130 "Ephesians and Acts", *Studies in Luke - Acts.* Edit. L. Keck and J. Martyn (London: SPCK, 1968) 291. See also "Epheserbrief", *RGG*3 II, 518–519.

Many have suggested that Ephesians was written to counteract heresy, specifically gnosticism. Yet others point out that Ephesians, which is heavily dependent on Colossians, omits all of the Colossian references to this type of heresy, and the high Christological statements that are used to counter them[131]. This criticism can be answered, however. There is mention of false teaching in the letter (4:14; 5:6). No specific mention is made of their identity or doctrines, and no overt effort is made to rebut them. The main counsel is to *avoid* them (5:7). In this, Ephesians is exactly like the Pastorals, and thus demonstrates a fundamentally different method of dealing with heresy, characteristic of a later era. Both emphasize instead the unity of the orthodox, apostolic church, though the Pastorals place more emphasis on the visible church, and Ephesians on the invisible. However muted the references, it seems clear that at least some of the problems of the letter stem from false teaching.

Whether that false teaching is best described as "gnosticism" is, however, another issue[132]. We simply do not know enough about the nature of the false teaching and practices in Ephesians. The debate still rages over whether the christology and ecclesiology of Ephesians can be regarded as deriving from and/or reacting to gnostic sources[133]. In light of this it is best to take the approach of J. Gnilka and say that Ephesians is written to counter the syncretistic, individualistic, and ahistorical influence of the popular Hellenistic religions near the turn of the century[134].

We have now mentioned anti-Semitism, false teaching, divisions, and moral laxity as part of the occasion for Ephesians. But how do these all relate? They all represent a fundamental threat to the identity and integrity of the Pauline communities. When Paul was alive, he maintained the unity of his churches by the force of his own person. But after his death, a great many forces would have been at work to dissolve those communities:

1. *Relation to Judaism* – As long as Paul was alive, there was little danger of a split with Judaism. But after his death, there was little incentive to maintain contact with Hebrew Christians. This was exacerbated by the destruction of Jerusalem and dispersal of the Palestinian Christians. The decline of the Jewish church confirmed the latent prejudices of Paul's followers.

2. *Relation to Hellenistic religions* – But in losing its grip on its Jewishness, Pauline Christianity also began to lose its grip on its distinctiveness. It was in danger of becoming one mystery religion among many. This especially laid it open to the influence of other religious thinking or false teaching, and Paul was no longer there to defend against it.

131 So K. Fischer, *Tendenz und Absicht des Epheserbriefes* (Göttingen: Vandenhoeck and Ruprecht, 1973) 14–15.

132 See P. Pekorný, *Der Epheserbrief und die Gnosis* (Berlin, 1965) 21. "Der Epheserbrief ist in der Auseinandersetzung mit der judaistischen Gnosis geschrieben".

133 For a history of the debate up to 1960, see C. Colpe, "Der Leib-Christi-Vorstellung im Epheserbreif", *Judentum, Urchristentum, Kirche*. Fest. J. Jeremias. Edit. W. Eltester (BZNW 26. Berlin: A. Töpelmann, 1960) 172–187. For further bibliography, see M. Barth, *Ephesians*, II, 404–405.

134 *Der Epheserbrief* (Freiburg: Herder, 1971) 45–49.

3. *Relation to each other* — This lack of distinctiveness easily led to a further indivi-
dualizing of the experience of salvation. Cut off from the Jewish appreciation of
corporate participation and responsibility, the Pauline communities were in danger
of fragmenting. A further result was a corresponding lack of concern for ethics.
When Paul's law-free gospel was separated from a Jewish understanding of the
moral demands of God (cf. Rom 3:1ff.), it was readily prone to licentiousness.

We can see then, that all of the problems of Ephesians stem from one fundamental problem: the loss of Paul as a unifying source of authority. The answer to Ephesians is an attempt to reintroduce the dynamic Pauline tension
of Jew and Gentile, faith and works, group and individual, by a comprehensive reinterpretation and application of Pauline tradition to the problem of
unity. The justification for the accomplishment of that task is now the subject of our further investigation.

5.3.2.3 *The Role of Paul in Ephesians*

As in the Pastorals, the letter of Ephesians regards Paul as an archetypical
figure, in both teaching and ethics. The apostle cannot be separated from his
tradition. We see this imagery foremost in the parenthetical insertion about
Paul's role in Ephesians 3:2–13. Not only is Paul's unique authority stressed,
but it is done so in a way that promotes the maximum continuity between
the apostle and his later followers. Thus Paul's place as the primary "apostle
to the Gentiles" is stressed (3:2), and as such is the one who serves as a source
of community-creating identity (3:2,8). These references are obviously an
allusion to Paul's own self-perceived role. (cf. Gal 1:12, 15–16). Yet even
here there is a distinctive emphasis. Whereas Paul's primary role was defined
in terms of evangelism, here the emphasis is more on his role as receiver and
guardian of the mystery (3:3,9; cf. 1:9). As Fischer puts it, "Paul appears
less as missionary than as mystagogue"[135]. This reflects the post-apostolic
Sitz im Leben of Ephesians: "The problem of Ephesians is no longer primarily missions, but the preservation of the unity of the church"[136]. Just as
the Pastorals stressed their continuity with Paul in terms of his role as teacher, here we have the continuity expressed in terms of the stewardship of mysteries.

Actually μυστήριον is singular, and not without significance. This itself
is an expression of the fundamental concern of Ephesians. Though it may
have many applications, there is in fact only *one* mystery, which indicates
the essential unity of the plan and will of God. This concern also explains
the distinctive use of the phrase, "holy apostles and prophets" in Ephesians
(3:5; cf. 2:20; 4:11). Defenders of authenticity have been hard put to explain
the veneration of foundational figures that this implies, but they also are
quick to point out that these phrases (cf. also 1:9f.) indicate that Paul was

---

135 *Tendez*, 99.
136 *Ibid.*

not regarded as the sole recipient of the mystery[137]. This is in fact true, but has no bearing on authenticity. Since the concern of Ephesians is to reintroduce the Pauline continuity with Judaism, it is natural that Paul's gospel would be identified with the gospel given to all the "apostles and prophets". The author of Acts accomplishes a similar task by placing the account of Peter's revelation about the centurion and defence of Gentile evangelism (Acts 10 and 11) after Paul's conversion (Acts 9) but before Paul's missionary journeys (Acts 13ff.). Similarly Paul himself, though he stresses his unique apostleship to the Gentiles (Gal 1:16; 2:7–8), also maintains a basic continuity of his gospel with that of Jerusalem (Gal 2:2). Given that the *Sitz im Leben* of Ephesians may reflect a Paulinism that had lost its Jewish roots, it is only natural that the author would reintroduce a similar theme of a universal gospel, while all the while making it clear that for his community Paul was the primary recipient and guardian of that tradition. Indeed, he may even be making a larger claim, to the effect that Paul is the foremost (though not exclusive) figure for the universal church (cf. Eph 3:9, "to make all men see what is the plan of the mystery"), a claim not unsimilar to that of many Protestants today.

In any case, in Ephesians the mystery is no longer given to all the saints (cf. Col 1:26,27), but to special representative figures. The apostles and prophets, Paul foremost among them, had become part of the tradition. Their role was unrepeatable and irreplaceable. This "canon-consciousness" of the apostolic role extends not only to the figure of the apostle, but to his literature as well. This is not to assert with Goodspeed that Ephesians serves as an introduction to a Pauline canon, a canon he thinks is alluded to in 3:3b[138]. However, while one cannot build too much on the enigmatic καθὼς προέγραψα ἐν ὀλίγῳ, it obviously refers to something. προγράφω can mean to write before in another document (cf. Rom 15:4; 1 Cor 5:9), to write above in the same document (cf. 1 Pet 5:2), or to write publicly (cf. Gal 3:1). The last alternative is unlikely here. A large number of scholars opt for the second alternative, that the writer is referring to the mystery (Eph 1:9–10) mentioned earlier in the letter (so, Robinson, Abbott, M. Barth, Westcott). Certainly this interpretation is grammatically and contextually possible. But though μυστήριον is mentioned earlier, it does seem rather artificial and unnecessary to refer to it in such a manner as Ephesians 3:3b. Since it is Paul's special role (as opposed to the more general 1:9) as apostle to the Gentiles that is in view here, it seems more likely that "as I have written briefly" refers to a previous writing of Paul's which also mentions his role. Nor is this alternative dependent on an assumption of non-Pauline authorship, since Paul does refer to material in previous letters (1 Cor 5:9–11; 2 Cor 2:3–4)[139].

---

137 See E. Percy, "Zu den Problemen", 189–190.
138 *Key*, x; *Meaning*, 42–45. However, that a whole body of writings is intended in 3:3 is ruled out by the adverbial clause ἐν ὀλίγῳ.
139 E.g. see L. Davies, "I write afore in few words. Eph iii 3", *ET* 46 (1934–35) 568, who thinks it is *Paul* alluding to Rom 16:25–27.

Though other passages might be proposed (e.g. Rom 16:25–27; Gal 1: 12ff.; 2 Cor 12:1ff.), it is likely that Ephesians 3:3b refers to the mystery mentioned in Colossians 1:26, since Ephesians 3:1–13 is heavily dependent on Colossians 1:23–29[140]. This suggestion is strengthened by the overall dependence of Ephesians on Colossians as well. If so, this is an indication that Paul's writings as well as his person and oral teaching had become part of the tradition. In the same manner as the Pastorals, though not to the same degree, even the literary expression of Pauline tradition was becoming fixed. It was recognized that authoritative Pauline tradition was expressed by Pauline letters.

Yet the recognition of the "canonical" value of Paul's writings did not signal their restriction to a fixed body. That they were considered foundational but not adequate is signalled by 3:4. The πρὸς ὅ is a rare expression that literally means "after the measure of which". A similar use of πρός with relative pronoun is found in 2 Corinthians 5:10, and means "according to, with reference to"[141]. The present participle ἀναγινώσκοντες makes it likely that the "reading" is not of a past document (which would require an aorist) but in fact refers to the present letter. *The intent of 3:4, then, is most likely to commend Ephesians as a further interpretation of the mystery that was mentioned briefly in an earlier Pauline letter.* "When you read this letter you can understand my insight into the mystery of Christ, which I wrote about briefly earlier" is the essential intent of 3:3b, 4. *As such this is a foundational statement of the principle of Vergegenwärtigung that we have noted elsewhere, and serves as a programmatic note to the whole purpose of this pseudonymous writing.*

Further collaboration of this can be seen in the principal theme of interpretation and understanding of the mystery that is found elsewhere in Ephesians. In Ephesians 1:17, Paul's prayer for the Ephesians is that God "may give you a spirit of wisdom and of revelation in the knowledge of him, having eyes of your hearts enlightened." This prayer is repeated in 3:14ff., "that he might grant you to be strengthened with might through his Spirit in the inner man ... that you ... may have power to comprehend with all the saints what is the breadth and length and height and depth ..."[142]. This theme and its connection with the Spirit shows that the author had a unitary understanding of tradition and revelation. No new mystery could be given. Only the apostles and prophets stood at the head of tradition. Yet because of the commonality of the Spirit, it was certainly possible to better understand the apostolically entrusted mystery.

This is precisely the intent of Ephesians, and it takes its cue from the document upon which it depends the most: Colossians. In Colossians 2:1–6, Paul is dealing with a community that he cannot visit, and that does not

---

140 See C.L. Mitton, *Ephesians* (NCB. Greenword, SC: Attic Press, 1976) 118: *idem,*
     Epistle, 291–295; E.J. Goodspeed, *Key,* 26–32.
141 M. Barth, *Ephesians,* I, 330.
142 See also 4:13f., 5:17, 18.

know him face to face. His desire is that they "have all the riches of assured understanding and the knowledge of God's mystery, of Christ". To that end he writes Colossians as a substitute for his apostolic presence (v.5) and in it calls them to hold fast to the traditions they received. This is exactly the agenda of Ephesians, and probably explains why it depends as heavily on Colossians. *The author of Ephesians wanted to promote the insight into the mystery that Paul himself desired, by using the same means that Paul himself used*[143].

But the insight itself is different in Ephesians from Colossians. This only makes sense, since if Colossians spoke directly to the needs of the "Ephesian" community, no *Vergegenwärtigung* would be needed. This explains why Ephesians is not a slavish imitation of Colossians, but a creative extrapolation and interpretation. Nowhere is this more clear than in the key term they share: μυστήριον. In Colossians, the focus of concern is primarily christological. Small wonder, then, that the μυστήριον in Colossians is Christ (Col 1:26–27; 2:2; 4:3). But the concern in Ephesians is different. Its interest is primarily ecclesiology. It comes as no surprise, then, that μυστήριον in Ephesians is related to the doctrine of the universal church, particularly its unity (Eph 1:9; 3:3,4,9; 5:32; 6:19).

This does not mean that μυστήριον in Ephesians is unrelated to its meaning in Colossians and elsewhere in Paul. Christology and ecclesiology are closely related in Ephesians, and it is particularly the cosmic aspect of the mystery (1:9) which facilitates a discussion of the mystery of the church as the one body of Christ. Similarly, Paul's use of "mysteries" to designate his apostolic ministry (1 Cor 4:1), especially the inclusion of the Gentiles in God's salvation (Col 1:27; Rom 16:25) is not inconsistent with what we find in Ephesians. It is just that μυστήριον is now related to a different *Sitz im Leben*. Rather than emphasizing Paul's revelation of a law free-gospel, and thereby the freedom of Gentiles *from* Judaism (or Jewish law), the μυστήριον of Ephesians 3:3,4,9; 6:19 is a proclamation of the unity of Gentiles *with* Jews. This does not contradict the former meaning, but is a reinterpretation of it to a new situation, when the problem was no longer inclusion of the Gentiles, but exclusion of the Jews. This is especially seen in 3:6, which explicitly describes the mystery as the Gentiles being συγκληρονόμα (co-heirs"), σύσσωμα ("co-incorporate") and συμμέτοχα ("co-participants").

---

143 The use of "mystery" in Ephesians has obvious parallels in the Qumran literature as well, but it is difficult to say if the influence is direct or if mediated through Paul and/or early Christianity. See further, M. Barth, *Ephesians*, I, 19–20; R.E. Brown, "The Semitic Background of the New Testament Mysterion (II)", *Bib* 40 (1959) 70–87 (reprinted by Philadelphia: Fortress Press, 1968); J. Coppens, "'Mystery' in the theology of Saint Paul and its parallels at Qumran", *Paul and Qumran*. Edit. J. Murphy - O'Connor (London: G. Chapman, 1968) 132–158; F. Mussner, "Contributions Made by Qumran to the Understanding of the Epistle to the Ephesians", *idem*, 159–163; K.G. Kuhn, "The Epistle to the Ephesians in Light of the Qumran Texts", *idem*, 118–119; C.C. Caragounis, *The Ephesian Mysterion, Meaning and Content* (Lund: Gleerup, 1977) 129–133.

However, as was noted earlier above, the concern of Ephesians is not solely with Jew/Gentile relations or even specific racial tensions. As a "wider spiritual crisis" it is reacting to the fragmentation of Pauline communities due to the loss of Paul. Because of this it does not limit the application of the mystery to the unity of Jew and Gentile. Indeed, the author begins at an even more fundamental level and affirms that the mystery begins with the plan[144] of God to unite (or reunite) all of creation in Christ (1:9–10). In the first three chapters of Ephesians the author seeks to re-establish the depth of the Paulinism of his communities, by reminding them of the central concern of Jewish salvation history: that the Creator might reconcile an estranged creation to himself, especially his foremost creation, man made in the image of God (Gen 1:26). *Both* Jew and Gentile are part of this plan, "that he might create in himself one new man ... and might reconcile us both to God." (2: 15, 16).

It is only after re-establishing the depth of the mystery and Paul's place in it that he is able to bring it to bear on the more immediate needs of his community: divisions within the church. It may well be that the experience of the Spirit had led them to make claims of liberation and independence (cf. 1 Cor 1–4). "Paul" thus reminds them that the Spirit-filled insight into the mystery leads to unity, not division: "maintain the unity of the Spirit ... there is one body and one Spirit ... " (4:3–4). This mystery of unity applies even to the relationship of individuals within the church, or smaller "institutions" within it, such as marriage. This is why the author can refer to the marriage union as "the great mystery ... Christ and the church" (5:32).

If Paul's role as recipient and guardian of the mystery of unity is emphasized in Ephesians, it is not done so only on an intellectual level. As in the Pastorals (and in Paul!), we see that the apostolic teaching or doctrine cannot be separated from his person. Just as Paul is a paradigm for teaching, so also is he a paradigm for praxis. We see this in Ephesians in the "larger than life" dimensions of Paul's role. In 3:8 he describes himself as "least of the saints", and thereby becomes a source of identification and emulation by the weakest Christian brother. This is based on 1 Corinthians 15:9, "least of the apostles", and represents a tendency to portray Paul's pre-Christian past in every darker terms[145]. The implication is that the apostle's life begins at the lowest point of sin and reaches the highest point of grace, so that no one might feel excluded from experiencing similar blessing[146].

---

144 οἰκονομία is used distinctively in Ephesians to refer to this plan (1:9; 3:2,9), and is virtually equivalent to μυστήριον (3:9). This is different than the Paulines, where οἰκουμία is used to refer to Paul's stewardship or commission (1 Cor 9:17; Col 1: 25).

145 See Luke's account of Paul in Acts; 1 Tim 1:15. See also Fischer, *Tendenz*, 95–98. He notes that even the word "least" is heightened from the comparative ἐλάχιστος in 1 Cor 15:9 to ελαχιστότερος in Eph 3:8.

146 Epist Barnabas 5:9, "And when He chose His own apostles who were to proclaim His gospel, that He might show that He came not to call the righteous but sinners *who were sinners above every sin"* (Lightfoot translation, italics mine).

Even more important is the post-conversion lifestyle of the apostle, and its relation to the *Sitz im Leben* of Ephesians. An important part of the apostolic vocation is *suffering* (Eph 3:1, 13; 4:1; 6:20), a suffering that almost takes on redemptive overtones (cf. 2 Tim 2:10; 4:6). This idea may be traced to Paul himself (2 Cor 4:10–12; Col 1:24). In any case, the lifestyle cannot be separated from the revelation of the mystery: "Die Leiden des Apostels werden als theologisch notwendig erkannt, um das zu verkundigende Mysterium ausmacht"[147]. Just as God's mystery of unity was accomplished by the death of his Son (2:16), so the revelation and proclamation of that mystery is accomplished by a similar lifestyle (6:19–20). The Ephesians' experience of the Spirit ought not to lead them to triumphalism, but to resolute suffering for the sake of the gospel (6:10–18).

It may be too strong to depict Ephesians as a testament, but the choice of the phrase "a prisoner of Jesus Christ (3:1; cf. Col 1:23; Phlm 1,9) shows that the author was identifying with a specific period in Paul's life, his last imprisonment. The author may have looked upon his work, then, as an attempt to secure the heritage of Paul after his passing. In that sense the pseudepigraphic framework of the letter is quite understandable.

The "universal" outlook and intent may also explain why there is almost no personal information in the letter. Though we do have an image of the suffering Paul, there is none of the elaborate historical allusions of the Pastorals, nor a specific call to imitate Paul. This is because the letter is not modelled on one to an exclusive Pauline community, but to one that has never met him face to face (1:15; 3:2; cf. Col 2:1). For that reason the call is to imitate God, not Paul (5:1; cf. Rom 15:7; Col 3:13). Now it may be that all of this is dictated by the close dependence on Colossians, a choice made, as we have seen, for other theological reasons. But it may also be possible that even the framework of the letter suits the purpose of the author. He may well be writing to communities who hold Paul as *an* authority but not as *the* authority, as in the Pastorals. In that case he could not make his appeal so personal. At the very least the framework of the letter serves very well its universal, "catholic" intent.

5.3.2.4 *Tradition and Literary Attribution in Ephesians*

We have seen that behind the pseudonymity of Ephesians lies a community in danger of fragmentation due to internal and external pressures after the death of their authority figure, Paul. Ephesians can be seen as a creative attempt to secure the Pauline heritage of these communities and to relate it to the church at large, by the actualization of the apostolic doctrine and

---

147 H. Merklein, "Paulinische Theologie in der Rezeption des Kolosser- und Epheserbriefes", *Paulus in den neutestamentlichen Spätschriften*. Edit. K. Kertelge (Freiburg: Herder, 1981) 30.

lifestyle. Yet this concern and this justification is denied by some. Most vociferous in his objections is D. Penny. After surveying how Ephesians uses Pauline themes and material, he concludes:

> In summary, Ephesians is not simply an attempt to transcribe Pauline theology for a new generation. Certainly the author has an interest in some Pauline themes: Christology, justification by faith, dying and rising with Christ, the *Charismata,* ecclesiology. But these themes are not presented for their own sake as summaries of Paul. Rather, the author has his own concerns, which are related primarily to the understanding of the church and especially to the relationship of Jewish and Gentile Christians in it ...[148].

Penny's use of words like "simply", "transcribe", and "summary" reveal a total lack of appreciation for how tradition was in fact actualized in Judaism and Christianity. Like Speyer, he would reject any *ausserliterarische Absicht* as inconsistent with legitimate pseudonymity[149]. Thus he rejects the idea of the pseudonymity of Ephesians as an "innocent deference to the master whose thought it presents"[150], and regards it as similar to other tendentious literature of the period. But as we have seen, the actualization of tradition is always related to the needs of the community, and often takes place in the midst of controversy over the proper interpretation of that tradition. It never displays a purely literary interest that would result in the production of a revised edition of Paul similar to Ardnt and Gingrich's (and Danker's) revision of Bauer's lexicon[151]. Ephesians is an occasional document, with its own agenda, but this does not detract from its serious effort to resolve a crisis by a fundamental actualization of Pauline thought and example.

Perhaps a more serious objection might be that the author of Ephesians is not so much interested in the wider application of Pauline theology as in the "Paulinization" of traditional material and contemporary philosophical concepts[152]. It is certainly true that Ephesians (like the Pastorals) makes use of non-Pauline materials. But the process of *Vergegenwärtigung* is never restricted to the original ideas and/or material of the founder of the tradition. It is always a creative weaving of old and new. Thus "interpretation of Paul" and "Paulinization of (other) traditional material" are not *ipso facto* mutually exclusive. How well they are combined is, of course, a matter of judgement. In this regard it might be instructive to look at how the author of Ephesians relates Pauline tradition and his own concerns in a treatment of justification, *Charismata,* and marriage.

---

148 *Deutero-Pauline,* 258. Cf. esp. 247–258.
149 W. Speyer, *Die Literarische Falschung im Altertum* (Munchen: C.H. Beck, 1971) 28.
150 Penny, *Deutero-Pauline,* 275–276.
151 This is exactly what Penny has in mind when he objects that Ephesians does not exhibit "a simple interest in updating Paul" (266), or that it does not represent "the kind of linear development and across-the-board reinterpretation of Paul which would in itself make the Pauline pseudonym self-evident." (248).
152 So H. Merklein, "Paulinische".

Though the statement of Ephesians 2:8–9 has been called the "quintessence of Paulinism"[153], there are in fact some significant differences. Resonance with Paul can certainly be found in the themes of grace (cf. Rom 3:24; 11:6), faith (Gal 2:16), gift (Rom 3:24), no boasting (Rom 3:27; 1 Cor 1: 28–31)[154]. Two major differences, however, stand out. First, in verse eight it is not the characteristic Pauline word δικαιόω that is associated with grace and faith, but σώζω. Though justification and salvation are at times nearly equated in Paul (cf. Rom 10:10), the most characteristic attitude of the apostle is that justification is present and salvation is future[155]. Here we have a more "realized" approach to soteriology/eschatology, which is characteristic of Ephesians, but it can also be regarded as making more explicit certain implicit Pauline ideas (cf. esp. Col 3:1–2; also Gal 4:26; 1 Cor 15:47–49; 2 Cor 12:2,3)[156]. Likewise the switch from justification to salvation terminology may be regarded as an attempt to make Pauline doctrine more meaningful to Gentiles whose grasp of Jewish legal ideas was limited.

Second, Ephesians 2:9 does not use the distinctive Pauline phrase "works of the law", but merely says "not by works". This generalization takes the issue away from the historical Judaizing/circumcision debate of Paul's time and applies it to the wider concern of any human effort. It can be regarded as an attempt to make Paul's doctrine applicable to a Gentile congregation which suffered no temptation to Judaize, but was in danger of regarding its salvation as needing the supplementation of human effort (cf. 2 Tim 1:9; Titus 3:5). The goal is no different than Paul's: "lest any man should boast" (Eph 2:9b; cf. Rom 3:27; 1 Cor 1:28–31). This is *precisely* the *Sitz im Leben* that we have described for Ephesians: a Gentile Christianity in danger of fragmentation from Judaism and within itself, open to the dangers of syncretism and self-exaltation (cf. Rom 11:18).

In Ephesians 4:1–16, we have a treatment of church order and the use of gifts that in many ways is reminiscent of Romans 12:1–8 and 1 Corinthians 12, particularly in the model of the church as a body (of Christ), and the concern for unity in the midst of diversity. Yet the author of Ephesians also displays some distinctive emphases[157]. While Paul does have a concept of a universal church, it is fair to say that his body imagery and even the term ἐκκλησία are always directed toward the local church. In Ephesians, however, the concern is solely with the universal church. Similarly, though unity is certainly one of Paul's concerns, in Ephesians it becomes of paramount importance. Even more significantly, though in Paul apostles and prophets

---

153 F.F. Bruce, "St. Paul in Rome: 4. The Epistle to the Ephesians", *BJRL* 49 (1967) 307f., using a phrase from A.S. Peake.
154 See C.L. Mitton, *Ephesians,* 13–14.
155 A. Lincoln, "Ephesians 2:8–10. A Summary of Paul's Gospel?", *CBQ* 45 (1983) 620. He cites Rom 5:9 as typical; "having been justified ... we shall be saved".
156 *Ibid.,* 621–622.
157 See esp. H.J. Klauck, "Das Amt in der Kirche nach Eph. 4, 1–16", *WiWei* 36 (1973) 81–110.

are contemporary figures, in Ephesians they belong to the past. This implies a foundational leadership that can be followed, but not repeated[158]. Finally, the key perspective of Ephesians is revealed in the list of gifts. Whereas in Paul the χαρίσματα are delineated as a hodge-podge of moral/spiritual qualities and administrative functions, in Ephesians the "gifts" are all official (4:11). In fact "gifts" (χαρίσματα) are not really even mentioned. Rather it is *people*, or more specifically, past and present leaders who are "given" (ἔδωκεν) to the church.

This priority given to the *unity* of the *universal* church, guaranteed by the supervision of "official" leaders, nowhere finds such forceful expression in Paul. It can be seen that these emphases relate directly to the central concern of Ephesians: to resist the fragmentation of the community by emphasizing a central authority. Though some would criticize this "early catholicism" as a betrayal of Paul's charismatic ecclesiology, this need not be the case. The purpose of the leaders is to supervise the practice of the *charismata*, not replace them. They are to "equip the saints for the work of the ministry" (4:12)[159]. A similar sort of supervisory priority is implicit in the order of the Pauline list in 1 Corinthians 12:28ff. Likewise, the "offices" of Ephesians 4:11, though more rigidly defined, must still be regarded as charismatic, as witnessed by the divine agency (ἔδωκεν). The ecclesiology of Ephesians 4:1–16, then, demonstrates a conscious attempt to highlight and extrapolate Pauline tradition for a new situation.

The teaching on marriage in Ephesians 5:21–33 is widely regarded as the most distinctly un-Pauline portion of the book, even by defenders of authenticity. Here it must be freely admitted that the author does not attempt to draw on Pauline tradition. But he does draw upon a more fundamental source of authority, the Jewish scriptures. J.P. Sampley has demonstrated that this passage is grounded in Jewish tradition, specifically Genesis 2:24; Leviticus 19:18, and the concept of the sacred marriage of Yahweh and Israel[160]. Since a fundamental feature of Ephesians is its concern to preserve the Jewish roots of Gentile Christianity, and it does so by stressing Paul's Jewishness, the treatment of marriage can be regarded as an attempt to associate Paul with the relevant Jewish tradition, a tradition which he would have affirmed. Here we have a demonstration of the configurational supplementation of (Pauline) tradition which we discussed earlier, which in the eyes of the author, at least, need not be regarded as anti-Pauline or an abandonment of Pauline tradition.

A thorough examination of the contents of Ephesians in search of its

---

158 Klauck, *ibid.,* 97–98, thinks that Eph 3:11 intends that evangelists should replace apostles (cf. Rev 21:8; 2 Tim 4:5), and that pastor-teachers should replace prophets.

159 Admittedly the meaning and referents of the three prepositions in 4:12 (πρός, εἰς, εἰς) are ambiguous, but the most natural and common reading takes πρός to refer to the officials, and εἰς (twice) to refer to the saints.

160 J.P. Sampley, *'And the Two Shall Become One Flesh'. A Study of Traditions in Ephesians 5:21–33* (Cambridge University Press, 1971).

relation to Pauline tradition is beyond the bounds of this work, but as we have seen above, the author can be regarded as having made a sincere and studied attempt to actualize and supplement the work of his "mentor" for a new generation. Those who would require more of him do so from a modern perspective that is not in keeping with the literary and religious milieu of Judaism and early Christianity. *Therefore we can conclude that literary attribution in Ephesians is primarily an assertion of authoritative Pauline tradition, not of literary origins.*

5.3.3 Excursus: Later Pauline Tradition

Though the primary focus of this investigation is the pseudepigraphical writings of the canonical period of Jewish and Christian writings, it may be helpful to examine Pauline literature written slightly later, to see how the patterns that we have discovered develop or alter. Here we will restrict ourselves to the second century works of 3 Corinthians and the Epistle to the Laodiceans[161].

There is great debate whether 3 Corinthians can even be regarded as an independent literary work. This pseudepigraphical correspondence between Corinth and Paul is found in the Acts of Paul and Thecla, dating from the end of the second century (cf. Tertullian, De Baptismo, 17). The question is whether it was incorporated into the work, or forms an integral part[162]. If independent, it cannot date more than a few decades earlier than the Acts of Paul. In any case, whether independent or part of the larger work, it is intended to read as a letter of Paul and can be examined as such[163].

The "occasion" for the correspondence is easily discovered: it is listed as a series of negative affirmations of the heretics in the letter of Corinth to Paul (1:10–15); (1) One must not use the prophets; (2) God is not almighty; (3) There is no resurrection of the flesh; (4) God did not create man; (5) The Lord did not come in the flesh, nor was born of Mary; (6) The world is

---

161 Two other documents are too late to be helpful: The apocryphal Correspondence Between Seneca and Paul (third century) and the Apocalypse of Paul (fifth century).

162 The arguments center on the textual evidence (esp. Coptic vs. Greek texts), and the contrasting style and contents of 3 Corinthians and the Acts of Paul. For a defence of its independence, see M. Testuz, *Papyrus Bodmer X–XIII* (Cologny - Geneve: Bibliotheque Bodmer, 1959) 23–26; *idem*, "La correspondance apocryphe de Saint Paul et des Corinthiens", *Litterature et Théologie Pauliniennes*. No edit (Paris: Desclée de Brouwer, 1960) 217–223; A.F.J. Klijn, "The Apocryphal Correspondence between Paul and the Corinthians", *Vig-Chr* 17 (1963) 2–23. For arguments for its unity with the Acts of Paul, see A. Harnack, "Untersuchungen über den apocryphen Briefwechsel der Korinther mit dem Apostel Paulus", *SPAW* 1 (1905) 3–35; W. Schneemelcher, "The Acts of Paul", *NTApocrypha*, II, 341–342.

163 The correspondence actually contains a letter from Corinth to Paul (1), the record of delivery (2), and Paul's reply (3). (2) is missing from the Greek text.

not of God but of the angels. What this describes is obviously some form of gnosticism, or perhaps the movement in general[164]

The response to this list of heresies is found in Paul's reply (3). Personal information is given, but it is hard to know if this is traditional information or just part of the literary framework. The work abounds in allusions to Paul and other parts of the NT, though quotations are few[165]. Why the pseudepigraphic appeal to Paul? The knowledge of lost letters might allow for the literary framework (1 Cor 5:9; 7:1; 2 Cor 10:10), but alone does not give sufficient warrant for the exercise. The choice of Paul was determined by the problem itself. We know that the gnostics, especially Marcion, appealed almost exclusively to Paul for the doctrines listed above. The response of 3 Corinthians, then, is to counter gnostic interpretation of Pauline tradition.

Penny rightly points out, however, that part of the thrust of 3 Corinthians is against an over-valuation of Paul. Though it holds him in high esteem, it *does not* view him as an apostle, but as subordinate to the Twelve.

> Paul is understood as the authoritative guardian of the tradition to whom one may appeal against heresy. However, his authority is derived from the apostles, whose gospel he hands down intact. No room is allowed for an appeal to a special Pauline teaching, since his message is none other than the common apostolic message, viz the catholic orthodoxy of the second century[166].

Nevertheless, this "devaluation" of Paul should not be taken too far. The widespread allusions to Pauline teaching in the letter make it apparent that this is no superficial "reformation" or "reclamation" of Paul, but the work of someone deeply influenced by his teaching[167]. Nowhere is this more apparent than his treatment of the resurrection, which takes up nearly a quarter of "Paul's" reply (3:6, 24—32). As Penny acknowledges, here the author expressed his concern to maintain the reality and corporeality of the resurrection by following Paul's argument[168]. The major (and crucial) difference is that 3 Corinthians stresses the resurrection of the flesh, while Paul talks about the resurrection of the body (cf. 1 Cor 15:37—38; 3 Cor 3:24,27).

Regardless of its success (or lack), 3 Corinthians can easily be regarded as an attempt by a devoted (but not exclusive) Paulinist to apply Pauline tradition to his own era. As we saw in Ephesians, even the use of other sources such as the Synoptic tradition and the Jewish scriptures in no way negates

---

164 See D. Penny, *Deutero-Pauline*, 307–309; A.F.J. Klijn, "Apocryphal", 18–22; M. Testuz, *P. Bodmer*, 16–18; M. Rist, "III Corinthians as a Pseudepigraphic Refutation of Marcionism" *ILiff Review* 26 (1969) 49–58.

165 D. Penny, *Deutero-Pauline*, 292–294, gives a helpful list of allusion and citations to Paul, Acts, the Synoptics and the OT. See also M. Testuz, *P. Bodmer*, 20–21.

166 In 1:4 he is distinguished from the other apostles, and in 3:4 he receives his gospel "from the apostles who were before me" (cf. Gal 1:17; 1 Cor 11:23). *Ibid.*, 303–306.

167 Thus the prebyter's protestation that he wrote the Acts of Paul (including 3 Corinthians, if not independent) "for love of Paul" (Tertullian, De. Bapt. 17).

168 *Ibid.*, 301–302. Cf. 3 Cor 3:24–26; 1 Cor 15:12–14, 18, 36–38.

the process of *Vergegenwärtigung*. Yet it must also be said that we can see the lines of developing orthodoxy that soon led to an end of this type of pseudonymous appeal. Perhaps the seeds are sown in the "one faith" of Ephesians 4:5 (cf. 1 Tim 1:2 *et al*), but certainly by the time of 3 Corinthians it is becoming difficult (if not theologically dangerous) to speak of a Pauline tradition, rather than of an apostolic "consensus" orthodoxy. This, of course, spells the demise of pseudepigraphy in the mode that we have discussed.

This demise can also be seen in our other letter under discussion, the Epistle to the Laodiceans. Here the difficulty is even more basic than that of 3 Corinthians. If the process of *Vergegenwärtigung* has been restricted by "consensus" orthodoxy in 3 Corinthians, in Laodiceans it has been virtually ended by the crystallization of the tradition process. Whereas 3 Corinthians still demonstrates a fluidity and ability to "think" theologically after the manner of Paul and the NT, the Epistle to the Laodiceans is nothing more than a catena of Pauline passages, taken mostly from Philippians, strung together to create a new Pauline letter[169]. Here we have simply mechanical reproduction on a grand scale, a "monument" to Paul that in fact spells the death of Pauline tradition in its biblical mode.

One might better appreciate this letter if it were at least directed toward some specific occasion or purpose. But it gives not one shred of evidence of any motive for production, save perhaps just to "fill the gap" left by Colossians 4:16. The Muratorian Fragment mentions an Epistle to the Laodiceans as a Marcionite forgery, but either the writer was mistaken or was referring to a different document than the one we now possess. The judgement of Lightfoot admirably sums up the work:

> Unlike most forgeries, it had no ulterior aim. It was not formed to advance any particular opinions, whether heterodox or orthodox. It has no doctrinal peculiarities. Thus it is quite harmless, so far as falsity and stupidity combined can ever be regarded as harmless[170].

Curiously, the decided failing of the Epistle to the Laodiceans becomes a virtue in the eyes of D. Penny[171]. This is because it is not tendentious, and fits very well his idea of legitimate pseudonymity as an "innocent" deference to a source. Since it is totally devoid of any influence by the pseudonymous author, it becomes an ideal "restatement" of Paul. As we have seen, however, this is completely out of keeping with the nature of biblical tradition. The Epistle marks in the granite of its own inflexibility the end of *Vergegenwärtigung* in the biblical mode, and it and its successors must be regarded not as innocent literary exercises, but as vacuous forgeries[172].

---

169 See esp. D. Penny, *Deutero-Pauline*, 322–324, for Pauline parallels. The author even follows the outline of Philippians.

170 *St. Paul's Epistles to the Colossians and to Philemon* (London: Macmillan, 1880) 281–282.

171 *Deutero-Pauline*, 324ff.

172 The date of the letter is uncertain, being placed anywhere from the second to the

5.3.4 *The Pauline Tradition: Summary*

At the conclusion of our treatment of NT revelation and the Jesus tradition (5.2), it was suggested that because of their link with community
foundations and the traditions that sustain them, it might be possible for
certain "apostolic" figures to give a distinctive expression to these traditions
by dint of their own personalities, and thus establish their own traditions.
This has certainly been demonstrated in the case of Paul. Not only is he an
apostolic figure with a sense of divine election; he also links that election to
a special foundational role as apostle to the Gentiles (Gal 1:16; 2:7; cf. Acts
9:15; 22:21; 26:16). For this reason he calls the (Jesus) tradition *my* gospel
(Rom 2:16; 1 Thess 1:5; 2 Thess 2:14; 2 Cor 4:3), exercises a patriarchal authority over his converts (1 Cor 4:15, 17; Phlm 10; Gal 4:19; 2 Cor 6:13),
and encourages them to imitate him in word and deed (1 Thess 2:11–15a; 2
Thess 3:6–9; Phil 3:15–17; 1 Cor 4:14–16; 10:31–11:1; Gal 4:12). Further,
he develops a distinctive means of communicating his authority or "apostolic presence" in his absence, through the use of emissaries, especially Timothy
(1 Thess 3:1–6; 1 Cor 4:17; 16:10–11; Phil 2:19–23) and Titus (2 Cor 8:
16–23; 12:18), and through the apostolic letter (Rom 15:15; Phlm 21; 1
Cor 4:14; 2 Cor 13:10).

When we turned to the (commonly regarded) pseudonymous epistles of
Ephesians and the Pastorals, we found that this sense of a distinctive Pauline
tradition had been preserved in a later era, and was consciously reapplied to
a new *Sitz im Leben*. Paul was regarded as an essential part of the communities' foundations (1 Tim 2:7–8; 2 Tim 2:8–10; Eph 3:2), a receiver and ex-
pounder of *revelation* (1 Tim 2:7; 2 Tim 1:11; Eph 3:3). This revelation was
considered as *autonomous*, readily applicable to the later church, (ὑποτύπωσις, 1 Tim 1:16; 2 Tim 1:13; μυστήριον, Eph 1:9; 3:3,4,9; 5:32; 6:19).
Likewise it was *unified* or *coherent*, for it was part of the shared work of the
Spirit (2 Tim 1:14; Eph 3:3; 1:17; 3:14ff.). For this reason it was a tradition
that could (and must) be further *interpreted* (2 Tim 1:15; Eph 1:17; 3:14ff.).

It is just such interpretation or *Vergegenwärtgung* that is the purpose of
these letters. The Pastorals address the issue of church leadership and use
Paul as archetype (1 Tim 1:16; 2 Tim 1:13) and Timothy (1 Tim 4:12) and
Titus (Titus 2:7) as types of the ideal Pauline leader who define the parameters of legitimate Christian experience and teaching which are to be reproduced in the current leadership (2 Tim 2:2). Pauline tradition is used further

---

fourth century. Likewise it is also uncertain whether it originated in Greek. See
further Lightfoot, *Colossians and Philemon*, 294–300; T. Zahn, *Geschichte des
neutestamentliche Kanon*, II (Erlangen: Deichert, 1890) 566–583; K. Pink, "Die
pseudopaulinischen Briefe II", *Bib* 6 (1925) 179–192; L. Vouaux, *Les Actes de
Paul et ses Lettres Apocryphes* (Paris: Librairie Letouzy et Ané, 1913) 315–322;
W. Schneemelcher, *NTApocrypha*, II, 128–132; A. Harnack, *Apokrypha IV: Die
apokryphen Briefe des Paulus an die Laodicener und Korinther* (Berlin: W. de
Gruyter, 1931[2]).

to address the problems of a paid ministry (1 Tim 5:17–18; cf. 1 Cor 9:6–8), and justification in light of the gnostic threat (2 Tim 1:9; Titus 3:5,7; cf. Gal 3 ; Rom 3–4). Ephesians depends heavily on Paul's letter to the Colossians, especially his theme of God's mystery, to address the problem of the fragmentation of Paulinism on many levels: heaven/earth (Eph 1); Jew/Gentile (Eph 2); individual/church (Eph 4:1–16); individual/society (Eph 5: 17–20; 6:1–9); husband/wife (5:21–33).

In both Ephesians (to a lesser degree) and the Pastorals (to a greater degree) we found a "canon-consciousness" that affected both the form and content of expression of Pauline tradition, especially its epistolary form (Eph 3:3; 1 Tim 3:14–15). The Pastorals in particular show an awareness that Pauline tradition is becoming increasingly identified with a corpus of apostolic letters, and may have even regarded these as scripture (2 Tim 3:16). This literary orientation probably explains the shape of the Pastorals as a three-fold corpus.

In conclusion, then, it can be affirmed that Ephesians and the Pastorals are another expression of the unique relationship of revelation and tradition or "pattern" of pseudonymity/anonymity that we discovered in the Jewish writings and Jesus tradition. The only difference is that of literary form, and its only role is to define the extent to which the author must be overtly pseudonymous. Since the epistle is the least adaptable in terms of anonymous redaction[173], it stands to reason that "Pauline" pseudonymity is more pronounced. *But as we saw, the epistolary framework is part of the Pauline tradition itself, i.e. the characteristic Pauline method of mediating his apostolic presence. Therefore the literary attribution of Ephesians and the Pastorals must be regarded primarily as an assertion of authoritative Pauline tradition, not of literary origins.*

5.4 The Petrine Tradition

When we turn to the issue of the Petrine literature in the NT, we are on much less sure footing than with Paul, because we possess no undisputed Petrine literature whereby we may assess the rest. Nevertheless, we do possess a variety of witnesses to the origin and growth of a "Petrine tradition" in the early church.

There is no disputing that apart from Paul (and Jesus!), no other figure dominates the NT like Peter. This is especially true in regard to the founda-

---

173 There are examples of such attempts of redactional actualization, e.g. Romans 16. See N. Dahl, "The Particularity of the Pauline Epistles as a Problem in the Ancient Church", *Neotestamentica et Patristica*. Fest. O. Cullmann (NTSupp 6. Leiden: Brill, 1962) 261–271; P. Trummer, *Paulustradition*, 102.

tions of the primitive community. Peter is always listed first among the Twelve, a point that is underscored (Matt 10:2). More important, Peter is connected in a unique way to authoritative tradition. His role as the spokesman for the disciples is attested in all the gospels. Likewise all four gospels, even the community of the beloved disciple (John), use the confession of Peter (Mark 8:27–30 pars) as a focal point or climax of their narratives, and use it to express fundamental Christian beliefs about Jesus and his ministry. Similarly it is Peter who first experiences and attests to the resurrection (Luke 24:34; 1 Cor 15:5; cf. Mark 16:7). This linkage of Peter and the primitive kerygma is strengthened in Acts, where Peter becomes the major spokesman, not just for the disciples, but for the primitive community. It is Peter who initiatives and presides over the election of Matthias (Acts 1:15–26). It is Peter who interprets the meaning of Pentecost (Acts 2:14–42), proclaims the new faith in the Temple (Acts 3:12–26), and defends it before the Sanhedrein (Acts 4:8–12; 5:29–32). It is Peter who gives the theological justification for taking the gospel to the Gentiles (Acts 10–11), and whose advocacy makes possible the circumcision-free mission of Paul (Acts 15:6–11). Paul seems to confirm this by his trip to Jerusalem to confer with Peter (Gal 1:18; see J.D.G. Dunn, *NTS* 28 (1982) 341–366).

Though the role of Peter in the gospels and Acts has undoubtedly been subject to the exaggeration or veneration of later generations, it would be hard to deny that Peter was a central figure in the community's origins. Though the absolute authority that is accorded Peter is probably a reflection of the later church (e.g. Matt 16:17–19), the fact that the tradition also records many of Peter's failures (e.g. Mark 8:33 par; 14:26–31 pars) shows that it is not simply a case of legend-mongering. *Certainly the picture we have is a consistent one of a strong (if impulsive) leader, who could hardly have failed to put his own personal stamp on the tradition.*

This link between Peter and the foundations of the community is strengthened when we consider the evidence for his missionary activity. It is difficult to know if the "fisher of men" label (Mark 1:17 pars) is authentic or the reflection of the later church, but since the Synoptics do not restrict the role to Peter, it is probably original. Certainly Paul recognized that Peter had an ordained mission "to the circumcised" (Gal 2:7–8), and Acts records his travels in Judea, Galilee, and Samaria (Acts 8:14; 9:32). But it is likely that Paul's clear-cut division between Jewish and Gentile missions was either a theological overstatement or simply impractical, because Peter felt free to travel to such essentially Gentile missions as Antioch (Gal 2:11), and his influence (if not his person) also extended to Corinth (1 Cor 1:12; 3:22). Thus it would seem that Peter was engaged in widespread missionary activity (1 Cor 9:5; cf. 1 Pet 1:1), a fact that receives support from the not insubstantial legend of his travel and martyrdom in Rome[174].

---

174 See esp. the treatment in O. Cullmann, *Peter. Disciple - Apostle - Martyr* (London: SCM, 1962²) 71–157.

Of course, it is impossible to tell how defined and organized this mission was. Tragically we have no mention of "Petrine" churches outside the Petrine literature, and no mention of any correspondence. Yet it should be remembered that Acts contains no reference to Paul's letters as well, and that our knowledge of Paulinism would be almost as anemic without the Pauline corpus. In any case, Peter's prominent place in the Jerusalem church and among the disciples of Jesus meant that the early Jesus tradition was linked with his person in a degree unparalleled by other figures. Furthermore, his "apostolic" ministry is regarded as contingent on divine revelation. His experience of the Transfiguration (Mark 9:2–13 pars), prophetic insight into the hearts of Ananias and Sapphira (Acts 5:1–11), visions (Acts 10:9–16; 12:7–9), inspired preaching (Acts 4:8), and intimacy with the earthly and risen Christ made him a revelatory figure in his own right. Thus it can be argued that there is a substantial basis for the birth and growth of a "Petrine tradition"[175], and it is now the task to determine whether such a tradition is the fundamental reality behind the Petrine epistles.

5.4.1 *1 Peter*

5.4.1.1 *The Problem of 1 Peter*

> 1 Peter is a notorious New Testament example of a document whose question of authorship is inseparably related to a wide range of disputed questions such as the letter's genre, destination, historical and social situation, place and date of composition, the traditions it incorporates, its literary style, its proximity to other New Testament writings, especially those of Paul and the Pauline circle, its suggested affinity with the Epistles and era of Pliny the Younger, the position of the Roman empire taken toward Christianity at the time of its composition, the function of pseudonymity within the early Christian literature, and of course, its theological message[176].

This observation of J.H. Elliott admirably sums up the troubling complexity of the outwardly simple and straightforward work labelled 1 Peter. Though some consensus may be achieved on what 1 Peter is *not*, very little exists in terms of what it *is,* in regard to authenticity, date, purpose, and other critical considerations. In this respect, little more than a summary of the debate can be presented here, chiefly from the perspective of authorship[177]. The external testimony to the work is substantial, cited as early as

---

175 For a fuller treatment of Peter inside and outside the NT, see O. Cullmann, *ibid.; Peter in the New Testament.* Edit. R.E. Brown *et al* (London: Chapman, 1973).

176 J.H. Elliott, "Peter, Silvanus and Mark in I Peter and Acts: Sociological and Exegetical Perspectives on a Petrine Group in Rome", *Wort in der Zeit.* Fest. H. Rengstorf. Edit. W. Haubeck and M. Bachmann (Leiden: Brill, 1980) 251.

177 Besides the standard introductions and commentaries, see J.A.T. Robinson, *Redating the New Testament* (London: SCM, 1976) 164–169; C.F.D. Moule, "The Nature and Purpose of I Peter", *ET* 59 (1948) 256–258; K. Shimada, *The Formul-*

2 Peter (3:1) and Polycarp (Phil 1:3; 21f.; 5:3; 7:2; 8:1f.; 10:2), in the first few decades of the second century. Irenaeus of Lyon (Adv. Haer. IV. 9,2; 16,5; V 7,2) is the first to mention it by name. Eusebius classes it among the undisputed books (H.E. iii.25.2)[178].

It is only internal arguments that carry any force against authenticity. A major argument of an earlier era was that the persecutions mentioned in 1 Peter (1:6,7; 3:13–17; 4:12–19) reflected a much later era of church history. In particular, the suffering "as a Christian" (4:15) was equated with the state-led, universal persecution of Christianity as a *religio illicita* mentioned in the Letters of Pliny the Younger, and thus dated in the time of Trajan (A.D. 98–117)[179]. However, more cautious examination reveals that the persecution in 1 Peter is local, and not one of policy. It stems from popular reaction to the Christian lifestyle, and could be dated almost anytime[180]. Robinson does make the valid point, though, that the surprise at the persecution (4:12, 17) and the optimism toward the state (2:13–14; cf. Rev 13) would argue for an earlier rather than a later first century date[181].

Another historical argument concerns the addresses of the letter (1:1). There is no sure evidence that Peter was involved in such widespread missionary activity in Asia Minor, and this field was in fact Paul's province. But it is well known that Peter did travel (Gal 2:11; 1 Cor 9:5). Furthermore, of the five areas mentioned, we have no record that Paul even set foot in three of them (Pontus, Bithynia, Cappadocia), nor is his activity in the others to be regarded as exclusive[182]. The mention of a "Peter party" in 1 Corinthians 1:12 shows that there were people willing to identify with Peter even within the Pauline mission. Related to this is the mention of Peter's associates, Mark

---

ary Material in First Peter (Ph.D., Union Theological Seminary, N.Y., 1966) 5–52; R.P. Martin, "The Composition of I Peter in Recent Study", *Vox evangelica*. Edit. R.P. Martin (London: Epworth, 1962) 29–42; F. Neugebauer, "Zur Deutung und Bedeutung des 1. Petrusbriefes", *NTS* 26 (1980) 61–86; E. Lohse, "Paränese und Kergyma im 1. Petrusbriefe", *ZNW* 45 (1954) 68–89; N. Brox, "Der erste Petrusbrief in der literarischen Tradition des Urchristentums", *Kairos* 20 (1978) 182–192; J.P. Love, "The First Epistle of Peter", *Interp* 8 (1954) 63–87; R. Thurston, "Interpreting First Peter", *JETS* 17 (1974) 171–182; B.H. Streeter, *The Primitive Church* (London: Macmillan, 1929) 115–136; D.H. Schmidt, *The Peter Writings: Their Redactors and Their Relationships* (Ph.D., Northwestern University, 1972) 7–18.

178 For full treatment of external witnesses, see C. Bigg, *A Critical and Exegetical Commentary on the Epistles of St. Peter and St. Jude* (Edinburgh: T and T Clark, 1902) xi–xii, 7–17.

179 J. Knox, "Pliny and I Peter: A Note On I Peter 4:14–16 and 3:15", *JBL* 72 (1953) 187–189.

180 See E.G. Selwyn, *The First Epistle of St. Peter* (London: Macmillan, 1947) 52–56; idem, "The Persecutions in I Peter", *BSNTS* 1950, 39–50; J.H. Elliott, "The Rehabitation of an Exegetical Step-Child: I Peter in Recent Research", *JBL* (1976) 251–252; F. Neugebauer, "Zur Deutung", 61–62.

181 *Redating*, 151f.

182 J.H. Elliott, *A Home for the Homeless: A Sociological Exegesis of I Peter, Its Situation and Strategy* (Philadelphia: Fortress Press, 1981) 277–278.

and Silvanus (5:12—13). It is objected that these are Paul's associates, not Peter's. While this is undoubtedly true[183], the relationship was not exclusive. Both Mark and Silvanus were part of the Palestinian church (Acts 12:12; 15: 22). Silvanus was the bearer of a letter which Peter helped draft (Acts 15: 22f.). A close relationship to Mark may be hinted at by Peter's relationship to his mother and the church at her house (Acts 12:12)[184].

A final historical argument is found in the usage of the term "Babylon" as a code name for Rome. Since this usage only occurs in Jewish apocalypses (4 Ezra, 2 Baruch, cf. also the Sibyllines) written after A.D. 70, 1 Peter must also date from this era[185]. But the identification of Rome with Babylon need not depend on the destruction of the temple. Already in Daniel, "Babylon" has become an eschatological symbol of a world power (1:1—8; 3:8—12; 6: 2—24). In Revelation (14:8; 17:5, 18; 18:2) it is used of Rome in reference to the persecution of the saints, not the destruction of Jerusalem. Thus there is nothing to prevent the rise of its usage in Christian apocalyptic circles before A.D. 70.

A theological and historical argument trained against 1 Peter is that it lacks direct references to the life and teachings of Jesus, and any personal reminiscences of Peter. Arguments from silence are always risky, but to make a decision based on what Peter "should" have included, when there are no other authentic documents for comparison, is simply untenable. 2 Peter *does* contain personal allusions, and yet these are regarded as part of the pseud-epigrapher's art. The subjective nature of these judgements is apparent.

A potentially decisive literary argument against authenticity can be found in the literary relationship of 1 Peter to the rest of the NT, particularly Ephesians. Though some might argue on the basis of Galatians 2:11—21 that *any* literary dependence on Paul would rule out Petrine authorship[186], this view is too biased by the dialectical approach of the Tübingen school to be objective. The real crux of the matter is dating, not theology. If 1 Peter can be demonstrated to be literarily dependent on a later work, such as Ephesians or Hebrews, then it could not have been written during the lifetime of Peter. There are undoubtedly numerous parallels between 1 Peter and other, particularly Pauline, NT documents[187]. Some argue that these demonstrate clear literary dependence on the part of 1 Peter[188]. Yet many more, even some

---

183 *Silvanus:* Acts 15:22—34; 15:40—18:5; 1 Thess 1:1; 2 Cor 1:19; 2 Thess 1:1; *Mark:* Acts 13:5,13; 15:37,39; Col 4:10; 2 Tim 4:11; Phlm 24.

184 It is difficult to know if the legend of Mark being Peter's disciple depends on 1 Peter 5:13 or is an independent witness. Cf. Eusebius, H.E. iii 39,15.

185 C.H. Hunzinger, "Babylon als Deckname für Rom und die Datierung des 1. Petrus-briefes", *Gottes Wort und Gottes Land.* Fest. H.W. Hertzberg. Edit. H. Reventlow (Göttingen: Vandenhoeck and Ruprecht, 1965) 67—77.

186 E.g. D.H. Schmidt, *Peter Writings*, 12—13.

187 See N. Brox, "Erster Petrusbrief", 183—187; A.E. Barnett, *Paul*, 51—69; L. Goppelt, *Der Erste Petrusbrief* (Göttingen: Vandehoeck and Ruprecht, 1978) 48—53.

188 C.L. Mitton, "The Relationship Between I Peter and Ephesians", *JThS* 1 (1950)

opponents of authenticity, regard the parallels as a consequence of a common (oral) source of catechetical traditions[189]. Even if a literary relationship could be established, the direction of influence would still be in doubt. 1 Peter could still be prior[190].

The most telling argument against authenticity is the language and style of 1 Peter. The Greek is quite good, and hardly fits in with the picture of Peter as "unlearned" (Acts 4:13). Similarly, the scripture quotations and allusions are taken from the LXX, and the dominical references are to the Greek synoptic tradition, not the Aramaic. The force of this argument perhaps appears more strong than it really is. It is hard to know if $ἀγράμμα$-$τος$ means "illiterate", or merely "untrained". In any case, a period of some twenty to thirty years separates the time of the incident in Acts with the possible (Petrine) date of this writing. How a man can or cannot develop in terms of linguistic ability in that period is open to question. The use of the LXX and the Greek synoptic tradition present no insuperable problems, since they were commonly used in the Palestinian as well as the Hellenistic communities. Nevertheless it may be admitted that the quality of writing is not consistent with what we would expect of Peter, even in his later years.

It is for this reason that defenders of authenticity often have recourse to a secretary theory. They usually point to Silvanus ($διὰ\ Σιλουανοῦ\ ...\ ἔγραψα$, 5:12)[191]. Yet this phrase is commonly used to designate the bearer of a letter, not its recorder (Acts 15:23; Polycarp, Phil 14:1; Ignat, Rom 10:1)[192]. Likewise there is no mention of Silvanus as co-author as in 1 Thessalonians 1:1; or any greeting, such as that of Tertius in Romans 16:22. The recourse to a secretary, Silvanus or otherwise, often raises as many problems as it solves, as its critics are quick to point out. If the secretary substantially impresses the document with his own personality, at what point does he become the real author[193]? Still, it must be said that there is no evidence to rule out what was a well known practice in antiquity.

A decision in regard to the authenticity of 1 Peter will inevitably be based more on surmise than on hard evidence in either direction. The force of the

---

67–73, reprinted in *Epistle*, 176–197; F.W. Beare, *The First Epistle of Peter* (Oxford: Blackwell, 1970³) 216–220; D.H. Schmidt, *Peter Writings*, 26–38, 57–58.

189 See esp. E.G. Selwyn, *First Peter*, 384–439; K. Schimada, *Formulary.* Also L. Goppelt, *Erste Petrusbrief*, 48–53; J.H. Elliott, "Rehabilitation", 246–248; N. Brox, "erste Petrusbrief", 183–187; W.G. Kummel, *Intro.*, 423.

190 C.L. Mitton, *Epistle*, 197, admits as much. See also J.H. Elliott, *ibid.*

191 L. Goppelt, *Erste Petrusbrief*, 347–348; E.G. Selwyn, *First Peter*, 9–17. Selwyn's attempt (369–384) to demonstrate the literary affinity of 1 and 2 Thessalonians and 1 Peter as proof of Silvanus' secretarial role has found little support. See F.W. Beare, *First Peter*, 212–216.

192 See J.A.T. Robinson, *Redating*, 167–168; N. Brox, "Tendenz und Pseudepigraphie im ersten Petrusbrief", *Kairos* 20 (1978) 111–112.

193 Some actually take this step and identity Silvanus as the *pseudonymous* author of the epistle. For criticism of this, see N. Brox, "Zur pseudepigraphischen Rahmung des ersten Petrusbriefes", *BZ* 19 (1975) 83–85.

language difficulty may be weak enough, or the strength of the secretary hypothesis may be adequate to allow defenders of authenticity to maintain their position. For others these problems are too great. E. Best, reflecting on theories regarding Petrine authorship, with or without a secretary, concludes,

> It must be frankly allowed that it is the difficulties in the above theories that suggest pseudonymity; there is nothing explicit in the body of the epistle, no anachronisms, no historical facts contrary to what we know of Peter, which necessitate this conclusion ....[194].

Since the force of the negative arguments do not carry sufficient weight to achieve consensus, a correspondingly greater weight is placed on the positive arguments. That is, what occasion or purpose suggests itself for the pseudonymity of 1 Peter?

5.4.1.2 *The Occasion and Purpose of 1 Peter*

As will be seen, this approach offers little in the way of clarification or consensus as well. One popular theory of the first half of this century was that 1 Peter was not really a letter at all, but a literary work or works with an epistolary (1:1f., 5:12–14) veneer. There were two main opinions regarding the source of this literature. One line of reasoning was that the body of 1 Peter represented an original baptismal liturgy, later given an authoritative *imprimatur* by a Petrine attribution[195]. The references to suffering in the "letter", then, could be regarded as having no historical referent, but merely represented elements of early Christian worship. The elaborate nature of these theories, however, was often proof of their limited feasibility.

A second line of reasoning sought to mitigate the difficulties of finding a structured liturgy in 1 Peter by attributing it to a more general "baptismal homily", addressed to new converts[196]. This view was usually held in conjunction with the belief that 1 Peter could be divided into two sources (plus the later epistolary framework)[197]. A major division was posited at 4:11, 12, with the suffering in the first half being regarded as only potential (1:6; 2: 20; 3:14, 17), and the second half as a reality (4:12, 14, 19; 5:6, 8). The

---

194 E. Best, *I Peter* (London: Oliphants, 1971) 59.

195 W. Bornemann, "Der erste Petrusbrief - eine Taufrede des Silvanus?", *ZNW* 19 (1919–20) 143–165; M.E. Boismard, "Une Liturgie Baptismale Dans la Prima Petri", *RB* 63 (1956) 182–208; *idem, Quatre Hymnes Baptismales dans la Première Épître de Pierre* (Paris: Éditions du Cerf, 1961); F.L. Cross, *I Peter. A Paschal Liturgy* (London: Mowbray, 1954); A.R.C. Leaney, "I Peter and the Passover: An Interpretation", *NTS* 10 (1964) 238–251.

196 B.H. Streeter, *Primitive;* F.W. Beare, *First Peter,* 25–28, 200–226; O.S. Brooks, "I Peter 3:21 – The Clue to the Literary Structure of the Epistle", *NT* 16 (1974) 290–305.

197 Though not all who held to a partition theory supported the baptismal homily approach. See C.F.D. Moule, "I Peter", 7–11.

first half was believed to be a pre-baptismal address to neophytes (to anticipate persecution), and the second half was generally regarded as real letter
(or sermon) to the church in the midst of (actual) persecution. This second
approach offered little real improvement over the strict liturgical theories.
The division of the letter by reference to potential and actual persecution is
artificial, and does not hold up to analysis (cf. esp. 1:6; 3:16; 4:4). The baptismal allusions are not specific enough to indicate an actual service or sermon
of baptism, but are simply part of the natural framework of early Christian
theology (cf. Rom 6:1ff.). Though few would deny the incorporation of
traditions from many sources in 1 Peter, the general consensus is that, whatever its sources, and whoever its author, it is a unified, epistolary composition[198].

An older theory regarding the occasion and purpose of 1 Peter that still
commands a wide following in variously modified forms is the *Unionsthese*
of F.C. Baur[199]. Though originally proposed in conjunction with a support
of authenticity, Baur soon attributed this purpose to the work of the later
church[200]. The fundamental thrust of this position is that 1 Peter represents
the work of a Paulinist who was seeking to reconcile the polar camps of
Gentile (Pauline) and Palestinian (Petrine) Christianity into a broader, inclu-
sive orthodoxy.

The union thesis rests on two assertions, both of which must be seriously
questioned. The first is that 1 Peter is a tendentious document reflecting a
Gentile/Jewish schism. Yet this idea is based on a dialectical approach to NT
history, and not the document itself. 1 Peter is in fact remarkable for its
absence of any reference to racial and/or religious tensions, such as one
might find in Ephesians or even the authentic Paulines. The letter evinces
only pastoral, and not any dogmatic interests[201].

Yet one might argue that a schism is best addressed not by mentioning it,
but by emphasizing the unity of the two positions. This leads to the second

---

198 For a full review and criticism of the liturgical/homiletical theories, see C.F.D.
Moule, "I Peter"; W.C. van Unnik, "Christianity According to I Peter", *ET* 68
(1956–57) 79–83; T.C.G. Thornton, "I Peter, a Paschal Liturgy?", *JThS* 12 (1961),
14–26; R. Martin, "I Peter": W.G. Kümmel, *Intro.*, 418–421; J.H. Elliott, "Rehabilitation", 248–249.

199 For further development and modification of this thesis, see W. Trilling, "Zum
Petrusamt im NT. Traditionsgeschichtliche Überlegungen anhand von Matthäus,
1 Petrus und Johannes", *ThQ* 151 (1971) 110–133, reprinted in *Theologische
Versuche*, IV (Berlin, 1972) 27–46; H. Goldstein, *Paulinische Gemeinde im Ersten
Petrusbrief* (Stuttgart: KBW Verlag, 1975).

200 See also V. McNabb, "Date and Influence of the First Epistle of Peter", *IER* 45
(1935) 596–613, who argues that 1 Peter is an authentic appeal of Peter to Disa-
spora Jewish Christians to accept a law free gospel!

201 N. Brox, "Tendenz", 116–118; *idem*, "Situation und Sprache der Minderheit im
ersten Petrusbrief", *Kairos* 19 (1977) 1–4. He notes that no mention is made of
the divisive theological issues such as Paul's idea of justification and his attitude
toward circumcision and the law.

assertion, that 1 Peter is really a Pauline document whose Petrine attribution is a way of stating (or achieving) the unity of the two camps. Laying aside the problem of the feasibility of such a subtle approach, the real difficulty with this assertion is that there is not enough in 1 Peter that can be labelled distinctively Pauline. The epistolary form, the addressees, and the associates Mark and Silvanus are identified with Paulinism, but not exclusively so. Moveover, the content of the letter is not uniquely Pauline. Proponents of the "Paulinism" of 1 Peter point to a similar ecclesiology (2:4f.; cf. Rom 9: 33)[202]. But the stone imagery is in fact a common one[203]. Completely lacking in 1 Peter is Paul's characteristic imagery of the church as the body of Christ. Though Paul does show some interest in the concept of the building metaphor (1 Cor 3:9ff.), it must be said that the nomenclature, and particularly the cultic terminology (1 Pet 2:9f.), is also indicative of Palestinian interests[204]. Furthermore, deutero-Paulinism included the apostolic figures as part of the foundation imagery (Eph 2:20; cf. 1 Tim 3:15), whereas 1 Peter (2:3ff.) reserves that imagery for Christ alone[205]. 1 Peter does use the Pauline phrase "in Christ" (3:16; 5:10, 14), but its usage lacks the distinctive Pauline idea of mystical union, and means little more than "as a Christian", or "in the Christian religion"[206]. The church organization of 1 Peter is also undeveloped. It mentions only the Palestinian concept of elder (5:1ff.), and shows no trace of bishops or deacons as in later Paulinism. 1 Peter 4:10–11 does reflect the unique Pauline teaching on *charismata*. Yet this passage also has elements in common with the primitive differentiation of function into the categories of teaching and practical ministry (Acts 6:1ff.), and thus its Paulinism seems to be tempered and less developed (cf. Rom 12; 1 Cor 12)[207]

The soteriology of 1 Peter is not particularly Pauline either. It does use the concepts of grace (1:2, 10, 13; 2:19f.) and election 1:15; 2:9, 21; 3:9; 5:10), but these are not exclusively Pauline. In fact the frequency of usage of the πίστις word group is significantly lower than in Paul, and a correspondingly greater emphasis is placed on ἐλπίς[208].

Many of the other "Pauline" parallels, particularly in the paranetic material, have been dealt with above in terms of the literary relationships of 1 Peter to the rest of the NT. It is not to be denied that 1 Peter shares a number of common traditions with Paulinism. This is to be expected. But there is

---

202 H. Goldstein, *Paulinische Gemeinde*, 50–53; D. Schmidt, *Peter Writings*, 58–81.
203 See N. Hillyer, " 'Rock-Stone' Imagery in I Peter", *Tyndale Bulletin* 22 (1971) 58–81.
204 For example, the designation of the church as ἔθνος ἅγιον. See E. Lohse, "Paränese", 75ff.
205 F. Neugebauer, "Zur Deutung", 72.
206 P.E. Davies, "Primitive Christology in 1 Peter", *Festschrift to honour F. Wilbur Gingrich*. Edit. E.H. Barth and R.E. Cocroft (Leiden: E.J. Brill, 1972) 119.
207 E.G. Selwyn, *First Peter*, 219. On 5:1–5 see also W. Nauck, "Probleme des frühchristlichen Amtsverständnisses (1 Ptr. 5,2f)", *ZNW* 48 (1957) 200–220.
208 F. Neugebauer, "Zur Deutung", 73f.

no quantity of distinctive Pauline concepts in it that would require 1 Peter to be attributed to an exclusive Paulinist, or further, to serve as a vehicle of unity between opposing ideologies. In fact the most characteristic Pauline doctrines, such as justification, the church as the body of Christ, and the work of the Spirit, are entirely absent from the letter. Though a certain amount of Pauline influence is likely, the degree of Paulinism in 1 Peter is far too small to support the union thesis[209].

The identification of the occasion and purpose of 1 Peter must be solved by an examination of the text itself, and not by patterns or formulas imposed from without. Taking the unity and occasional nature of the letter at face value, the problem that the communities addressed by 1 Peter face is persecution, both a present reality and a growing threat (1:6; 2:19ff.; 4:4, 12ff.; 5:10). More generally, it is evidence of a growing alienation between the church and society[210]. While it is true that no date can be placed on the document with regard to the nature of the persecution, there are several elements that would argue for an earlier rather than a later (turn of the century) date[211]. The late Book of Revelation is obsessed with the role of the state in persecution (cf. Rev 13) and is generally pessimistic. But 1 Peter makes only a general reference to the state, and that in a most positive attitude (2:12–17; 3:13ff.). Likewise the other Johannine writings take the hate of the world for granted (John 15:18f.; 1 John 3:13), but 1 Peter evinces surprise at the hostility (4:12, 17) and remains hopeful that good conduct will be rewarded (2:14; 3:13). Similarly, missionary activity ($\kappa\eta\rho\acute{\upsilon}\sigma\sigma\omega$ and $\epsilon\grave{\upsilon}\alpha\gamma\gamma\epsilon\lambda\acute{\iota}\zeta o\mu\alpha\iota$) has disappeared in late writings, and "witness" ($\mu\alpha\rho\tau\upsilon\rho\acute{\epsilon}\omega$) takes its place. But martyr terminology is almost totally lacking in 1 Peter (though see 5:1), while missionary activity is very present (1:12, 25; 3:19; 4:6, 17). Finally, the late writings exhibit a concern not only with outward threat, but also with inner conflict, particularly of the gnostic variety (Rev 2–3; 1 John 2:19), and make a strong appeal for unity (Eph 4:1ff.; John 17:21). But there is no evidence of inner church conflict in 1 Peter; the threat is all from outside (2:12; 3:1f., 15f.).

Beside the issues directly related to the problem of suffering, there are other indications of an early date as well. As we have seen above, the church order and exercise of spiritual gifts is simple and undeveloped (4:10–11; 5:1ff.). Likewise the letter shows a primitive doctrinal development, such as the archaic tradic formula (1:2) and the identification of Jesus with the Suffering Servant (2:21ff.)[212]. Perhaps most important is the vivid convic-

---

209 This applies particularly to the novel thesis of Schenke and Fischer, *Einleitung*, 200–203 that 1 Peter was originally attributed to Paul, and a scribal error changed *Paulos* to *Petros* in 1 Peter 1:1.
210 See esp. J.H. Elliott, *A Home*.
211 See esp. F. Neugebauer, "Zur Deutung", 64.
212 J.N.D. Kelly, *A Commentary on the Epistles of Peter and Jude* (London: Black, 1969) 30.

tion of an imminent parousia (4:7). 1 Peter gives no evidence of the problem of delay that is so characteristic of later writings.

How, then, does this evidence for the date and occasion of 1 Peter fit into a theory of its purpose? Basically three choices lie open to us. The first possibility is the least likely: 1 Peter is a pseudonymous document written to counsel Christians in distress, with no real connection to Peter. This is particularly the view of N. Brox: "Man muss den 1 Peter im Rahmen der *praeparatio ad martyrium* lesen, die von der frühen Kirche zu leisten war"[213]. The attribution serves the purely formal function of identifying the message as apostolic[214]. The choice of Peter was dictated by the literary venue of Rome (5:1) and Peter's traditional association with it[215]. But J.H. Elliott rightly calls this a "counsel of despair"[216]. It is not that the purpose is insufficient. As a threat to the community, persecution is reason enough for a recourse to pseudonymity. But such an innocuous use of a pseudonym as Brox suggests is contrary to the community-creating and sustaining roles of tradition and traditional figures that we have discussed before. The crux of the problem is dating. In order to justify his thesis, Brox must place 1 Peter at the end of the first century or later, where a homogeneous orthodoxy was, in fact, beginning to exert itself. He himself recognizes a stronger concern for individuality in earlier writings, particularly the deutero-Paulines[217]. But everything that we have examined in 1 Peter argues for an earlier dating as well. Indeed to classify the writing as a "preparation for martyrdom" along with the writings of the second century fails to recognize the fundamental optimism of 1 Peter in contrast to the martyr ideology of a later era[218]. In short, 1 Peter must be placed in an earlier, tradition conscious era that demands some reason for the use of a pseudonym.

A second possibility for the purpose of 1 Peter lies with the claim to authenticity. It may well reflect an attempt by Peter to address the needs of the Christian communities during his closing years. According to F. Neubebauer, the *best* parallel to 1 Peter is the early Pauline letter 1 Thessalonians 2:14f.: "... for you suffered the same things from your own countrymen as they did from the Jews, who killed both the Lord Jesus and the prophets,

---

213 "Situation", 9.
214 "Der einzelne Name garantiert generall die Apostolizität, weil ganz früh schon das dogmatische Interesse an 'den Aposteln' nicht verschiedene Profile derselben zur Kenntnis nahm, sondern die totale Übereinstimmung zwischen allen behauptete. Man muss in der Tat von einer Entindividualisierung der Apostel reden." "Rahmung", 92. See also "Tendenz", 118–120; *Das erste Petrusbrief* (Zurich: Benziger, 1979) 34.
215 See 1 Clem 5:4; Ign, Rom 4:3. N. Brox, "Tendenz", 115; "Rahmung", 95.
216 "Peter, Silvanus", 252.
217 "Tendenz", 119, n.46. But he tries to mitigate this by saying it is not meant to distinguish Paul from other Christian theologians, but from heretics. The distinction seems artificial.
218 See F. Neugebauer, "Zur Deutung", 75–77.

and drove us out ..."[219]. It is in the sixth and seventh decades of the first century that conflict with the world enters full swing. In particular the reign of Nero marks a sinister development and increase in persecution, though it need not be labelled official or universal. The suspicion and hatred of Christians (4:4), the potential of false accusations (4:14–16), and the reference to a fiery trial (1:7; 4:2), as well as the threat (if not the actuality) of widespread persecution is consistent with what we know of Nero's era and its aftermath. The διασπορά (1:1) could either be Christians dispersed from Rome during the Neronian excesses, or simply Christian communities who had heard of those excesses and were either anticipating or experiencing repercussions in their own locale[220].

The early dating and occasion of 1 Peter does not, however, necessitate a defence of its authenticity. Peter was probably martyred during the time of Nero, and the letter could have as easily been written in the years after Peter's death as during his lifetime. And even if it could be dated before Peter's death, it would not be absolute proof of its authenticity. This leads us to the third possibility, that 1 Peter is a pseudonymous document, written probably shortly after Peter's death, in order to give a word of encouragement to his surviving communities. The difference between this possibility and that of Brox is that here the choice of the pseudonym is more than a formality. It is a deliberate attempt to identify with Peter and his community creating tradition, and to actualize that tradition for a later situation. That this is a possibility is rejected by N. Brox, who is critical of attempts to determine a Petrine tradition or stream in the NT[221]. What follows is an examination of 1 Peter in light of the NT evidence.

5.4.1.3 *Petrine Tradition in 1 Peter*

There are essentially three areas of the NT witness where a correspondence of "Peter tradition" with 1 Peter are sought. First is the dominical tradition that has a particular association with Peter. Second is the "Petrine kerygma" as found in the speeches of Acts. Third is what might be called the "Peter

---

219 *Ibid.*, 65.
220 See R. Thurston, "Interpreting", 174–178. G. Selwyn's suggestion, *First Peter,* 57f., that these may in part be Jewish Christians scattered after James' execution (A.D. 62) is unlikely, given the clear indication of a Gentile audience in 1:14,18; 2:10; 4:4.
221 "Tradition", 187–190. He says this in regard to the earlier elaborate and uncritical theories of E. Scharfe, *Die petrinische Strömung der neutestamentlichen Literatur* (Berlin, 1893); B. Weiss, Der Petrinische Lehrbegriffe (Berlin, 1855); W. Elert, *Die Religiosität des Petrus. Ein religions-psychologischer Versuch* (Leipzig, 1911); J. van Dodewaard, "Die sprachliche Übereinstimmung zwischen Markus-Paulus und Markus-Petrus. II. Markus-Petrus", *Bib* 30 (1949) 218–238; as well as the more circumspect theories of C. Spicq, J.H. Elliott, R. Gundry and E. Best (see below).

legend", i.e. the portrait of key experience and roles of Peter that we find in the NT.

In regard to the first two areas, it must be speedily admitted with H. Goldstein that "Der Komplex der Überlieferung als des kompendiumhaften Lehrgutes fehlt im 1 Petrusbrief völlig"[222]. There is no mention of such things as "deposit" ($\pi\alpha\rho\alpha\vartheta\dot{\eta}\kappa\eta$) or "sound teaching" such as we have in the Pastorals. But this in itself is not a denial of the force or use of tradition, but only an observation about the stage of its development. It is in fact another witness to the early and undeveloped nature of the teaching in 1 Peter. It is still in an age where the traditions are quite malleable.

The first attempt to trace a Petrine tradition (or authentic Petrine teaching) is connected with the dominical sayings in 1 Peter. These Jesus *logia* have often been used as evidence of the Peter who sat at the feet of Jesus[223]. The most recent and critical attempt is that of R. Gundry, who maintains that the *verba Christi* of 1 Peter exhibit a "Petrine pattern", That is, they refer to contexts and/or fundamental interests of Peter according to the gospel tradition[224]. He isolates ten such parallels:

1. Saying about freedom from human authority (1 Pet 2:13–17; Matt 17:24–27) occurs in Jesus' conversation with Peter over the temple tax.
2. 1 Peter 1:13; 4:7; 5:8f. from Olivet Discourse (Matt 24:49; 25:13; Mark 13:33, 35,37; Luke 21:31,34,36) which is spoken privately to Peter, James, John and Andrew.
3. 1 Peter 1:4,13; 5:2 from Luke 12:32–38. Luke 12:41 records Peter's particular interest and participation.
4. 1 Peter 4:7, command to watch and pray reflects Gethsemene story (Mark 14: 32–42 par) where Peter is singled out for special rebuke and exhortation.
5. 1 Peter 2:4,7, stone motif (cf. Mark 12:10 par). Peter would have held special interest in this because of the name given him by Jesus (Matt 16:18). Cf. also Acts 4:11.
6. 1 Peter 5:3–5, Jesus' remarks about overlordship and humble service. Cf. Mark 10:35–45; Matt 20:20–28, dispute of James and John over seats in kingdom threatens Peter's leadership. Also Luke 22:24–30, dispute takes place in Upper Room, where Peter figures prominently.
7. 1 Peter 1:21f.; 3:8; 4:8; 5:3–5 on love and humility, also from Upper Room. Cf. esp. phrase believers $\epsilon\dot{\iota}\varsigma$ God $\delta\iota\dot{\alpha}$ (Christ) which is spoken by Christ to Peter (John 14:1,6; cf. 1 Pet 1:21).
8. 1 Peter 1:6; 2:12, 18ff.; 3:14; 4:13f. are from the Sermon on the Mount according to Luke (6:17ff.). This took place right after his choice of the 12, which would have been a memorable occasion to Peter as leader.
9. 1 Peter 5:2 "shepherd the flock" recounts Jesus' words to Peter, "shepherd my sheep" (John 21:16). Cf. also 1 Peter 5:2,4; John 10:11, 14.
10. 1 Peter 1:10–12 comes from Jesus' sayings to the Emmaus disciples (Luke 24: 26). These disciples reported to Peter, who had a similar experience[225].

---

222 *Paulinische Gemeinde*, 102.
223 See C. Spicq, "La Iᵃ Petri et le témoignage évangélique de sainte Pierre", *StTh* 20 (1966) 37–61.
224 "'Verba Christi' in I Peter: Their Implications Concerning the Authorship of I Peter and the Authenticity of the Gospel Tradition", *NTS* 13 (1966) 336–350.
225 *Ibid.*, 345–348.

Gundry maintains that this "Petrine pattern" could not be due to accident, and is too well-woven into the text to be the work of a pious forger, so it must be by Peter. Yet both premises are false. The connections with Peter of many of the *logia* are tenuous at best (e.g. nos. 2,6,8,10). Given Peter's prominence in all the Synoptic records, it ought to be possible to find some connection with most *logia*. His second premise is based on the unsubstantiated belief that a pseudepigrapher (a more neutral term) has to be stupid or clumsy. E. Best has made a telling critique of Gundry's evidence, noting that when you omit all his parallels with the Synoptics which also occur in John and the rest of the NT, you are only left with 2:4, hardly enough on which to build a case[226]. Equally important, the parallels are based on a developed and Greek tradition, which makes the likelihood of an original (Petrine) source more unlikely[227]. The use of Jesus *logia* in 1 Peter as an independent witness gives no support whatever for authenticity, and only slightly less support for a body of "Petrine tradition". But this is not to say that the material is un-Petrine. All of it *can* be connected with Peter in some way, but it is sufficiently neutral not to require any connection. Some further indication would be needed.

A second area of correspondence between the Petrine witness of 1 Peter and the NT is in the speeches and other material of Acts[228]. E. Best summarizes the most important parallels:

1. Fulfillment of prophecy (Acts 2:16ff.; 3:18; 1 Pet 1:10ff., 20).
2. Insistence on the cross as the foreordained action of God (Acts 2:23; 1 Pet 1:20. But cf. Luke 22:22; Mark 8:31; Eph 1:3–12).
3. Close connection of resurrection and exaltation (Acts 2:32ff.; 1 Pet 1:21; 3:22. But cf. Phil 2:8–11; Eph 1:20; Col 3:1).
4. Call to repentance and faith/baptism (Acts 2:38, 40; 1 Pet 3:20ff. But cf. Rom 6:1–14; Col 2:11–3:11; Titus 3:15).
5. Christ as judge of the living and dead (Acts 10:42; 1 Pet 4:5. But cf. 2 Tim 4: 1)[229].

As Best demonstrates, these shared kerygmatic traditions are not uniquely Petrine. They may give some evidence for early dating[230], but are no independent witness to either authenticity or a separate Petrine tradition. Again, however, they are not *un*-Petrine. There does remain, as well, one particular association that in its own form is uniquely associated with Peter in the

226 E. Best, "I Peter and the Gospel Tradition", *NTS* 16 (1970) 95–113. See also *idem, I Peter* (London: Oliphants, 1971) 52–53; N. Brox, "Tradition", 188–190.

227 Gundry's reply, "Further *Verba* on *Verba Christi* in First Peter", *Bib* 55 (1974) 211–232, disagrees that Peter would have only used his own translation from the Aramaic, and not appealed to developed tradition, citing the Gospel of John as evidence to the contrary. While this may be true, Best's criticism still undermines the use of the *verba Christi* as a uniquely (authentic) Petrine witness.

228 J. van Dodeward, "Übereinstimmung", C. Spicq, "La Iᵃ Petri", 53–59; J.H. Elliott, "Peter, Silvanus", 262–264; E.G. Selwyn, *First Peter*, 33–36.

229 E. Best, *I Peter*, 53.

230 P.E. Davies, "Primitive", 117.

speeches of Acts. This is the use of παῖς θεοῦ (Acts 3:13, 26; 4:27, 30) as an expression of a Suffering Servant Christology. That this usage is connected to Peter's speeches may be an indication that this was a primitive Christology held in association with Peter[231]. In any case, Servant Christology is also the central affirmation of 1 Peter (1:19; 2:22ff.; 3:18), and as we shall see, is the key hermeneutic of the author in addressing the problem of persecution. Though this theological perspective is not so uniquely Petrine as to demand a recognition of Petrine tradition, the strong associations in the speeches of Acts cannot be ignored.

Here is where the third area of correspondence between 1 Peter and the NT, the "Peter legend", brings clarification to the issue. The portrait of Peter in 1 Peter is fourfold: apostle, witness, participant, and fellow-elder. The first role we meet in 1 Peter is undoubtedly the foundational one: apostle (1:1). There is, of course, no difficulty in establishing this as a traditional role of Peter. No one had better claim to the title. The use of that title in 1 Peter is itself a claim to an authoritative message. The question is, is the linking of the name Peter with that title merely for the purpose of a formal authorization, or does it go deeper?

The other three roles or titles show that it does. The second designation of the author is μάρτυς, "witness" (5:1). Here is an allusion to the crucial role of an apostle, his physical proximity to the historical Jesus. Hints of this are found in 1:8. "Without having seen him, you love him" may imply that the author has. Witness to the passion of Jesus is the emphasis in 5:1. μάρτυς τῶν τοῦ χριστοῦ παθημάτων is admittedly a vague enough expression that a historical referent is not required, but the allusion is a natural one. It may well be that the author deliberately used this ambiguous expression to heighten the identification of later suffering Christians with the apostolic witness (cf. further on "fellow-elder", below). The identification of the apostolic witness with the passion does not specifically tie the tradition to Peter[232], but at least it eliminates one important rival: Paul. Allusion to the apostolic witness of the resurrection may also be implied in the "we" form of 1:3 (cf. Luke 24:21; 1 Cor 15:15; Acts 2:32). Most other attempts to see allusions to events in the life of Jesus and Peter meet with less than success[233].

One other allusion to an event in the life of Peter is certainly indicated in the third self-designation of the author as ὁ τῆς μελλούσης ἀποκαλύπτεσθαι δόξης κοινωνός (5:1). That this was intended as an allusion to the Transfig-

---

231 The Servant Christology is also associated with a "ransom" soteriology (1 Pet 1: 18, 19) that is also found in Mark (10:45) and may serve as supportive evidence for a Petrine tradition in this regard.

232 F. Neugebauer, "Zur Deutung", 71, suggests that 2:22f. is an allusion (by way of contrast) to Peter's denial of Jesus, but it is more likely just due to its dependence on Isaiah 53:9.

233 For further treatment of the Peter legend in the early church, see W. Bauer, "The Picture of the Apostle in Early Christian Tradition. 1. Accounts", *NTApocrypha*, 45–50.

uration is clear from the earliest interpretation we have of this verse: 2 Peter 2:16ff. This designation is important because it not only dissociates the author from Paul, but makes it highly likely that a specifically Petrine tradition is being identified. Not just any apostle, but one who has experienced the Transfigured glory of Christ is the authority behind the message of 1 Peter.

But why is this specific identification so important? This leads us to the fourth self-designation, which serves as the hermeneutical key for understanding the purpose of 1 Peter and the use of the Petrine attribution. The author calls himself συμπρεσβύτερος, "fellow-elder" (5:1). While we have no other historical referent to Peter as an elder, it is easy to see how this title could be associated with him, particularly in its pastoral associations. J.H. Elliott has demonstrated that the understanding of church order and ministry in 1 Peter 5:1–5 is remarkably similar to the account of John 21:15–23, especially in relation to the central figure of Peter. He lists eight affinities:

1. The person of Peter. Cf. also Luke 22:31–34.
2. The shepherd/sheep metaphor for ministry. Cf. also Luke 12:32–40, 41–48.
3. Clothing metaphor expressing either deferment to the will of another (John 21: 18b) or humility before others (1 Peter 5:5b).
4. Theme of discipleship.
5. Reference to the Lord's final appearance.
6. Common glory/glorification motif.
7. Issue of rank raised by both.
8. Both related to John 13[234].

Elliott suggests that these points of contact, as well as others with Mark 10:35–45 and par. suggest a common tradition of ministry and church order associated with the role of Peter[235]. At the very least we can say that 1 Peter makes a deliberate attempt to identify the role of Peter with the task facing the leaders of the communities, and to ground that role in a peculiar Petrine experience of the gospel record. 1 Peter 5:1–5 is in some ways similar to Paul's address to the Ephesian elders in Acts 20:17–35, where the apostolic experience is alluded to and the elders are encouraged to be similarly devoted to their duties (cf. Acts 20:28; 1 Pet 5:2f.). As one who received the charge of the Risen Lord to "shepherd my sheep" (ποίμαινε, John 21:16), he as apostolic "fellow-elder" (5:1) can charge the church leaders to do likewise (ποιμάνατε, 5:2). Peter both identifies with them and stands above them as an apostolic prototype, who can encourage them also to be "examples" (τύποι) to their flocks (5:3; cf. 1 Tim 4:12; Titus 2:7).

Yet this apostolic prototype or example is also derived, being based on the supreme example (ὑπογραμμός 2:21) of Christ, the "chief shepherd" (5:4; cf. 2:25). Here is where the full panoply of Petrine tradition comes into

---

234 "Ministry and Church Order in the NT. A Traditio-Historical Analysis (1 Peter 5, 1–5 and plls)", *CBQ* 32 (1970) 383–384.
235 He also cites the role of Peter in Acts 1:15–26; 5:1–11 in church organisation (election of Matthias) and discipline (Ananias and Sapphira).

play. The basic problem of 1 Peter is how Christians are to respond to persecution. That problem is addressed using many allusions to the dominical tradition. Foremost among these is the identification of Jesus as the Suffering Servant (1:19; 2:21–25; 3:18), a role that is further identified with that of the Shepherd (2:25; cf. 5:4; John 10:11), who suffers on behalf of those entrusted to him. As we saw, it was in association with Peter's speeches in Acts (παῖς θεοῦ, 3:13, 26; 4:27, 30) that Jesus' role as Servant is most strongly portrayed. The paradigm for Christian suffering is found in the passion of Christ, a *theologia crucis,* as taught by Peter.

Not only is this theology bound up with the teaching tradition of the apostle. It is tied to the example of the apostle as well. He who was a μάρτυς τῶν τοῦ Χριστοῦ παθημάτων was called to reincarnate the Shepherd role of Christ in his care for the flock (John 21:15–19). If the author is not Peter, then the reference to his "witness" (μάρτυς) may in fact also be an allusion to the martyrdom of Peter, the ultimate in sacrificial living. In any case, the figure (and teaching) of Peter stands as the exemplary link between Christ's attitude to suffering and the leadership of the communities to whom 1 Peter is addressed. Like Peter, and the Lord whom he served, they are to give of themselves sacrificially for the sake of God's flock and to lead them in the path that he led (5:2, 3).

Finally, the promise of reward parallels that of Jesus and Peter as well. As God vindicated Him who abandoned all to God, likewise his imitators will share in his glory (δοξῆς, 5:4). As proof of this is the apostle Peter, who was uniquely privileged to taste of this glory in the Transfiguration, (ὁ τῆς μελλούσης ἀποκαλύπτεσθαι δόξης κοινωός, 5:1). It is particularly signigicant that it is the Transfiguration, and not the resurrection, that is used as the paradigm of this glory. Not only does this give a pre-eminent role to Peter as an apostolic witness to the promise of this glory, but it also heightens the futurity of that glory. By emphasizing the Transfiguration rather than the resurrection, 1 Peter assures that no *theologia gloriae* is possible in the present circumstances. It seems no accident that a very similar approach is taken by the roughly contemporaneous gospel of Mark, which has strong traditional associations with Peter.

In summary, we can see that though 1 Peter contains a great deal of tradition material that in isolation can only be regarded as general in nature, this material is woven together with a particular image of the experiences or roles of Peter that makes it part of a fabric that must be labelled a "Petrine" tradition. By collecting and arranging this material, and heightening its effect by making the explicit identification of Peter with the leaders of the communities (συμπρεσβύτερος, 5:1), the author has achieved a contemporary application of traditional Petrine material to the new situation of persecution, or in short, *Vergegenwärtigung.* The idea of pseudonymity in 1 Peter as an appeal to Petrine tradition must be maintained as a viable option.

5.4.1.4 *Vergegenwärtigung and the Authorship of 1 Peter*

An option, however, is not a conclusion. The question needs to be asked, what does the presence of a Petrine tradition and *Vergegenwärtigung* in 1 Peter imply for an understanding of its authorship? Essentially two negative assertions need to be made, which will, however, also entail some positive affirmations.

First the presence of a Petrine tradition in 1 Peter does not necessarily mean that a school or any such group is responsible for its production[236]. Of course this remains a possibility. Because of the affinities of 1 Peter with Mark[237] and Peter's traditional association with Rome, the capital of the empire is usually cited as the location of this Petrine organization[238]. The thesis remains, at best, a tantalizing possibility, but with no support from any of the other Petrine literature[239].

What the presence of Petrine tradition *does* mean is that the communities who received the letter, whether it was written by a group or an individual, regarded Peter and his associated traditions as a source of identity. This need not be an exclusive identification, since we know that Peter had elements of support even in Pauline communities (1 Cor 1:12). Nor do many of the traditions need to be identified with Peter in an exclusive sense, especially taken in isolation. It is the combination of the traditional role of Peter with various dominical and kerygmatic traditions that give evidence of the kind of tradition thinking that regards Peter as an authoritative source and might lead to pseudepigraphic attribution.

Second, the presence of *Vergegenwärtigung* in 1 Peter, using a reinterpretation of Petrine tradition to address the newly arisen problem of persecution, does not necessarily require that the letter be regarded as pseudonymous. Since 1 Peter does not reveal a developed sense of "canon-consciousness" in regard to the use of the traditional material (cf. possibly 1:12), and since there is no overwhelming evidence of a post-Petrine *Sitz im Leben* in the

---

236 This applies both to the formal concept of a school or tannaite system of elders (P. Carrington, *The Primitive Christian Catechism*. Cambridge: University Press, 1970, 71; E. Best, *I Peter*, 59–63) and the less formal idea of circle or community (J.H. Elliott, "Peter, Silvanus"; *idem*, "Rehabilitation", 246–248; E. Lohse, "Paränese", 83–85; L. Goppelt, *Erste Petrusbrief*, 30–37, 66–70, 345–355).

237 E. Best, *I Peter*, 60, cites three: (1) a similar interpretation of Jesus' death as bearing punishment for men's sins (rather than defeat of evil powers), (2) a view of that death as ransom, and (3) a like interest in the Woes of the Messiah as involving persecution for the church, and not just a terrible time for the world as a whole.

238 J.H. Elliott is the most thoroughgoing advocate of this approach. See esp. "Peter, Silvanus", and *A Home*, 267–295. Elliott suggests that part of the purpose behind 1 Peter is to assert the influence of the Petrine group in Rome over all of Rome (contra the Paulinists) and the rest of the Christian World. Though he denies it, this smacks of the union thesis, and is open to many of its criticisms.

239 See D.H. Schmidt, *Peter Writings*, who demonstrates that the Petrine literature cannot be attributed to an organically related, geographically centralized Petrine group of disciples or school.

letter, the most that we can say is that the pseudonymity of 1 Peter is possible. It is true that other elements of the "pattern" in the relationship of revelation and tradition which we discovered are also found in 1 Peter. Thus the author clearly regards the *kerygma* as *divinely inspired* (1:12), and that it is part of a *unified* or *coherent* plan of God (1:10–11), a plan that had to have been spiritually *interpreted* (1:12). Further, this revelation, past and present, is part of the *autonomous* word of God, which has a life of its own. Thus after the author cites Isaiah 40:6–8 (1 Pet 1:24), he remarks "That word is the good news which was preached to you" (1 Pet 1:25). Thus he regards the *kerygma* (and probably his own writing) as equal in authority to the Jewish scriptures. Yet as we said earlier, the "pattern" cannot be used to *prove* pseudonymity, only explain it[240].

The important result for the purpose of this investigation, however, is that the integrity of the pattern remains. If 1 Peter is pseudonymous (and the jury is still very much out on the matter), then the only viable alternative is to understand it in light of an actualization of Petrine tradition, perhaps suggested by the tradition of Peter "strengthening the brethren" after his own trials (Luke 22:31–32; cf. 1 Pet 5:12). *In either case, the result is that attribution in 1 Peter remains an assertion of authoritative tradition.*

5.4.2 2 Peter

5.4.2.1 *The Problem of 2 Peter*

No document included in the NT gives such thorough evidence of its pseudonymity as does 2 Peter. The arguments against authenticity are overwhelming[241]. No work had greater difficulty in acceptance into canon. Eusebius (H.E. iii.2, 1–2) lists it as non-canonical, and it is unknown in the West until the fourth century[242]. Literarily the work is dependent on the Epistle of Jude[243]. There is no problem in the Apostle Peter using it in this manner, even if Jude is now judged to be pseudonymous. The problem is that, authentic or not, Jude is usually dated after the lifetime of Peter[244].

---

240 For similar sentiments, see R.E. Brown (edit.), *Peter,* 154.
241 Beside the standard introductions and commentaries, see esp. T. Fornberg, *An Early Church in a Pluralistic Society: A Study of 2 Peter* (Lund: Gleerup, 1977). For a defense of authenticity, see E.M.B. Green, *2 Peter Reconsidered* (London: Tyndale Press, 1961); J.A.T. Robinson, *Redating,* 169–199.
242 See D.H. Schmidt, *Peter Writings,* 168–172; C. Bigg, *The Epistles of St. Peter and St. Jude,* 199–215 for full attestation.
243 See T. Fornberg, *Early Church,* 33–59; and the commentaries of A. Leany and E. M. Sidebottom for the list of parallels and discussion.
244 Though occasionally the priority of 2 Peter is asserted (see C. Bigg, *Epistles of St. Peter,* 216–224), the usual tack of defenders of authenticity is to appeal to a common tradition behind both. See B. Reicke, *The Epistles of James, Peter and Jude* (Garden City, N.Y.: Doubleday, 1964) 189–190; E.M.B. Green, *2 Peter,* 50–55.

The language and style of 2 Peter is very different from that of 1 Peter. The two works could not have come from the same man[245]. Similarly, 2 Peter reveals a later, Hellenistic perspective in its theology and language, even when dealing with same subjects as 1 Peter[246]. Finally, 2 Peter demonstrates an unquestionably post-Petrine *Sitz im Leben*. One of the central problems of 2 Peter is the delay of the parousia. The argument of the heretics, "Where is the promise of his coming? For ever since the fathers fell asleep, all things have continued as they were from the beginning of creation" (3:4), would have been impossible if Peter were alive (cf. Mark 9:1)[247]. Likewise, 2 Peter 3:15–16 refers to Paul's letters as "scripture", a development of the concept of a NT canon that dates well after the death of the apostles[248].

In face of the preponderance of arguments against authenticity, it is only with heroic (and ingenious) tenacity that a few retain their defence of the Petrine attribution. By their own admission, their defence is really based on a prior and more fundamental objection to pseudonymity. E.M.B. Green is typical in his remarks that 2 Peter is manifestly superior to other pseudonymous Petrine writings, and does not exhibit any (heretical) motive that would require pseudonymity[249]. A similar appeal to a lack of motive is made by D. Guthrie, who adds that only heretics needed pseudonymity to get their views across, since "orthodox" writers already had acceptance[250]. But these presuppositions are based more on a theological *a priori* than on historical facts.

But the fact that 2 Peter contains all but five verses of Jude (the epistolary frame-work) makes this approach hardly credible.

245 See esp. J.B. Mayor, *The Epistle of St. Jude and the Second Epistle of St. Peter* (New York: Macmillan, 1907) lxviii–cv. Recourse by defenders of authenticity is usually made to a secretary, or actually *two* secretaries, one for each letter. See E.M.B. Green, *2 Peter,* 11–14; C. Bigg, *Epistles of St. Peter,* 242–247. Occasionally an appeal is made to a fragment hypothesis to justify the Petrine attribution (e.g. E.I. Robson, *Studies in the Second Epistle of St. Peter* (Cambridge: University Press, 1915), but the unity of the letter is so apparent that E.M.B. Green rightly asks, "Why bother?".

246 For instance, 1 Peter refers to the return of Christ as a "revelation" (ἀποκάλυψις, 1:7,13; 4:13), while 2 Peter calls it an "arrival" (παρουσία, 1:16; 3:4, 12). Cf. also Cf. also 1 Peter 1:19 "salvation of your souls", and 2 Peter 1:4 "partakers of the divine nature".

247 Contrast this with the fervent expectation of 1 Peter 4:7. Defenders of authenticity argue that "fathers" (3:4) refer to OT patriarchs. See E.M.B. Green, *2 Peter,* 29–30; D. Guthrie, *Intro.,* 836–837. But even J.A.T. Robinson, *Redating,* 180, rejects this, citing 1 John 2:13f.; Acts 21:16. Some Jesus logia place the parousia in the context of the first generation (see B.S. Crawford, "Near Expectation in the Sayings of Jesus", *JBL* 101 (1982) 225–244), and later works give a clear connection to the passing of the Christian "fathers" and the problem of delay (1 Clem 23:3; 2 Clem 11:2).

248 Robinson, 181–184, and Green, 30–32, appeal to Paul's own consciousness of his authority, but this is different than (though necessarily prior to) regarding them as *scripture*.

249 *The Second Epistle General of Peter and the General Epistle of Jude* (London: Tyndale Press, 1968) 30–31.

250 *Intro.,* 845–848.

The division between heresy and orthodoxy, either in content or method, was not that clear in the first and early second century. Their common appeal to legitimation by the apostolic tradition opened the opportunity for the use of pseudonymity by both camps. If 2 Peter is a superior document to the others, this is a theological judgement of canon (written from the perspective of an orthodox "winner" in the struggle), and not a relevant criterion for the historical-critical question of authorship. The issue of a motive is a legitimate one, however, if it is not restricted to "heresy". It is precisely the motive for the pseudonymity of 2 Peter that is now the focus of our concern.

5.4.2.2 *The Occasion and Purpose of 2 Peter*

The problem that gave rise to 2 Peter is readily apparent: the active presence of heresy. This heresy had both doctrinal and moral implications. The heretics were denying fundamental principles of the faith, such as the parousia, perhaps advocating a cyclical view of history in its stead (3:3–4). Their behaviour is morally reprehensible (2:11–16), and seem to be based on an antinomian doctrine of freedom (2:19). They are a seditious group, threatening to entice members away from the regular church fellowship into their own organization and practices (2:13–14, 18; 3:17). There is little reason to doubt that this was some form of gnostic sectarianism[251].

There is no doubt that the fundamental issue was one of *interpretation.* Both sides seem to have recognized or appealed to common authorities, whether it be the Jewish scriptures (1:20), Paul (3:15–16) or perhaps Peter (3:1)[252]. Indeed, the appeal to these sources reveals a highly developed sense of "canon-consciousness". The Jewish scriptures were, of course, long recognized as the church's scripture. However, in a manner far clearer than even the Pastorals, now Paul's letters are similarly regarded (3:15–16), transforming them from occasional letters to documents of universal significance. Of special note is the reference to the *divine inspiration* of these Pauline scriptures. They are a result of wisdom being given to Paul, the divine passive an indication of their source (3:15, cf. Wisd 9:17)[253]. This link between wisdom and inspiration is one that we have met frequently in both Jewish Wisdom and Apocalyptic, and demonstrated the consciousness of a *unity and continuity* between an original recipient of a revelation and his later followers.

---

251 For further attempts to identify the nature of the heretics and the *Sitz im Leben* of 2 Peter, see J. Klinger, "The Second Epistle of Peter: An Essay in Understanding", *St. Valdmir's Theological Quarterly* 17 (1973) 152–169; T. Fornberg, *Early Church,* 111–148; J.H. Neyrey, *The Form and Background of the Polemic in 2 Peter* (Ph.D., Yale, 1977).

252 It is uncertain if the heretics appealed to Peter. It seems likely that he was an authority figure to them, for otherwise the pseudepigraphic refutation by Peter would carry no weight.

253 T. Fornberg, *Early Church,* 21.

This is why the misinterpreters are labelled "ignorant" (ἀμαθεῖς, 3:16), since they do not partake, in even a secondary manner, of the revelational wisdom given to Paul.

The epistle of 1 Peter, too, is the focus of this developed "canon-consciousness", though it is not specifically labelled "scripture" (2 Pet 3:1; cf. 1:12–15)[254]. It at least demonstrates that, like the Pastorals for Paul, authoritative Petrine tradition was now expected to take literary form.

Where the sides differed was not in primary sources of authority, but in the derived authority that comes through interpretation. This is the heart of the issue in 2 Peter. When it is said that the heretics "despise authority" (2:10), what is really meant is that they disregard the authority of the "orthodox" interpreters, not the primary authorities themselves (Jewish scripture, Paul, Peter). The libertinism and emphasis on personal knowledge of the gnostic sect had undoubtedly led to an individualistic hermeneutic. This is confirmed by 1:20, which makes the explicit counter-claim that "no prophecy of scripture is a matter of one's own interpretation"[255]. The implication is that the purity of doctrine and its interpretation is now in the hands of an official teaching office, a concept that we met with in the Pastorals. Furthermore, the mention of the Holy Spirit as the source of prophetic inspiration (1:21) has ramifications for the teaching office as well. *The argument that scripture cannot be privately interpreted because it is Spirit-inspired can only make sense if the Spirit of interpretation has been given to an authorized body of teachers. This hermeneutical assumption of 2 Peter, then, becomes a clear indication of the perceived continuity between a Spirit-inspired source of tradition and its later interpreters which, as we have seen, is the fundamental justification of pseudonymity.* The clash of 2 Peter, then, is over who has the right to be designated as legitimate (Spirit-led) interpreters of scripture, which includes the writings of the apostles.

That this "interpretation" is regarded as continuous with, but secondary to, the primary inspiration of scripture may also be seen in the designation of the heretics as ψευδοδιδάσκαλοι (2:1). Though there is admittedly a blurring of distinctions between prophecy and teaching in the NT, as we discussed earlier in the Pauline tradition, there is a growing tendency to relegate prophecy to the earlier, "apostolic" age of the church (cf. Eph 2:20; 3:5) and to stress the continuity of the apostles and their followers in terms of teaching (cf. 2 Tim 1:11; 3:10). It is significant, then, that in contrast to the OT false prophets, the heretics are labelled *false teachers,* a *hapax.* It may be that 2 Peter represents the last stage in the early church development, where

---

254 A few commentators (Spitta, Zahn) think 3:1 refers to a lost letter, not 1 Peter; and M. McNamara, "The Unity of Second Peter: A Reconsideration", *Scripture* 12 (1960) 13–19, based on his thesis of disunity, argues it refers to a previous letter now found in chapters 1 and 2. Both positions are unlikely.

255 The phrase ἰδίας ἐπιλύσεως οὐ γίνεται is subject to a number of translations and interpretations, but the idea of private or individual interpretation seems paramount. See J.T. Curran, "The Teaching of 2 Peter 1:20", *TS* 4 (1943) 347–368.

prophecy had in fact died out, and only inspired interpretation was considered legitimate.

In any case, the focus of 2 Peter is on correct or authoritative interpretation, witnessed also by the themes of understanding (1:20, 3:3, 16) and knowledge (1:2, 3, 5, 8; 2:20; 3:18). This backward looking attitude is also confirmed in the explicitly stated purpose in 1:12—15, the only part of the letter where the author uses the first person singular. Three times the theme of "reminding" is raised (ὑπομιμνήσκειν, v.12; ὑπομνήσει, v.13; μνήμην, v. 15; cf. also ὑπομνήσει 3:1; and μνησθῆναι, 3:2), a clear indication that the author is not intending to say something new, *but to appeal to an authoritative tradition.* The threat to the integrity of the community, the "canon-consciousness" that identifies Peter as a source of that community-creating identity, the conviction of a continuity with the apostles through a divine spirit of wisdom and interpretation, and the determination to address the crisis by an appeal to the primary source of tradition (*Vergegenwärtigung*) are all part of the classic pattern of pseudonymity that we have established in our investigations. It now remains to see if and how Petrine tradition is actually used to address the problems of 2 Peter.

5.4.2.3 *Petrine Tradition in 2 Peter*

There are some who would doubt that 2 Peter depends in any way on 1 Peter or other sources of Peter tradition. Yet 3:1 makes it clear that *at least* 1 Peter is in mind. This is confirmed when we compare the salutations of the two letters. They are almost identical (apart from the material about the addressees). The major variation is that Συμεών is added to Peter's name, which is perhaps a reflection of the usage by James in Acts 15:4. The unique similarity of these two salutations suggests that the author of 2 Peter was in some way intending to pattern his work after 1 Peter.

But how? Though they appear to have radically different *Sitzen im Leben,* G.H. Boobyer suggests that the connection was made between two similar concerns: holiness and the Second Coming[256]. The "reminder" (1:13; 3:1), then, is to use the similar topical arguments of 1 Peter to address new situations. The first indication of this reapplication of Petrine material comes in the salutation itself. Though the shared material is nearly identical, there is one significant addition in 2 Peter (1:2b): to the πληθυνθείη is added ἐν ἐπιγνώσει τοῦ θεοῦ καὶ Ἰησοῦ τοῦ κυρίου ἡμῶν. As we saw, "knowledge" is a major theme of 2 Peter, and relates to the problem of false teaching. Further indications of this problem can even be found in the material describing the addressees, which of course, would not be parallel with 1 Peter.

---

256 "The Indebtedness of II Peter to I Peter", *New Testament Essays: Studies in Memory of T.W. Manson.* Edit. A.J.B. Higgins (Manchester: University Press, 1959) 34—53.

There is a certain parallel of content, since each stress the theme of holiness. But while 1 Peter (1:2) places this in the context of their divine election, thus accenting its own theme of reassurance in persecution, 2 Peter (1:1) places it in the context of a "faith of equal standing with ours (i.e. the apostles)". This change of emphasis most likely is a counter to the divisiveness and assumption of spiritual position that was so much a part of gnostic sectarianism.

According to Boobyer, the following arguments in 1 Peter 1:3–9; 2 Peter 1:3–11 are then paralleled, not in terms of literary dependence, but in thought and structure:

1 Peter 1:3–4	2 Peter 1:3–11
Through the resurrection of J.C. we have a hope of an incorruptable and undefiled inheritance, reserved for us in heaven.	Christ's divine power and glory are sources of all things pertaining to life and godliness, as well as of previous promises, enabling us to become partakers of the divine nature and avoid terrestial corruption.
This inheritance is for those guarded by faith until salvation "in the last time", and is a cause of rejoicing in the grief of present trials or temptations.	To faith other virtues must be added. This will promote the necessary knowledge of J.C. and be in keeping with cleansing from former sins.
But faith, tested and proved, will issue in glory, honor, and the salvation of your souls at the revelation of J.C. (i.e. the second avent).	In this manner, make your calling and election sure, as well as your entry into Christ's eternal kingdom (i.e. at the Parousia).[257]

As Boobyer points out, the major difference lies in the middle section. Though both use faith as a connecting link, 2 Peter digresses to make a point about the nature of faith, that it needs to be "supplemented" (i.e. with works). This may well be a response to an antinomian use of Paul (3:16)[258]. Similarly, even where the topics are paralleled, the distinctive vocabulary of 2 Peter reveals its concern. Thus we meet with the issue of knowledge repeatedly (1:3, 5, 6, 8), and it is closely identified with εὐσέβεια, "godliness" (1:3). 2 Peter may even be appealing to Petrine tradition in Acts 3:12. There the issue is over the source of Peter's "power" and "godliness", and Peter affirms that both come from God. In 2 Peter 1:3 this is the *same* assurance, and in its connection to knowledge may serve as a counter to the individualistic spirituality of the sectarians. To those Christians who are beleagured by the claims and allures of gnostic appeals, the apostle "Peter" assures them by relating their experience of Christ to his. He assures them that they need not fear that they are lacking anything (e.g. "knowledge"), for their standing in the faith is equal to his (1:1), because its common source is God (1:3).

This appeal to the experience of Peter as the basis of its argument shows the tradition orientation of 2 Peter, and leads to the heart of the issue it ad-

---

257 *Ibid.*, 40f.
258 See J. Klinger, "Second Epistle", 163, who demonstrates how this is done from a Hellenistic perspective, rather than a Jewish one (as in James).

dresses. As we said earlier, the problem of 2 Peter is really one of authority. It is no accident, then, that 2 Peter uses the same sources of authority as does 1 Peter. In 1 Peter 1:10:12 the authority for the teaching regarding the suffering and glory of Christ is found in the Jewish scriptures, (the Spirit of) Christ, and the apostles (early kerygma). 2 Peter 1:12–21 (cf. 3:1–2) repeats this pattern, and uses it to support its arguments regarding the parousia, as well as its ethical appeals[259]. Furthermore, that appeal to tradition and authority is predicated on a uniquely Petrine experience – the witnessing of the Transfiguration (2 Pet 1:16-18). This may well be an exegesis of 1 Peter 5:1, but at the very least is an important part of the Synoptic Petrine tradition. Not only does this confirm the concern of the author to root his argument in the experience of Peter, it also reveals an astute attack upon the sectarian theology. Since the parousia was most often denied through some sort of spiritualizing of the resurrection (cf. 1 Cor 15), the author bases his argument for the parousia not on the common apostolic witness of the resurrection, but on Peter's experience of the Transfiguration. This method may also have been used to counter an exclusive dependence on Paul by the heretics[260].

After 1 Peter 1:12 comes a paranetical section, and 2 Peter 2 begins one as well. H. Boobyer suggests that here the author departs from his dependence on 1 Peter and uses a source more appropriate to his task – Jude[261]. Since he is now describing the heretics in some detail, he needs an invective against opponents that 1 Peter lacks. It is significant that the material is still given a Petrine "anchor" by a common treatment of the figure of Noah and the Flood (1 Pet 3:19, 20; 2 Pet 2:4, 5), linking both with angels who fell. Here is a prime example of configurational *Vergegenwärtigung*.

Space will not allow for a more detailed investigation of 2 Peter's use of sources. We have seen, however, how the author uses a number of traditional authorities to refute the doctrines of the sectarians. Note that this confirms the "canon-consciousness" that we discussed earlier, that the letter recognizes both Jewish scriptures and the apostolic writings (Peter, Paul) as "scripture" or at least as authoritative. Also remember that the heretics appealed to similar authorities. It would seem, then, that after coming full circle we have returned to the same problem, that of interpretation. What was to prevent the opponents mentioned in 2 Peter from rejecting the arguments of the author on the basis that the author had misinterpreted the (commonly held) authorities?

Here the author of 2 Peter offers an answer quite similar to the Pastorals: Peter has arranged not only for a body of authoritative writings (including 2 Peter); he has also provided for an authorized body of interpreters. This is seen in the pivotal verses, 1:12–15. We have a reference here to Peter's ap-

---

259 G. Boobyer, "Indebtedness", 42–43. He notes that "these things" (1:12, 17) cover the items in both vv 3–11 and 16–21.
260 Though it is not a rejection of Paul himself. Cf. 3:15, "our beloved brother Paul".
261 "Indebtedness", 44.

proaching death, "as our Lord Jesus showed me". Though there is no little disagreement over the source of this reference[262], its clear intent is to depict 2 Peter as a testament[263]. As the last words of Peter, they are intended to make provision for the continuance of his "apostolic" doctrine in his absence. "I will see to it that after my departure you may be able at any time to recall these things" (1:15) at a minimum refers to 2 Peter (and 1 Peter), but it is likely that there is something more. Though more implicit than 2 Timothy, the intent is the same. The way that Petrine (like Pauline) doctrine would maintain its vitality and relevance is not just through scriptural writings (since these could be misinterpreted), but through an official teaching office, a primitive form of *magisterium* (2 Pet 1:20–21). This is the final refutation of the heretics (and any subsequent ones), and like 2 Timothy sets the scene for a fundamental alteration in the growth and application of biblical tradition. *Thus it is clear that attribution in 2 Peter is intended primarily as an assertion of authoritative tradition, not literary origins.*

5.4.3 *Excursus: Later Petrine Tradition*

As with the Pauline tradition, it may be helpful to take a cursory glance at later Petrine tradition, to see if any continuity and/or development can be discerned. Two documents will be examined, the Apocalypse of Peter and the Gospel of Peter[264].

The first difference is, of course, that these documents are a different literary genre than the epistles of 1 and 2 Peter. Though pseudonymity is not tied to any particular genre, it does mean that for the later Petrine tradition, the letter form was not an inherent part of the tradition, as it was for 2 Peter (3:1) or the deutero-Paulines. The Apocalypse of Peter (not to be confused with the gnostic Apocalypse) is a quite early document, usually dated around A.D. 135[265]. It is generally regarded as subsequent to 2 Peter, but their actual literary relationship is subject to debate[266]. Since this is the

---

262 It may be a reference to John 13:36–37; 21:18–19; the *Quo Vadis* legend (Acts of Peter 35); or an interpretation of 1 Peter 5:1. See H. Boobyer, "Indebtedness", 44–51; T. Fornberg, *Early Church*, 10.

263 See O. Knoch, *Die Testament*.

264 The second-century Kerygma Petrou might be helpful, but it is too fragmentary. See *NTApocrypha*, II, 94–101. The Kerygmata Petrou is a third century document not attributed to Peter in the first instance. See *NTApocrypha*, II, 102–127. Both the Epistle of Peter to Philip and the Apocalypse of Peter found at Nag Hamimadi are gnostic, and do not appear in any church canons. Also to be excluded are writings *about* Peter (e.g. Acts of Peter).

265 See *NTApocrypha*, II, 664.

266 For arguments for the priority of 2 Peter, see A.E. Simms, "Second Peter and the Apocalypse of Peter", *Exp* 5/8 (1898) 460–471; F. Spitta, "Die Petrusapokalypse und der zweite Petrusbriefe", *ZNW* 12 (1911) 237ff. (N.V.). The issue of literary dependence is complicated by the debate over the accuracy of the sources. See D.H. Schmidt, *Peter Writings*, 112–116.

case, we will examine the work without any assumption of clear literary dependence on 2 Peter[267]

Written in the first person singular, the author gives explicit identification of himself as Peter (A.P. *Eth* 2, 3, 14). His role as primary recipient of revelation is also made clear (A.P. *Eth* 14, cf. also 2, 3, 16), a role that includes the dissemination of that revelation to the whole world. How was this to be done? Here we see the importance of the idea of tradition. Apocalypse of Peter *(Eth)* 1: "Make known unto us what are the signs of thy Parousia and of the end of the world, that we may perceive and mark the time of the Parousia, and *instruct those who come after us,* to whom we preach the word of thy Gospel, *and whom we install in thy church,* in order that they, when they hear it, may take heed to themselves that they mark the time of thy coming." Like the Pastorals and 2 Peter, we see how Petrine tradition has been passed on, both in the form of "apostolic" literature (i.e. the Apocalypse of Peter), and in an official teaching office of interpreters. This verse also gives us the occasion of this writing: the threat to the community caused by the delay of the Parousia.

According to D.H. Schmidt[268], the author depends on two main sources, both Jewish: the gospel of Matthew and 1 Enoch. The framework of the Apocalypse of Peter is to use the little apocalypse according to Matthew and weave in material from 1 Enoch, concluding with a (supplemented) visionary account of the Transfiguration. In all the book the role of Peter is heightened, and the material harmonized in almost midrashic fashion[269]. It seems that the author is undertaking a fundamental restatement and supplementation of the apocalyptic traditions in both Christianity and Judaism.

As a Christian Jew, apostle to the circumcision (Gal 2:7), Peter was the natural choice to stand at its head. Here the Transfiguration account is crucial, since it gives Peter a unique position as an eyewitness of the Parousia which is still to come (cf. 1 Pet 5:1; 2 Pet 1:16–18). Since he stands as a primary apocalyptic witness, then by right any authoritative (Jewish) apoclyptic traditions can be attributed to him. This conviction of the unity of revelation is confirmed by the presence of a familiar apocalyptic feature in Apocalypse of Peter *(Eth)* 16: the heavenly books. At the Transfiguration Peter read and "understood that which is written in the book of my Lord Jesus Christ" (cf. also A.P. *Eth* 17, "book of life"). Since Peter saw all apocalyptic revelation at the Transfiguration, then any authoritative apocalyptic tradition could be attributed to him.

The Gospel of Peter dates from around mid-second century, based on the testimony of Serapion[270]. Originally accepted for use in the Syrian church, it

---

267 Though it does in fact share a number of Petrine topics, e.g. the account of the Transfiguration (AP *Eth* 15–17; 2 Pet 1:16–18); and the prophecy of world conflagration (AP *Eth* 4–5; 2 Pet 3:10–13).

268 *Peter Writings,* 116–127, 131–134.

269 *Ibid.*

270 In Eusebius, H.E. vi, 12. For texts and bibliography see C. Mauer, *NTApocrypha,* I, 183; D.H. Schmidt, *Peter Writings,* 216–219.

was later rejected by the Bishop as containing heresy, particularly the docetic variety. Since we only possess a fragment, it is difficult to know precisely to what Serapion objected, since the fragment displays no overt docetic doctrine[271].

There are only two references in the fragment that give evidence of a Petrine attribution. In Gospel of Peter 26f., the speaker identifies himself with those mourners who hid from the Jews. In Gospel of Peter 58ff., the author specifically identifies himself as "I, Peter". D.H. Schmidt notes that this use of the first person singular is a departure from the anonymity of the canonical gospels, and reflects a desire to tie the gospel testimony to the apostles[272]. It also reflects a changing attitude toward the authorship of these traditions. The gospels are now the gospels of the apostles, not the gospel of Jesus[273].

Nevertheless, the Gospel of Peter does not display the rigidity in its use of tradition that we find characteristic of later writings (e.g. Epistle to Laodiceans, Diatessaron). It still feels free to use oral and written traditions in a fluid manner. The author depends mostly on the gospels of Matthew and Mark, but also uses a good deal of legendary material from popular tradition[274]. Beside the explicit charge of docetism by Serapion, the most obvious *Tendenz* of the writing is in its vilification of the Jews (cf. Gospel of Peter 2, 5, 13, 26, 33, 38, 50, 52, 54), heightening their opposition to Christianity. Schmidt suggests that Gospel of Peter 26 "were sought after by them (the Jews) as evil doers and as persons who wanted to set fire to the temple" may be a further indication of the letter's purpose – to aid in the struggle with the Jews of the day, who may have blamed Christians for the destruction of the Temple.

The fragmentary preservation of the Gospel of Peter makes it difficult to· assess the nature and purpose of the pseudepigraphic attribution. There is no developed Peter legend, nor any real attempt to apply Petrine tradition to a new *Sitz im Leben*. As was stated earlier, the apostolic attribution of the gospel genre was a new development, that may well indicate that the traditio-historical process was in the process of disintegration. Though it does not display the formal rigidity of the later Epistle to the Laodicean's, the Gospel of Peter shows no real appreciation for the linkage of the material that it uses to the firgure of Peter. *Vergegenwärtigung* in the biblical mode may well be at an end.

---

271 The substitution of "my power" for "my God" in the cry of dereliction (GP 5) is the most likely suspect. See C. Mauer, *NTApocrypha*, I, 181–182, who suggests that three docetic *tendencies* can be discovered in GP: (1) a move from history into the realm of myth, (2) an abandonment of OT salvation-history, and (3) a lack of understanding of Christ's death as expiatory.

272 *Peter Writings*, 155–156.

273 This is confirmed by Justin (A.D. 165), who says that the gospels were being looked upon as the written memoirs of the apostles (I Apol 66, as cited by Schmidt, *ibid.*).

274 *Ibid.*, 141–155. See esp. the tables on 150–151.

5.4.4 *The Petrine Tradition: Summary*

At the end of our treatment of NT revelation and the Jesus tradition, it was suggested that because of their unique link to the authoritative (Jesus) traditions which were part of the foundations of the primitive Christian communities, it might be possible for at least some "apostolic" figures to impress the tradition so strongly with their own personalities that they become *part* of the tradition itself, i.e. to create their own individual tradition. We found this to be true with the figure of Paul, and now it can be concluded, though with less certainty, that this is the function of Peter as well. Despite later veneration by the church, it is indisputable that Peter was a primary leader among the disciples (Matt 10:2) and the early Church (Gal 1:8). More important, he was uniquely linked to authoritative traditions concerning the identity of Jesus (Mark 8:27–30 pars), his resurrection (Luke 24:34; 1 Cor 15:5), the early *kerygma* (Acts 2:14–42; 3:12–26), and even the Gentile mission (Acts 10–11; 15:6–11). Though some of this may be embellishment, it is certain that he was an active missionary figure, at least to the "circumcision" (Gal 2:7–8; cf. Acts 8:14; 9:32), and probably to the Gentiles as well (Gal 2:11; 1 Cor 9:5; cf. 1 Cor 1:12; 3:22; Acts of Peter 35). Further, he was regarded as a receiver of revelations (Mark 9:2–13 pars; Acts 4:8; 5:1–11; 10:9–16; 12:7–9).

Thus the stage was set for an authoritative Petrine tradition, and this is the phenomenon that we discovered in the Petrine literature. In both 1 and 2 Peter the "pattern" in the relationship of revelation and tradition that we isolated in the Jewish background, Jesus tradition, and Pauline literature was repeated. Both deal with material or tradition regarded as *divinely inspired* (1 Pet 1:12; 2 Pet 1:19), part of the *unified* or *coherent* plan of God 1 Pet 1: 10–11; 2 Pet 3:5–7), a plan that needs to be understood and *interpreted* (1 Pet 1:12; 2 Pet 1:20; 3:15–16). Because of this connectedness, this revelation or word of God is *autonomous,* taking on a life of its own, and is not restricted to one individual or place (1 Pet 1:23–25; 2 Pet 1:15; 3:1, 15–16). 2 Peter in particular shows a highly developed sense of "canon-consciousness", placing the writings of Paul (3;16) and probably that of 1 Peter (2 Pet 3:1) on a level with the Jewish scriptures.

The above "pattern" makes it possible for authoritative tradition to be actualized to meet the demands of a new *Sitz im Leben.* In the case of 1 Peter, however, it does not demand that the letter be regarded as pseudonymous. After examining the various theories of the occasion of 1 Peter, it was concluded that the letter was either authentic or a pseudonymous application of Petrine tradition. If pseudonymous, it draws on dominical sayings (e.g. 2: 4, 7; cf. Mark 12:10 par), the speeches of Acts (1:19; 2:22ff.; 3:18; cf. Acts 3:13, 26; 4:27, 30) and the image of Peter as apostle (1:1), witness of Christ's suffering (5:1), participant in his (transfigured) glory (5:1), and above all as "fellow-elder" (5:1) to make a point of contact between Peter's experience of the gospel and the recipients' (cf. John 21:15–23). By linking Peter's experience to that of a later generation, and both to Christ the Suffering Servant who is also the "Chief Shepherd" (1 Peter 5:4; cf. 2:25), the author gives both meaning and hope to the persecuted Christians of his day.

In 2 Peter, the great issue is one of authority (2:10), or more precisely, authoritative tradition and interpretation (1:20—21). To counter the threat of gnostic libertinism, the author engages in a type of thematic *Vergegenwärtigung,* whereby he both affirms and expands on themes in 1 Peter (cf. 1 Pet 1:3—9; 2 Pet 1:3—11). To quell gnostic excess, the author both affirms the role of faith and knowledge as found in 1 Peter, but qualifies it as the type of faith that issues in "godliness" (2 Pet 1:3, 5ff.; cf. 1 Pet 1:5; Acts 3: 2). Similarly it appeals to the same sources of authority as 1 Peter (cf. 1 Pet 1:10—12; 2 Pet 1:12—21; 3:1—2) to support its ethical appeals. To more specifically address the heretics, however, it uses a configurational type of *Vergegenwärtigung,* borrowing from Jude (2 Pet 2) and linking it to Petrine tradition via a similar Noah typology (cf. 1 Pet 3:19—20; 2 Pet 2:4—5).

In 2 Peter we find the testamentary features to be quite strong (1:12—15), and together with its emphasis on a magisterium (1:20—21) is quite similar to the Pastorals. Since the author does reveal a knowledge of Paul's writings (3:15—16), it may well be that his concept of authoritative tradition is influenced by Paulinism, and that his "reminder" (1:12—15; 3:1—2) is intended, like the Pastorals, to be a mediation of the apostolic presence in Peter's absence ("after my departure", 1:15). *At the very least we can say that in the Petrine epistles, attribution is primarily an assertion of authoritative tradition, not literary origins.*

5.5 Tradition and Attribution in the NT: Summary

At the outset of this investigation (Chap 1) it was suggested that an examination of the relationship of revelation and tradition in pre-Christian Judaism might help us to understand the problem of pseudonymity in the NT. After examining the prophetic (Chap 2), wisdom (Chap 3), and apocalyptic (Chap 4) traditions of Judaism, a fundamental "pattern" emerged which had a direct bearing on literary attribution. After summarizing these findings, we have attempted in this chapter to compare our results with the phenomenon of the NT. Though not all of the NT documents were treated, it is safe to say that this "pattern" is overwhelmingly reproduced in the growth of the Jesus tradition:

1. The subject matter is regarded as the product of *divine revelation.* Jesus compared his ministry with the prophets (Mark 6:4f. par; Luke 13:33), and attributed his authority to the Spirit (Matt 12:28 par; Mark 3:28—30 pars). The early church shared the same experience of the eschatological rebirth of prophecy (Acts 2:17— 18), and in addition to the universal gift of the Spirit had a number of regular types of ministries which had (at least in part) a revelatory function: apostles (Acts 2:43; 1 Cor 12:8; Eph 4:11), prophets (Acts 11:27—30; 13:1; 15:32; 1 Cor 10:12), and teachers (1 Cor 14:6, 26; Rom 12:7; Eph 4:11; Acts 6:14—7:53).

2. That revelation is considered to be *unified* or *coherent,* part of the unfolding plan or will of God. This is why the central thought of both Jesus and the early church is the fulfillment of the Jewish scriptures, Thus Jesus' proclamation is encapsuled in the announcement that the kingdom of God "is at hand" (e.g. Mark 1:15), and the church could identify that kingdom with Jesus (e.g. Acts 2:22–36). Further because the eschatological Spirit was the Spirit of Jesus (Acts 16:7; Rom 8:9; Gal 4:6 *et al*), the risen Christ could still address his church (Rev 2–3; OdesSol 42:6).

3. Similarly, that revelation is regarded as *autonomous* or "living", and not just tied to the moment. This was how both Jesus and the church treated the Jewish scriptures, and how the church treated the words of Jesus, preserving them orally for over thirty years.

4. Finally, that revelation is regarded as *interpretative,* part of an on-going process. Both Jesus (e.g. Matt 5:21–48) and the early church (e.g. Acts 1:20; 4:11; Rom 15:9–12) interpreted the Jewish religious traditions, and it is characteristic of the church's attitude to the Jesus tradition as well. Thus we saw that in the Bread of Life Discourse contained in John 6, the Jesus tradition was further interpreted or actualized to better address the needs of the church. This was made possible by the interpretive ministry of the Spirit or Paraclete, (John 14:25–26; 16:13–15).

The reproduction of the Jewish "pattern" in the formation of the Jesus tradition helped us to understand the phenomenon of anonymity in the gospels. Since it is the "gospel of Jesus Christ" (Mark 1:1), no other attribution is needed. It was also suggested that something similar may be at work in the pseudonymous literature of the NT, since the conviction of authoritative tradition stands behind both anonymity and pseudonymity in the Jewish literature we studied. Because certain "apostolic" figures were quickly granted supreme authoritative status in the early church (1 Cor 12:8; Eph 2:20; 1 Thess 2:6; 2 Pet 3:2; Rev 18:20; Acts 1:2), and this status seems to be linked to their role in founding the various communities and proclaiming/defining their religious traditions (Acts 2:42; 4:33; Jude 17 ;2 Thess 2:15; Phil 4:9), it was proposed that some of these figures might have been able to make such an impression on those traditions that they became *part* of the tradition, or started their own individual traditions.

This was precisely what we found in our examination of the deutero-Pauline and Petrine literature. Both Peter and Paul were individuals who had placed their personal stamp on the kerygmatic traditions of the primitive communities. Paul, as apostle to the Gentiles (Gal 2:7), was able to call the tradition *my* gospel (Rom 2:16; 1 Thess 1:5 *et al*), exercise patriarchal authority over his converts (1 Cor 4:15, 17; Gal 4:19), and encourage them to imitate him in word and deed (1 Thess 2:11–15a; Phil 3:15–17; 1 Cor 10: 31–11:1 *et al*). He even developed a distinctive means of mediating his apostolic presence: the emissary (1 Cor 4:17; 2 Cor 8:16–23) and the apostolic letter (Rom 15:15; Phlm 21; 1 Cor 4:14). Similarly Peter was a primary leader among the disciples (Matt 10:2) and early church (Gal 1:18), and was uniquely linked to authoritative traditions concerning the identity of Jesus (Mark 8:27–30 pars), his resurrection (Luke 24:34; 1 Cor 15:5), the early *kerygma* (Acts 2:14–42; 3:12–26), and even the Gentile mission (Acts 10–11; 15:6–11). As an active missionary figure, he travelled both to Palestinian (Gal 2:7–8; Acts 8:14; 9:32) and Gentile fields (Gal 2:11; 1 Cor 9:5).

When we turned to the letters of Ephesians, the Pastorals and 1 and 2 Peter, we discovered that the same "pattern" in the relation of revelation and tradition as we found in our previous studies was reproduced. Thus both Paul and Peter are regarded as recipients of divine *revelation* (1 Tim 2:7; 2 Tim 1:11; Eph 3:3; 1 Pet 1:12; 2 Pet 1:19), a revelation that was considered *autonomous*, readily applicable to the later church (1 Tim 1:16; 2 Tim 1:13; Eph 3:3–4; 1 Pet 1:23–25; 2 Pet 1:15; 3:1–2). Likewise it was *unified* or *coherent*, part of the shared work of the Spirit revealing the mind of God (2 Tim 1:14; Eph 3:3–4; 1 Pet 1:10–11; 2 Pet 3:5–7). Thus it is a revelation that must be *interpreted* (2 Tim 1:15; Eph 1:17; 1 Pet 1:12; 2 Pet 1:20).

The reproduction of this "pattern" of revelation and tradition, coupled with the strong personalization of the kerygmatic traditions in Peter's and Paul's ministries made it possible for the authors of the Pastorals, Ephesians, and 1 and 2 Peter to address the pressing needs of their communities by *Vergegenwärtigung* or a new actualization of authoritative Petrine and Pauline traditions. The Pastorals address the issue of church order by using Paul as archetype (1 Tim 1:16; 2 Tim 1:13) and Timothy and Titus as types (1 Tim 4:12; Titus 2:7) of the ideal Pauline leader which define the parameters of legitimate Christian experience and teaching. Ephesians uses Paul's letter to the Colossians and Paul's theme of God's mystery to address the problem of the fragmentation of Paulinism on many levels (e.g. Jew/Gentile, Eph 2; individual/church, Eph 4:1–16; husband/wife, Eph 5:21–33). 1 Peter, pseudonymous or not, combines the tradition of Peter as witness of Christ's suffering, participant in his transfigured glory, and shepherd or fellow-elder (1 Peter 5:1–5; cf. John 21:15–23) and links them to the role of the Suffering Servant who is also the chief Shepherd (1 Pet 5:4; 2:25). Through these exemplary roles the author offers meaning and hope to the persecuted Christians of his day. 2 Peter counters the excesses of gnosticsim by stressing that faith is linked with godliness (2 Pet 1:3, 5f.; cf. 1 Pet 1:5; Acts 3:2).

In their attempts to actualize the Petrine and Pauline traditions, we noted that the authors of these letters display varying levels of "canon-consicousness", which appear to parallel the relative ages of the traditions and dates of the letters. Thus Ephesians and 1 Peter (both first century), display a free and fluid use of tradition, while the Pastorals and 2 Peter (both early second century) are much more rigid and stress the *traditum* more than the *traditio*. The implications of this will be explored in the next chapter. But regardless of the varying degrees of "canon-consciousness" or the crystallization of tradition, that "consciousness" governs one aspect in at least three of the four cases we examined: the literary *form* of the tradition. In both Ephesians (3:3–4) and the Pastorals (1 Tim 3:14–15) it is recognized that authoritative Pauline tradition is communicated via the epistle. Similarly, 2 Peter is aware that this is how previous Petrine teaching was expressed (2 Pet 3:1–2). Only in 1 Peter do we not find any linkage of literary form and tradition, and this just adds one more question to the puzzle of its authorship. *But aside from that puzzle, we can note a consistent relationship between the development of the Petrine and Pauline traditions and the literary forms which they take. The pseudonymous epistles, then, are simply different members of the same family that we found in the "anonymous" gospels and various literary genres of the prophetic, wisdom, and apocalyptic traditions. In other words by now quite familiar, attribution in the pseudonymous Pauline and Petrine epistles must be regarded primarily as an assertion of authoritative tradition, not of literary origins.*

Chapter 6

Pseudonymity and Canon

At the outset of this investigation, it was suggested that an examination of the role of revelation and tradition in Jewish writings might provide a "pattern" of pseudonymity that would shed light on a similar practice in the NT, and this has in fact proved to be the case. Since neither all Jewish nor all Christian documents were examined, it cannot be said, however, that this "tradition theory" of pseudonymity is applicable to all the Christian documents of the NT era. Though a case can certainly be made for its relevance to the Johannine literature, James, Jude, and other suspected pseudepigrapha, the substantiation of this must wait for separate, subsequent investigations. Certainly one can say, at least, that the reproduction of the Jewish pattern of pseudonymity in the Petrine and Pauline traditions goes a long way towards a resolution of the impasse between literary-critical and dogmatic/theological concerns.

Two tasks remain, however, before this investigation can be regarded as complete. First, though our examination of the NT documents was more concerned to discover a "theology" of authorship and revelation, rather than reconstructing the actual mechanics of pseudonymous literary production, it would be helpful to suggest plausible historical models for the development of this literature. Any reconstruction is by its very nature speculative, and our prior investigations are dependent upon it only in the sense that some plausible historical model must be forthcoming. Since it was suggested that there may have been a development in the process of *Vergegenwärtigung* that led to a qualitative distinction between the writings of the NT era and later Christian writings, the value of an historical reconstruction is even more obvious.

A second task is to relate our findings to both ancient and modern concepts of (closed) canon. Though many theological observations have already been made in the course of this investigation, a more comprehensive treatment is needed to understand the relationship of pseudonymity and canon.

6.1 The Historical Development of Early Christian Pseudepigrapha

6.1.1 *Literary Origins*

There are three questions of an historical nature that are of interest for our further investigation. The first is the basic question as to who was responsible for the origin and promulgation of the Christian pseudepigrapha that we have considered. Though this has been touched upon in Chapters 1 and 5, a full enumeration of the possibilities is required. Naturally some proposals will be more suitable for some documents than others.

The possibility of a Pauline or Petrine school has been mentioned. There is virtually no evidence at all for a Petrine school, and evidence for a Pauline school is far more circumstantial than, say, for the Johannine school. The only possible Pauline pseudepigrapha that may be due to a "school", loosely defined, is the Pastorals. Here we have a highly structured community with absolute allegiance to Paul, concerned with the preservation and propagation of properly interpreted Pauline doctrine through visibly organized means.

This emphasis on teaching and lack of "ecumenical" interest in other apostolic traditions may serve as evidence that the Pastorals originated among the leaders of these Pauline communities. Probably for two or three decades after the death of Paul, no need was felt to give literary and theological articulation to their Pauline inheritance. Pauline teaching and "historical" information was passed on orally, and the leadership that evolved to serve these communities may have gone unquestioned, perhaps due to their actual acquaintance with Paul or one of his associates. But in the first decade of the second century, the third generation of leadership of these communities had lost their physical proximity to their Pauline foundations. The rise of heresy constituted a challenge to both their interpretation of Pauline tradition and their right to authoritative Pauline "succession". The growth of persecution in the time of Domitian probably also initiated the sense of urgency to secure the communities' foundations (2 Tim 1:7–14). This threat to the integrity of oral tradition, as was similar with the Jesus traditions, gave rise to the fixation of those traditions in writing. In particular, certain cherished legendary material (not without historical value) was woven together with a theological essay justifying the right of the church hierarchy to a continuity of succession in authoritative Pauline interpretation. Since we have argued that the distinctive nature of the Pastorals as a three-fold "canon" (not necessarily in the closed sense) may argue for the awareness of a larger Pauline collection, this may serve as a reason why little need was felt to record, in the manner of the Synoptics, a compendium of Pauline teaching and activities. What was needed was a supplement, an "epilogue", so to speak. It is difficult to know whether each book was written separately over a period of a few years, or if all were constructed together. In any case the literary period of the origin of the Pastorals was probably brief, and as it stands was intended to be received as a unified corpus, a collection.

Another possible origin of certain Christian pseudepigrapha would be from actual disciples of the pretended author. Naturally this would only be feasible with those documents that may be dated relatively early, such as Ephesians and 1 Peter. The evidence here is much more speculative but not without some foundation. The mention of Pauline disciples by Luke (Acts 9:25) and the portrayal of Timothy and Titus as Pauline disciples in the Pastorals may reflect some knowledge of Pauline practice, even if mistaken in particulars. Certainly Paul "took under his wing" certain young men in his missionary work (e.g. John Mark, Acts 13:5; Timothy, 1 Cor 4:17), and it is not unlikely that some developed a deep sense of personal loyalty, even if no strict master-disciple relationship was intended by Paul. There is no certain evidence that Ephesians was written by a direct disciple of Paul, but it is certainly plausible. The intimacy of the writer with Pauline thought, and the very fact that the work was so readily received as the work of Paul, may serve as indirect testimony to the closeness of the writer to his master. This needs to be appreciated in light of the rapidity with which a true appreciation of Pauline theology receded in the early church. In the second decade or so after the apostle's death, it is precisely this "slippage" or disintegration of true Paulinism that one of Paul's disciples may have wished to prevent, and the great theological essay on unity that is Ephesians was the result. We do have external testimony to a Petrine mission, but not to a school. All we have in 1 Peter is a document that is relatively undeveloped in its theology, and its writing *might* fit in very well with a "disciple" writing in the aftermath of Peter's martyrdom, preparing the church for what might lie ahead.

Though some pseudepigraphers may have more direct, organized links to their pseudonyms, the likely possibility is that many do not. These might be designated "admirers" or "followers" of their hero, but not disciples in the technical sense. This is most certainly the case with the Apocalypse and Gospel of Peter, 2 Peter, and 3 Corinthians. It is very difficult to ascertain much about the author of 2 Peter, but his dependence on 1 Peter and Jude and the relatively late date of the letter (AD 125) make it likely that his only acquaintance with Peter is literary. His commitment to a hierarchical teaching body might suggest the possibility of a school, but the lack of focused Petrinism such as we find in the Paulinism of the Pastorals or in the Johannine theology of that school makes it rather unlikely. The Apocalypse of Peter shows a high regard for its pseudonym, and the author seems to have constructed his work with both synoptic material and other apocalyptic traditions, probably both written and oral. The Gospel of Peter is too fragmentary to gain much information on the author's attitude toward his pseudonym. In the case of 3 Corinthians, if it is by the same author as of the Acts of Paul and Thecla, we have a direct witness to the attitude of the author, who wrote "for the love of Paul"[1]. There is nothing in Tertullian or the letter itself to suggest that 3 Corinthians is the product of anything more than an individual, whose proximity to Paul was only emotional or theological.

A final possibility of the literary origin of the Christian pseudepigrapha we have discussed may be designated neutrally by the term "other". It is difficult to refrain from a more negative evaluation such as "imitators", or "plagiarist", since the Epistle to the Laodiceans comes under this category. The author may have been an admirer of Paul, but its wooden method of

---

1 Tertullian, De Bapt. 17.

stringing together Pauline texts seems to testify more to a pure literary interest in "reconstructing" a lost Pauline letter than to a desire to recapture Pauline thought.

Though it has already been pointed out that these historical reconstructions are only surmise, and open to revision, an even more important point needs to be underscored in summary. The "legitimacy" of the pseudonymity of these documents is not affected by their location in any of these possible categories, except the last one. Thus, for example, if one were to argue that the Pastorals were written by an "admirer" of Paul, and not by a school or disciple, it would not affect the rationale or "pattern of pseudonymity" that we discovered earlier in our investigation. This is because pseudonymity as we discovered it was based on a perceived continuity of revelation and tradition (expressed through *Vergegenwärtigung*), and not on any physical proximity, continuity, scholastic organisation, or technical master-disciple relation. All of these factors are compatible with the pattern of pseudonymity, but are not required by it.

6.1.2 *Means of Propagation*

A second historical question concerns the practical but important inquiry into how the pseudepigrapha actually entered circulation. Here is where the issue of "deception" enters the scene, but it must be said at the outset that this word must be radically qualified as a result of our investigations. "Deception" runs on two levels. On one level is the question of authenticity or literary origins: who actually wrote the book? On the second level is the question of truth: are the ideas presented in the book actually those of the (purported) author, or are they someone else's? In modern practice these two levels cannot be separated, and it is their *combination* that enables one to equate deception and forgery. But in the Jewish and Christian literature that we have investigated, these two levels are in fact separate. Literary authenticity and (doctrinal) truth are two related but distinct issues, and all the evidence points to a sense of moral culpability in deception only on the second, doctrinal level. Attribution of literary origins played the subsidiary, *theological* function of sanctioning the far more important enterprise, the recording of authoritative tradition. Though modern theologians can quite readily note the difference in thought between a pseudepigrapher and his pseudonym (where original, authentic documents exist), such a dispassionate evaluation was not and could not be part of the pseudepigrapher's reckoning. Whether heretic or orthodox (as judged by the later church), the writer was convinced of the *truth and continuity* of his assertions with those of his pseudonym, and therefore the charge of deception at the second level of ideas (*geistiges Eigentum*) is difficult to lay at his door. Therefore when we examine the issue of "deception" in literary propagation, it is with the understanding that the word is not used in its modern configuration, and applies only to the first level, that of literary origins. There are essentially three operative models at this level.

The first model, the least likely, is that the various pseudepigrapha were composed and promoted openly, as a transparent fiction. The inadequacy of this view was treated in Chapter 1. However, one cannot entirely rule out one permutation of this theory. If any of the documents that we discussed had an origin in a "school", then *within the school* the work would most likely have been openly known and acknowledged to be pseudonymous (though no less authoritative). The Pastorals are the most likely candidate. Yet even here the work is not intended for just the Pauline leaders, but for the communities as a whole, and the knowledge of its pseudonymous origins would be counter-productive to its use against heretics within the congregation. There is an overwhelming likelihood, therefore, that there is an element of "deception" with all the pseudepigrapha, and this leads to the other two options.

For those documents that were written near to the death of their pseudonym, a possible second model is that these letters were actually sent to the communities to whom they are addressed. 1 Peter is the most likely possibility, because its nature as a circular letter could have allowed it to be sent many years after Peter's death. A less likely candidate is Ephesians, since the theory of its origin as a circular letter is now in disrepute.

The third model is applicable to the majority of the pseudepigrapha. This is that the documents were variously "discovered" and presented to the churches as authentic. A later example of this technique is the Apocalypse of Paul, which relates the story of its own discovery in the foundations of Paul's house in Tarsus. It may be that the textual mutilation of Ephesians 1:1 is a deliberate attempt to suggest an original address while as the same time obscuring its origins. Since I have already suggested that the Pastorals may have been written to supplement a growing Pauline collection, it is easy to see how several more Pauline "letters" would be readily accepted, and the personal nature of their address (to Timothy and Titus, rather than churches) would be sufficient explanation for the lateness of their arrival on the scene. 2 Peter also gives an awareness of a collection of Pauline letters (3:16) as well as of 1 Peter (3:1). It is highly likely that 2 Peter was circulated as a rediscovered circular letter of Peter, in an era where interest in the recovery of apostolic literature was growing. This is probaby also the case for the other pseudepigrapha we have discussed. If 3 Corinthians is not an independent work, its inclusion in the "historical" work of the Acts of Paul and Thecla may have served as a cover for its pseudonymous origins.

No doubt the admission of "deception" even on the literary level is highly unsettling for some. Yet one ought to hesitate before making hasty judgements. Today we regard slavery as incompatible with the Christian gospel, yet this was not the case in the NT era. Indeed, it took Christianity nearly two thousand years to come to our current opinion. Even more important than changing moral sensitivities, however, is our whole way of regarding attribution and authorship. The greater part of our revulsion to pseudonymity lies in its association with forgery, and as we have seen, this is manifestly not the case with the documents that we have considered. The consciousness of standing within an inspired stream of tradition, an attitude that can be traced back into Judaism nearly a thousand years before the New Testament, has effected an approach to literary attribution that is entirely foreign and highly appropriate to the modern mind. For this reason the moral objection to the deception of the recipients of the apostolic pesudepigrapha is mitigated by the realization that the pseudepigrapher really felt that he was a spokesman for the apostle. *The more blatantly "deceptive" form of canonical epistolary pseudonymity is just the result of historical accident, the conjunction of a fundamentally Jewish understanding of authorship and revelation with a fundamentally Greek form of literature.*

6.1.3 "Canon-consciousness" and the Crystallization of Tradition

The third historical question concerns the mode of development of Christian tradition. Throughout our investigation we have used the term "canon-consciousness" to designate the growing awareness on the part of the authors and their communities of the authoritative nature of the traditions they were handling, and the increasingly rigid form that those traditions took in both content and literary expression. As such it is different from a "history of the canon", an account of how the documents of the Bible were delimited into a collection of writings in which nothing could be added or taken away (closed canon). Yet the two processes are obviously related, in that because of the crystallization of tradition that is represented by a growth of "canon-consciousness", the literary development of multi-layered books had to be "closed". Yet there was nothing to prevent that tradition from being taken up again under the same authority but in a separate work and form (e.g. Deuteronomy, Epistles of John).

What has been intimated in Chapter 5, however, is that in the second century A.D., the practice of *Vergegenwärtigung,* the heart of the tradition process, was becoming increasingly rare and difficult to practice *in the biblical mode.* That is, the actualization of tradition through anonymous supplementation of multi-layered works or the pseudonymous production of "sequels" was becoming less of a possibility. It is not that there was not a desire to re-apply apostolic tradition, but rather that there emerged a consciousness of a fundamental discontinuity between "apostolic" and "ecclesiastical" tradition[2]. *What this. represents is a qualitatively different attitude toward tradition which could not fail to have dramatic implications for literary attribution.*

Now it is freely admitted that not enough work has been done to substantiate this hypothesis entirely. The primary aim of this work has been to demonstrate the *continuity* of the NT with its Jewish background, not its

---

2 See O. Cullmann, "The Tradition", *The Early Church* (London: SCM, 1956), 59–99.

discontinuity with the age of the fathers. A proper substantiation of the latter would be the work of another monograph. Our treatment of the Petrine and Pauline traditions, however, shows that the hypothesis is not without mertit. There is a marked ossification in the development of these traditions, and a corresponding alteration in attitude toward tradition itself. The Pauline tradition begins with the creative and fluid work of Ephesians, which, though heavily dependent on Colossians, except for two verses (6:21–22, part of the epistolary framework) never actually "quotes" Paul. By the time of the Pastorals, however, great blocks of traditional material have become so stabilized that they can only be associated with Paul through the use of a semi-quotation formula ("faithful is the word", 1 Tim 1:15; 3:1; 4:9; 2 Tim 2:11; Titus 3:8) rather than simply be attributed to Paul. Yet a great deal of Pauline thought and legend is still freely woven into the text of the writing. The mid-second century 3 Corinthians still reveals a somewhat fluid use of Paul, though its construction is based more on a restatement of Pauline phrases rather than a deep understanding of the apostle's thought (cf. esp. 1 Cor. 15). More important, however, is the attitude of the author toward Paul. Though he may have "loved" the apostle, the clear subordination of Paul to the "other apostles before (him)" (3:4), even to the point of attributing the source of Paul's distinctive ideas on the resurrection to the Twelve, is indicative of a growing "consensus orthodoxy" that makes an appeal to a distinctive Pauline tradition neither helpful nor possible. This may be the reason why the Epistle to the Laodiceans, written at least fifty years later (the dating is uncertain), shows no real sign of *Vergegenwärtigung*. It seems to be a mere literary exercise, designed to fill in the gaps of a Pauline collection with a collection of Pauline citations strung together to make a new Pauline "letter". There is no way of telling if *any* possibility of further actualization of Pauline tradition existed at this stage, but the trajectory we have traced would seem to mitigate against it.

The Petrine tradition shows a similar, though less discernible trajectory. 1 Peter, if pseudonymous, achieves a creative mixture of elements of Petrine tradition with a host of other sources. 2 Peter is more stylized, both in its appeal to the Peter legend and in its use of its sources. The roughly contemporaneous Apocalypse of Peter shows a similar measure of fluidity, joining well defined blocks of apocalyptic material from Matthew and 1 Enoch with a legendary account of Peter's participation in the Transfiguration. Though fragmentary, the very attribution of the mid-second century Gospel of Peter to Peter is an indication that a fundamental shift in tradition consciousness has taken place. It is now no longer the gospel of *Jesus Christ* that is anonymously expanded, but the gospel is now treated as an apostolic "memoir". There seems to be no real consciousness of a distinctive Peter tradition.

Since any further verification of this proposed trajectory must await the opportunity of another investigation, a more helpful approach is an historical inquiry into *why* it may have been so. That is, what historical factors can be cited as possible reasons for the demise of *Vergegenwärtigung* in its biblical mode?

Two factors seem paramout. First, there is the loss of what might be called the "Jewish matrix" of biblical tradition. Scholars do not often take enough account of the fact that in contrast to the literature of the fathers, the NT is written almost entirely by Jews or writers who were intimately acquainted with Judaism (such as Luke). It is true that even Palestinian Judaism had been thoroughly exposed to Hellenistic culture for several centuries prior to the writing of the NT. Indeed, the adoption of Greek literary forms, especially the epistle, did represent a major obstacle to the free progress of tradition building which the older Jewish oracular, historical, hymnodic, and proverbial literature afforded. Yet as long as Israel remained the focal point of salvation history, the fundamental and distinctive Jewish attitudes toward tradition and revelation could continue, and *Vergegenwärtigung* was carried on even by means of the recalcitrant Greek genres. But as soon as the focus of salvation-history shifted to the Gentiles, the dynamic tension between Jewish thought and Greek form was lost. The rift between Judaism and Christianity, exacerbated by the destruction of Jerusalem and the decline of the Jewish church, meant that at the end of the NT era, the production of Christian thought and literature was almost universally in the hands of Gentiles who had no first-hand knowledge of Judaism, a complete reversal of the earlier state of affairs. This could not fail to have a significant impact on the perception of tradition and attribution in all subsequent literature[3].

Yet it must be said that this alone is not enough to account for our proposed phenomenon. For it was not only Christianity which closed its canon, but at least portions of Judaism as well. Indeed, in post-70 A.D. Rabbinic literature there is a decided emphasis on properly attributed *halakah,* in contrast to the anonymity that was generally characteristic of an earlier era[4]. Though space will not allow for a detailed examination of the Jewish development, canonical forces may include the need for self-definition over against Christianity, and the reaction to those apocalyptic elements of Jewish tradition which contributed to the disasters of A.D. 70 and A.D. 135[5].

---

3 Indeed, D.L. Dungan, "The New Testament Canon in Recent Study", *Interp* 29 (1975), 350 asserts that the idea of closing the canon (and thus ending *Vergegenwärtigung* in the biblical mode) is due to Hellenism and its concern for the "ideal", an eternal standard by which the world is to be judged.

4 See A. Guttmann, "The Problem of the Anonymous Mishnah", *HUCA* 16 (1941) 137–155.

5 The latter point is, of course, debated. See L. Ginzberg, "Some Observations on the Attitude of the Synagogue Towards the Apocalyptic-Eschatological Writings". *JBL* 41 (1922) 115–136; W.D. Davies, "Apocalyptic and Pharisaism", *Christian Origins and Judaism* (London: Darton, Longman, and Todd, 1962) 19–30; J. Stiassny, "L'occultation de l'apocalyptique dans le Rabbinisme", *Apocalypses et Théologie de L'Espérance.* Edit. L. Monloubou (Paris: Éditions du Cerf, 1977) 179–203; A.J. Saldarini, "Apocalyptic and Rabbinic Literature", *CBQ* 37 (1975) 348–358; *idem,* "The Uses of Apocalyptic in the Mishna and Tosepta", *CBQ* 39 (1977) 396–409; *idem* "Apocalypses and 'Apocalyptic' in Rabbinic Literature", *Semeia* 14 (1979) 187–205.

The need for self-definition over against Judaism was certainly a factor in the development of the NT scriptures, but is not sufficient reason in itself why the process of tradition was ended and the canon closed. Why could not *Vergegenwärtigung* continue as it had? Here we come to the second historical factor, the rise of "heresy", or perhaps more accurately, the problem of discerning between true and false prophecy and tradition. The problem was not a new one, and indeed may have been the reason for the demise of classical prophecy in Israel (cf. Ezek 12:21–25; Zech 13:2–6). Early on the problem of the proper interpretation of tradition arose (2 Tim 2:15; 2 Pet 1:20). This problem was multiplied by the rise of the great Gnostic systems of the mid-second century, which not only "misinterpreted" the literature of Paul and others, but also appealed to a secret oral tradition traceable back to the apostles. The growing problem of interpretation was exacerbated by the rise of the "New Prophecy" of Montanism in the late second century. Though it is difficult to reconstruct a complete picture of the phenomenon, at least in its latter stages this movement was not satisfied to supplement the prophecies of the NT era, but rather intended to supercede them[6].

The "orthodox" reaction to these problems began as early as the late first century, and developed in a number of discernible features. A rapid development was the rise of a "consensus orthodoxy". There is neither time nor point in discussing whether it is at all legitimate to speak of a strict orthodoxy in the earliest period of the Christian church[7]. At any rate, by the turn of the century there is no doubt that many writers had become more "apostolic" than the apostles. That is, because of the growing diversity of interpretation of various apostolic writings and legends, particularly those of Paul, it became part of policy to stress that *all* of the apostles agreed on *everything*. There was no difference in the teaching of Paul and Peter, or between the Synoptic records. Only the heretics would exalt one portion of the NT scriptures against another, or even recognize fundamental distinctions within it. Obviously it became increasingly difficult, if not theologically dangerous, to try to actualize a *distinctive* tradition after the manner of the biblical pattern which we have discussed.

In tandem with "consensus orthodoxy" was another early development, the rise of a magisterium or authoritative body of interpreters, the roots of which go back to the NT itself. Interpretation was now no longer in the hands of anyone who felt led by the Spirit, but reposed in the offices of the church. It is this development that probably lies at the heart of the growing distinction between apostolic and ecclesiastical tradition. Instead of the polymor-

---

6 See H. von Campenhausen, *The Formation of the Christian Bible* (Philadelphia: Fortress, 1972) 221–231, and the literature cited there. Also H. Kraft, "Vom Ende der urchristlichem Prophetie", *Prophetic Vocation in the New Testament and Today*. Edit. J. Panagopoulos (NT Supp 45. Leiden: E.J. Brill, 1977) 162–185.

7 See W. Bauer, *Orthodoxy and Heresy in Earliest Christianity* (Philadelphia: Fortress, 1971[2]); J.D.G. Dunn, *Unity and Diversity in the New Testament* (London: SCM, 1977).

phous anonymous and pseudonymous expansion of tradition, there was now just apostolic word and church interpretation, scripture and tradition.

The final blow to *Vergegenwärtigung* in the biblical mode was the closure of the canon. With the decisive rejection of Montanism and delimitation of the NT, it was guaranteed that the "apostolic" writings could not be significantly expanded in any fashion, either anonymously or pseudonymously. (The Western textual tradition of Acts may have been an exception: cf. E.J. Epp, *The Theological Tendency of Codex Bezae Cantabrigiensis in Acts* (Cambridge: University Press, 1966). In any case, the production of scripture eventually came to an end, and with it the distinctive phenomenon of the growth of biblical tradition.

6.2 Authorship and Canon

6.2.1 *Ancient Criteria for Canonicity*

From the discussion above, it is obvious that the demise of *Vergegenwärtigung* (and therefore of attribution) in the biblical mode is prior to but intimately connected with the closure of the canon. The historical factors in both were often shared. For this reason it is necessary to correlate the corresponding theological criteria for the definition and delimitation of canon with the findings of our previous investigation. This does not mean that we can become involved in all the historical debates about the origins of the OT and NT canon[8]. Nor can we even be involved in a discussion of all the various

---

8 In addition to the standard introductions and reference works, on the OT see the series of articles edited by S. Z. Leiman in *The Canon and Masorah of the Hebrew Bible* (New York: KTAV, 1974); *idem, The Canonization of Hebrew Scripture: The Talmudic and Midrashic Evidence* (Hamendon, Conn.: Archon, 1976); A. Saldarini, "Apocalyptic and Rabbinic"; G. Ostborn, *Cult and Canon. A Study in the Canonization of the Old Testament* (Uppsala: Lundequistska, 1950); A.C. Sundberg, "The Old Testament of the Early Church: A Study in Canon", *HTR* 51 (1958) 205–226; *idem, The Old Testament of the Early Church* (Cambridge: Harvard University Press, 1964); J.N. Lightstone, "The formation of the biblical canon in Judaism of late antiquity: Prolegomenon to a general reassessment", *SR* 8 (1979) 135–142; E.R. Kalin, "How Did the Canon Come to Us? A Response to the Leiman Hypothesis", *Currents in Theology and Mission* 4 (1977) 47–51; R.C. Newman, "The Council of Jamnia and the Old Testament Canon", *WThJ* 38 (1976) 319–349. For the NT, see J.N. Aletti, "Le Canon des Écritures. Le Nouveau Testament", *Études* 349 (1978) 109–124; N. Appel, "The New Testament Canon: Historical Process and Spirit's Witness", *TSI* 32 (1971) 627–646; F.F. Bruce, "New Light on the Origins of the New Testament Canon", *New Dimensions in New Testament Study*. Edit. R. Longenecker and M. Tenney (Grand Rapids: Zondervan, 1974) 3–18; H. von Campenhausen, *Formation*; K.L. Carroll, "Towards a Commonly Received New Testament", *BJRL* 44 (1962) 327–349; I. Frank, *Der Sinn*

theological grounds for the inclusion of a book in the NT[9]. Rather we must concern ourselves with two related ancient criteria for canonicity which are relevant to our topic: apostolicity and authenticity of authorship.

The first criterion is rather easily dispensed with. Even for the early church, the criterion of apostolicity was more of a theological title, signifying *Urkirchlichkeit*, than an actual reference to the apostolic authorship of all of the NT[10]. Even the early fathers realized that certain books of the NT were not directly authored by apostles (e.g. Tertullian, Adv. Marcion IV 5), and indicated that they were more concerned about preservation of apostolic *doctrine*. This attitude has always been characteristic of Protestants[11], and is reflective of modern Catholic thought as well. Canonicity does not depend on (actual) authorship by an apostle.

Though this does not directly relate to the problem of pseudonymity, it does mean that in our modern estimation if a work is pseudonymous that in itself is no barrier to its *apostolicity*. The real problem lies in the second criterion: authenticity. Would the early Church (second century onward) have accepted a work as "canonical" if it were known to be inauthentic? Here the evidence is ambiguous, for the evaluation of apostolic authorship is invariably intertwined with the question of apostolic *doctrine*. The literary-critical tools of the fathers were not used dispassionately, but were coloured by their ideological concerns[12].

Space will not allow for a comprehensive treatment, but a few of the better known examples will illustrate the difficulty of discerning the minds

---

der Kanonbildung (Freiburg: Herder, 1971); R.F. Collins, "The Matrix of the New Testament Canon", *Biblical Theology Bulletin* 7 (1977) 51–59; D.L. Dungan, "The New Testament Canon in Recent Study", *Interp* 29 (1975) 339–351; R.M. Grant, *The Formation of the New Testament* (New York: Harper and Row, 1965); D.E. Groh, "Hans von campenhausen on Canon. Positions and Problems", *Interp* 28 (1974) 331–343; S.J. Kistemaker, "The Canon of the New Testament", *JETS* 20 (1977) 3–14; R. Murray, "How Did the Church Determine the Canon of Scripture?", *HeyJ* 11 (1970) 115–126; S. Pederson, "Die Kanonfrage als historisches und theologisches Problem", *Studia Theologica* (Oslo) 31 (1977) 83–136; A.C. Sundberg, "Canon Muratori: A Fourth-Century List", *HTR* 66 (1973) 1–41; *idem*, "A Revised History of the NT Canon", *StEv* 4 (1968) 452–461; L.P. Trudinger, "The Churches' Rôle in the Making of Scripture", *ET* 85 (1974) 342–343; A. Sand, *Kanon* (Freiburg: Herder, 1974). For further bibliography on both OT and NT canon, see S.J.P.K. Riekert, "Critical Research and the one Christian canon comprising two Testaments" *Neotestamentica* 14 (1981) 38–41.

9 See esp. K.H. Ohlig, *Die theologische Bergründung des neutestamentliche Kanons in der alten Kirche* (Dusseldorf: Patmos, 1972).

10 *Ibid*, 57–156.

11 An often quoted position is that of Luther: "That which does not teach Christ is still not apostolic, even if it were the teaching of Peter and Paul. Again that which preaches Christ, that were apostolic, even if James, Annas, Pilate and Herod preached it" (from *Werke XIV*, translated by Westcott).

12 See W. Speyer, *Die Literarische Fälschung im Heidnischen und Christlichen Altertum* (München: C.H. Beck, 1971) 201–218. Thus there was a blurring of distinctions between forgery of documents (*Fälschung*) and falsification of doctrine (*Verfälschung*).

of the ancient authorities. In the NT itself we have evidence of a concern over authenticity. Paul refers to a false letter (2 Thess 2:2), and seems to take pains to authenticate his own document by his distinctive signature (3:17). Yet it is clear from Chapter Two of 2 Thessalonians that Paul's main concern is purity of eschatological doctrine. All that we can safely say is that he was condemning pseudonymity in the service of heresy, and not necessarily the inauthenticity of the letter *per se.* The example of Tertullian's defrocking of a presbyter for writing the Acts of Paul seems to be a much clearer expression of disapproval of pseudonymity (De. Bapt. 17). Yet here too there are theological concerns, for the reprimand is given in the context of promoting a false doctrine through the document, that is, the right of women to baptize. This is clearly seen in Tertullian's counter that this doctrine would have been impossible to attribute to Paul. Once again, then, it is doctrine, not authenticity, that is of paramount concern. The third example is the use of the Gospel of Peter by the Syrian church. At first this was permitted by Serapion, bishop of Antioch, and only subsequently forbidden when he discovered its (docetic) heretical contents (Eusebius, H.E. vi 12). Though Serapion states that he rejects writings which falsely bear the names of apostles, his casual approach at first to the matter demonstrates that he was not really concerned with literary authenticity in the abstract, but with preserving purity of doctrine. Finally, the Muratorian canon mentions by way of rejection the "forged" letters of Paul to the Laodiceans and Alexandrians (63—67). Yet again the main concern is doctrine, testified by the metaphor of mixing gall and honey, and the specific mention of Marcionism as the driving force behind these writings.

As can be seen from the examples above, there exists a great deal of confusion over the precise attitude of the early church toward literary authenticity. Indeed, this confusion probably reflects the actual state of affairs of the church at the time. It is probably not legitimate to talk about "the" attitude of the church in some monolithic fashion. The fact that a presbyter could write the Acts of Paul in the middle of the second century is evidence that things were in a state of flux, and if there was an "official" attitude, it had not yet filtered down to all the rank and file.

It is probably more legitimate to talk about a *developing* attitude toward literary attribution, stretching from the NT era itself to the fourth century and beyond. Though it might be difficult to isolate what precisely was the position in any given decade or indeed century, it might be possible to characterize the *trend of development.* In this case there seems to be an increasing objection to both anonymity and pseudonymity, and a correspondingly growing emphasis on orthonymous writing. Thus in the second century we witness the concern to specify the "apostolic" authorship of the anonymous gospels[13], and other writings, such as Hebrews, and the denigration of con-

---

13 See R. Pesch, "Die Zuschriebung der Evangelien an apostolische Verfasser", *ZKTh* 97 (1975) 56—71.

temporary works that lack any attribution[14]. As we saw in the case of Tertullian and the presbyter, pseudonymity was also being discouraged.

Why would the history of the early church witness an increasing rejection of anonymity and pseudonymity? The reasons are most likely the same as those enumerated for the demise of *Vergegenwärtigung* and the closure of the canon: the loss of a Jewish matrix and the problem of orthodoxy/heresy. The latter is the most important issue, for within it rises the whole problem of *control* of doctrine. The production of anonymous and pseudonymous documents in the biblical mode runs counter to the efforts of the early church to secure the parameters of doctrinal development. The authors of anonymous and pseudonymous literature cannot be identified, and therefore cannot be countered or controlled. This concern for control probably led to the three essential counter-measures of the growing church hierarchy: the role of the magisterium, the closure of the canon, and the stress on orthonymous writing and attribution. Thus we cannot rule out the concern for literary authenticity in the early church, but we have to recognize that it was part of a larger process of theological articulation that gained clarity as the church developed.

It is for this reason that the *strictly literary* criterion of authenticity in the *modern* sense cannot be related to the ancient church's criteria for canonicity without considerable qualification[15]. This is even more the case when we consider the earliest church, the period of the composition of the NT. There is good reason to maintain that there was a quantitatively (if not qualitatively) different attitude toward pseudonymous and anonymous authorship in the NT era from that pertaining in subsequent generations. We must never forget that many of the deliberations regarding the "authenticity" and "canonicity" of many NT canonical and apocryphal pseudepigrapha took place long after their origins were forgotten and their usage (or lack of it) had been established in the church. As we have emphasized elsewhere, there is not only a "history of the canon", where the inclusion or exclusion of certain books are decided, but there is also a "canonical process" or growing "canon-consciousness", where traditions and their literary expressions gain authoritative status in the communities which they sustain. Before the history of the NT canon began, the canonical process was well developed, and it is this factor more than any other that explains the presence of canonical pseudepigrapha.

How then, does authorship or authenticity relate to canon? The suggestion of B.S. Childs regarding the relation of Moses to the Pentateuch is instructive. He notes that both conservatives and liberals have erred by treating the issue merely as an *historical* problem. For Moses' writing activity is

---

14 Thus Tertullian despises anonymous works as not being able to "lift up their heads".

15 See K.H. Ohlig, *Bergründung*, 59 ff.

closely tied to his mediatorial role in receiving the divine law[16]. This indicates that authorship is not so much an historical, but a *theological* designation. That is, it is not a statement of modern research ("Moses wrote this"), but a statement of authority ("This is Mosaic"). It indicates the acceptance of a given body of tradition as authoritative and continuous (in harmony) with the law as given to Moses on Sinai.

In our investigations we have seen that this phenomenon of the growth of tradition continues in Jewish culture into the era and milieu of the NT itself. This is not to say that there were not any historical or literary concerns in Jewish culture. The later superscriptions to the prophetic writings and the ascription of the Psalms to various events in David's life reveals a need to root their traditions in the peculiarity of history and indeed of individuals. But these historical and literary concerns are subsidiary to the main focus of Jewish thought: the continuity of authoritative tradition. In both multi-layered and independent works, pseudonymity and anonymity furthered the goal of *Vergegenwärtigung*.

This fundamental process continued with renewed vigor in the life of the NT church. The growth of the Jesus tradition is a well recognized phenomenon. But similar to the OT, this is not to say that there was no concern for historicity or individual peculiarity, nor were the gospel redactors at liberty to totally rewrite salvation-history (an admittedly theological construction in itself). Contrary to the opinions of some more radical scholars, there was some effort to maintain a continuity with the Jesus of history. The "kerygmatic Christ" or spirit of prophecy could not just say anything[17]. The same could be said for "deutero-Paul". As we have seen, there is a decided effort on the part of the deutero-Paulines to extrapolate and harmonize with Pauline tradition, however the results might be judged today. The same may be posited of the Peter tradition, though with less confidence. In any case it is this affinity for the furtherance of *Vergegenwärtigung* in the biblical mode, that is, through anonymous and pseudonymous expansion of tradition, which must lie at the heart of much of the NT canonical pseudepigrapha, both in its production and acceptance. Indeed, the rapid acceptance of this literature, in contrast to the more highly articulated (and skeptical) literary and theological period of the post-apostolic church, should tell us something about the real nature of the "canonicity" of the NT. It is because of this fundamental distinction between the era of the NT and the later church that we can make the assessment, that *in the context of the canonical process, authorship is not primarily a statement of literary origins, but of authoritative tradition. Taken from a modern literary perspective, authorship cannot determine canonicity, and canonicity cannot determine authorship.*

---

16 *Introduction to the Old Testament as Scripture*. London: SCM, 1979, 132–133.

17 See J.D.G. Dunn, "Prophetic 'I'-Sayings and the Jesus Tradition: The Importance of Testing Prophetic Utterances Within Early Christianity", *NTS* 24 (1977–78) 188–192.

6.2.2 *Modern Criteria For Canonicity*

Having related our findings to the ancient criteria of apostolicity and authenticity, it remains to address the distinctive modern attitude toward canon. Once again the scope must be severely restricted. No substantial interaction can be made with the current debate over the nature and function of the canon[18]. What is important for our consideration is the *modern use* of the (ancient) criterion of inspiration and how this relates to authorship and canonicity. In the course of our discussion we will make two negative assertions: 1. inspiration cannot be limited to individual authorship, and 2. inspiration cannot be limited to the canon.

Though it may be said that even most conservatives have rejected the mechanical dictation theory of inspiration, the truth is that modern theology as a whole is still obsessed with *individual* inspiration. The underlying assumption is that revelation can only be focused, and therefore guaranteed, in the isolated act of the inspired individual. Though dictation is renounced, the image is still of the solitary Moses on the mountain top, or Jeremiah or Isaiah in the market-place, or Paul sitting in his prison. In other words, it is the *prophetic* model that has dominated theories of inspiration in the church almost from the very beginning[19]. While the validity of the prophetic mode of inspiration has never been called into question, the discovery of modern criticism as to how the Bible actually came about has made this model inappropriate for the inspiration of the Bible as a whole. Yet it must be said that both conservative and liberal (simplistic, but necessary distinctions) have been reluctant to adjust their thinking.

Even when acknowledging the role of tradition in the Bible, conservatives tend to think of this in terms of a static *depositum* to be handed down, faithfully and precisely preserving this *ipsissima verba* (or *vox*) of the inspired individual. Because of this, conservatives have often been openly hostile to the findings of historical-critical and traditio-historical disciplines. Similar to the fundamentalist-modernist controversy of the early twentieth century, where every rock and bone became the ground for a pitched battle with modern views of evolution, anthropology, geology, and archaeology, so today conservatives become stuck in the quagmire of arguing over the authenticity of every verse of scripture. By placing such high stakes on the authenticity of each and every passage (to lose one battle is to lose the war!), conservatives have placed themselves in a hermeneutical straight-jacket which has hindered them from dispassionately weighing the evidence, and from appreciating the role of tradition in biblical writings.

---

18 Particularly the debate over the "canon within the canon". See the collection of essays collected and reprinted by E. Käsemann, *Das Neue Testament als Kanon* (Göttingen: Vandenhoeck & Ruprecht, 1970); and the literature cited in D.L. Dungan, "New Testament Canon".

19 For a history of the doctrine, see B. Vawter, *Biblical Inspiration* (London: Hutchinson, 1972), and more circumspectly, J.T. Burtchaell, *Catholic Theories of Biblical Inspiration Since 1810* (New York: Cambridge University Press, 1969).

Yet liberals cannot be said to have reacted much more positively. In the face of critical findings liberals have for the most part simply ceased to speak of inspiration. This is because their concept of inspiration as the expression of *individual religious genius* was so closely tied to the prophetic model. This commitment to individual inspiration is still seen in the hermeneutical priority of some liberals to strip away any accretions of a tradition to arrive at what is for them the essential and authoritative words of the "inspired" individual[20].

Rather than reject either the findings of modern criticism or the wholistic inspiration of the Bible, a more satisfactory solution is to recognize that *inspiration cannot be limited to individual authorship in the prophetic mode. For this reason it is more helpful to put the locus of inspiration in tradition and the community which both creates it and is sustained by it.* This is exactly the emphasis given in the most recent works on inspiration. The first and most articulate of these have been the "social theory" of inspiration promoted by the Catholic theologians K. Rahner and J. McKenzie[21], though more recent Protestant works have also addressed the problems helpfully[22]. These Catholic scholars stress the divine election of Israel and the Church, and argue that inspiration belongs to these communities as a whole, rather than to individuals within them.

While it is not within the scope of this study to fully expound and criticize this (or any other) theory, a fundamental concern which does arise is whether there is any place for the individual in this framework? It is at precisely this point that the social inspiration theory has come under fire[23]. While it is true that certain tradition based societies can stifle individual self-conscious-

---

20 In a far too sweeping judgement J.A. Sanders remarks, "Historical criticism in its handling of the Bible has by-passed the ancient communities which produced it and shaped it. It has focused, in good modern Western fashion, on individual authors. Liberals and conservatives alike have done the same: the one simply attributes less of a text to the early 'author' than the other. They both located authority almost solely in individuals and original speakers: conservatives claim the individual said all the words of a book or passage while liberals peel away accretions." J.A. Sanders, "Canonical Context and Canonical Criticism", *Horizons in Biblical Theology* 2 (1980) 183. See also P.J. Achtemeier, *The Inspiration of Scripture* (Philadelphia: Westminster, 1980) 99–104. The problem, however, is not with the historical critical method, but with individual misuse or over-emphasis of certain of its phases.

21 K. Rahner, *Inspiration in the Bible* (New York: Herder and Herder, 1961); J.L. McKenzie, "The Social Character of Inspiration", *CBQ* 24 (1962) 115–124. See also P. Benoit, *Aspects of Biblical Inspiration* (Chicago: Priory, 1965) 13–35; R.A.F. Mackenzie, "Some Problems in the Field of Inspiration", *CBQ* 40 (1958) 1–8; L.J. Topel, "Rahner and McKenzie on the Social Theory of Inspiration", *Scripture* 16 (1964) 33–44; B. Vawter, *Inspiration*.

22 See J. Barr, "The Bible as a Document of Believing Communities", *The Scope and Authority of the Bible. Explorations in Theology*, Vol. 7 (London: SCM, 1980) 111–133; P.J. Achtemeier, *Inspiration*; W.J. Abraham, *The Divine Inspiration of Holy Scripture* (Oxford: Oxford University Press, 1981).

23 See D.J. McCarthy, "Personality, Society, and Inspiration", *TS* 24 (1963) 553–576.

ness, this was certainly not the case with Israel or the Church. Indeed it may
be said that the decisive character of Israelite and Christian religion is due to
individuals. Though an anonymous (or pseudonymous) tradition process
could collect, sift, and supplement God's revelation, the role of the inspired
individual in the prophetic mode is irreplaceable.

Without recourse to the precision of a detailed theological essay, it might
be suggested that the relation of the inspired individual to tradition is two-
fold. First, he (or she!) is an *initiator* of tradition. Though it would be an exercise in futility to try to prove the historical core of all the traditions of
Israel and Christianity, it can be said that the great majority of them owe
their existence to an actual inspired individual: a Moses, an Isaiah, a Jesus, a
Paul. Second, the inspired individual acts as a *critic* of tradition. The prophets
especially had the unique position of both moving in the stream of tradition,
and yet standing in judgement over it.

If there is any truth in the above, then the prophetic model of inspiration
must not be lost to the equally valid concept of social inspiration, but the
efforts of systematic theologians must be turned to capture the dialectical
tension inherent in the biblical witness. As a New Testament scholar I pru-
dently identify the need and wait for the efforts of someone more qualified
than I. What is important for our purposes is to maintain the inadequacy of
relying on a model of individual inspiration as we try to relate to the role of
authorship and canon.

It is at this point that we can consider how inspiration relates to canon in
modern thinking. The predominant position in modern theology is to nearly
equate the two terms. The remarks of P.J. Achtemeier are illustrative:

> ... the canon is a key element in understanding the inspiration of Scripture, since it
> delimits the area within which inspiration is understood to have operated. God in-
> spired the canonical books, with no exception, and no noncanonical books are in-
> spired, with no exception[24].

Yet this position engenders insuperable difficulties. It creates such a wide
gulf between the Bible and other Jewish and Christian literature of the era
that the non-canonical books simply drop from our reckoning. But this hardly squares with the usage of the church of the first four centuries. Furthermore, the very concept of inspiration was not limited, even in the post-apostolic age, to the biblical authors. The fathers often referred to themselves as
"inspired", and seem to indicate by it a continuity with authoritative tradition[25]. Thus it must be affirmed that *for the early church, inspiration was not
limited to the closed canon, nor can it be now*[26].

---

24 *Inspiration*, 119.
25 See E.R. Kalin, "The Inspired Community: A Glance at Canon History", *CTM* 42
   (1971) 541–549; *idem. Arguments from Inspiration in the Canonization of the
   New Testament* (Harvard Ph.D., 1967); A Sundberg, "The Bible Canon and the
   Christian Doctrine of Inspiration", *Interp* 29 (1975) 352–371.
26 See further T.A. Hoffman, "Inspiration, Normativeness, Canonicity, and the
   Unique Sacred Character of the Bible", *CBQ* 44 (1982) 447–469.

The reason for this limitation of inspiration to canon is the same over-dependence on the prophetic model of inspiration that we discussed above. Even Achtemeier, who discusses the failings of this model at length, fails to see the implications for our understanding of canon. But fundamentalists clearly understand the link between the prophetic model and canon. R.L. Harris writes,

> It is clear from the foregoing that regardless of what one may himself believe concerning the Pentateuch, ancient Israel believed that Moses wrote it as the spokesman for God. There is no dissenting voice. And is it not clear that this is precisely why ancient Israel received it as authoritative, i.e. canonical? It was not canonized because of its antiquity, linguistic phenomena, beautiful style, royal imposition, or ecclesiastical decision. The principle for canonizing the Pentateuch which guided ancient Israel as far as we have any evidence at all, is, Was it from God's great spokesman, Moses? The human author, admitted by all to be a spokesman for the divine author, guaranteed the writing[27].

Since a canonical writing can only be written by an inspired individual, called a "prophet" by Harris, then by implication the entire Bible must have been written by prophets. This fantastic thesis is exactly what he endeavours to prove. Yet one ought not to allow the extreme features of this particular author to blind one to a much more common misconception. What Harris has done has been to carry an exclusive dependence on the prophetic model of inspiration to its logical conclusion in relation to canon. The conclusion that *only* canonical works are inspired is the result of using individual (prophetic) authors to guarantee the canonicity of a writing, just as the individual (prophetic) author was used to guarantee its inspiration. In other words, an inspired individual writes a book, which because of his acknowledged authority, is "received" into the canon. This effectively removes the religious community from any participation in either inspiration or the formation of the canon, a position with which Harris readily agrees[28].

But if, as we have seen, this over-reliance on the prophetic model is a distortion of how the Bible was written, it is also a distortion of how the canon was formed. What is lacking is a full appreciation of how tradition relates to canon. In this regard, there are two recent developments in Biblical Studies that help to shed light on this relationship. First is the application of the principles of sociology to reconstruct the setting of the biblical text. In particular, recent works from a sociological perspective have stressed the *social* nature of authority, that it is not something just exercised by the force of the individual personality, but is shaped and conferred by the community or social

---

27 *Inspiration and Canonicity of the Bible. An Historical and Exegetical Study* (Grand Rapids: Zondervan, 1969) 159.

28 In relation to the canon he writes, "We have no knowledge of a sifting of a prophet's work by his contemporaries or successors. It was not that people chose what to preserve. *This would place the burden of forming a canon on uninspired people, rather than leaving it in the hands of God's inspired teachers*", *Inspiration*, 175 (italics mine).

context in which it operates[29]. Second is the rise of "canon criticism" as developed by its leading proponents, B.S. Childs and J.A. Sanders[30]. They stress that critical historical studies have often isolated the elements of the biblical text from the needs of the community which collected and preserved them[31]. To insure the sustenance and survival of the community of Israel, a source of authority was needed to give it identity and purpose. This is exactly the function of canon, and canon is thus a *community* concern.

According to Sanders, there are four criteria that an authority source must meet for it to be an effective focus of identity for the community. It must be

1. an indestructible element in society
2. a commonly available element,
3. a highly adaptable element, and if necessary,
4. a portable element[32].

Only one element in Israelite society meets these criteria: tradition. As Sanders puts it, "Only the traditional can become canonical"[33]. Only Israel's tradition had the power to reach out and unify disparate elements of society. Only tradition had the stability to weather the vicissitudes of history, such as the Babylonian captivity. And only tradition had the adaptability to remain relevant to a society that was in a constant state of flux.

Though Childs' and Sander's work have been mostly restricted to the OT[34], we have seen in this investigation how their ideas have been applicable to the NT as well, particularly their stress that the formation of canon was not a process extrinsic to the production of the biblical literature, but a long series of developments stretching from the first expression of a tradition to its final delimitation in a specific literary corpus. The process of canon, then, runs parallel to the process of tradition, or put another way, tradition is the arena of the canonical process.

This is not to say, however, that everything that is traditional is canonical. Indeed, it may be well to say that tradition is the *battleground* of the canonical process. In the OT and NT we see evidence of many and often conflicting traditions. Nowhere is this clash of traditions more prominent than in the

---

29 For an OT and NT example, see B. Long, "Prophetic Authority as Social Reality", *Canon and Authority. Essays in Old Testament Religion and Theology*. Edit. G. Coats and B. Long (Philadelphia: Fortress, 1977) 3–20; B. Holmberg, *Paul and Power. The Structure of Authority in the Primitive Church as Reflected in the Pauline Epistles* (Philadelphia: Fortress, 1980).

30 The term "canon criticism" is Sanders' term, and one Childs would reject. For their agreements and disagreements, see J.A. Sanders, "Canonical Context".

31 See esp. B.S. Childs, *Introduction*, 41.

32 "Adaptable for Life: The Nature and Function of Canon", *Magnalia Dei: the mighty acts of God*. Fest. G.E. Wright. Edit. J.M. Cross, W.E. Lemke, P.D. Miller (Garden City, N.Y.: Doubleday, 1976) 539.

33 *Ibid*, 542.

34 The first attempt to address the NT from this perspective, see J.D.G. Dunn, "Levels of Canonical Authority", *Horizons in Biblical Theology* 4 (1982) 13 60. Recently, see B.S. Childs, *The New Testament as Canon* (Philadelphia: Fortress, 1984).

problem of true and false prophecy. Though the subject cannot be treated in depth[35] at least one illustration will demonstrate the problem of the authority of conflicting traditions. The classic example is the clash of Jeremiah and Hananiah in Jeremiah 28. Both represent different traditions, or at least interpretations of tradition. Hananiah represents a tradition of continuity, stressing the divine oversight and deliverance of Israel from their bondage (Isa 9:4; 14:25). Jeremiah represents a tradition of discontinuity and judgement (Hos 10:11). Though from our *post eventum* position we sit in judgement upon Hananiah, one must recognize that his arguments must have had great cogency and authority, and indeed even won the day! As Sanders suggests, it was probably not until the time of the Babylonian captivity and beyond that the oracles of Jeremiah and others of the canonical prophets established their validity as "true" as opposed to false prophecy[36]. No attempt can be made to resolve the hermeneutical problems involved in this struggle[37]. What is important to point out from the canonical perspective is that the *community* is the final arbitrator in the clash of authoritative traditions. No matter how "inspired" or correct an individual's message may be, it cannot become "canonical" until the community recognizes it as such[38]. This is not to say that the community was always right in its decisions, and a period of testing of traditions may lead to a reversal of opinion, as in the case of Jeremiah. But in the final analysis, the formation of canon belongs to the community.

Thus the picture that Harris presents of a prophet whose authority guarantees the canonicity of his writing puts the cart before the horse. It is the community recognition (sooner or later) that the prophet's words are *authoritative* (i.e. canonical) that help it to recognize or affirm the (divinely-given) *authority* of the prophet.

The opposition of most (Protestants) conservatives to this way of thinking has come by way of a perceived threat to the principle of *sola scriptura*. This idea of the role of the community (Israel, Church) smacks of ecclesiastical councils "creating" the canon by official pronouncement. But this is manifestly not the case here. It is simply the recognition that the divine involvement takes place along the whole continuum of the tradition process, from inspired individual to the delimitation of writings. The inspired individual is not totally separate from the community, but both influences and is in-

---

35 See J.L. Crenshaw, *Prophetic Conflict. Its Effect Upon Israelite Religion* (Berlin: W. De Gruyter, 1971).

36 J.A Sanders, "Adaptable For Life", 547–549.

37 See J.A. Sanders, "Hermeneutics in True and False Prophecy", *Canon and Authority*. Edit. G. Coats and B. Long (Philadelphia: Fortress, 1977) 21–41.

38 In Deuteronomy, if a prophecy does not come true, it is proof that it is a false prophecy (Dt 18:20–22). Yet the opposite is not true. Even if a prophecy comes true; it is not considered to be true prophecy if it does not accord with the community's religious tradition (Dt. 13–1–5). The issue is obviously more complex than this, but at least here we have an emphasis on the community as arbiter.

fluenced by it. Similarly, community and tradition lie in a dialectical relationship, each creating and shaping the other, the fruit of which is canon[39].

This crucial role of the community also explain why even when a certain figure had acknowledged authority in the manner that Harris posits, not all of that figure's works were considered of equal value or preserved. Thus, for example, the Apostle Paul would fit in best as a NT example of the prophetic model, writing and exercising authority by virtue of a special call. Yet we know for a fact that not all of Paul's writings were preserved as part of the NT canon, (1 Cor 5:9; 2 Cor 2:3–4; Col 4:16). Now on a purely "historical" level one might account for this as mere accident. This may be the reason for the loss of the letter to the Laodiceans, because of that church's slide into oblivion. But the fact that some of the Corinthians letters were preserved while others were lost suggests that the community itself had a role in deciding which writings were of more permanent value (cf. also "Q"). If this is the case, then once again we must emphasize that the *community* is the focus of canon formation, and not the prophetically inspired individual. *Inspired (individual) authorship does not guarantee canonicity.*

It is for the above reasons that the modern criterion of inspiration for canonicity, based as it is on the prophetic model, is an inadequate approach to both the historical and theological definition of canon. It is representative of the kind of "top-down" approach to authorship and authority that characterizes so much of our ecclesiastical thinking. Though one would not wish to detract from the force of the inspired individual in the Judaeo-Christian tradition, it must be said that in the majority of cases, both in writing and in the process of canonization, the "inspired community" plays an equally crucial role.

Furthermore, it must also be said that inspiration cannot be restricted to the (closed) canon. The possibility of divine inspiration will last as long as God continues to create a community for Himself through His revelation, and in both Jewish and Christian thought this means forever. Inspiration can only serve as a negative criterion, i.e. what is *not* inspired is not canonical. But inspiration was and will continue to be a broader phenomenon than canon. What then, is the role of canon in relation to inspiration? Here we can take a clue from the Pauline ὑποτύπωσις analogy in the Pastorals[40]. The ὑποτύπωσις of Pauline doctrine and lifestyle was not meant to be an expression of *all* Christian experience or thought but a foundational outline or archetype for further elaboration. This is also the function of canon. It does not encompass all of Christian theology or inspiration, but serves as an inviolable ὑποτύπωσις:

---

39 G. Gleoge relates "Überlieferung ist also eine Funktion der durch Offenbarung begründeten Gemeinschaft. Was fur das altisraelitische Gottesrecht gilt, das gilt in gewissen Umfang auch von der Überlieferung im A.T. Offenbarung konstituiert Gemeinschaft- und Gemeinschaft übernimmt und überliefert Offenbarung." *Offenbarung und Überlieferung: Ein dogmatischer Entwurf* (Göttingen: Vandenhoeck & Ruprecht, 1967) 27.

40 1 Tim 1:16; 2 Tim 1:13. See Chapter 5.

Thus, in forming the canon, the church acknowedged and established the Bible as the measure or standard of inspiration in the church, not as the totality of it. What concurs with canon is of like inspiration; what does not is not of God[41].

6.3 Summary

It now remains to draw together our reflection on canon and the findings of this investigation. In the beginning we noted how the problem of NT pseudonymity has plagued biblical scholarship ever since the advent of critical studies, and suggested that a long neglected investigation of Jewish background, particularly with respect to tradition and revelation, might prove helpful in easing the tension between historical and theological concerns. In fact we discovered a "pattern" of anonymity/pseudonymity in the prophetic, wisdom, and apocalyptic traditions of Israel and post-biblical Judaism that could be tested against Christian literature for similar features. Foremost among these features was the principle of *Vergegenwärtigung,* the recurring need to actualize a tradition for a future generation, and the common conviction of a continuity of revelation and interpretation which made this possible, *regardless of literary genre.*

This fundamental pattern was found to be paralleled in the NT literature that was examined. Though the NT understandably demonstrated its own peculiarities (particularly the more overtly pseudonymous character of the epistolary genre), the repetition of the pattern in the NT era demonstrates a strong continuity with its Jewish background, and offers a substantial case for regarding this as the fundamental motivation behind the use of authorship and attribution in the NT. When we then tried to relate these findings to the question of canon, we ran into the difficulty arising from the separation of the period when these documents were authored and first used from the time when these documents were formed into a (closed) canon. It was suggested that the continuity of the NT writers with their Jewish predecessors begins to erode after the NT era, and that the period of the fathers witnessed a gradual rejection of *Vergegenwärtigung* in the biblical mode. Naturally, further work must be done to substantiate this.

What then, is the relationship between pseudonymity and canon? The relationship is a complex one, and this study is not sufficient to answer that question in its entirety. What we can say is that for many if not most of the Jewish and Christian religious writings which we examined, both inside and outside the "canon", *the discovery of pseudonymous origins or anonymous redaction in no way prejudices either the inspiration or the canonicity of*

---

41 A. Sundberg, "The Bible Canon and Inspiration", 371.

*the work. Attribution, in the context of canon, must be primarily regarded
as a statement (or assertion) of authoritative tradition*[42].

6.4 Addendum: *Vergegenwärtigung* and the Closure of the Canon

Though this investigation can be regarded as complete, our concern with
the role of canon and tradition or *Vergegenwärtigung* makes it important to
mention in retrospect something that has been identified as one of the central
issues of our generation[43]. The question arises, why bother about the (closed)
canon at all? Given that inspiration has not ended, nor the need to actualize
God's revelation, what is the purpose of a fixed, authoritative body of writings?

Almost all scholars agree on the nature of the growth of biblical tradition,
and on the historical factors that led to its demise through the closure of the
canon. Where the agreement ends is over the question whether this can be
regarded as legitimate *theologically*. At the heart of the issue are two contrasting attitudes toward the locus of authority or revelation.

On one side are those who would see the *process* of tradition as the locus
of revelation and authority. According to R. Lauren, while the development
of a scripture and the canonizing process was a legitimate search for authority, final canonization was an illegitimate closure of that process in one moment in history[44]. D. Knight agrees, and establishes the theological foundations for this position by his essay, "Revelation Through Tradition"[45].
According to Knight and others, canon can only function authoritatively as
a dynamic process, not a static event. He stresses that revelation comes
through tradition by way of personal encounter. Process theology has further
elaborated the implications of this hermeneutic[46].

On the other side are those who would regard the *product* of tradition
(i.e. the canon) as the locus of revelation and authority. Though B.S. Childs

---

42 It cannot be denied that literary concerns also arise in some documents, but even
    when they do they are always related to the larger issue of authoritative tradition,
    and are not treated in isolation.
43 See B.W. Anderson, "Tradition and Scripture in the Community of Faith", *JBL*
    100 (1981) 5–21, the Presidential Address delivered at the centennial meeting of
    the Society of Biblical Literature.
44 "Tradition and Canon", *Tradition and Theology in the Old Testament*. Edit. D.A.
    Knight (Philadelphia: Fortress, 1977) 261–274.
45 *Idem*, 143–180.
46 See P. Hanson, *Dynamic Transcendence: The Correlation of Confessional Heritage
    and Contemporary Experience in a Biblical Model of Divine Activity* (Philadelphia:
    Fortress, 1978).

and J.A. Sanders differ in their hermeneutical approach to the scriptures[47], both agree that the canon embodies the whole history of biblical tradition, and is authoritative as such. The closure of the canon is not qualitatively different from the process of canon in the growth of tradition. It is just the final act, the logical conclusion to the process.

Though the issue is far too complex to be argued at length, it seems that the latter position offers a more fruitful approach. The great problem with a process hermeneutic is that it engenders theological solipsism. It has no mechanism for assuring a continuity between how God worked among His people in the past, and how He works now. Furthermore, it destroys any sense of uniqueness or election in the divine economy. Tradition becomes equated with the human struggle in general[48]. The great value of canon is that it is both a preserving and liberating force. It both assures a continuity of salvation-history and serves as a catalyst for further theological reflection. It is not a monolithic list of doctrines, but a dialogical record of the interaction of God and those He calls, and as such serves as the locus of both the unity and diversity of God's people[49].

But what is the *theological* justification for the closure of the canon? Undoubtedly it has to reside in the once-for-all nature of the events that it records and reflects. If the growth of tradition is in any way connected to the unfolding revelation of God, and if we believe that the decisive act of God's revelation is in Jesus Christ, then there must be some way of registering that claim in the authority structure of God's people. This is the function of (closed) canon, serving as a focal point for tradition prior and subsequent to the Christ-event.

Just as canon denotes the standard but not the extent of inspiration, likewise it represents the standard but not the extent of tradition. God's word has been and always must be actualized to meet the needs of its contemporary listeners. *Vergegenwärtigung* can and will continue, but now only under the biblical *model,* and not in the biblical *mode.* That is, tradition and the *Vergegenwärtigung* that is its driving force must continue, but it is now a process that is *extrinsic* to the biblical text and corpus. It cannot follow the

---

47 Sanders would not assign any greater authority to the different levels of tradition, while Childs would reserve normative authority for the final text. The differences stem mainly from Sander's existential hermeneutic. For a discussion of the many issues raised by "canon criticism", see the reviews of Childs' book, *Introduction to the Old Testament as Scripture* (1979) in *JSOT* 16 (1980), and *Horizons in Biblical Theology* 2 (1980). For Childs' argument against the existential hermenuetic in tradition formation, see B.S. Childs, *Memory and Tradition in Israel* (London: SCM, 1962).

48 See D. Knight, "Revelation", 168.

49 If we remember that a perennial problem of the growth of tradition has been the discernment of true and false prophecy/interpretation, then the canon can be regarded as a creative solution. To use the words of J.D.G. Dunn, the canon both recognizes the validity of diversity of religious expression, and marks out the limits of acceptable diversity. *Unity and Diversity,* 376–379. Some form of magisterium

biblical mode and become part of the text or corpus itself. Rather, following the ὑποτύπωσις analogy of the Pastorals (1 Tim 1:16; 2 Tim 1:13), it is both *legitimated* by the canonical outline or archetype and *judged* by it.

---

can also be seen in this light, though not necessarily as it has found expression in the Roman Catholic Church.

Selected Bibliography

The bibliography below represents works (excluding general reference works) dealing with the broad topics of authorship, revelation, canon and tradition in Judaism and earliest Christianity. Bibliographic treatment of individual Jewish and Christian writings can be found in the chapter footnotes.

Abraham, W.J. *The Divine Inspiration of Holy Scripture*. Oxford: University Press, 1981.

Achtemeier, P.J. *The Inspiration of Scripture*. Philadelphia: Wesminster, 1980.

Ackroyd, P.R. *Continuity. A Contribution to the Study of the Old Testament Religious Tradition*. Oxford: Blackwell, 1962.

— — "Continuity and Discontinuity: Rehabilitation and Authentication," *Tradition and Theology in the Old Testament*. Edit. D.A. Knight. Philadelphia: Fortress, 1977, 215–234.

— — "The Vitality of the Word of God in the Old Testament. A Contribution to the Study of the Transmission and Exposition of Old Testament Material," *ASTI* 1 (1962) 1–23.

Aland, K. "Falsche Verfasserangaben? Zur Pseudonymität im frühchristlichen Schrifttum," *ThRv* 75 (1979) cols. 1–10.

— — "The Problem of Anonymity and Pseudonymity in Christian Literature of the First Two Centuries," *The Authorship and Integrity of the New Testament*. Edit. K. Aland. London: SPCK, 1965, 1–13, reprinted from *JThS* 12 (1961) 39–49.

Aletti, J.-N. "Le canon des Écritures. Le Nouveau Testament," *Études* 349 (1978) 109–124.

Anderson, B.W. "Tradition and Scripture in the Community of Faith," *JBL* 100 (1981) 5–21.

Appel, N. "The New Testament Canon: Historical Process and Spirit's Witness," *TS(1)* 32 (1971) 627–646.

Bahnsen, G.L. "Autographs, Amaneunses and Restricted Inspiration," *EvQ* 45 (1973) 100–110.

Baldwin, J.G. "Is there pseudonymity in the Old Testament?" *Themelios* 4 (1978) 6–12.

Balz, H.R. "Amonymität und Pseudepigraphie im Urchristentum: Überlegungen zum literarischen und theologischen Problem der urchristlichen und gemeinantiken Pseudepigraphie," *ZThK* 66 (1969) 403–436.

Bardy, G. "Faux et fraudes littéraires dans l'antiquité chrétienne," *RHE* 32 (1936) 5–23, 275–302.

Barnett, A.E. *Paul Becomes a Literary Influence*. Chicago: University Press, 1941.

Barr, J. *Holy Scripture: Canon, Authority, Criticism*. Philadelphia: Westminster, 1983.

— — *Old and New in Interpretation*. London: SCM, 1966.

— — "The Bible as a Document of Believing Communities," *The Scope and Authority of the Bible. Explorations in Theology* 7. London: SCM, 1980, 111–133.

Bauer, H. "Die hebräischen Eigennamen als sprachliche Erkenntnisquelle," *ZAW* 48 (1930) 73–80.

Bauer, W. *Orthodoxy and Heresy in Earliest Christianity*. Philadelphia: Fortress, 1971[2].

Benoit, P. *Aspects of Biblical Inspiration*. Chicago: Priory, 1965.

Berger, K. "Apostelbrief und apostolische Rede. Zum Formular frühchristlichen Briefe," *ZNW* 65 (1974) 190–231.

Berger, P.L. "Charisma and Religious Innovation: The Social Location of Israelite Prophecy," *ASR* 28 (1963) 940–950.

Best, E. "Scripture, Tradition and the Canon of the New Testament," *BJRL* 61 (1979) 258–289.

Betz, O. *Offenbarung und Schriftforschung in der Qumransekte.* Tübingen: Mohr, 1960.

Blenkinsopp, J. *Prophecy and Canon: A Contribution to the Study of Jewish Origins.* London: University of Notre Dame Press, 1977.

Boring, M.E. "Christian Prophecy and the Sayings of Jesus: The State of the Question," *NTS* 29 (1983) 104–112..

–– *Sayings of the Risen Jesus.* Cambridge: University Press, 1982.

Brockington, L.H. "The Problem of Pseudonymity," *JThS* 4 (1953) 15–22.

Brownlee, W.H. "Biblical Interpretation Among the Sectaries of the Dead Sea Scrolls," *BA* 14 (1951) 54–76.

–– "The Background of Biblical Interpretation at Qumran," *Qumrân: Sa piété, sa théologie et son milieu.* Edit. M. Delcor. Paris: Duculot, 1978, 183–193.

Brox, N. *Falsche Verfasserangaben. Zur Erklärung der frühchristlichen Pseudepigraphie.* Stutgart: KBW, 1975.

–– "Methodenfragen der Pseudepigraphie Forschung," *ThRv* 75 (1979) 275–278.

–– "Pseudo-Paulus und Pseudo-Ignatius. Einige Topoi altchristlichen Pseudepigraphie, *VigChr* 30 (1976) 181–188.

–– (edit.) *Pseudepigraphie in der heidnischen und jüdisch-christlichen Antike.* Darmstadt: Wissenschaftliche Buchgesellschaft, 1977.

–– "Zum Problemstand in der Erforschung der altchristlichen Pseudepigraphie," *Kairos* 15 (1973) 10–23, reprinted in *Pseudepigraphie* (Edit. N. Brox) above, 311–334.

Bruce, F.F. *Biblical Exegesis in the Qumran Texts.* Grand Rapids: Eerdmans, 1959.

–– "New Light on the Origins of the New Testament Canon," *New Dimensions in New Testament Study.* Edit. Zondervan, 1974, 3–18.

–– "Scripture and Tradition in the New Testament," *Holy Book and Holy Tradition.* Edit. F.F. Bruce and E.G. Rupp. Manchester: University Press, 1968, 68–93.

–– "Some Thoughts on the Beginning of the New Testament Canon," *BJRL* 65 (1983) 37–60.

–– *Tradition Old and New.* Grand Rapids: Zondervan, 1970.

Bultmann, R. *The History of the Synoptic Tradition.* New York: Harper and Row, 1963.

Burtchaell, J.T. *Catholic Theories of Biblical Inspiration Since 1810.* New York: Cambridge Unversity Press, 1969.

von Campenhausen, H. *The Formation of the Christian Bible.* Philadelphia: Fortress, 1972.

Candlish, J.S. "On the Moral Character of Pseudonymous Books," *Exp* 4 (1891) 91–107, 262–279.

Carroll, K.L. "Towards a Commonly Received New Testament," *BJRL* 44 (1962) 327–349.

Childs, B.S. *Introduction to the Old Testament as Scripture.* (Not an ordinary introduction) London: SCM, 1979.

–– *Memory and Tradition in Israel.* London: SCM, 1962.

–– "The Canonical Shape of the Prophetic Literature," *Interp* 32 (1978) 46–55.

–– "The Exegetical Significance of Canon for the Study of the Old Testament," *Congress Volume: Göttingen, 1977.* Edit. J.A. Emerton *et al.* VTSupp 29. Leiden: Brill, 1978, 66–80.

–– *The New Testament as Canon. An Introduction.* Philadelphia: Fortress, 1984. (Not an ordinary introduction.)

Clements, R.E. "Patterns in the Prophetic Canon," *Canon and Authority: Essays in Old Testament Religion and Theology.* Edit. G.W. Coats and B.O. Long. Philadelphia: Fortress, 1977, 42–55.

−− *Prophecy and Tradition.* Atlanta: Knox, 1975.

Collins, J.J. "Pseudedonymity, Historical Reviews and the Genre of the Revelation of John," *CBQ* 39 (1977) 329−343.

Collins, R.F. "The Matrix of the New Testament Canon," *BTB* 7 (1977) 51−59.

Cothenet, É. "Les prophètes chrétiens comme exégètes charismatiques de l'ecriture," *Prophetic Vocation in the New Testament and Today.* Edit. J. Panagopoulos. *NTSupp* 45. Leiden: Brill, 1977, 77−107.

Cullmann, O. *The Johannine Circle.* London: SCM, 1976.

−− "The Tradition," *The Early Church.* London: SCM, 1956, 59−99.

Culpepper, R.A. *The Johannine School.* Missoula: Scholars Press, 1975.

Dautzenburg, G. *Urchristliche Prophetie: Ihr Erforschung, ihre Voraussetzung im Judentum und ihre Struktur im ersten Korintherbrief.* Stuttgart: Kohlhammer, 1975.

−− "Zur urchristlichen Prophetie," *BZ* 22 (1978) 125−132.

DePury, A. "Sagesse et Revelation dans l'Ancien Testament," *RThPh* 27 (1977) 1−50.

Dibelius, M. *From Tradition to Gospel.* New York: Scribners, 1935.

Dietrich, E.L. "Das religiös-emphatische Ichwort bei jüdischen Apokalyptikern, Weisheitslehren, und Rabbinen," *ZRGG* 4 (1952) 1−22.

Dillistone, F.W. "Wisdom, Word and Spirit. Revelation in the Wisdom Literature," *Interp* 2 (1948) 275−287.

Dodd, C.H. *According to the Scriptures: the sub-structure of New Testament Theology.* London: Nisbet, 1952.

Doty, W.G. *Letters in Primitive Christianity.* Philadelphia: Fortress, 1973.

−− "The Classification of Epistolary Literature," *CBQ* 31 (1969) 183−199.

Dungan, D.L. "The New Testament Canon in Recent Study," *Interp* 29 (1975) 339−351.

Dunn, J.D.G. *Jesus and the Spirit.* London: SCM, 1975.

−− "Levels of Canonical Authority," *Horizons in Biblical Theology* 4 (1982) 13−60.

−− "Prophetic 'I'-Sayings and the Jesus-Tradition: The Importance of Testing Prophetic Utterances Within Early Christianity," *NTS* 24 (1977−78) 175−198.

−− *Unity and Diversity in the New Testament.* London: SCM, 1977.

Ehrlich, E. *Der Traum im Alten Testament. BZAW* 73. Berlin: Töpelmann, 1953.

Ellis, E.E. "Prophecy in the New Testament Church − and Today," *Prophetic Vocation in the New Testament and Today.* Edit. J. Panagopoulos. *NTSupp* 45. Leiden: Brill, 1977, 46−57.

Evans, D. "Protestant and Roman Views of Revelation. I. Protestant Views," *CJR* 10 (1964) 258−265.

Fenton, J.C. "Pseudonymity in the New Testament," *Theology* 58 (1955) 51−56.

Finegan, J. "The Original Form of the Pauline Collection," *HTR* 49 (1956) 85−103.

Finkel, A. "The pesher of Dreams and Scriptures," *RdQ* 4 (1963−64) 357−370.

Fischer, H.A. "The Transformation of Wisdom in the World of Midrash," *Aspects of Wisdom in Judaism and Early Christianity.* Edit. R.L. Wilken. Notre Dame: University Press, 1975, 67−102.

Fisher, J.A. "Pauline Literary Forms and Thought Patterns," *CBQ* 39 (1977) 209−233.

Fischer, K.M. "Anmerkungen zur Pseudepigraphie im Neuen Testament," *NTS* 23 (1976) 76−81.

Fishbane, M. "Revelation and Tradition: Aspects of Innerbiblical Exegesis," *JBL* 99 (1980) 343−361.

−− "Torah and Tradition," *Tradition and Theology in the Old Testament.* Edit. D.A. Knight. Philadelphia: Fortress, 1977, 275−300.

Flack, E.E. "Motives for Pseudonymity in the Apocalypses. A Study in the Continuity of Revelation," *LCQ* 9 (1936) 1−17.

Fohrer, R. "Tradition und Interpretation im Alten Testament," *ZAW* 73 (1961) 1−30.

Forster, L. "The Earliest Collection of Paul's Epistles," *BETS* 10 (1967) 44−55.

Frank, I. *Der Sinn der Kanonbildung.* Freiburg: Herder, 1971.

Freer, K.O. *A Study of Vision Reports in Biblical Literature.* Ph.D., Yale University, 1975.

Füglister, N. "Für Jahwe begeistert – Künder des Wortes. Geschichte und Struktur des Prophetismus in Israel," *Wort und Botschaft.* Edit. J. Schreiner. Wurzburg: Echter Verlag, 1967, 118–142.

Gamble, H. "The Redaction of the Pauline Letters and the Formation of the Pauline Corpus," *JBL* 94 (1975) 403–418.

Gerhardsson, B. *Memory and Manuscript.* Uppsala: Gleerup, 1961.

Gese, H. "Erwägungen zur Einheit der biblischen Theologie," *ZThK* 67 (1970) 417–436.

— "Tradition and Biblical Theology," *Tradition and Theology in the Old Testement.* Edit. D.A. Knight. Philadelphia: Fortress, 1977, 301–326.

Gevaryahu, H.M.I. "Biblical colophons: a source for the 'biography' of authors, texts, and books," *Congress Volume: Edinburgh, 1974.* Edit. G.W. Anderson *et al. VT-Supp* 28. Leiden: Brill, 1975, 42–59.

Gloege, G. *Offenbarung und Überlieferung: Ein Dogmatischer Entwurf.* Volksdorf: Reich, 1954.

Goodspeed, E.J. "Pseudonymity and Pseudepigraphy in Early Christian Literature," *New Chapters in New Testament Study.* New York: Macmillan, 1937, 169–188.

Grant, R.M. "Literary Criticism and the New Testament Canon," *JSNT* 16 (1982) 24–44.

— *The Formation of the New Testament.* New York: Harper and Row, 1965.

Grelot, P. "L'Inspiration Scripturaire," *RSR* 51 (1963) 337–382.

— "Tradition as Source and Environment of Scripture," *Conc (GB)* 2, 10 (1966) 5–15.

Gribomont, J. "De la notion de 'Faux' en litterature populaire," *Bib* 54 (1973) 434–436.

Groh, D.E. "Hans von Campenhausen on Canon. Positions and Problems," *Interp* 28 (1974) 331–343.

Grudem, W.A. *The Gift of Prophecy in I Corinthians.* Washington: University Press of America, 1982.

Guillaume, A. *Prophecy and Divination Among the Hebrews and Other Semites.* London: Hodder and Stoughton, 1938.

Guthrie, D. "Acts and Epistles in Apocryphal Writings," *Apostolic History and the Gospel.* Fest. F.F. Bruce. Edit. W.W. Gasque and R. P. Martin. Exeter: Paternoster, 1970, 328–345.

— *Early Christian Pseudepigraphy and Its Antecedents.* Ph.D., London University, 1961.

— "Epistolary Pseudepigraphy," *New Testament Introduction.* London: Tyndale, 1970[3], 671–684.

— "The Development of the Idea of Canonical Pseudepigrapha in New Testament Criticism," *Vox Evangelica,* I. Edit. R.P. Martin. London: Tyndale, 1962, 43–59, reprinted in *The Authorship and Integrity of the New Testament.* Edit. K. Aland. London: SPCK, 1965, 14–39.

— "Tertullian and Pseudonymity," *ET* 67 (1956) 341–342.

Haag, H. "'Offenbarung' in der herbräischen Bibel," *ThZ* 16 (1960) 251–258.

Habel, N.C. "Appeal to Ancient Tradition as a Literary Form," *Society of Biblical Literature 1973 Seminar Papers,* I. Edit. G. MacRae. Cambridge: SBL, 1973, 34–54.

Haefner, A.E. "A Unique Source for the Study of Ancient Pseudonymity," *AThR* 16 (1934) 8–15.

Hahn, F. "Die heilige Schrift als älteste christliche Tradition und als Kanon," *EvTh* 40 (1980) 456–466.

Hammer, P.L. "Canon and Theological Variety: A Study in the Pauline Tradition," *ZNW* 67 (1976) 83–89.

Hanson, A.T. "The Domestication of Paul: A Study in the Development of Early Christian Theology," *BJRL* 63 (1981) 402–418.

Hanson, P.D. *Dynamic Transcendence.* Philadelphia: Fortress, 1978.

Hanson, R.P.C. *Tradition in the Early Church.* London: SCM, 1962.

Haran, M. "From Early to Classical Prophecy: Continuity and Change," *VT* 27 (1977) 385–397.

Harnack, A. *Die Briefsammlung des Apostels Paulus und die anderen vorkonstantinschen christlichen Brief- sammlungen.* Leipzig: Hinrich, 1926.

Harrelson, W. "Life, Faith, and the Emergence of Tradition," *Tradition and Theology in the Old Testament.* Edit. D.A. Knight. Philadelphia: Fortress, 1977, 9–30.

Harrington, W. "The Inspiration of Scripture," *IThQ* 29 (1962) 3–24.

Harris, R.L. *Inspiration and Canonicity of the Bible.* Grand Rapids: Zondervan, 1969.

Hecker, K. "Tradition and Originalität in der altorientalischen Literatur," *ArOr* 45 (1977) 245–258.

Heinrici, C.F.G. "Zur Charakteristik der litterarischen Verhältnisse des zweiten Jahrhunderts," *Pseudepigraphie in der heinnischen und jüdisch-christlichen Antike.* Edit. N. Brox. Darmstadt: Wissenschaftliche Buchgesellschaft, 1977, 74–81, reprinted from *Beiträge zur Geschichte und Erklärung des Neuen Testament*, I. Leipzig: Dürr, 1894, 71–78.

Hengel, M. "Anonymität, Pseudepigraphie und 'Literarische Falschung' in der jüdisch-hellenistischen Literatur," *Pseudepigrapha* I. Edit. K. von Fritz. Vandoeuvres-Geneve: Fondation Hardt, 1972, 231–308, with discussion 309–329.

–– *Judaism and Hellenism.* Two volumes. London: SCM, 1974.

Herrman, S. *Ursprung und Funktion der Prophetie im alten Israel.* Opladen: Westdeutscher Verlag, 1976.

Hertzberg, H.W. "Die Nachgeschichte alttestamentlichen Texte innerhalb des Alten Testaments," *Werden und Wesen des Alten Testaments.* Edit. P. Volz. *BZAW* 66. Berlin: Töplemann, 1936, 110–121.

Heschel, A.J. "Prophetic Inspiration. An analysis of prophetic consciousness," *Jdm* 11 (1962) 3–13.

Hill, D. "Christian Prophets as Teachers or Instructors in the Church," *Prophetic Vocation in the New Testament and Today.* Edit. J. Panagopoulos. *NTSupp* 45. Leiden: Brill, 1977, 108–130.

–– *New Testament Prophecy.* London: Marshall, Morgan and Scott, 1979.

–– "On the Evidence for the Creative Role of Christian Prophets," *NTS* 20 (1974) 262–274.

Hoffman, T.A. "Inspiration, Normativeness, Canonicity, and the Unique Sacred Character of the Bible," *CBQ* 44 (1982) 447–469.

Horgan, M.P. *Persharim: Qumran Interpretation of Biblical Books.* Washington: CBA, 1979.

Horst, F. "Die Visionsschilderungen der alttestamentlichen Propheten," *EvTh* 20 (1960) 193–205.

Käsemann, E. (edit.) *Das Neue Testament als Kanon.* Göttingen: Vandenhoeck and Ruprecht, 1970.

Kalin, E.R. *Arguments from Inspiration in the Canonization of the New Testament.* Ph.D., Harvard University, 1967.

–– "The Inspired Community: A Glance at Canon History," *CTM* 42 (1971) 541–549.

Kapelrud, A.S. "The Spirit and the Word in the Prophets," *ASTI* 11 (1977–78) 40–47.

–– "Tradition and Worship: The Role of the Cult in Tradition Formation and Transmission," *Tradition and Theology in the Old Testament.* Edit. D.A. Knight. Philadelphia: Fortress, 1977, 101–124.

Karavidopoulos, I. "To problēma tēs Pseudepigraphias," *Deltion Biblikon Meleton* 5 (1977–78) 178–188.

Knibb, M.A. "Prophecy and the emergence of the Jewish apocalypses," *Israel's Prophetic Tradition.* Fest. P.R. Ackroyd. Edit. R. Coggins *et al.* Cambridge: University Press, 1982, 155–180.

Knierim, R. "Offenbarung im Alten Testament," *Problem biblischer Theologie.* Fest. G. von Rad. Edit. H.W. Wolff. München: Kaiser, 1971, 206–235.

Knight, D.A. *Rediscovering the Traditions of Israel*, Revised. Missoula: Scholars Press, 1975.
– – "Revelation through Tradition," *Tradition and Theology in the Old Testament.* Edit. D.A. Knight. Philadelphia: Fortress, 1977, 143–180.
Knight, H. *The Hebrew Prophetic Consciousness.* London: Lutterworth, 1974.
Koch, K. *The Rediscovery of Apocalyptic.* London: SCM, 1972.
Kraft, H. "Das besondere Selbstbewusstsein der Verfasser der neutestamentlichen Schriften," *Modern Exegese und historische Wissenschaft.* Edit. J.M. Hallenbach and J. Staudinger. Trier: Spee, 1972, 77–93.
– – "Vom Ende der urchristlichen Prophetie," *Prophetic Vocation in the New Testament and Today.* Edit. J. Panagopoulos. *NTSupp* 45. Leiden: Brill, 1977, 162–185.
Lambert, W.G. "A Catalogue of Texts and Authors," *JCS* 16 (1962) 59–77.
– – "Ancestors, Authors, and Canonicity," JCS 11 (1957) 1–14.
Laube, F. "Falsche Verfasserangeben in neutestamentlichen Schriften. Aspekte der gegenwärtigen Diskussion um die neutestamentliche Pseudepigraphie," *TThZ* 89 (1980) 228–242.
Lauren, R.B. "Tradition and Canon," *Tradition and Theology in the Old Testament.* Edit. D.A. Knight. Philadelphia: Fortress, 1977, 261–274.
Lea, T.D. "The Early Christian View of Pseudepigraphic Writings," *JETS* 27 (1984) 65–75.
Leihman, S.Z. "Inspiration and Canonicity: Reflections on the Formation of the Biblical Canon," *Jewish and Christian Self-Definition*, I. Edit. E.P. Sanders. London: SCM, 1981, 56–63.
– – (edit.) *The Canon and Masorah of the Hebrew Bible.* New York: KTAV, 1974.
– – *The Canonization of Hebrew Scripture.* Hamden: Archon, 1976.
Leivestad, R. "Das Dogma von der Prophetlosen Zeit," *NTS* 19 (1973) 288–299.
Lewis, J.P. "The Schools of the Prophets," *RestQ* 9 (1966) 1–10.
Lightstone, J.N. "The formation of the biblical canon in Judaism of late antiquity: Prolegomenon to a general reassessment," *SR* 8 (1979) 135–142.
Lindblom, J. *Prophecy in Ancient Israel.* Oxford: Blackwell, 1962.
– – "Symbolic Perceptions and Literary Visions," *The Bible in its Literary Milieu.* Edit. J. Maier and V. Tollers. Grand Rapids: Eerdmans, 1979, 67–76, reprinted from *Prophecy* (above), 137–148.
Long, B.O. "Prophetic Authority as Social Reality," *Canon and Authority. Essays in Old Testament Religion and Theology.* Edit. G. Coats and B.O. Long. Philadelphia: Fortress, 1977, 3–20.
– – "Prophetic Call Traditions and Reports of Visions," *ZAW* 84 (1972) 494–500.
– – "Reports of Visions Among the Prophets," *JBL* 95 (1976) 353–365.
McCarthy, D.J. "Personality, Society, and Inspiration," *TS* 24 (1963) 552–576.
Mack, B.L. *Logos und Sophia.* Göttingen: Vandenhoeck and Ruprecht, 1973.
McKane, W. "Prophecy and the Prophetic Literature," *Tradition and Interpretation.* Edit. G.W. Anderson. Oxford: University Press, 1979, 163–188.
McKenzie, J.L. "The Social Character of Inspiration," *CBQ* 24 (1962) 115–124.
MacKenzie, R.A.F. "Some Problems in the Field of Inspiration," *CBQ* 40 (1958) 1–8.
Marshall, I.H. *Biblical Inspiration.* London: Hodder and Stoughton, 1982.
Martin, R.P. "Authority in the Light of the Apostolate, Tradition, and the Canon," *EvQ* 40 (1968) 66–82.
Martucci, J. "Protestant and Roman Views of Revelation. 2 A Roman Catholic Commentary," *CJT* 10 (1964) 265–270.
Metzger, B.M. "Literary Forgeries and Canonical Pseudepigrapha," *JBL* 91 (1972) 3–24.
Meyer, A. "Besprechung von Frederik Torm: Die Psychologie der Pseudonymität im Hinblick auf die Literatur des Urchristentums (1932)." *ThLZ* 58 (1933) 354–357; reprinted in *Pseudepigraphie in der heidnischen und jüdisch-christlichen Antike.* Eidt. N. Brox. Darmstadt: Wissenschaftliche Buchgesellschaft, 1977, 149–153.
– – "Religiöse Pseudepigraphie als ethisch-psychologisches Problem," *ZNW* 35 (1936) 262–279, reprinted in *Pseudepigraphie* (Edit. N. Brox, above) 90–110.

-- "Religiöse literarische 'Falschungen'," *WuL* 14 (1920–21) 741–756, 823–837.

Mitton, C.L. *The Formation of the Pauline Corpus of Letters.* London: Epworth, 1955.

Müller, U.B. *Prophetie und Predigt im Neuen Testament.* Gütersloh: Mohn, 1975.

Murray, R. "How Did the Church Determine the Canon of Scripture?" *HeyJ* 11 (1970) 115–126.

Myers, J.M. and E.D. Freed, "Is Paul Also Among the Prophets?" *Interp* 20 (1966) 40–53.

Nel, P. "Authority in the Wisdom Admonitions," *ZAW* 93 (1981) 418–426.

Newman, R.C. "The Council of Jamnia and the Old Testament Canon," *WThJ* 38 (1976) 319–349.

Niditch, S. "The Visionary," *Ideal Figures in Ancient Judaism.* Edit. J.J. Collins and G.W.E. Nickelsburg. Chico: Scholars Press, 1980, 153–179.

Nielsen, E. *Oral Tradition.* London: SCM, 1954.

Neilsen, C.M. "Polycarp, Paul, and the Scriptures," *AThR* 47 (1965) 199–216.

-- "Scripture in the Pastoral Epistles," *Perspectives in Religious Studies* 7 (1980) 4–23.

Noth, M. "The 'Re-presentation' of the Old Testament in Proclamation," *Essays on Old Testament Interpretation.* Edit. C. Westermann. London: SCM, 1963, 76–88.

Oppenheim, A.L. "The Interpretation of Dreams in the Ancient Near East," *TAPhS* 46 (1956) 179–255.

Osswald, E. "Zum Problem der *Vaticinia ex eventu*," *ZAW* 75 (1963) 27–44.

von der Osten-Sacken, P. *Die Apokalyptik in ihrem Verhältnis zu prophetie und Weisheit.* München: Kaiser, 1969.

Patzia, A.G. "The Deutero-Pauline Hypothesis : An Attempt at Clarification," *EvQ* 52 (1980) 27–42.

Penny, D.N. *The Pseudo-Pauline Letters of the First Two Centuries.* Ph.D., Emory University, 1980.

Perls, A. "Das Plagium," *MGWJ* 58 (1914) 305–322.

Pesch, R. "Die Zuschreibung der Evangelien an apostolische Verfasser," *ZKTh* 97 (1975) 56–71.

Petersen, D.L. *The Roles of Israel's Prophets.* Sheffield J SOT Press, 1981.

Pfeiffer, R.H. "Wisdom and Vision in the Old Testament," *ZAW* 11 (1934) 93–101, reprinted in *Studies in Ancient Israelite Wisdom.* Edit. J . Crenshaw. New York: KTAV, 1976, 305–313.

Pinnock, C. *Biblical Revelation.* Chicago: Moody, 1971.

Piper, J . "The Authority and Meaning of the Christian Canon: A Response to G. Sheppard on Canon Criticism," *JETS* 19 (1976) 87–96.

Pokorný, P. "Das theologische Problem der neutestamentliche Pseudepigraphie," *EvTh* 44 (1984) 486–496.

Quinn, J.D. "p[46] – The Pauline Canon?" *CBQ* 36 (1974) 379–385.

Rahner, K . *Inspiration in the Bible.* New York : Herder and Herder, 1958.

Reiling, J . *Hermas and Christian Prophecy.* NTSupp 37. Leiden: Brill, 1973.

-- "Prophecy, the Spirit and the Church," *Prophetic Vocation in the New Testament and Today.* Edit. J. Panagopoulos. *NTSupp* 45. Leiden : Brill, 1977, 58–76.

Rendtorf, R. "The Concept of Revelation in Ancient Israel," *Revelation as History.* Edit W. Pannenberg. New York: Macmillan, 1968, 23–53.

Richter, W. "Traum und Traumdeutung im Alten Testament," *BZ* 7 (1963) 202–220.

Rist, M. "Pseudepigraphic Refutations of Marcionism," *JR* 32 (1942) 39–62.

-- "Pseudepigraphy and the Early Christians," *Studies in New Testament and Early Christian Literature.* Fest. A.P. Wikgren. Edit. D.E. Aune. Leiden: Brill, 1972, 75–91.

Robinson, H.W. *Corporate Personality in Ancient Israel.* Philadelphia Fortress, 1964, an expansion of "The Hebrew Conception of Corporate Personality," *Werden und Wesen des Alten Testaments.* Edit. P. Volz. *BZAW* 66. Berlin: Töpelmann, 1936, 49–62.

-- *Inspiration and Revelation in the Old Testament.* Oxford: Clarendon, 1946.

—— "The Council of Yahweh," *JThS* 45 (1944) 151–157.

Robinson, T.H. *Prophecy and the Prophets in the Old Testament.* London: Duckworth, 1944[2].

Rogerson, J.W. "The Hebrew Conception of Corporate Personality: A Re-examination," *JThS* 21 (1970) 1–16.

Roller, O. *Das Formular der paulinischen Briefe.* Stuttgart: Kohlhammer, 1933.

Ross, J.F. "The Prophet as Yahweh's Messenger," *Israel's Prophetic Heritage.* Fest.J. Muilenburg. Edit. B.W. Anderson and W. Harrelson. London: SCM, 1962, 98–107.

Rowland, C. *The Open Heaven. A Study of Apocalyptic in Judaism and Early Christianity.* London SPCK, 1982.

—— "The Visions of God in Apocalyptic Literature," *JSJ* 10 (1979) 137–154.

Russell, D.S. *The Method and Message of Jewish Apocalyptic 200 B.C.–A.D. 100.* London: SCM, 1964.

Rylaarsdam, J.C. *Revelation in Jewish Wisdom.* Chicago: University Press, 1946.

Sand, A. *Kanon. Von den Anfängen bis zum Fragmentum Muratorianum.* Freiburg: Herder, 1974.

—— "Überlieferung und Sammlung der Paulusbriefe," *Paulus in den neutestamentlichen Spätschriften.* Edit. K. Kertelge. Freiburg: Herder, 1981, 11–23.

Sanders, J.A. "Adaptable for Life: The Nature and Function of Canon," *Magnalia Dei: the Mighty Acts of God.* Fest. G.E. Wright. Edit. F.M. Cross *et al.* Garden City: Doubleday, 1976, 531–560.

—— "Biblical Criticism and the Bible as Canon," *USQR* 32 (1977) 157–165.

—— "Canonical Context and Canonical Criticism," *Horizons in Biblical Theology* 2 (1980) 173–197.

—— "Reopening Old Questions About Scripture," *Interp* 28 (1974) 321–330.

—— *Torah and Canon.* Philadelphia: Fortress, 1972.

Schenke, H.-M. "Das Weiterwirken des Paulus und die Pflege seines Erbes durch die Paulus-Schule," *NTS* 21 (1974–75) 505–518, reprinted in *Einleitung in die Schriften des Neuen Testaments,* I. Edit. H.-M. Schenke and K.-M. Fischer. Gütersloh: Mohn, 1978, 233–247.

Schmidt, D.H. *The Peter Writings: Their Redactors and Their Relationships.* Ph.D., Northwestern University, 1972.

Schmidt, K.W. "Prophetic Delegation: A Form-Critical Inquiry," *Bib* 63 (1982) 206–218.

Schmithals, W. "On the Composition and Earliest Collection of the Major Epistles of Paul," *Paul and the Gnostics.* Nashville: Abingdon, 1972, 239–274.

Schmitt, J. "L'autoritée de la tradition aux temps apostoliques," *RevSR* 53 (1979) 209–219.

Schökel, L.A. "The Psychology of Inspiration," *The Bible in its Literary Milieu.* Edit. J. Maier and V. Tollers. Grand Rapids: Eerdmans, 1979, 19–56, reprinted from *The Inspired Word.* London: Seabury, 1967, 177–215.

Schwank, P.B. "Das Probleme der Pseudepigraphie im Neuen Testament. Zum Commentar von K.H. Schelke über die Petrusbriefe und den Judasbrief: Erbe und Aufrag," *BenM* 38 (1962) 133–136.

Schwartz, J. "Le Voyage au Ciel dans la Littérature Apocalyptique," *L'Apocalyptique.* Edit. M. Philonenko and M. Simon. Paris: Geuthner, 1977, 89–126.

Scott, R.B.Y. "Priesthood, Prophecy, Wisdom, and the Knowledge of God," *JBL* 80 (1961) 1–15.

Shaw, R.D. "Pseudonymity and Interpretation," *The Pauline Epistles.* Edinburgh: Clark, 1903, 477–486.

Sheppard, G.T. "Canon Criticism: The Proposal of B.S. Childs and an Assessment for Evangelical Hermeneutics," *StBibT* 4 (1974) 3–17.

—— "Canonization: Hearing the Voice of the Same God through Historically Dissimilar Traditions," *Interp* 36 (1982) 21–33.

—— *Wisdom as a Hermeneutical Construct. BZAW* 151. Berlin: de Gruyter, 1980.

Sint, J.A. *Pseudonymität im Altertum. Ihre Formen und ihre Gründe.* Innsbruck: Universitätsverlag Wagner, 1960.

Smith, M. "Pseudepigraphy in the Israelite Literary Tradition," *Pseudepigrapha I.* Edit. K. von Fritz. Vandoeuvres-Geneve: Fondation Hardt, 1972, 189–215, with discussion 216–227.

Souter, A. and C.S.C. Williams, *The Text and Canon of the New Testament.* London: Duckworth, 1954².

Speyer, W. *Die literarische Fälschung im Altertum.* München: Beck, 1971.

– – "Fälschung, pseudepigraphische freie Erfindung und 'echte religiöse Pseudepigraphie'," *Pseudepigrapha I.* Edit. K. von Fritz. Vandoeuvres-Genève: Fondation Hardt, 1972, 333–366 with discussion 367–378.

– – "Religiöse Pseudepigraphie und literarische Fälschung im Altertum," *Pseudepigraphie in der heidnischen und jüdisch-christlichen Antike.* Edit N. Brox. Darmstadt: Wissenschaftliche Buchgesellschaft, 1977, 195–263, reprinted from *JAC* 8/9 (1965–66) 82–125.

Stanley, D.M. "'Become imitators of me': The Pauline Conception of Apostolic Tradition," *Bib* 40 (1959) 859–877.

Steck, O.H. "Theological Streams of Tradition," *Tradition and Theology in the Old Testament.* Edit. D.A. Knight. Philadelphia: Fortress, 1977, 183–214.

Stone, M.E. "Apocalyptic – Vision or Hallucination?" *Milla wa-Milla* 14 (1974) 47–56.

– – "Lists of Revealed Things in the Apocalyptic Literature," *Magnalia Dei: the Mighty Acts of God.* Fest. G.E. Wright. Edit. F.M. Cross *et al.* Garden City: Doubleday, 1976, 414–452.

Sundberg, A.C. "A Revised History of the New Testament Canon," *StEv* 4 (1968) 452–461.

– – "Canon Muratori: A Fourth-Century List," *HThR* 66 (1973) 1–41.

– – "The Bible Canon and the Christian Doctrine of Inspiration," *Interp* 29 (1975) 352–371.

Syme, R. "Fraud and Imposture," *Pseudepigrapha I.* Edit. K. von Fritz. Vandoevres-Genève: Fondation Hardt, 1972, 1–17, with discussion 18–21.

Topel, L.J. "Rahner and McKenzie on the Social Theory of Inspiration," *Scrip* 16 (1964) 33–44.

Torm. F. *Die Psychologie der Pseudonymität im Hinblick auf die Literatur des Urchristentums.* Gütersloh: Bertelsmann, 1932, reprinted in *Pseudepigraphie in der heidnischen und jüdisch-christlichen Antike.* Edit. N. Brox. Darmstadt: Wissenschaftliche Buchgesellschaft, 1977, 111–140.

Trudinger, L.P. "The Church's Role in the Making of Scripture," *ET* 85 (1974) 342–343.

Tucker, G.M. "Prophetic Superscriptions and the Growth of a Canon," *Canon and Authority.* Edit. G.W. Coats and B.O. Long. Philadelphia: Fortress, 1977, 56–70.

van Unnik, W.C. "First Century A.D. Literary Culture and Early Christian Literature," *Nederlands Theologisch Tydschrift* 25 (1971) 28–43.

Vawter, B. *Biblical Inspiration.* London: Hutchinson, 1972.

Vögtle, A. "Die Pseudepigraphische Briefschreibung," *BiLe* 12 (1971) 262–264.

Wegenast, K. *Das Verständnis der Tradition bei Paulus und in den Deuteropaulinen.* Neukirchen-Vluyn: Neukirchener Verlag, 1962.

Wengst, K. "Der Apostel und die Tradition. Zur theologischen Bedeutung urchristlicher Formeln bei Paulus," *ZThK* 69 (1972) 145–162.

Westermann, C. *Basic Forms of Prophetic Speech.* London: Lutterworth, 1967.

White, J.L. "Saint Paul and the Apostolic Letter Tradition," *CBQ* 45 (1983) 433–444.

Widengren, G. *Literary and Psychological Aspects of the Hebrew Prophets.* Uppsala: Lundequist, 1948.

– – *The Ascension of the Apostle and the Heavenly Book.* Uppsala: Lundequist, 1950.

Widmann, H. "Die literarische Fälschung im Altertum. Bemerkung zu Wolfgang Speyers Monographie," *Antiquariat* 23 (1973) 169–174.

Willi, T. "Das Erlöschen des Geistes," *Jud* 28 (1972) 110–116.

Willi-Plein, I. "Das Geheimnis der Apokalyptik," *VT* 27 (1977) 62–81.

Williams, R.B. "Reflections on the Transmission of Tradition in the Early Church," *Encounter* 40 (1979) 273–285.

Willrich, H. *Urkundenfälschungen in der hellenistisch-jüdischen Literatur.* Gottingen: Vandenboeck and Ruprecht, 1924.

Wilson, R.R. *Prophecy and Society in Ancient Israel.* Philadelphia: Fortress, 1980.

Zahn, T. *Geschichte des neutestamentlichen Kanons.* Two volumes. Erlangen: Deichert, 1890.

Zeitlin, S. "An Historical Study of the Canonization of the Hebrew Scriptures," *The Canon and Masorah of the Hebrew Bible.* Edit. S.Z. Leiman. New York: KTAV, 1974, 164–201.

–– "Dreams and their Interpretation from the Biblical Period to the Tannaitic Time: An Historical Survey," *JQR* 66 (1975) 1–18.

Zimmerli, W. "Offenbarung im Alten Testament," *EvTh* 22 (1962) 15–31.

–– "Prophetic Proclamation and Reinterpretation," *Tradition and Theology in the Old Testament.* Edit. D.A. Knight. Philadelphia: Fortress, 1977, 69–100.

Zmijewski, J. "Apostolische Paradosis und Pseudepigraphie im Neuen Testament. 'Durch Erinnerung wachhalten' (2 Petr 1, 13; 3, 1)," *BZ* 23 (1979) 161–171.

–– "Die Pastoralbriefe als pseudepigraphische Schriften – Beschreibung, Erlärung, Bewertung," *Studien zum Neuen Testament und seiner Umwelt* 4 (1979) 97–118.

Index of Passages

A. Old Testament

B. New Testament

C. Jewish Literature

3. Dead Sea Scrolls

4. Rabbinic Literature

Index of Authors

Index of Subjects